- THE ORIGINAL HOT AND HOT FISH CLUB RULES -

RULE X
DUTY OF EACH MEMBER IN ROTATION

It shall be the duty of each member in rotation to furnish sugar for the Club for one season.

RULE XI
PRIZE RULE

Should any member become the parent of twins, each member shall, in rotation, furnish one basket of champagne for the Club; the names of the twins to be announced after the removal of dinner, in an appropriate toast by the President.

RULE XII

Whenever a member has an additional compliment to his family, he shall compliment the Club with a basket of champagne.

RULE XIII

Any unmarried member who practically illustrates his preference to matrimony by being wedded, shall be complimented by each unmarried member, through the Club, with a basket of champagne, in commemoration of that event.

RULE XIV

Any member of this Club, who shall be elected or appointed to any distinguished office in the State, shall for each and every such compliment furnish for the use of the Club one box of champagne.

RULE XV

Each member shall contribute annually five dollars, for the contingent fund of the Club, the same to be paid on the second Friday in June, to the Treasurer of the Club.

RULE XVI
ORDER

It shall be competent for the presiding officer or for any member of the Hot and Hot Fish Club, through the President, to call the Club to order, during the introduction or discussion of any subject, and there shall be no appeal from the Chair at that meeting: any member persisting, shall be considered as severely censured by the Club generally.

RULE XVII
OF MEMBERS ABSENT FROM THE PARISH
(PASSED JULY, 1860)

It shall be lawful from and after the first day of August, 1860, for any member intending to be absent from All Saints Parish for more than one year, to acquaint the Secretary and Treasurer with such intention, and from and after such notice given, the said member shall not be liable for any pecuniary dues to the Club, until he shall, by appearing again at the Club, resume his rights and privileges of membership. But if a member shall be absent for a fraction of a year, beyond the first twelve months, then he shall not be liable for any dues owing during any part of that year. And members so absent, shall not be counted as members on the roll, in cases where the Rules require a majority of two-thirds.

RULE XVIII

No alteration or amendment of the foregoing Rules shall be made, unless notice of the substance of the proposed alteration be given at a previous meeting, and the motion for such shall be renewed at the subsequent meeting, and two-thirds of the members on the roll of the Club shall be necessary to carry the same.

HOT AND HOT
FISH CLUB
COOKBOOK

A CELEBRATION OF

FOOD, FAMILY, & TRADITIONS

CHRIS AND IDIE HASTINGS

WITH KATHERINE COBBS

RUNNING PRESS
PHILADELPHIA • LONDON

THIS BOOK IS DEDICATED TO THE MEMORY OF

ANGELICA CRANFORD HASTINGS, CHRIS' MOTHER,

AND AMERINO JAMES MORANO, IDIE'S DAD.

Library of Congress Control Number: 2008943528
ISBN: 978-0-7624-3552-4

All photography by Jason Wallis, unless noted.

Design by Joshua McDonnell
Edited by Geoffrey Stone

Additional Photography by Howard Lee Puckett:
pp. 118,121, 162–62, 262, 265, 267

Running Press Book Publishers
2300 Chestnut Street
Philadelphia, Pennsylvania 19103-4371

Visit us on the web!
www.runningpresscooks.com

TABLE OF CONTENTS

6   FOREWORD

8   ACKNOWLEDGMENTS

10   INTRODUCTION: FOOD MEMORIES
A Lifetime of Living Seasonally

LIFESTYLE MENU

16   CHAPTER 1: MAY & JUNE
School is Out and Life Begins

60   An Outdoor Sunday Picnic and Fly-Fishing

70   CHAPTER 2: JULY & AUGUST
Seven Summers with Grandma Morano

118   Beach Dinner at the "Happy House"

124   CHAPTER 3: SEPTEMBER & OCTOBER
Harvest Moon, Pumpkins, and Lessons On Growing Up

166   Father-son Dove Hunt

174   CHAPTER 4: NOVEMBER & DECEMBER
Family Memories and Food Traditions

216   Italian Christmas with the Moranos (Idie's family)

228   CHAPTER 5: JANUARY & FEBRUARY
Catch Our Breath, Slow Things Down, and Run the Dogs

264   Crawfish, Football, Beer, and Boudin with the Staff and Friends

274   CHAPTER 6: MARCH & APRIL
The Art of Foraging, Rejuvenation, Creative Thinking, and Gobbling Turkeys

324   When In Rome

332   CHAPTER 7: BASIC RECIPES & TECHNIQUES
334 Sauces & Stocks | 343 Dressings & Vinaigrettes | 349 Condiments & Garnishes | 353 Breads, Grains & Dough | 361 On the Sweet Side | 368 Side Dishes | 374 Miscellaneous Basics | 377 Vegetables

380   APPENDIX | SOURCES GUIDE

384   IDIE'S LARDER

386   INDEX

FOREWORD

"For us, food is magic" write Chris and Idie Hastings in these pages. And magic, we have been told by the Great Houdini, is practice. The practice of preparing and consuming good food, and the manifold joys and solaces that practice provides, is what this marvel of a cookbook is about. What makes it as richly satisfying a creation as a perfect béchamel sauce is that the making and eating of food is not only magical to the Hastings but sacramental: the outward and visible sign of the graces that attend celebrations with friends and family; paying attention and due respect to the places and seasons in our lives; taking pains. What you hold in your hands is not only one of the best cookbooks you will ever come across, but a manual on living fully and well.

This should come as no surprise to anyone who knows Chris and Idie. These are well-spiced people, who bring a big-flavored, generous zest to both their work and their play and refuse to acknowledge much distinction between the two. During our annual woodcock and grouse shooting week in New Brunswick, Chris is always the first one in the kitchen at night after a long day in the coverts, stepping over and around exhausted bird dogs and rattling the humble pots and pans of the backwoods chalet we stay in with the same exuberant panache he puts on show each night at Hot and Hot. No matter where Chris and Idie cook, what they are after is what they call herein "memory cuisine"—meals like the ones we have in New Brunswick that will stay with you all the way to the walker and the drool-cup: the food itself a flashbulb illuminating in your memory the people you were with, the wine you drank, the stories that were told, the evanescent preciousness of human intimacy.

Memory cuisine as practiced by the Hastings, and as on display in this book, is all about intimacy. Despite the fact that nothing warms the cockles of the heart or is as basic to our animal natures as eating, many cookbooks are as chilly and austere as Jesuit ruminations on the Ontological Argument. Not so this one. In this one we become members of a family: accompanying Chris and Idie and their sons, Vincent and Zeb, on trips to the Gulf Coast, to dove hunts and pumpkin-carving parties and Italian Christmas meals with Idie's relatives. We meet—in wonderful profiles scattered throughout the book—the farmers and food purveyors (oystermen, cheese makers, beekeepers) who enable the Hastings to practice in their cooking the crucial and disappearing intimacy of knowing the exact provenance of food. The importance of such knowledge, along with that of the additional, deep intimacy of eating seasonally and locally—of cleaving to a cuisine that honestly reflects its terroir—are guiding principles in the Hastings culinary philosophy and in this book.

With all these various intimacies at work, we are welcomed into these pages as easily and fondly as if into a party of old friends, and the voice of the writing is as unpretentious and engaging as the conversation of such friends. This makes for a cookbook that is, for a change, fun to read. As I have had the galleys for a number of weeks, I can also tell you it is that equally rare cookbook that is fun to cook out of. The recipes here are as elegantly form-following-function contrivances as a Le Corbusier chair: unprissy, unhistrionic, uncomplicated, and honest. And the food they produce! The superb and sturdy food they produce is simply magic. Memory cuisine.

The bad-boy French writer Céline once commented that "the mark of true aristocracy in humankind is the legs." One is led to wonder about and perhaps envy the research that led him to that conclusion. Equally, one could envy me the years of research into Hastings cooking that have led me to this corollary: The mark of a true lover of life is the taste buds.

Read on, and pleasure yours.

Charles Gaines

January 2009, Lake Tadpole, AL

ACKNOWLEDGMENTS

Writing *Hot and Hot Fish Club Cookbook: A Celebration of Food, Family, and Traditions* while running a restaurant, consulting company, developing products, and managing our family has been an exciting and challenging process. The first pages of this book were written many years ago in the kitchens of our mothers and grandmothers. It has been a lifelong process and we are indebted to the many individuals who have guided, assisted, and helped us in writing and producing this book over the years. If it weren't for their tireless efforts, we might still be hard at work on this labor of love. While there's no way to acknowledge everyone individually who has helped with this project over the years, there are a few people we would like to extend our special debt of gratitude.

We are privileged to live in a city with a rich culinary heritage. We are grateful to all of the independent Birmingham chefs and restaurateurs who have mentored, supported, and encouraged us along the way.

Lisa Ekus-Saffer, our publicist, agent, and friend, believed in our project from the beginning and championed our vision every step of the way. We appreciate her advice, guidance, and encouragement and are inspired by her love of seasonal cuisine.

Geoffrey Stone, our dedicated editor at Running Press, jumped in midway through the process and carried us through to the finish line. He helped our voice shine on every page and was always patient and available when we had questions and concerns about the book.

Laura Zapalowski, who patiently tested each recipe with us, lent a critical eye to the edits of both the recipes and text and kept us organized and motivated throughout this entire process. We cannot thank Laura enough for her calming presence coupled with her uncanny proficiency in everything she did. Once, in the middle of a deadline her computer crashed—completely crashed, with all the data lost—Laura painstakingly went back over each page and every detail to put the process back on track. In the chaos of coordinating photo shoots, editing the cookbook, and managing the restaurant's day-to-day business, she knew our schedules better than we did and she approached every task with a positive, cheerful attitude.

Katherine Cobbs effortlessly compiled our writing and our thoughts into a seamless manuscript. We are grateful for her advice and experience throughout this process. Her careful eye and thoughtful conversations with our purveyors were invaluable, and her assistance during our computer failure was greatly appreciated.

To Jason Wallis, whose beautiful photographs gave life to our recipes and purveyors, we appreciate his hard work and dedication to this project. To Howard Lee Puckett, who began this exciting journey with us, we are thankful for his beautiful photographs.

To Joshua McDonnell, our talented designer at Running Press, we are grateful for his hard work and patience.

We are grateful to our entire kitchen staff, past and present, at Hot and Hot Fish Club, including our Chef de Cuisine Chris Zapalowski and Sous Chef Bill Schleusner who helped us with recipe testing, tasting, and food for photography, and kept a watchful eye on the restaurant while we were working on this book.

To the servers, waiter's assistants, bartenders, and our Sommelier, John Ruseicki, who each and every night attend to our guests with warmth and professionalism.

To the many loyal customers and acquaintances who agreed to prepare recipes at home and give us their honest opinions including: Brooke Michael Bell, Beth Borak, Kitty and Tucker Brown, Robin Burgess, Rosemarie Childress, Martha Chitwood, Rhoda Tishler Fleisig, Pamela Helms, Stephanie Hixon, Jennifer Walker Journey, Katie S. Kloster, Lynn Leishman, Lynne Morris, Dean and Carol Mueller, Glenda and Paul Nagrodzki, Pam Pritchard, Gail Rubin, Rebecca P. Sikorski, and Julianne Sneckenberger.

To the many extraordinary farmers, purveyors, and fishermen whose amazing products bring our menu to life, we appreciate their hard work and disproportionate passion that defines their personal greatness as well as the products they bring us.

To the individuals and business who lent us their beautiful products for photography, including: Issam Bajalia, Andy Boyles, Judy Bridgers, Rachel Gaudel, The Cook's Store, Hen House Antiques, Adam Norris Home, Mulberry Heights Antiques, and Table Matters, we are thankful.

Joe and Ivette Immormino lent us their home for photography and helped us test old family recipes. We are blessed to have such a wonderful family and always have so much fun when we visit.

To the people who have advised, mentored, and inspired us over the years, we are extremely grateful for all you've taught us: Bradley Ogden, Danny Meyer, Scott Peacock, Tyler Florence, Dean Max, Ted and Matt Lee, Mike Lata, Tory McPhail, Ken Vedrinski, John Currence, Hugh Acheson, Scott Jones, Julia Rutland, Andrew Knowlton, John T. Edge, Pete Wells, Dan Huntley, Corbin Day, Dixon Brooke, Sam Upchurch, Lee Styslinger, Elton B Stephens Sr., Rod Wilson, Charles Gaines, and John and Susan Vawter.

To our sons, Zeb and Vincent, who lovingly encouraged us to take on this project, we are blessed to be their parents and hope this book becomes our legacy to them for years to come.

INTRODUCTION

WITH A TRAILER IN TOW, IN 1989 WE JOURNEYED THREE THOUSAND MILES FROM BIRMINGHAM, ALABAMA, TO SAN FRANCISCO—A HOTBED OF GREAT FOOD IN AMERICA—IN JUST TWO DAYS. WE SET UP OUR APARTMENT IN RECORD TIME, TOO. WITH EVERYTHING IN PLACE, WE PASSED OUT FROM EXHAUSTION, NOT REALIZING THAT WHEN WE AWOKE OUR ADVENTURE WOULD TRULY BEGIN. IT WAS 1989 AND LIFELONG DREAMS WERE COMING TRUE FOR BOTH OF US. CHRIS LANDED A JOB AS SOUS CHEF UNDER BRADLEY OGDEN, WHO WE HAD ADMIRED FOR SOME TIME, AND HELPED OPEN THE NOW FAMED LARK CREEK INN IN MARIN COUNTY. IDIE DECIDED TO ATTEND THE CALIFORNIA CULINARY ACADEMY TO PURSUE HER ENDURING PASSION FOR THE CULINARY ARTS.

Our rented studio apartment was in the basement of a building called "Marie's Place" in Pacific Heights. To say our new home was small is an understatement. There was barely room to move around, but we weren't home enough for it to matter. We both worked long hours for little pay. We did not have much, but we had never been happier. In the lucky event that we shared a day off, we would stroll through our neighborhood in search of fresh ingredients from which to prepare dinner at home. Idie would select a crusty loaf of bread from the nearby bakery while Chris picked out the perfect little bottle of wine at the corner wine shop. Together again, we would wander through the farmers' market, selecting fresh meat from a vendor and just-harvested vegetables to round out our dinner. Cooking together in our tiny kitchen, we lost ourselves in long conversations about our hopes and dreams. As we played cards until the wee hours of the morning (we did not have a TV), sipping the last few drops of wine, our future together came into focus.

One such evening was a pivotal, defining moment for us. It was autumn, and fresh porcinis were abundant at the farmers' market, along with a colorful array of root vegetables. We picked up a small, organic chicken and prepared it quite simply—just a bit of olive oil, salt, and pepper, with some fresh herbs, earthy root vegetables, and porcinis scattered around it. Idie opened a bottle of Salice Salentino while our meal cooked. We tossed a simple salad of arugula procured from a local farm and sliced the crusty loaf—perfect! As we sat and began to

enjoy what seemed an ordinary meal, we were struck by its magic. It was one of the most delicious meals we had ever experienced together.

Though the ingredients were quite humble, each was at the height of freshness. We were certain that the vegetables had just been picked from local farms and the chicken had been butchered perhaps that very day. As we talked about the merits of the meal, we concluded that eating foods so close to their source, prepared in a fashion that allowed their pure, unadulterated flavors to shine, must have been the key to the meal's success. It wasn't as if we had set out to create the greatest dish of all time, yet by letting the essence of such undeniably fresh ingredients come through, we had experienced our own sort of culinary nirvana. Re-creating that magical dining experience for others, hopefully in our own restaurant one day, became our united mission from that moment.

Over the next decade, we sought out—and developed relationships with—farmers and purveyors of the finest products. Through these ties, we continue to source the uncommon quality ingredients necessary to replicate the enchanting aspect of that defining meal for our patrons. The lesson we learned that night has become the philosophy behind what we do at Hot and Hot Fish Club. Our food at the restaurant is unassuming and uncomplicated because we want our customers to experience the sheer pleasure of tasting a ripe heirloom tomato, freshly picked from Dave Garfrerick's farm, or the delight of savoring a slice of cheese made using milk from a nearby dairy. This is why we have chosen to share the profiles of some of our favorite purveyors. They are the real heroes of Hot and Hot—the ones who share our unequivocal passion for great products and hard work. Whether oysterman, farmer, cheese maker, or beekeeper, each producer provides us access to the very best ingredients available in America. By introducing you to our sources, as well as providing you with tips for ways to develop your own sourcing relationships, we hope you will broaden and diversify your arsenal of ingredients and, therefore, your cooking.

For us, food is magic. We see its restorative power and the delight it brings people every day. This book is our attempt to share with you the magic of that same food that moved us so long ago. Now, one restaurant and two children later, we feel the time is right to offer readers more than a taste of the restaurant through the recipes we love. Because of our respective rich food heritages and combined passions, we go a step further and invite you to join us at our table—both at Hot and Hot Fish Club and at home.

The pages that follow offer a glimpse of our family life on a monthly basis, especially how we gather at the table with friends and family and celebrate life through great seasonal meals. Each chapter has a final section called lifestyle menus in which we invite you to experience a part of our lives through story and food. The lifestyle menus include recipes that we enjoy during certain events in our lives. We've paired wines—or beer in the case of the crawfish boil and football menu—with each menu. In these pages we will take you on a journey with us through the many micro-growing seasons, our major family events, and the seasonal evolution of our restaurant menus. This book is as much a view into our creative process at the restaurant as it is an example of living seasonally. It is also very much a family history. We are honored to have you be a part of it.

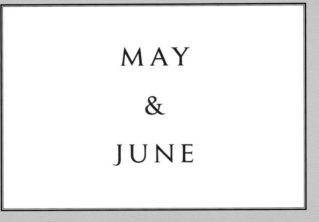

CHAPTER I

MAY
&
JUNE

OF ALL MONTHS, MAY AND JUNE REMIND CHRIS OF CHILDHOOD SUMMERS SPENT ON PAWLEYS ISLAND DURING HIS FORMATIVE YEARS. THESE MONTHS CENTERED AROUND FORAGING, FOOD, AND FUN AND PROFOUNDLY INFLUENCED THE WAY HE APPROACHES COOKING TODAY. CHRIS IS THE FIRST TO ADMIT HE WAS NOT A VERY FOCUSED STUDENT, PREFERRING THE BACK ROW OF THE CLASS FOR THE OPPORTUNITY IT AFFORDED HIM TO STARE, UNNOTICED, OUT THE WINDOW, DAYDREAMING ABOUT FISHING AND HUNTING. MOST OF HIS YEAR WAS SPENT IN ANTICIPATION OF MAY, WHEN HE FELT LIFE TRULY BEGAN. FROM THE MOMENT THAT FINAL SCHOOL BELL RANG, MORE MINUTES OF HIS DAY WOULD BE SPENT OUTDOORS THAN IN, FISHING ON THE WATER, HUNTING, AND GATHERING FOOD IN THE WOODS. EACH DAY CULMINATED AT THE DINING TABLE, SHARING STORIES WITH HIS FAMILY AND MANY MATERNAL RELATIVES.

These summer months of freedom were a welcome break from school yet provided him a different sort of education as "creek boy," a role he considered his true calling. Each generation someone in his mother's family was the designated "creek boy." It was a badge of honor bestowed only on the capable few who could be sent out in the morning and return at dinnertime with the star attraction for the table. Chris' job each day of summer was to catch as much seafood as he could for family meals. Each evening his mother and aunts would prepare the most delicious meals using everything he and his cousins had gathered during their daily adventures at the water's edge. Looking back, Chris appreciates the valuable lessons such early foraging experiences offered—the joy and perfection of eating just what is available at a given moment in time, while respecting the land and environment that offers up such treasures.

Today at our restaurant, we greet May and June with equal childlike fervor. These months provide us with products that we haven't seen in a long while and reenergize our creative process. The farmers and gardeners who supply us from around the state and beyond are bringing us an amazing variety of lettuces, herbs, and vegetables. The cooks in our kitchen react like kids on Christmas morning when great boxes of produce arrive.

In early May, we increase our early morning visits to the Jefferson County Farmers' Market downtown to catch up with our farmer friends and select the freshest tomatoes, squash, and peas each has to offer. Summer produce in all its prolific diversity provides such inspiration for us at Hot and Hot Fish Club. It breathes new life and freshness into our menu, energizes our cooks and servers and, in turn, enlivens the crowd in our dining room. The first warm weather dishes make their short-lived appearance—Roasted Squash Blossoms with Blue Crab, Cherry Tomatoes, and Cucumbers and Creamed Field Pea and Summer Squash Salad reminiscent of a southern childhood. Our patrons order these delights again and again until there are no more.

Today, May still signals a new beginning in our minds. In Birmingham, May is a time when spring matures into summer's full glory and heat and humidity settle over the city. It is also the time Chris grows most restless at his desk, attending to restaurant business. Just like the student daydreamer back in the classroom, he gets excited with anticipation knowing that school is almost out and summer is just around the corner. Even today, for our family, this is when life begins again.

THE ORIGINAL HOT AND HOT FISH CLUB

A century and a half ago, Chris' great- great- great- great-grandfather, Hugh Fraser, arrived on American soil from Edinburgh, Scotland, and settled in South Carolina near Pawleys Island. Somehow this man from the Scottish hills was drawn to the Low Country's ample swampland. He purchased a tract and began growing rice.

Pawleys Island was a draw for many and actually may have been one of the country's first true resort areas. Robert Mills, the great American architect, wrote after a visit to Pawleys Island: "The good things of this life, are here really enjoyed by the inhabitants in abundance; for the land and the ocean lay their treasures at their feet." The region's inhabitants, mostly made up of rice plantation owners, did indeed take time to celebrate the area.

Hugh Fraser, and the men of his new community, began to gather near Murrells Inlet on "Drunken Jack" Inlet every Friday from May through October to fish the salt marshes. Afterwards, they joined back up to discuss the day's catch and clean their fish. Each member of the group supplied his own day's catch for a communal meal, as well as provisions from his own plantation, such as rice, game, vegetables, bread, and desired condiments. The day always culminated with a huge meal at a long harvest table in the clubhouse. These meetings were truly a celebration of land and life where one could shed the worries of the week, relax, and enjoy a simple meal with friends.

In 1845 the group officially established themselves as an epicurean gentleman's club, calling themselves The Hot and Hot Fish Club, and developed a set of rules and regulations, which governed membership. As far as we can tell, the term "hot and hot" may have been part of the local vernacular. It emphasized that the meals were not only freshly cooked but were served piping hot with the steam still rising.

With the Civil War came less time for fishing and festivities and the Hot and Hot Fish Club was forced to dismantle. Today, Murrells Inlet is a shifting sandbar and the original structure for the Hot and Hot clubhouse is only a memory. Chris has found great inspiration and wonder in learning about his family's Low-Country history and ancestral traditions. Southerners are a culture of storytellers and Chris grew up hearing about the Hot and Hot Fish Club and his family's history through stories passed down by his parents, grandparents, aunts, and uncles. Those stories, histories, and traditions have shaped the way he looks at life and have been the greatest inspiration behind his career as a chef.

In the fall of 1995, we opened the modern-day Hot and Hot Fish Club, a restaurant in the historic Southside district of Birmingham, Alabama. We built a restaurant that is a tribute to the original members of the Hot and Hot Fish Club and the ideals for which the original club stood. In the same vein, we strive to ensure that our guests enjoy a warm and inviting atmosphere that is never pretentious with great food and service to match. It is a place where people come to shed the worry and pretense of the day and reconnect over a great meal.

We believe that the bonds formed so many years ago through fishing, foraging the marshland, and coming to the table together continue each night at our restaurant. Although the original South Carolina Hot and Hot Fish Club no longer exists, we work hard to keep the spirit of the club alive and flourishing at our restaurant and in our way of life.

- THE ORIGINAL RULES -

RULE I TIME AND PLACE OF MEETING
It is the duty of members to meet, at or about 12 o'clock p.m., at the Club House, at Midway sea shore, on each Friday, from the first Friday in June, to the last Friday, but on, in October.

RULE II ADMISSION OF MEMBERS
Any person, wishing to become a member, must be proposed by the President, and if elected by a majority, shall, after subscribing to the rules, and paying his admission fee of fifty dollars to the Treasurer, be entitled to all the rights and privileges of a member.

RULE II QUORUM
Not less than two-thirds of the members shall constitute a quorum for the transaction of business.

RULE IV OFFICERS
There shall be a President and Vice-President, to preside at the meetings, and a Secretary and Treasurer, to record the proceedings, and to take charge of the funds of the Club.

RULE V DUTIES OF THE PRESIDENT
Each member, in rotation, and in order of residences, shall act as President. He shall furnish a ham, and good rice, and also attend to the preparation for dinner, to be on table at 2 o'clock p.m., or not later than half-past 2. He must preserve order, and select sides with the Vice-President for games. If absent, he must send his ham and rice.

RULE VI DUTIES OF THE VICE-PRESIDENT
The Vice-President shall, in addition to his dish and wine, supply the Club with water and ice, and attend to the games. If the President is absent, the Vice-President will preside, and his next neighbor officiates for him. He must also announce whether champagne will be brought at the ensuing Club meeting.

RULE VII DUTIES OF SECRETARY AND TREASURER
The Secretary and Treasurer shall keep a record of the proceedings of Club, take charge of the funds, receive or disburse, according to the vote of the Club. He shall also keep an account of the debts due by, and to the Club, and furnish an annual report at the first meeting in October.

RULE VIII DUTIES OF MEMBERS
Each member shall contribute at least one substantial dish for dinner, also one bottle of wine, unless it shall have been previously announced that champagne will be furnished. He must also bring not less than two knives and forks, two tumblers, two wine glasses, two plates, and one dish.

RULE IX DUTY OF CERTAIN MEMBERS
Each unmarried member shall be permitted in rotation to furnish a pudding, in lieu of that required under Rule VIII.

RULE X DUTY OF EACH MEMBER IN ROTATION
It shall be the duty of each member in rotation to furnish sugar for the Club for one season.

RULE XI PRIZE RULE
Should any member become the parent of twins, each member shall, in rotation, furnish one basket of champagne for the Club; the names of the twins to be announced after the removal of dinner, in an appropriate toast by the President.

RULE XII
Whenever a member has an additional compliment to his family, he shall compliment the Club with a basket of champagne.

RULE XIII
Any unmarried member who practically illustrates his preference to matrimony by being wedded, shall be complimented by each unmarried member, through the Club, with a basket of champagne, in commemoration of that event.

RULE XIV
Any member of this Club, who shall be elected or appointed to any distinguished office in the State, shall for each and every such compliment furnish for the use of the Club one box of champagne.

RULE XV
Each member shall contribute annually five dollars, for the contingent fund of the Club, the same to be paid on the second Friday in June, to the Treasurer of the Club.

RULE XVI ORDER
It shall be competent for the presiding officer or for any member of the Hot and Hot Fish Club, through the President, to call the Club to order, during the introduction or discussion of any subject, and there shall be no appeal from the Chair at that meeting: any member persisting, shall be considered as severely censured by the Club generally.

RULE XVII OF MEMBERS ABSENT FROM THE PARISH (PASSED JULY, 1860)
It shall be lawful from and after the first day of August, 1860, for any member intending to be absent from All Saints Parish for more than one year, to acquaint the Secretary and Treasurer with such intention, and from and after such notice given, the said member shall not be liable for any pecuniary dues to the Club, until he shall, by appearing again at the Club, resume his rights and privileges of membership. But if a member shall be absent for a fraction of a year, beyond the first twelve months, then he shall not be liable for any dues owing during any part of that year. And members so absent, shall not be counted as members on the roll, in cases where the Rules require a majority of two-thirds.

RULE XVIII
No alteration or amendment of the foregoing Rules shall be made, unless notice of the substance of the proposed alteration be given at a previous meeting, and the motion for such shall be renewed at the subsequent meeting, and two-thirds of the members on the roll of the Club shall be necessary to carry the same.

WATERMELON MARTINI

MAKING WATERMELON JUICE IS EASY AND DOESN'T REQUIRE A FANCY JUICER. CUT A FRESH, RIPE WATERMELON INTO TWO-INCH CHUNKS AND PROCESS IN A BLENDER OR FOOD PROCESSOR UNTIL PURÉED. STRAIN THE PURÉE THROUGH A FINE-MESHED STRAINER AND DISCARD ANY SEEDS OR SOLIDS. IN THIS MARTINI WE ADD A SMALL AMOUNT OF SIMPLE SYRUP TO ENHANCE THE WATERMELON'S NATURAL SWEETNESS. IF YOU ARE USING AN EXTRA SWEET MELON VARIETY LIKE THE SUGAR BABY, THE SIMPLE SYRUP MAY NOT BE NECESSARY.

YIELD: 1 SERVING

1½ OUNCES (3 TABLESPOONS) CITRUS-FLAVORED VODKA
3 OUNCES (¼ CUP PLUS 2 TABLESPOONS) FRESH WATERMELON JUICE
½ OUNCE (1 TABLESPOON) SIMPLE SYRUP (PAGE 362)
1 LEMON TWIST, FOR GARNISH

Chill a martini glass for at least 20 minutes before serving.

Combine the vodka, watermelon juice, and syrup in a martini shaker filled halfway with ice. Shake until well chilled. Strain into the chilled martini glass and garnish with a twist of lemon. Serve immediately.

SOUTHERN LEMONADE COCKTAIL

WHAT COULD BE MORE SOUTHERN THAN FRESH MINT, BOURBON, AND LEMONADE SERVED OVER ICE? THIS REFRESHING COCKTAIL IS A HIT WITH OUR FRIENDS AND CUSTOMERS IN THE SUMMERTIME. IF YOU DON'T MIND TAKING THE TIME TO MUDDLE THE MINT IN SMALL BATCHES, THIS IS A WONDERFUL RECIPE TO SERVE IN LARGE PITCHERS AT PARTIES AND COCKTAIL HOURS.

YIELD: 1 SERVING

10 FRESH MINT LEAVES, 3 TO 4 TABLESPOONS
2 OUNCES (¼ CUP) MAKER'S MARK OR OTHER GOOD-QUALITY BOURBON
1½ OUNCES (3 TABLESPOONS) FRESH LEMON JUICE
1 OUNCE (2 TABLESPOONS) SIMPLE SYRUP (PAGE 362)
2 OUNCES (¼ CUP) CLUB SODA OR SPARKLING WATER
1 FRESH MINT SPRIG, FOR GARNISH

Fill a martini shaker one-third full with ice. Tear the mint leaves and add them to the ice; muddle until the mint is bruised and fragrant, about 1 minute. Add the bourbon, lemon juice, and syrup. Shake until the mixture is well chilled.

Strain the muddled mint and lemonade mixture into one (12-ounce) Collins glass filled with ice. Top with the soda water and stir gently to combine. Garnish with a sprig of fresh mint and serve immediately.

BOILED PEANUTS

WHEN WE OPENED HOT AND HOT FISH CLUB WE WANTED TO OFFER SOMETHING SALTY FOR OUR GUESTS TO NIBBLE ON AT THE COCKTAIL BAR. BOILED PEANUTS HAVE BEEN A SOUTHERN STAPLE SINCE THE CIVIL WAR AND CAN BE FOUND AT ROADSIDE STANDS THROUGHOUT THE SOUTH. FROM MAY THROUGH SEPTEMBER, WE OFFER OUR GUESTS AT THE BAR SMALL BOWLS OF THIS SOUTHERN SPECIALTY. IF YOU HAVE TROUBLE FINDING THE RAW, GREEN (FRESHLY HARVESTED) PEANUTS, YOU CAN USE REGULAR RAW PEANUTS. THE GREEN PEANUTS ARE SMALLER AND BEST FOR BOILING. REGULAR RAW PEANUTS ARE MORE MATURE, SO THEY ARE LARGER IN SIZE AND WILL NEED TO SIMMER A LITTLE LONGER THAN THE GREEN PEANUTS.

YIELD: ABOUT 2 POUNDS

2 POUNDS RAW, UNSHELLED GREEN PEANUTS
¾ CUP PLUS 2 TABLESPOONS KOSHER SALT
4 QUARTS COLD WATER

Rinse the peanuts in cold water to remove any excess dirt. Pick through and discard any broken nuts.

Place the peanuts and salt in a large stockpot and add enough water to cover, about 4 quarts. Bring the mixture to a boil, reduce the heat to low, cover, and simmer for 3½ to 4 hours, adding additional water, to cover, as needed. Taste the peanuts occasionally to determine the correct amount of cooking time. When done, the peanuts will be tender and soft with a slight texture or bite.

Remove the peanuts from the heat and allow them to cool at room temperature in the brine for at least 1 hour. Drain half of the liquid off of the peanuts and serve warm. Refrigerate any leftover peanuts covered in their brine for up to 1 week.

HOLLOW SPRING FARM AND FARMER CHRIS BENNETT

Hollow Spring Farm is a small farm situated in the dip of a fertile valley just east of Birmingham near Pell City owned by one of our former employees, Chris Bennett and his family. He supplies our kitchen with incredible cultivated and wild ingredients. Because we have worked side by side with him in our restaurant kitchen for a number of years, we know that he is not only a very capable chef with a great pedigree, but a passionate outdoorsman and dedicated grower with a specialized understanding of what chefs want.

Chris Bennett approached us several years ago to share his dream of creating an organic farm on his family's land with the ultimate goal of becoming one of our suppliers. We knew it would be a tough way to scratch out a living, but like so many "callings" sometimes the draw is just too strong to resist. He simply had to go down that road to see if working the land was indeed his calling. As beneficiaries of his harvests, we are so glad he took the leap of faith.

Perhaps more interesting than what he cultivates is what he has been able to harvest in the wild on his property—a spit of land simply overflowing with assorted edibles. He has made it a point to comb the property in order to forage for us a number of things—sassafras, wild ginger, tiny strawberries, elderberries, huckleberries, persimmons, earthy mushrooms, and honeysuckle blossoms so sweet they bring tears to your eyes. It is exciting to know that he has only just scratched the surface. He discovers new delicacies all the time and spends a fair amount of time researching many of the plants growing so abundantly on his property. He recently found highbush berries, a wild blueberry…small, sweet, and unbelievable in flavor. Cultivated blueberries, found in supermarkets, are just giant, diluted hybrids of this untamed variety. Chris Bennett's discoveries allow us to provide our patrons with a truly unique culinary experience. The primitive ingredients he brings to us predate "heirloom" because they predate cultivation. He harvests what Mother Nature planted. Quite frankly, most folks don't get to taste such ingredients these days. The flavor of a highbush blueberry, for instance, is the most powerful essence of blueberry you can imagine because it is the archetype. Unfortunately, so much of what we eat today has moved away from its original wild flavor, due to the need for mass production. The wild fruits and vegetables Chris Bennett provides are a rare gift.

Access to wild harvests from Hollow Spring Farm is like having a culinary treasure chest opened up for us time and time again as the calendar unfolds. We talk so much about seasonality and about our dishes being of-the-moment and this philosophy is certainly reflected in our relationship with this small farm. It has enabled us to provide our guests a taste of something truly of its time and place—it goes beyond the family farm and artisanal grower to Mother Nature herself.

It is awe-inspiring to know that for a mere two weeks out of the year, you can come into our restaurant and savor tiny wild strawberries—the sweetest strawberries you have ever tasted bar none—just foraged at Hollow Spring Farm. We often serve them with our Lemon Buttermilk Tart (page 314), with huckleberries, elderberries, and honeysuckle simple syrup made with perfect fleeting blossoms found growing there. Dishes like this are ephemeral and pure excitement both to prepare and eat. This is the type of cooking that separates our restaurant from the pack. We aren't serving just some unique organic variety cultivated someplace, but sun-ripened, wild strawberries discovered clinging haphazardly to some rocky slope at Hollow Spring Farm right where nature dictated. The berries are superb, rare, momentary and so unique that no other strawberry can compare. Incorporating a bit of the wild into our dishes allows us to give our customers explosive "wow" moments that create indelible food memories.

We never stop saying that our purveyors are the real heroes of our restaurant. Certainly the bounty Chris Bennett harvests enables us to take our cooking to new heights. As beneficiaries of his wild, foraged foods, we are forced to approach cooking in a new way. His ingredients elevate both our craft and our cuisine. After all, chefs have limited creative ability. Talent and skill can take a cook just so far before one moves beyond good common sense when it comes to cooking. The only other vehicle for true creativity is access to phenomenal products. Otherwise, cooking can become static or, worse, misguided. Foam is a good example. If the products are exceptional, it does not add to or improve a dish. So, our hats are off to our purveyors, like Hollow Spring Farm's Chris Bennett, who allow us to constantly raise the bar at our restaurant and keep our passion for food and cooking alive.

VEGETABLE MINESTRONE
with *Pesto*

Working for Bradley Ogden at the Lark Creek Inn taught Chris a great deal about the value of the farmer and choosing fresh ingredients that are at the peak of their season. Our weekly visits to the Marin County Farmers' Market further cemented the philosophy of the benefits of living from farm to table. This soup reflects the purity and clarity of flavors that a well-timed trip to the farmers' market can accomplish. You can use the vegetable scraps from this dish to make your own vegetable stock. It's a quick stock to make and it will add an extra depth of flavor to this dish. Serve this soup with a crusty baguette for a filling meal or appetizer.

YIELD: 8 CUPS OR 8 SERVINGS

2 TABLESPOONS EXTRA-VIRGIN OLIVE OIL
½ CUP FINELY DICED YELLOW ONION
½ CUP FINELY DICED LEEKS
1 TEASPOON MINCED GARLIC
½ CUP FINELY DICED FENNEL
½ CUP FINELY DICED CELERY
½ CUP PEELED AND FINELY DICED CARROTS
½ CUP FINELY DICED ZUCCHINI
½ CUP FINELY DICED YELLOW SQUASH
½ CUP SEEDED AND FINELY DICED TOMATOES
4 CUPS VEGETABLE STOCK (PAGE 334)
½ CUP FRESH ENGLISH PEAS
½ CUP COOKED AND DRAINED BRAISED VEGETARIAN
  WHITE BEANS (PAGE 371)
1 CUP COOKED SMALL-SHAPED PASTA, SUCH AS ELBOW,
  DITALINI, OR ORZO
1½ TEASPOONS KOSHER SALT
⅛ TEASPOON FRESHLY GROUND BLACK PEPPER
½ CUP BASIL PESTO (PAGE 350)
4 TEASPOONS LEMON OIL (PAGE 382)

Heat the extra-virgin olive oil in a large saucepan over medium heat. Add the onion, leeks, and garlic and cook until the vegetables are tender and translucent, about 5 minutes. Add the fennel, celery, and carrots and cook, stirring occasionally for 5 minutes. Add the zucchini, squash, and tomatoes and cook for an additional 3 minutes.

Add the stock and bring the soup to a simmer. Stir in the peas, white beans, and pasta and return the mixture to a simmer. Allow the soup to simmer for 1 to 2 minutes, or until the soup is heated through. Season the soup with the salt and pepper.

Place 1 tablespoon of the pesto in the bottom of each of eight warm soup bowls. Ladle about 1 cup of soup into the bowls and drizzle each bowl with ½ teaspoon of the lemon oil and serve immediately.

SHRIMP AND AVOCADO SALAD
with Carolina Gold Rice

CAROLINA GOLD RICE IS A LONG-GRAIN VARIETY THAT WAS NEARLY EXTINCT AFTER THE CIVIL WAR. IT IS NAMED FOR THE GOLDEN HUE OF THE RICE FIELDS AND IS PRIZED FOR ITS SUPERIOR FLAVOR AND TEXTURE. THIS IS ALSO THE SAME VARIETY OF RICE THAT CHRIS' ANCESTORS AND FOUNDERS OF THE ORIGINAL HOT AND HOT FISH CLUB PLANTED AND GREW NEAR PAWLEYS ISLAND. THANKS TO PEOPLE LIKE GLENN ROBERTS, THE OWNER AND FOUNDER OF ANSON MILLS, YOU CAN PURCHASE THIS RICE DIRECTLY FROM THE MILL (PAGE 380). SINCE THIS IS AN HEIRLOOM VARIETY, THE COOKING TIME IS VERY DIFFERENT FROM REGULAR LONG-GRAIN RICE. FOLLOW THE DIRECTIONS PROVIDED BY ANSON MILLS WHEN COOKING THEIR PRODUCTS. IF CAROLINA GOLD RICE IS UNAVAILABLE, YOU CAN SUBSTITUTE REGULAR LONG-GRAIN RICE FOR THE RICE IN THIS RECIPE.

YIELD: 4 SERVINGS

- 1 CUP COOKED ANSON MILLS CAROLINA GOLD RICE (PAGE 353)
- ½ CUP GREEN GODDESS DRESSING (PAGE 347)
- ⅛ TEASPOON KOSHER SALT
- PINCH OF FRESHLY GROUND BLACK PEPPER
- 4 RIPE HAAS AVOCADOS, HALVED, PITTED, AND PEELED (ABOUT 1½ POUNDS TOTAL)
- 16 RIPE CHERRY TOMATOES, HALVED (ABOUT 1½ CUPS)
- 12 MEDIUM (25 TO 30 COUNT) BOILED AND PEELED SHRIMP
- 1 TABLESPOON FRESH LEMON JUICE
- 2 TABLESPOONS EXTRA-VIRGIN OLIVE OIL

Combine the rice and the dressing in a mixing bowl and season with the salt and pepper. Spoon the rice mixture evenly into each avocado half, placing about ¼ cup in each avocado. Arrange 1 stuffed avocado on each of four salad plates.

Toss the tomato halves and the shrimp in a small bowl with the lemon juice and the extra-virgin olive oil. Season the shrimp mixture with a pinch of salt and pepper, if needed. Spoon the shrimp and tomato mixture over and around each avocado, placing about 3 shrimp on each avocado half and serve immediately.

CAROLINA GOLD RICE

Carolina Gold rice is a particularly important staple of our restaurant, as it was to those of the original Hot and Hot Fish Club of long ago. Only recently, has this prized grain undergone a revival. Anson Mills, a commercial grower and on-demand miller of organic heirloom, some near-extinct grains, stumbled upon this particular old-fashioned variety of rice growing wild on antebellum plantations in the Low Country. It is a variety that for centuries served as the cash crop of the region. Rice was then to South Carolina what tobacco was to North Carolina or cotton to Texas and Mississippi.

The Low-Country topography and natural river systems are perfectly suited to rice cultivation. Growers would drain swamps and clear them to create sections to seed. They would then re-flood the swamp in order to propagate the rice. Carolina Gold is a long-grained variety with a distinctive texture and flavor that was sought after around the world, making it the premier rice of its time.

In South Carolina rice was a staple at every meal. Most all pre–Civil War plantation owners grew it. It was their "golden ticket" and, quite possibly, one reason the rice came to be called "Carolina Gold." As we've delved into the history of the original Hot and Hot Fish Club, we discovered Carolina Gold was the exact variety its members grew one hundred eighty years ago. One of the original rules required members to contribute a certain amount of "good" rice to the club. That meant good-quality, whole-grain Carolina Gold rice, not broken grains or lesser varieties. Much like paying dues, contributing fine rice to the table was a condition of membership.

The rediscovery and resuscitation through cultivation of this heirloom rice variety by Anson Mills has been a great gift to the culinary world. They were able to trace their find back genetically to the original Carolina Gold, restoring a long lost commodity in the process.

Six years after we opened our restaurant doors, we discovered that Anson Mills was ready to offer the first fruits of its production of Carolina Gold rice and we jumped at it. While they had discovered it years before, it required years of propagation to get stocks up enough to be able to meet commercial demand. It has been extremely gratifying for us to now have access to the very same rice that our ancestors grew and to be able to share it with the patrons of our restaurant. It is the starring rice on our menu and we serve it in all manners—even rice pudding. Thankfully, Carolina Gold is not just a food memory, but instead a grain that can be shared for generations to come.

SHRIMP AND CORN FRITTERS
with Chive Aïoli

SEAFOOD FRITTERS WERE ALWAYS SERVED AT THE BEACH WHEN CHRIS WAS A CHILD. FRITTERS HAVE LONG BEEN AN IMPORTANT PART OF THE SOUTHERN DIET AND HE GREW UP EATING THEM FOR LUNCH ALONG WITH SLICED TOMATOES AND SUCCOTASH. HIS GRANDMOTHER LOVED TO SERVE THEM WITH A DOLLOP OF HOMEMADE MAYONNAISE. TODAY WE SERVE THESE FRITTERS AS HORS D'OEUVRES FOR COCKTAIL RECEPTIONS OR SNACKS AT THE BEACH WITH CHIVE AÏOLI INSTEAD OF THE MAYONNAISE. FOR A DIFFERENT TWIST, TRY SUBSTITUTING FRESH CLAMS OR LUMP CRABMEAT FOR THE SHRIMP.

YIELD: ABOUT 50 FRITTERS

1 POUND FRESH, PEELED MEDIUM (25 TO 30 COUNT) SHRIMP, DEVEINED AND CUT INTO ½-INCH PIECES

1½ CUPS FRESH CORN KERNELS, ABOUT 2 EARS

½ CUP FINELY DICED RED BELL PEPPER

½ CUP FINELY DICED YELLOW BELL PEPPER

½ CUP FINELY DICED POBLANO PEPPER

¾ CUP CHOPPED GREEN ONIONS (GREEN PART ONLY)

1½ TEASPOONS KOSHER SALT

¾ TEASPOON FRESHLY GROUND BLACK PEPPER

¼ TEASPOON CAYENNE PEPPER

½ CUP ALL-PURPOSE FLOUR

1 TEASPOON BAKING POWDER

2 QUARTS PEANUT OIL, FOR FRYING

3 LARGE EGG WHITES

1 CUP CHIVE AÏOLI (PAGE 342), FOR SERVING

Combine the diced shrimp, corn, peppers, and green onions in a large bowl; cover and refrigerate for 1 hour. Once chilled, season the shrimp mixture with the salt, pepper, and cayenne, stirring until well seasoned. In a separate bowl, combine the flour and baking powder. Add the flour mixture to the shrimp and vegetables and toss until the vegetables and shrimp are well coated with the flour. Cover and refrigerate for 30 minutes.

Pour the oil into a deep-sided skillet to a depth of 3 inches. (Alternately, a deep fryer can be filled with peanut oil.) Preheat the oil to 350°F.

In a separate bowl, whisk the egg whites until medium-stiff peaks form. Gently fold one-third of the whipped egg whites into the shrimp and vegetable mixture. Repeat with the remaining egg whites, making sure the egg whites are incorporated before adding the next third. (At this point, the fritter batter can be used immediately or chilled for up to 2 hours before serving.)

Carefully drop rounded tablespoon-size scoops of the fritter batter into the preheated oil and fry for about 2 minutes or until golden brown. Remove the fritters with a slotted spoon and drain on a paper towel–lined plate. Season the fritters with additional salt, if needed. Serve the fritters in towel–lined baskets or on platters alongside a small bowl of chive aïoli.

SOFT-SHELL CRAB BLT

BEGINNING IN MID-MAY, THE BLUE CRABS BEGIN TO SHED THEIR HARD SHELL, FOR A DAY OR TWO, IN ORDER TO GROW. IN ITS LIFETIME OF ONLY A FEW YEARS, A BLUE CRAB WILL SHED ITS HARD SHELL AN AVERAGE OF TWENTY TIMES. BLUE CRABS' SILKEN SKIN CAN BE COOKED AND EATEN AS IS, NO PEELING REQUIRED. IF YOU LIVE NEAR THE COAST, ANYWHERE FROM NEW JERSEY TO TEXAS, LOOK FOR SOFT-SHELL CRABS THAT ARE LIVELY AND STILL MOVING. THAWED FROZEN, SOFT SHELLS CAN BE SUBSTITUTED IF FRESH ARE NOT AVAILABLE.

YIELD: 4 SERVINGS

1 QUART PEANUT OIL, FOR FRYING
4 FRESH SOFT-SHELL CRABS, CLEANED AND DRAINED
1 CUP BUTTERMILK
½ CUP FINELY GROUND YELLOW CORNMEAL
½ CUP CORN FLOUR
½ CUP ALL-PURPOSE FLOUR
1½ TEASPOONS KOSHER SALT, DIVIDED
¼ TEASPOON CAYENNE PEPPER
8 (½-INCH-THICK) SLICES SOURDOUGH BREAD OR FRENCH BAGUETTE, GRILLED
½ CUP BASIL AÏOLI (PAGE 342)
2 HEIRLOOM TOMATOES, ABOUT 1½ POUNDS, THINLY SLICED INTO 4 SLICES EACH
2 CUPS LOOSELY PACKED ARUGULA
8 SLICES APPLEWOOD SMOKED BACON, COOKED UNTIL CRISPY

Pour the oil into a deep-sided skillet to a depth of 3 inches. (Alternately, a deep fryer can be filled with peanut oil.) Preheat the oil to 360°F.

Place the crabs in a small bowl with the buttermilk, and toss until evenly coated.

Combine the cornmeal, corn flour, all-purpose flour, 1¼ teaspoons of the salt, and the cayenne in a separate bowl or shallow dish. Remove the crabs one at a time from the buttermilk, and dredge in the cornmeal mixture, tossing until the crabs are well breaded.

Add the crabs to the hot oil and fry for 2½ to 3 minutes, or until golden brown and crispy. Remove the crabs from the oil with a slotted spoon and place on a paper towel–lined plate. Season the crabs with the remaining ¼ teaspoon of the salt, if needed.

Place a slice of bread on each of four plates. Spread 1 tablespoon of the aïoli on each bread slice. Slightly overlap 2 tomato slices on each bread slice and top each with a small handful (about ½ cup) of the arugula. Arrange 2 slices of the bacon and 1 fried crab on top of each portion. Spoon an additional tablespoon of the aïoli over each crab and top with remaining bread slice. Serve hot.

CLEANING SOFT-SHELL CRABS

This task is not as daunting as it may sound and is well worth the effort. It is best to use live soft-shell crabs to ensure the freshness of the dish and because the shells begin to harden as soon as the crabs die. To clean soft shell-crabs, cut off the face of the crab with kitchen shears. Pull off and discard the bottom flap or "apron" of the crab then clean out and discard the lungs (grayish, finger-like portion on the inside of the main cavity, just under the top shell). Place the cleaned crabs on a jelly roll pan lined with a kitchen towel and refrigerate them for about 15 minutes. This allows any excess liquid to drain from the crabs, which are now ready to be cooked according to the recipe directions.

ROASTED SQUASH BLOSSOMS

with Blue Crab, Cherry Tomatoes, and Cucumbers

ONE OF OUR KEY SUPPLIERS IS THE CHEF'S GARDEN LOCATED IN HURON, OHIO. WE BEGAN DOING BUSINESS WITH FARMER LEE JONES ABOUT FIFTEEN YEARS AGO. LEE AND HIS FAMILY WERE TYPICAL AMERICAN FARMERS STRUGGLING TO KEEP UP WITH THE LARGE MARKET DEMANDS. ONE DAY A CHEF CAME TO VISIT THE FARM AND WANTED TO BUY THE SQUASH BLOSSOMS, NOT THE SQUASH. LEE REALIZED THAT CHEFS WERE THE CUSTOMERS HE NEEDED TO FOCUS ON. FARMER JONES SOON BEGAN DEVELOPING ALL KINDS OF HYBRIDS AND HEIRLOOMS FROM SEEDS HE COLLECTED ALL OVER THE WORLD. TODAY THE CHEF'S GARDEN IS THE LEADING SUPPLIER OF ARTISANAL PRODUCE IN THE UNITED STATES TO TOP CHEFS AND RESTAURANTS. THIS RECIPE IS A TRIBUTE TO FARMER LEE JONES, HIS FAMILY, AND THOSE FIRST SQUASH BLOSSOMS HE SOLD ALMOST TWENTY-TWO YEARS AGO. WE EXTEND OUR HEARTFELT THANKS TO LEE, BOB SR., BOB JR., AND ALL OF THE PEOPLE AT THE CHEF'S GARDEN WHO MAKE OPENING A BOX OF THEIR PRODUCE AS EXCITING AS OPENING THAT FIRST PRESENT ON CHRISTMAS MORNING!

YIELD: 12 STUFFED BLOSSOMS OR 6 SERVINGS

¼ CUP DAY-OLD BREADCRUMBS, FINELY GROUND

8 OUNCES (ABOUT 1½ CUPS) FRESH, LUMP BLUE CRAB-MEAT, PICKED THROUGH FOR SHELLS AND CARTILAGE

3 TABLESPOONS UNSALTED BUTTER, MELTED AND COOLED SLIGHTLY

1½ TABLESPOONS GRATED LEMON ZEST

3 TABLESPOONS CHOPPED FRESH CHIVES, DIVIDED

1 TABLESPOON FINELY CHOPPED FRESH PARSLEY

1 TABLESPOON FINELY CHOPPED FRESH BASIL

¾ TEASPOON KOSHER SALT, DIVIDED

¼ TEASPOON FRESHLY GROUND BLACK PEPPER, DIVIDED

12 FRESH SQUASH BLOSSOMS

2 TABLESPOONS UNSALTED BUTTER

1 LARGE CUCUMBER, PEELED, SEEDED, AND SLICED

1 PINT CHERRY TOMATOES, HALVED LENGTHWISE

¼ CUP THINLY SLICED FRESH OPAL (PURPLE) BASIL, DIVIDED

¼ CUP EXTRA-VIRGIN OLIVE OIL

2 TO 3 TABLESPOONS FRESH LEMON JUICE

Preheat the oven to 350°F.

Combine the breadcrumbs, crabmeat, melted butter, lemon zest, 2 tablespoons of the chives, the parsley, and basil in a medium bowl. Season the stuffing with ½ teaspoon of the salt and ¼ teaspoon of the pepper. Open the squash blossoms and gently fill each blossom with 1 to 2 tablespoons of the breadcrumb mixture. Fold the tip of the blossoms closed and chill for at least 15 minutes.

Add the butter to a large, ovenproof skillet. Arrange the stuffed blossoms in an even layer around the butter and bake for 12 minutes, turning halfway through to ensure even browning.

While the blossoms are roasting, combine the cucumber slices, tomatoes, 2 tablespoons of the opal basil, and the remaining tablespoon of chives in a medium mixing bowl. Drizzle the extra-virgin olive oil and lemon juice over the cucumber mixture and season with the remaining ¼ teaspoon of salt and a pinch of pepper. Allow the salad to marinate at room temperature for about 10 minutes, tossing occasionally.

Divide the cucumber salad evenly among six salad plates. Arrange 2 of the roasted squash blossoms on top of each salad. Garnish each plate with a pinch of the remaining sliced opal basil and serve immediately.

RABBIT TAMALES

with Black Bean Salsa

IF RABBITS ARE UNAVAILABLE, YOU CAN PREPARE THE FILLING RECIPE USING PORK, CHICKEN, OR DUCK. ANY, INEXPENSIVE, TOUGHER CUT OF MEAT THAT NEEDS TO BE BRAISED FOR LONG PERIODS OF TIME WILL WORK WELL. PREPARING THE DIFFERENT COMPONENTS OF THIS APPETIZER CAN BE TIME CONSUMING, SO WE LIKE TO MAKE A DAY OF IT. WE GATHER OUR BOYS INTO THE KITCHEN AND GIVE EVERYONE A SPECIFIC TASK. IT MAKES THE WORK MORE FUN AND GIVES US TIME TOGETHER AS A FAMILY. OF COURSE, THE TAMALES CAN ALSO BE SERVED WITHOUT THE ADDITIONAL ACCOMPANIMENTS, IF YOU'RE PRESSED FOR TIME.

YIELD: 16 TAMALES

RABBIT FILLING:

¼ CUP OLIVE OIL, DIVIDED

1 (2 TO 2½-POUND) WHOLE RABBIT, CUT INTO 6 PIECES

1½ TEASPOONS KOSHER SALT, DIVIDED

½ TEASPOON FRESHLY GROUND BLACK PEPPER

2 CUPS DICED YELLOW ONION, ABOUT 1 LARGE ONION

2 GARLIC CLOVES, PEELED AND ROUGHLY CHOPPED

2 FRESH THYME SPRIGS

2 POBLANO PEPPERS, CHARRED, PEELED, STEM AND
   SEEDS REMOVED, AND CHOPPED, ABOUT 1¼ CUPS

1 DRIED ANCHO CHILE PEPPER, REHYDRATED IN WARM
   WATER AND CUT INTO THIRDS

1 TABLESPOON ANCHO CHILI POWDER

1 TABLESPOON GROUND CUMIN

3 CUPS CHICKEN STOCK (PAGE 335)

TAMALE DOUGH:

16 EARS FRESH CORN WITH HUSKS INTACT

3½ CUPS HEAVY CREAM

2 POBLANO PEPPERS, STEM AND SEEDS REMOVED, AND
   CHOPPED (ABOUT 1¼ CUPS)

1¼ TEASPOONS KOSHER SALT, DIVIDED

¼ TEASPOON FRESHLY GROUND BLACK PEPPER, DIVIDED

4 CUPS MASA HARINA (CORN FLOUR)

FOR SERVING:

1 CUP ANCHO CHILI SAUCE (PAGE 337)

5⅓ CUPS BLACK BEAN SALSA (PAGE 350)

2 CUPS CILANTRO CRÈME FRAÎCHE (PAGE 352)

FRESH CILANTRO SPRIGS, FOR GARNISH

(CONTINUED ON NEXT PAGE)

To Prepare the Rabbit Filling:

Heat 2 tablespoons of the olive oil in a Dutch oven or medium saucepan over medium-high heat. Season the rabbit pieces on both sides with 1 teaspoon of the salt and the pepper. Add the rabbit pieces to the hot oil and sear until well browned on all sides, about 5 minutes. Remove the browned rabbit from the pan and set aside.

Heat the remaining 2 tablespoons of olive oil in the same pan. Add the onion, garlic, and thyme sprigs to the pan and cook until softened, about 2 minutes. Stir in the poblanos, Ancho pieces, chile powder, and cumin. Cook, stirring for 30 seconds, or until the chile peppers are lightly toasted. Deglaze the pan with the chicken stock, stirring to scrape any brown bits from the bottom of the pan and return the rabbit to the skillet. Bring the mixture to a boil, cover, and reduce the heat to low. Allow the mixture to simmer for 45 to 50 minutes or until the meat is tender.

Remove the rabbit from the broth and set aside to cool. Place the broth in a blender and process on high until smooth; set aside at room temperature. When the rabbit is cool enough to handle, remove the meat from the bones and cut into 2 to 3-inch pieces. Discard any excess fat and bones. Combine the shredded rabbit meat and the puréed broth in a medium saucepan and bring to a boil over medium-high heat. Reduce the heat to low and simmer for 1 hour or until the meat is tender and most of the cooking liquid is evaporated. Season the meat mixture with the remaining ½ teaspoon of salt. Using two forks stir and shred the rabbit meat and set aside to cool completely.

To Prepare the Tamale Dough:

Pull off the outer, darker husks of the corn and set aside. Make sure to leave enough corn husks to completely surround the corn, without any gaps. Pull back the remaining husks and cut the corn cob off, leaving a ¼-inch piece of corn in the base of the husks. Trim the pointed base of the corn cob. Repeat with remaining corn husks and cobs. Set aside 2 of the corn cobs for the poblano cream and reserve remaining corn cobs for another use such as the Sweet Corn Succotash (page 105).

Remove the kernels from the two reserved corn cobs. Combine the corn kernels, cream, and poblanos in a medium saucepan. Bring the mixture to a gentle boil, reduce the heat to low, and simmer for 10 minutes. Remove mixture from the heat, cover, and steep for 10 more minutes. Transfer the cream mixture to a blender or food processor and process on high until puréed. Season the cream with ¾ teaspoon of the salt and a pinch of pepper. Refrigerate the cream mixture until well chilled.

Place the masa harina, the remaining ½ teaspoon of salt and ¼ teaspoon of pepper into a large mixing bowl. Gradually add enough of the poblano cream to the masa harina to create a stiff but pliable dough. Make sure enough of the poblano cream is added so that the dough does not crack when rolled out.

Using your hands, pat a ⅓ cup portion of the tamale dough into a 5-inch circle, about ¼-inch thick. Form about 3 tablespoons of the rabbit filling into a 3-inch-long cylinder. Place the meat on the tamale dough and wrap the dough around the filling, pinching to close and seal. Set the tamale inside a corn husk, making sure the corn husk completely covers the tamale. Pull the reserved corn husks into long strips. Use a strip to tie the top of the stuffed corn husk together. Repeat with remaining tamale dough and husks. Using scissors, trim the tops of the corn husks to ½ inch above the tie. Tamales can be steamed immediately or chilled for up to three days.

Set a bamboo steamer inside a wide roasting or braising pan. Fill the pan with enough water to come halfway up the sides of the steamer. Bring the water to a simmer and add the tamales to the top of the steamer basket, in a single layer. Cover and steam for 7 to 8 minutes, or until heated through.

To Serve the Tamales:

Spread 1 tablespoon of the ancho sauce in a circle on each appetizer plate. Mound ⅓ cup of the black bean salsa on each plate. Pull the corn husks down on one side of the steamed tamales and place on each plate, folding the husks behind the tamales. Drizzle 1 to 2 tablespoons of the crème fraîche over each tamale and garnish with several cilantro sprigs. Serve immediately.

ROASTED YOUNG CHICKEN BREAST
with Blackberry Vinaigrette

WE OFTEN USE POUSSIN (YOUNG CHICKEN) BREASTS FOR APPETIZER PORTIONS AT THE RESTAURANT. THE REMAINING POUSSIN LEGS AND THIGHS CAN BE BRAISED AND USED TO MAKE TAMALES OR COOKED IN STOCKS OR SOUPS. IF POUSSINS ARE UNAVAILABLE, CUT TWO REGULAR-SIZE CHICKEN BREASTS HALVES INTO THIRDS. THIS APPETIZER CAN EASILY BE ADAPTED FOR A LUNCHEON ENTRÉE BY DOUBLING THE AMOUNT OF FRISÉE AND VINAIGRETTE IN THIS RECIPE.

YIELD: 6 SERVINGS

6 (1½ TO 2-OUNCE) SKIN-ON, BONELESS POUSSIN OR
   CORNISH GAME HEN BREAST HALVES
1 TEASPOON CHOPPED FRESH THYME
1 TEASPOON CHOPPED FRESH PARSLEY
1 TEASPOON CHOPPED FRESH CHIVES
1 TEASPOON FRESHLY GROUND BLACK PEPPER
2 TABLESPOONS EXTRA-VIRGIN OLIVE OIL
1½ CUPS FRESH BLACKBERRIES
¼ CUP PLUS 1 TABLESPOON HERB VINAIGRETTE (PAGE
   348), DIVIDED
1½ TABLESPOONS VEGETABLE OIL
1 TABLESPOON PLUS ¼ TEASPOON KOSHER SALT, DIVIDED
3 CUPS FRISÉE LETTUCE
6 ROASTED SHALLOTS (PAGE 378), PEELED AND HALVED

Combine the chicken breasts with the thyme, parsley, chives, pepper, and extra-virgin olive oil. Cover and marinate the chicken in the refrigerator for at least 1 hour or up to overnight. After marinating, allow the chicken to sit at room temperature for 20 minutes before cooking.

Preheat the oven to 350°F.

Combine the blackberries and 3 tablespoons of the vinaigrette in a medium mixing bowl, tossing until berries begin to tint the vinaigrette purple. Set aside.

Heat the vegetable oil in a large, heat-proof skillet over medium-high heat. While the oil is heating, season the chicken breasts on both sides with 1 tablespoon of the salt, using about ¼ teaspoon per breast half. Add the chicken to the hot oil, skin side down and cook for 4 to 5 minutes or until golden brown. Turn the chicken and place the skillet in the oven. Roast the chicken for about 4 minutes or until brown on both sides and cooked through. Allow the chicken to rest in the pan for 5 minutes before serving.

Add the frisée and shallots to the macerated blackberries and toss until combined. Season the salad with the remaining ¼ teaspoon of salt and a pinch of black pepper. Evenly divide the lettuce mixture among six appetizer plates. Top each plate with a warm chicken breast and drizzle the remaining 2 tablespoons of vinaigrette over each portion. Serve immediately.

HERB-CRUSTED FLOUNDER

with Watercress Salad and Lemon Butter Sauce

When purchasing flounder, ask your local fishmonger or seafood market for "gigged" flounder that is locally caught. Because it is caught in small quantities, you can be assured of its freshness, and the fishmonger will usually sell out quickly. If gigged flounder is unavailable, choose a regular flounder by asking the fishmonger to hold up the flounder by its head and point the tail at you. If the fish's tail droops and the fish is not flat and stiff it is not fresh and should not be purchased. To save time, have the fishmonger fillet the fresh flounder for you, leaving the skin on.

YIELD: 6 SERVINGS

6 (6-ounce) skin-on flounder fillets
1 tablespoon plus 1¾ teaspoons kosher salt, divided
1¾ teaspoons freshly ground black pepper, divided
1½ cups all-purpose flour
2 large eggs, lightly beaten
5 cups finely ground fresh breadcrumbs
2 tablespoons grated lemon zest, about 3 large lemons
½ cup chopped fresh parsley
½ cup chopped fresh chives
2 tablespoons chopped fresh tarragon (optional)
2 tablespoons chopped fresh chervil (optional)
¼ teaspoon cayenne pepper
¼ cup plus 2 tablespoons peanut oil, divided
6 cups cleaned watercress
2 tablespoons Lemon Dijon Vinaigrette (page 346)
¾ cup Lemon Butter Sauce (page 341)

Preheat the oven to 200°F.

Season the fillets on both sides with 1 tablespoon of the salt and 1½ teaspoons of the pepper, using ½ teaspoon of salt and ¼ teaspoon of pepper per fillet and set aside. Place the flour and the eggs in separate shallow bowls. Combine the breadcrumbs and the next 6 ingredients (lemon zest through cayenne) in a large shallow bowl and season with 1½ teaspoons of the salt. Dredge the seasoned fillets in the flour until evenly coated and shake off any excess flour. Dip the fillets one at a time in the beaten eggs and turn to coat both sides. Lift the fillets out of the egg mixture, allowing any excess egg to drip off before placing the fillets in the breadcrumbs. Dredge the fillets in the breadcrumbs, pressing lightly until well coated.

Heat 3 tablespoons of the peanut oil in a large, nonstick pan over medium-high heat. Just before the oil begins to smoke, add 3 of the breaded fillets, skin-side up and cook for 2 minutes or until golden brown. Turn the fillets and cook an additional 2 to 2½ minutes or until golden brown and cooked through. Remove the fish from the skillet and place on a wire rack set over a jelly roll pan. Place the pan in the oven to keep warm at 200°F until ready to serve. Carefully wipe the skillet clean and repeat with remaining peanut oil and breaded fillets.

Place the watercress in a large bowl with the vinaigrette and the remaining ¼ teaspoon of the salt and pepper. Toss until the watercress is lightly coated and arrange 1 cup of the salad on each of six dinner plates. Place 1 warm fillet next to each mound of greens and drizzle each with 2 tablespoons of the sauce. Serve immediately.

FLOUNDER GIGGERS

The flounder giggers of Apalachicola Bay are a unique breed of fishermen tied to the cycles of the Bay—tonging for oysters part of the year, pulling up nets of bay shrimp at other times, and gigging flounder for a stretch twice each year. For three months at a time, from around May through June and again from September to November, flounder journey from deeper Gulf waters to the shallows of Apalachicola Bay when water temperatures signal it's time to spawn again.

Apalachicola has a long history of flounder gigging and the quality of the flounder there is impressive. As an avid outdoorsman, the process of gigging has fascinated Chris. As "creek boy," from the banks of Pawleys Island, he gigged flounder for his family table before, but never from a boat the way the commercial fishermen do it in Apalachicola. There they maneuver shallow-running boats, sometimes in a mere six inches of water. The only other tools of the trade are a bright light and a long, three-pronged spear. When illuminated, the flounder remain perfectly still in the clear water. The goal of the gigger is to prong the fish right at the gill so the flesh doesn't get mangled.

It is no surprise that Chris jumped at an opportunity to join the giggers who provide our restaurant with such impeccable fish. He headed out on Apalachicola Bay one night with Captain Dwayne Allen and a couple of other guys. Typically two guys venture out in a boat. One steers the boat while the other mans the bow, gigging. Like most things in the natural world, the conditions must be just right. You have to hit the window when the fish are spawning and do so on a calm, still night. If it is windy, the water becomes choppy, churning up the silt from the floor of the bay and clouding the water, making it impossible to gig. Water clarity is crucial.

At the end of a successful night, the giggers take the flounder to the icehouse and ice them down at the docks. Delivery trucks arrive at dawn to load them up to bring to us in Birmingham later that same morning. We get to serve these beautiful fish less than a day out of the water! Dwayne and his buddies are commercial "creek boys" in the purest sense. They are mostly the workers of the bay—harvesting its oysters, bay shrimp, clams, flounder, and mullet. Other fishermen work deeper waters beyond, fishing for snapper, grouper and the big shrimp out in the Gulf.

Chris' experience gigging in the company of these guys who grew up on Apalachicola Bay, as did their fathers and grandfathers, resonated with him in many ways. The bay is a remarkably pristine environment considered one of the cleanest of its kind in America. The bay teems with such a diversity of fish and sea life it leaves you determined to preserve it. The giggers are passionate about the bay and what they do. Who wouldn't be? It is magical to be out on boats under a million stars on a clear night watching the occasional porpoise blow and sharing their stories. In their own unique cadence they convey the importance of preserving and respecting this bay. After all, their lives and livelihoods are intertwined with it. At Hot and Hot we are doing all we can to promote their products while simultaneously helping them preserve the bay they call home.

SEARED TUNA ON ASIAN VEGETABLE SLAW

with Wasabi Aïoli

WHEN WE LIVED IN SAN FRANCISCO, WE WERE EXPOSED TO THE RICH TAPESTRY OF THAT CITY'S FOOD CULTURE. AN IMPORTANT PART OF THAT TAPESTRY IS THE CITY'S ASIAN COMMUNITY ALONG WITH ITS MARKETS AND RESTAURANTS. HAVING NEVER BEEN EXPOSED TO AN ASIAN MARKET, OUR FIRST VISIT TO ONE IN SAN FRANCISCO WAS UNFORGETTABLE. THE SIGHTS, SOUNDS, SMELL AND MYRIAD EXOTIC INGREDIENTS REALLY SPARKED OUR CURIOSITY. IT WAS THERE THAT CHRIS FIRST BEGAN TO FORMULATE IDEAS AND ASIAN FLAVOR PROFILES THAT WE WOULD EVENTUALLY USE AT HOT AND HOT FISH CLUB. THE BEAUTY OF THIS DISH IS THAT IF YOU DON'T HAVE ACCESS TO AN ASIAN MARKET, YOU CAN MAKE IT WITH ANY OF THE FRESH VEGETABLES THAT YOU FIND IN YOUR LOCAL GRO-CERY STORE. HERE IN BIRMINGHAM, WE GO TO A LOCAL MARKET CALLED CHAI'S GROCERY (PAGE 380). MR. CHAI ALWAYS STOCKS A VARIETY OF PRODUCE SUCH AS BOK CHOY, MIRLITON SQUASH, BEAN SPROUTS, AND CHINESE CABBAGES.

YIELD: 6 SERVINGS

SEAFOOD BROTH:

1 CUP VEGETABLE TRIMMINGS SAVED FROM TRIMMING THE BOK CHOY, SNOW PEAS, AND BELL PEPPERS (BELOW)

2 LEMONGRASS STALKS, THINLY SLICED

1 KAFFIR LIME LEAF

1 FRESH THAI CHILE PEPPER, SLICED

1 TEASPOON KOSHER SALT

2 CUPS FISH STOCK (PAGE 334)

TUNA:

6 (6-OUNCE) SUSHI-GRADE TUNA STEAKS (ABOUT 1 INCH THICK)

1¼ TEASPOONS KOSHER SALT, DIVIDED

½ TEASPOON FRESHLY GROUND BLACK PEPPER, DIVIDED

3 SMALL BOK CHOY, TRIMMED AND QUARTERED LENGTHWISE

¾ CUP SESAME VINAIGRETTE, DIVIDED (PAGE 345)

1 CUP THINLY SLICED NAPA CABBAGE

1 CUP JULIENNED FRESH SNOW PEAS

1 CUP FRESH BEAN SPROUTS

½ CUP SEEDED AND THINLY SLICED YELLOW BELL PEPPER

½ CUP SEEDED AND THINLY SLICED RED BELL PEPPER

2 TABLESPOONS JULIENNED FRESH THAI CHILI PEPPERS

2 CUPS COOKED CELLOPHANE NOODLES

3 TABLESPOONS PEANUT OIL

1 CUP FRESH PEA TENDRILS

½ CUP WASABI AÏOLI (PAGE 342)

TO PREPARE THE SEAFOOD BROTH:

Combine the vegetable trimmings, lemongrass, lime leaf, Thai chile, salt, and fish stock in a medium saucepan over high heat. Bring the mixture to a boil, reduce heat, and simmer for 30 minutes. Strain the broth through a fine-meshed sieve. Keep warm over low heat until ready to serve.

TO PREPARE THE TUNA:

Season the tuna steaks on both sides with 1 teaspoon of the salt and ¼ teaspoon of the pepper. Toss the bok choy with 3 tablespoons of the vinaigrette and set aside until ready to use. Combine the cabbage, snow peas, bean sprouts, bell peppers, chile peppers, and cellophane noodles with ½ cup of the vinaigrette. Season with the remaining ¼ teaspoon of salt and ¼ teaspoon of pepper and set aside.

Heat the peanut oil in a large, heavy skillet over medium-high heat. Add the tuna steaks and sear for 1 to 2 minutes on each side (for medium-rare) or until desired degree of done-ness. Remove the steaks from the skillet and keep warm until ready to serve. Add the bok choy and sesame vinaigrette to the same skillet over medium-high heat and cook for 3 min-utes, or until heated through. Remove from the heat.

To plate, ladle ¼ cup of the warm broth into six large soup bowls. Arrange about 1 cup of the slaw and noodle mixture in the center of each bowl. Place 1 tuna steak on top of each mound of slaw. Arrange 2 quarters of the bok choy around each dish. Toss the pea tendrils with the remaining tablespoon of the vinaigrette. Drizzle each dish with 2 teaspoons of the aïoli and garnish with the dressed pea tendrils. Serve immediately.

WHOLE ROASTED SNAPPER

with Vidalia Onions, Lemon, Basil, and Extra-Virgin Olive Oil

USING FRESH, GOOD-QUALITY SEAFOOD ENSURES THAT THE FISH WILL BE THE STAR OF THIS DISH. WE SERVE THIS SIMPLE PREPARATION OFTEN IN THE SUMMERTIME WITH A VARIETY OF SIDE DISHES SUCH AS SLICED HEIRLOOM TOMATOES, RATATOUILLE (PAGE 370), OR CREAMED FIELD PEA AND SUMMER SQUASH SALAD (PAGE 64). THE CLEAN FLAVOR OF FRESH FISH DOES NOT NEED TOO MANY FLAVORS THAT MAY INTERFERE OR OVERPOWER IT.

YIELD: 6 SERVINGS

- **3 (2-POUND) WHOLE RED SNAPPERS, SCALED, GILLS REMOVED, CAVITIES CLEANED, AND FINS TRIMMED**
- **2 TABLESPOONS KOSHER SALT, DIVIDED**
- **1 TABLESPOON FRESHLY GROUND BLACK PEPPER, DIVIDED**
- **1½ LEMONS, THINLY SLICED**
- **1½ BUNCHES (3 OUNCES) FRESH BASIL, DIVIDED**
- **3 LARGE VIDALIA ONIONS, PEELED AND SLICED INTO 4 (¾-INCH-THICK) SLICES EACH**
- **18 FRESH THYME SPRIGS**
- **¾ CUP EXTRA-VIRGIN OLIVE OIL**
- **¼ CUP PLUS 2 TABLESPOONS FRESH LEMON JUICE**
- **3 TABLESPOONS CHOPPED FRESH PARSLEY**

Preheat the oven to 400°F.

Rinse the fish cavities under cold running water and pat dry. Gently pat the outside of the fish until dry. Season the inside of each cavity with 1 teaspoon of the salt and ½ teaspoon of the pepper. Divide the sliced lemons into 3 equal portions and place one portion in each cavity (about ½ lemon per cavity). Roughly chop half of the basil (about 1½ ounces) and evenly stuff each cavity with chopped basil. Set aside.

Arrange the onion slices in three rows on a jelly roll pan. Sprinkle the onions on both sides with 1½ teaspoons of the salt and ¾ teaspoon of the pepper. Place 6 thyme sprigs on each portion of onions and divide the remaining basil over the top of the thyme. Arrange 1 stuffed fish over each portion of onions and herbs. (The fish tails may be slightly longer than the jelly roll pan and can hang over the edge of the pan, if needed.) Bake for 25 to 30 minutes or until cooked through and the flesh flakes easily when tested with a fork. Set aside to rest for 5 minutes before serving.

Whisk together the extra-virgin olive oil, lemon juice, parsley, and remaining 1½ teaspoons of salt and remaining ¾ teaspoon of pepper in a small bowl. Arrange two slices of the onions on each of six dinner plates. Drizzle 1 teaspoon of the olive oil mixture over each portion of onions. Once the fish has rested, transfer to a clean cutting board and gently peel away the skin using a large fork or fish knife. Carefully remove the top fillet off each fish and place one fillet over each portion of onions. (If the fish is cooked through, the flesh will easily pull away from the bones.) Remove the backbone of each fish (which should also pull away easily) and carefully remove the bottom fillet of each fish. Place the remaining fillets on the remaining dinner plates and drizzle the olive oil mixture evenly over each fillet. Serve immediately.

BRUCE MCCULLOUGH – WILD AMERICAN SHRIMPER

It is of supreme importance to us to educate the public about shrimp. We want folks to understand that shrimp are not just shrimp. There are many varieties of shrimp, seasons for shrimp, and flavor profiles of shrimp. Quite simply, wild American shrimp are a far superior product from a quality and flavor standpoint than farmed, imported shrimp. Like a good wine's ties to its terroir, a shrimp's habitat and diet dictate its unique flavor. Understanding the nuances of the many types of shrimp opens a world of opportunity for the chef and home cook. We strive to do all we can to promote the value of wild American shrimp and to advocate for the shrimpers who provide us with this wonderful culinary resource. Like small farmers, shrimpers are getting pounded by rising fuel prices and imports, jeopardizing shrimping communities throughout the southeastern states.

We've had the good fortune to get to know a standout, wonderful shrimper named Bruce McCullough who provides us with top-quality fresh bay shrimp. There are two types of shrimping: bay shrimping and deepwater shrimping. Typically, bay shrimpers do not freeze or artificially preserve their catch; they simply drag their nets for an evening and ice down whatever they get for the return trip to the docks. There, they head the shrimp and sort them by size to sell the next day. A very small portion of their catch is left with the head on. We prefer to purchase and use the head-on bay shrimp as they lend a particularly rich, sweet flavor to the dishes we prepare with them.

Bruce has been a great resource for us for a long time and he truly makes his living, supporting his wife and nine children, by living off the water. He loves the bay and is doing what his family has done there for generations. Besides feeling pinched by diesel prices and the import market, the real tragedy comes from the reality that many restaurants along the Gulf Coast are actually buying imported shrimp to stretch their dollar and calling it "local" shrimp without understanding how they are actually killing their own economy.

While Bruce's expenses have risen at record pace, the price he gets per pound of shrimp has stayed the same since his father was a shrimper forty years ago. His exasperation about the plight of the shrimper is understandable. "Sometimes I'm catching around 600 to 800 pounds a night and I'm still selling shrimp for about $3.00 a pound the same as shrimpers have for half a century only I am forced to spend four times as much to do it. I'm spending easily $40k a year on fuel alone. Imported shrimp are killing us. If our government won't put enough tariff tax on imported shrimp to stop it from coming or at least slow it down, we won't have a fighting chance," Bruce laments.

It would be a tremendous tragedy to stand by and watch our shrimping industry die. At Hot and Hot we are on a crusade to make sure that the decline of the American shrimping industry does an about-face. You can help by learning about the shrimp varieties, buying only Wild American shrimp, and making a conscious effort to avoid imported, farm-raised shrimp at all costs. Your actions will directly support over seventy thousand shrimping jobs, including those of processors, netmakers, and boatbuilders in the United States.

HOT AND HOT CREAMY SHRIMP AND GRITS

with *Country Ham*

At a young age, Chris learned that food was not to be wasted. He and his cousins used to catch small, brown creek shrimp for his mother to use in a traditional Low-Country boil to serve at dinnertime. Leftover boiled shrimp were peeled and placed in a quick pickle brine and refrigerated overnight. In the morning the pickled shrimp were served for breakfast over warm grits along with bacon and eggs. That was the original shrimp and grits. At Hot and Hot Fish Club, we serve shrimp and grits every night. Although this version is different from the one Chris ate as a child, the main elements still remain: shrimp, grits and an acidic sauce. In this recipe we use verjus to give the shrimp sauce an extra zing. Verjus is an acidic, tart liquid made from unripe grapes and can sometimes be found at specialty food stores (pages 380–85). You can also substitute cider vinegar for the verjus with similar results.

YIELD: 4 SERVINGS

1 POUND MEDIUM (25 TO 30 COUNT) SHRIMP, PEELED
  AND DEVEINED

1¼ TEASPOONS KOSHER SALT, DIVIDED

½ TEASPOON FRESHLY GROUND BLACK PEPPER, DIVIDED

1 CUP (2 STICKS) UNSALTED BUTTER, DIVIDED

¼ CUP MINCED SHALLOTS

1 TEASPOON CHOPPED FRESH THYME

½ CUP EQUAL PARTS FINELY DICED CARROTS, CELERY,
  AND ONION (MIREPOIX)

½ CUP BLOND VERJUS OR CIDER VINEGAR

1 CUP SEEDED AND FINELY DICED TOMATOES

3½ TABLESPOONS FRESH LEMON JUICE

1 TABLESPOON CHOPPED FRESH PARSLEY

2 CUPS COOKED MCEWEN AND SONS YELLOW STONE-GROUND
  GRITS (PAGE 354)

¼ CUP THINLY SLICED COUNTRY HAM, JULIENNED

2 TABLESPOONS CHOPPED FRESH CHIVES, FOR GARNISH

Season the shrimp with 1 teaspoon of the salt and ¼ teaspoon of the pepper.

Melt ¼ cup (½ stick) of the butter in a large sauté pan or rondeau over medium-high heat. Add the shallots and thyme and sauté for 1 minute, being careful not to let the shallots brown. Add the mirepoix and continue to cook for 2 to 3 minutes, stirring frequently. Add the seasoned shrimp and cook, stirring frequently, until the shrimp are cooked halfway, about 2 minutes.

While the shrimp are cooking, dice the remaining ¾ cup (1½ sticks) butter and set aside. Deglaze the pan with the verjus and stir in the tomatoes. Cook for 3 to 4 minutes or until the tomatoes and shrimp are cooked through and the liquid has reduced by half. Reduce the heat to low and stir in the lemon juice. Add the diced butter, a few pieces at a time, stirring until each portion is incorporated before more butter is added. Season the sauce with the remaining ¼ teaspoon of salt and ¼ teaspoon of pepper. Remove the pan from the heat and stir in the parsley.

Place ½ cup of the grits on four dinner plates and spoon equal amounts of the shrimp and sauce mixture over each portion of grits. Garnish each plate with 1 rounded tablespoon of country ham and ½ tablespoon of fresh, chopped chives. Serve immediately.

OVER-ROASTED DUCK BREAST ON CRAWFISH RISOTTO
with Spicy Ham Hock Broth

EACH SEASON BRINGS OPPORTUNITIES TO COMBINE INGREDIENTS THAT ARE SIMPLY MEANT TO BE TOGETHER. THIS DISH IS THE PERFECT EXAMPLE: CRISPY DUCK BREAST, PLUMP CRAWFISH, SWEET VIDALIA ONIONS, AND SMOKY TASSO COMBINE FOR AN INTENSE TASTE OF LATE SPRING. FOR A SIMPLE MEAL AT HOME, THE CRAWFISH RISOTTO WORKS WELL ON ITS OWN.

YIELD: 6 SERVINGS

DUCK:
6 (6-OUNCE) DUCK BREASTS, FAT SIDE SCORED
2 TEASPOONS KOSHER SALT
½ TEASPOON FRESHLY GROUND BLACK PEPPER
2 TEASPOONS PEANUT OIL

RISOTTO:
¼ CUP (½ STICK) UNSALTED BUTTER, DIVIDED
1 TABLESPOON MINCED SHALLOTS
1 TEASPOON CHOPPED FRESH THYME
3 MEDIUM SPRING ONIONS, CUT IN HALF AND THINLY SLICED (BOTH WHITE AND GREEN PARTS)
¼ CUP FINELY CHOPPED TASSO HAM OR OTHER CAJUN-SPICED AND SMOKED HAM
3 CUPS BASIC RISOTTO (PAGE 355)
3 CUPS CHICKEN STOCK (PAGE 335), SIMMERING
1 TEASPOON KOSHER SALT
¼ TEASPOON FRESHLY GROUND BLACK PEPPER
2 CUPS COOKED CRAWFISH TAILS

FOR SERVING:
2 TEASPOONS CHOPPED FRESH PARSLEY
2 TEASPOONS CHOPPED FRESH TARRAGON
2 TEASPOONS CHOPPED FRESH CHIVES
1½ CUPS SPICY HAM HOCK BROTH (PAGE 336)

TO PREPARE THE DUCK:
Preheat the oven to 400°F.

Season the duck breasts on both sides with the salt and pepper. Heat the peanut oil in a large, cast-iron skillet over medium heat. Place the duck breasts, fat side down into the skillet and cook until golden brown and crispy, about 6 minutes. Turn the duck breasts and place the skillet in the oven. Roast the duck for 3 to 4 minutes (for medium-rare), or until desired degree of doneness. Remove the duck breasts from the skillet and slice each breast into ¼-inch-thick, diagonal slices. Keep covered on a warm plate while you prepare the risotto.

TO PREPARE THE RISOTTO:
Melt 2 tablespoons of the butter in a wide saucepan or small rondeau over medium-low heat. Add the shallots and thyme and cook for 1 minute, stirring frequently. Increase the heat to medium, add the sliced onions and cook, stirring frequently, until softened but not browned, about 8 minutes. Add the tasso and cook, stirring, for 2 minutes.

Stir the risotto into the onion mixture and cook for 30 seconds or until warmed through. Add ½ cup of the simmering stock and stir constantly with a wooden spoon until all of the liquid is absorbed. Repeat this process, adding ½ cup of the stock each time, until all of the stock has been added. Season the risotto with the salt and pepper and fold in the crawfish tails. Remove the risotto from the heat and stir in the remaining 2 tablespoons butter, parsley, tarragon, and chives.

TO SERVE:
Evenly divide the risotto among six dinner plates. Arrange one sliced duck breast over each plate of risotto. Spoon ¼ cup of the broth around each mound of risotto. Serve immediately.

ANCHO-RUBBED PORK CHOPS
with Arepa Cake and Peach Mojo

AREPA REFERS TO A TYPE OF BAKED OR FRIED CORNMEAL CAKE OF COLOMBIAN OR VENEZUELAN ORIGIN. ALTHOUGH TRADITIONALLY SERVED WITH MEAT AND CHEESE, LIKE A SANDWICH, IT'S SERVED HERE AS A SIDE DISH FOR THE PORK. IN OUR VERSION, WE ALSO ADD SOME FRESHLY SHAVED SWEET CORN THAT'S AVAILABLE THIS TIME OF YEAR. WE HAVE A VARIETY OF BEAUTIFUL PEACHES FROM CHILTON COUNTY, ALABAMA, THAT WE USE IN THIS PEACH MOJO. IN THE FALL, WE PREPARE THE MOJO WITH PEARS INSTEAD OF PEACHES.

YIELD: 4 SERVINGS

2 CUPS PEANUT OIL, FOR FRYING
1 LARGE PLANTAIN
4 (8-OUNCE) 1½-INCH-THICK CENTER-CUT, BONE-IN PORK CHOPS
1½ TABLESPOONS HASTINGS CREATIONS ANCHO PORK SALT (PAGE 381) OR KOSHER SALT
4 AREPA CAKES (PAGE 360)
6 CUPS MIXED BABY LETTUCE GREENS
¼ CUP LEMON DIJON VINAIGRETTE (PAGE 346)
¼ TEASPOON KOSHER SALT
PINCH FRESHLY GROUND BLACK PEPPER
1⅓ CUPS PEACH MOJO (PAGE 351)

Pour the oil into a deep-sided skillet to a depth of ½ inch. (Alternately, a deep fryer can be filled with peanut oil.) Preheat the oil to 360°F. Use a candy thermometer to check the oil temperature as it's important to bring it to the correct temperature when frying the plantains.

Peel the plantain and slice it lengthwise into thin strips using a vegetable peeler or mandoline. Fry the plantain slices in the peanut oil for 2 to 3 minutes, or until golden brown and crispy. Remove from the oil and set aside on a paper towel–lined plate. Keep in a warm place until ready to serve.

Preheat the oven to 400°F.

Season the pork chops on all sides with the ancho salt. Heat 3 tablespoons of the peanut oil in a large, ovenproof skillet over high heat. Add the pork chops and sear for 3 minutes on each side, or until well browned. Place the pork chops in the oven and roast for 10 to 12 minutes (for medium-well) or until desired degree of doneness. Remove the chops from the skillet.

Arrange 1 Arepa Cake on each of four plates. Place lettuce greens in a large bowl with the vinaigrette, salt, and pepper; toss until well combined. Evenly divide the dressed greens among each plate over the cake. Place 1 pork chop on each plate and spoon ⅓ cup of the mojo over each chop. Garnish each plate with 2 fried plantains. Serve immediately.

ROAST LEG OF LAMB

with Ratatouille, Tapenade, and Garlic Crème Fraîche

IDIE'S FAMILY ALWAYS SERVED LAMB FOR EASTER, A TRADITION THAT WAS STARTED BY HER FATHER. WHEN WE MARRIED, CHRIS CREATED THIS DISH TO SERVE AT OUR FIRST EASTER WITH OUR FAMILY. IT WAS A HIT AND WE NOW SERVE IT REGULARLY AT THE RESTAURANT IN THE SPRING. MANY OF THE COMPONENTS CAN BE MADE AHEAD OF TIME AND REFRIGERATED UNTIL READY TO SERVE. THIS MEAL IS DEFINITELY WORTH THE EXTRA EFFORT.

YIELD: 8 SERVINGS

1 (5-POUND) BONELESS LEG OF LAMB
1 TABLESPOON PLUS ½ TEASPOON KOSHER
   SALT, DIVIDED
2½ TEASPOONS FRESHLY GROUND BLACK
   PEPPER, DIVIDED
1 TABLESPOON CHOPPED FRESH THYME
1 TABLESPOON CHOPPED FRESH SAVORY
3 CUPS FRESH SAUSAGE STUFFING (PAGE 374)
¼ CUP OLIVE OIL
5 CUPS EQUAL PARTS ROUGHLY CHOPPED ONIONS,
   CELERY, AND CARROTS (MIREPOIX)
2 CUPS BEEF BROTH OR VEAL STOCK (PAGE 335)
1 CUP GARLIC CRÈME FRAÎCHE (PAGE 352)
1 CUP TAPENADE (PAGE 349)
2 CUPS RATATOUILLE (PAGE 370)
1 TABLESPOON SEA SALT

Arrange the lamb on a clean work surface and remove and reserve the elastic twine bag used in packaging. Open up the lamb, cutting the top if necessary, to allow the leg to lie flat. Season the inside portion of the leg with 1 teaspoon of the salt and ½ teaspoon of the pepper. Sprinkle the thyme and savory over the inside of the leg and top with the sausage stuffing. Fold the leg around the stuffing and tie the center with a piece of butcher's twine to secure. Fit the reserved elastic bag around the stuffed lamb (alternately the lamb can be tied at 2-inch intervals with butcher's twine). Season the outside of the lamb with the remaining 2½ teaspoons of salt and 2 teaspoons of pepper.

Preheat the oven to 350°F.

Heat the olive oil over high heat in a large, ovenproof rondeau or roasting pan. Add the stuffed lamb and cook until well browned on all sides, 10 to 12 minutes. Remove the lamb roast from the skillet. Reduce the heat to medium and add the mirepoix. Cook, stirring frequently, until the vegetables are softened and well browned, 3 to 4 minutes. Remove the roasting pan from the heat and arrange the seared lamb roast on top of the vegetables.

Roast the lamb and mirepoix in the oven for 1 hour and 10 minutes or until the lamb reaches an internal temperature of 130°F. Remove the roast from the oven and allow the lamb to rest for 15 minutes on a rack in a warm place.

Place the roasting pan with the vegetables and lamb drippings on the stove over medium-high heat. Add the beef broth and bring to a boil. Allow the liquid to reduce by half, about 5 minutes. Remove from the heat and strain the liquid through a fine-meshed strainer. Discard the vegetables and reserve the lamb jus.

Using 1 tablespoon of the crème fraîche, form a quenelle (torpedo) shape and place the crème fraîche on a dinner plate, near the rim. Repeat with the remaining crème fraîche on seven remaining dinner plates. Form the tapenade into 1 tablespoon quenelles and place one on each plate next to the garlic crème fraîche. Spoon ½ cup of the ratatouille in the center of each plate. Slice the lamb into 8 (1-inch-thick) pieces. Arrange 1 slice of the lamb over each portion of ratatouille. Spoon several tablespoons of the reserved lamb jus over the lamb and sprinkle lightly with the sea salt. Serve immediately.

CHRIS' MEMORIES FROM THE STRAWBERRY PATCH

Growing up, I was an admitted mama's boy. Without realizing the uniqueness of it at the time, I recall how my mom, Angelica, so often talked about food, planned family trips around food, sought out that perfect ingredient, or just spent time chatting with me and letting me taste her creations while she cooked. Every year during the spring berry season, Mom organized a family trip to a "u-pick" strawberry farm. It was a family ritual to bring home overflowing baskets of plump, ripe berries and to hull them to use in all manners of ways—from strawberry ice cream to strawberry shortcakes—if it could be done with strawberries, Mom most likely attempted it.

These forays afield were just a part of growing up in the Hastings clan. Family vacations had an element that revolved around gathering food for the family meal. It all seemed natural to me at the time, but in hindsight I have come to understand that these experiences, championed by my mom, led to my becoming a chef. The childhood lessons she doled out in the kitchen and strawberry patch and the time spent as her "creek boy" were the most powerful and profound influences on my culinary life.

As a schoolboy, whether I was under the weather or just playing hooky, my mother would take me on an outing. A favorite spot of hers was a place called Leo's Deli where we would go to linger over lunch and have long talks. Our discussions inevitably turned to food. Mom might say something dramatic (Angelica was an actress after all) like, "if you were dying and today was your last day on earth, what would you choose for your last meal?" We would debate the finer points of various dishes, rarely making up our minds, before moving on to other things. Afternoons back home would be spent in her kitchen, bent over a frying pan, tasting the chicken gizzards she'd prepared or sampling the ice cream just churned for our evening's dessert. Events that seemed routine to me at the time are priceless memories today.

My mom died of cancer when I was just eighteen. She would have loved to see me as a chef and restaurateur. Despite the fact that she didn't get to know my wife, Idie, and our boys, Zeb and

Vincent, I wish she could have had the opportunity see my adult love of food and cooking—born of her own passion. My mom taught me that food is magic . . . that it is a very powerful thing that brings people together and forms us as children in ways we can't even begin to understand, and, in turn, those experiences influence the adults we become.

Over the years, many friends have expressed to me how sad it is that my mom died before seeing my success as a chef. I always tell them that after the profound sadness of her death, I came to understand that she is still with me. My strength is Angelica's. My confidence is Angelica's. In a nutshell, if you know me then you know my mother. She is the parent that I am, the lover of food that I am, and the passionate lover of life that I am. I have become my mom!

RHUBARB AND STRAWBERRY
TAPIOCA PUDDING

TAPIOCA PUDDING IS A DISH THAT WE FEEL HAS BEEN A LITTLE LOST TODAY, BUT AS A CHILD, CHRIS REMEMBERS HIS GRANDMOTHER SERVING IT OFTEN. SHE LIKED TO COOK DOWN FRESH SOUTH CAROLINA STRAWBERRIES WITH A LITTLE BIT OF SUGAR AND SERVE THEM OVER WARM TAPIOCA PUDDING. TODAY, I ADD RHUBARB TO THE STRAWBERRY COMPOTE WHICH PROVIDES A BRIGHT, TARTNESS TO THE DISH AND COMPLIMENTS THE SWEETNESS OF THE STRAWBERRIES. THIS DESSERT IS A WELCOME CHANGE FROM THE HEAVY, OFTEN SUPERSWEET DESSERTS THAT SOUTHERNERS TEND TO SERVE.

YIELD: 6 SERVINGS

PUDDING:

½ CUP PLUS 2 TABLESPOONS (3½ OUNCES) LARGE
   PEARL TAPIOCA

2¼ CUPS WATER

3 CUPS WHOLE MILK

½ CUP HEAVY CREAM

PINCH OF SALT

2 LARGE EGG YOLKS

½ CUP GRANULATED SUGAR

1 TEASPOON GRATED LEMON ZEST

COMPOTE:

¾ POUND FRESH RHUBARB STALKS, ABOUT 2 LARGE STALKS

½ CUP GRANULATED SUGAR

¼ CUP FRESH LEMON JUICE, ABOUT 2 LARGE LEMONS

½ CUP DRY ROSÉ WINE

2 CUPS SMALL RIPE STRAWBERRIES, HULLED AND QUARTERED

TO PREPARE THE PUDDING:

Combine the tapioca and water in a large bowl and set aside at room temperature for 2 hours or until the tapioca pearls are tender.

Drain the tapioca in a fine-meshed sieve and place in a large saucepan along with the milk, cream, and salt. Bring the mixture to a boil over medium-high heat, reduce the heat to low and simmer the tapioca mixture until tender, 45 to 50 minutes, stirring frequently to keep from sticking.

Whisk together the egg yolks and sugar in a large bowl. Ladle ¼ cup of the cooked tapioca into the egg mixture while whisking constantly. Continue adding the tapioca, ¼ cup at a time until half of the tapioca mixture has been added. Pour the tapioca egg mixture into the remaining tapioca along with the lemon zest and stir to combine. Return the tapioca to the stove and cook over medium heat, stirring constantly until slightly thickened, 12 to 14 minutes. Cover the pudding and set aside to keep warm until ready to serve.

TO PREPARE THE COMPOTE:

Peel the rhubarb stalks with a vegetable peeler or pairing knife. Slice the stalks into ½-inch-thick slices. (You will need about 2¼ cups, sliced.) Combine the sliced rhubarb, sugar, lemon juice, and wine in a small stainless steel saucepan. Bring the mixture to a boil over high heat, stirring occasionally until the sugar is dissolved. Reduce the heat to medium low and simmer for 20 minutes. Stir in the strawberries and cook for an additional 3 minutes. Remove from the heat and set aside to cool slightly, about 5 minutes.

To serve, spoon ½ cup of the pudding into each of six bowls and top each with 3 to 4 tablespoons of the compote. Serve warm.

FIRST-OF-THE-SEASON STRAWBERRY SHORTCAKES
with Honeysuckle Crème Fraîche

As a child, Chris' family and would go out each May and pick strawberries from the local "pick your own" farms around Charlotte, North Carolina, where they lived. His mother was a great cook and she loved the adventure of foraging for food as much as she did cooking. The smell and taste of a perfectly ripe strawberry that is still warm from the sun is one of his favorite food memories. Sadly, juicy ripe strawberries are hard to find these days. Look for fresh strawberries at your local farmers' market that are red all the way through and are naturally sweet with a slight tanginess. You can use this shortcake recipe throughout the summer, switching out the strawberries for whatever berry is in season.

YIELD: 8 SERVINGS

STRAWBERRIES:

1 (16-OUNCE) CONTAINER FRESH STRAWBERRIES, HULLED AND QUARTERED (ABOUT 2½ CUPS)

3 TABLESPOONS GRANULATED SUGAR

2 TABLESPOONS FRESH LEMON JUICE

SHORTCAKES:

2 CUPS ALL-PURPOSE WHITE LILY FLOUR, PLUS MORE FOR ROLLING OUT DOUGH

1 TEASPOON BAKING POWDER

½ TEASPOON SALT

1 TABLESPOON GRANULATED SUGAR

½ CUP (1 STICK) CHILLED UNSALTED BUTTER, DICED

¾ CUP PLUS 1 TABLESPOON BUTTERMILK, DIVIDED

1 TABLESPOON COARSE, RAW SUGAR

1½ CUPS HONEYSUCKLE CRÈME FRAÎCHE (PAGE 352)

TO PREPARE THE STRAWBERRIES:

Combine the strawberries, sugar, and lemon juice in a small glass or stainless steel bowl. Cover and chill for at least 30 minutes, stirring occasionally.

TO PREPARE THE SHORTCAKES:

Mix together 2 cups of the flour, the baking powder, salt, and granulated sugar in a large bowl. Cut the butter into the flour mixture until pea-sized pieces are formed. Refrigerate the flour and butter mixture, until well chilled, about 30 minutes.

Slowly add ¾ cup of the buttermilk into the chilled flour mixture until a dough begins to come together. Be careful not to overmix or the shortcakes will be tough.

Preheat the oven to 425°F.

Pour the dough out onto a lightly floured work surface and pat down into a 1-inch-thick circle. Using a 1½-inch round cutter, cut as many shortcakes as you can out of the dough. Gently pull together the dough scraps and pat into a 1-inch-thick circle. Continue cutting out shortcakes with the remaining dough.

Place the shortcakes onto an ungreased baking sheet and brush the tops with the remaining tablespoon of buttermilk. Sprinkle the raw sugar evenly over the tops of the shortcakes. Bake for 13 to 15 minutes or until golden brown, remove from the oven, and cool slightly.

Cut the shortcakes in half, horizontally, and place 2 halves on each of eight dessert plates. Spoon ¼ cup of the macerated strawberries and their juices onto the bottom half of each shortcake. Place 2 to 3 tablespoons of the crème fraîche over each of the strawberries and top each with the top half of the shortcake. Serve immediately.

RASPBERRY AND WHITE CHOCOLATE BREAD PUDDING
with Raspberry Coulis

AFTER WEEKS OF TESTING BREAD PUDDINGS, IDIE DEVELOPED THIS RECIPE. DIFFERENT BREADS WERE TRIED FROM FRENCH BAGUETTE TO BRIOCHE AS WELL AS DIFFERENT SIZES AND CUTS OF BREAD. THE AMOUNT OF CUSTARD WAS ADAPTED TO WORK WITH THE TYPE OF SOFT BREAD WE CHOSE. WE KNEW WE WANTED A MOIST, DELICATE BREAD AND THE RIGHT AMOUNT OF WHITE CHOCOLATE IN THE CUSTARD MIXTURE. THEN THE PUDDING IS GENTLY TOSSED WITH THE FRUIT. AS THE SEASONS CHANGE SO DOES THE FRUIT IN THIS RECIPE. IN THE EARLY SUMMER WE USE BLUEBERRIES OR BLACKBERRIES, RASPBERRIES IN LATE SUMMER, APPLES IN THE FALL, AND DRIED CRANBERRIES IN THE WINTER. WHICHEVER VERSION YOU PREFER, WE ARE SURE YOU WILL ENJOY OUR RENDITION OF THIS CLASSIC DESSERT.

YIELD: 9 SERVINGS

2 CUPS HEAVY CREAM
½ CUP PLUS 3 TABLESPOONS GRANULATED SUGAR, DIVIDED
½ VANILLA BEAN, SPLIT
3 LARGE EGGS, LIGHTLY BEATEN
½ (16-OUNCE) FRESH FRENCH BAGUETTE, CUT INTO ½-INCH SQUARES
1 PINT FRESH RASPBERRIES, DIVIDED
4 OUNCES GOOD-QUALITY WHITE CHOCOLATE ROUGHLY CHOPPED
1 TABLESPOON UNSALTED BUTTER, AT ROOM TEMPERATURE
1 CUP PLUS 2 TABLESPOONS WHITE CHOCOLATE SAUCE (PAGE 362)
1 CUP PLUS 2 TABLESPOONS RASPBERRY COULIS (PAGE 363)
1 CUP WHIPPED CREAM (PAGE 367)

Combine the cream and ½ cup of the sugar in a medium saucepan over medium heat. Scrape the vanilla bean into the cream mixture and add the vanilla pods. Bring the mixture to a simmer and then remove the pan from the heat. Set aside until the mixture is cool enough to touch.

Whisk the eggs into the cooled cream mixture and set aside to cool completely.

Stir together the cooled cream mixture, bread cubes, three-fourths of the raspberries, and the chopped white chocolate in a large mixing bowl. Allow the mixture to stand at room temperature for 1 hour.

Preheat the oven to 350°F.

Lightly grease an 8 x 8-inch baking dish with the butter. Sprinkle the remaining 3 tablespoons of sugar into the dish and turn until the bottom and sides of the baking dish are evenly coated. Spoon the bread pudding mixture into the prepared dish, pouring any remaining custard over the top of the pudding. (The mixture may still be slightly liquidy at this point.)

Pour the remaining raspberries on top of the pudding. Cover the pan with aluminum foil and set inside a larger baking dish. Fill the larger pan with enough water to come halfway up the sides of the pudding. Bake the pudding at 350°F for 25 minutes and remove from the oven.

Increase the oven temperature to 375°F. Remove the foil from the top of the pudding, return to the oven, and bake for 35 to 40 minutes, or until the top is golden brown. Remove the pudding from the water bath and set aside to cool slightly.

Cut the cooled bread pudding into 9 equal squares. Serve each portion lightly drizzled with 2 tablespoons of the white chocolate sauce, 2 tablespoons of the coulis, and topped with 1½ to 2 tablespoons of the whipped cream. Serve warm.

ELTON B. STEPHENS AND ELTON'S CHOCOLATE SOUFFLÉ

Elton's Chocolate Soufflé, an Idie creation, has been a mainstay on our dessert menu at Hot and Hot Fish Club since our opening. Idie created the soufflé for our dear friend, Elton B. Stephens. Mr. Stephens was an entrepreneur and great philanthropist for the city of Birmingham and the state of Alabama. He spent his life promoting the arts, health, banking, and education in Alabama. He was a firm believer in the unity of family and importance of one's civic duty and his life and career exemplified these values. Elton and Idie shared a love for chocolate and one day he requested she make him a chocolate soufflé. After several attempts and the sort of tinkering pastry chefs are driven to do, Idie developed a rich chocolate soufflé that was so to Elton's liking; it will never leave our dessert menu.

It has been an honor and great pleasure for Idie to have watched her creation become a signature recipe on the menu and to witness the faces of those in the dining room tasting that first bite of pure chocolate heaven. Idie and our staff stay on top of the very best chocolate varieties available and have found that Belgian dark chocolate is ideal for the richness it brings. At the table the server pours crème anglaise into the center of the hot soufflé then tops it off with a dollop of whipped cream to serve. On occasion we have tried to change up the dessert menu, trading the chocolate soufflé with a lemon one, but our customers always request that we go back to the chocolate.

When we travel, if Idie sees a chocolate soufflé on a restaurant dessert menu, she orders it to compare it to her own recipe. Hands down, we still believe that after thirteen years Idie's recipe does not need a single tweak or adjustment. It is soufflé perfection, so why change or adapt it? The proof is in our customers' reactions and the soufflé bowls that always return to the kitchen empty.

ELTON'S CHOCOLATE SOUFFLÉ
with *Crème Anglaise and Whipped Cream*

WHILE SOUFFLÉS ARE NOTORIOUS FOR INTIMIDATING THE AVERAGE COOK, THIS RECIPE IS EASY AND YIELDS CONSISTENT RESULTS. IDIE TAKES GREAT CARE IN HOW THE EGG WHITES ARE BEATEN AND FOLDED INTO THE BATTER. THE KEY IS TO INCORPORATE AS MUCH VOLUME AS POSSIBLE WHEN BEATING THE WHITES. THIS CAUSES THE "PUFF" OF THE SOUFFLÉ AS IT RISES. IT IS IDEAL TO WHIP THE EGG WHITES BY HAND IN A COPPER BOWL. IF YOU DON'T HAVE A COPPER BOWL, USE A MIXER WITH A WHISK ATTACHMENT AND ADD A PINCH OF CREAM OF TARTAR TO STABILIZE THE EGG WHITES. HAVE FUN WITH THIS RECIPE WHICH IS SURE TO DAZZLE YOUR GUESTS!

YIELD: 8 SERVINGS

1⅓ CUPS (8.75 OUNCES) ROUGHLY CHOPPED
  BITTERSWEET CHOCOLATE
¼ CUP PLUS 1 TABLESPOON UNSALTED BUTTER
4 LARGE EGG YOLKS
PINCH OF SALT
12 LARGE EGG WHITES
PINCH OF CREAM OF TARTAR

5 TABLESPOONS GRANULATED SUGAR
2 TABLESPOONS SOFTENED UNSALTED BUTTER,
  FOR GREASING THE RAMEKINS
½ CUP GRANULATED SUGAR, FOR SUGARING
  THE RAMEKINS
2 CUPS VANILLA CRÈME ANGLAISE (PAGE 361)
1 CUP WHIPPED CREAM (PAGE 367)

Preheat the oven to 400°F.

Place the chocolate in a clean, dry mixing bowl set over a pot of simmering water. (Do not allow the bottom of the mixing bowl to touch the simmering water or the chocolate may scorch.) Stir the chocolate with a heat-proof, rubber spatula until melted and smooth. Remove the bowl from heat and add ¼ cup plus 1 tablespoon of the butter, whisking until melted. Set chocolate mixture aside to cool, about 5 minutes.

Whisk the egg yolks and salt into the cooled chocolate mixture until smooth; set aside.

Combine the egg whites and the cream of tartar in the bowl of a standing mixer. Whisk the whites on medium-low speed and add the sugar, 1 teaspoon at a time, increasing the speed gradually. Continue mixing until the whites are soft, glossy and tripled in volume (medium-stiff peaks).

Fold one-third of the whites into the chocolate mixture, being careful not to overmix. When folding the egg whites into the chocolate mixture, make a figure 8 motion with a rubber spatula, making sure to scrape the bottom of the bowl and then back up. Take care not to overfold the egg whites

which will deflate the volume, making the soufflé loose and runny. It is also important to coat the sides and bottom of the soufflé dish evenly with butter. This enables the soufflés to climb to the very top of the dish and rise evenly. Add the remaining whites, one-third at a time, until all of the whites have been incorporated.

Liberally coat eight 8-ounce ramekins with softened butter and sugar, making sure to cover the bottom, sides, and rims thoroughly. Tap out any excess sugar.

Spoon ¾ cup of soufflé batter into each prepared ramekin. (At this point, the soufflés can be chilled for up to 2 hours, if desired.) Bake the soufflés at 400°F for 12 to 15 minutes, or until the tops are puffed and the edges are lightly brown.

Remove the soufflés from the oven and serve immediately. At the table, cut an X in the top of each soufflé and pour several tablespoons of the crème anglaise into each soufflé. Top with a generous dollop of whipped cream.

AN OUTDOOR SUNDAY PICNIC AND FLY-FISHING

In the late spring and early summertime when the moon is full, bream will go to their beds and spawn for several weeks. It is during that time that you will find our family out in the local ponds and lakes, fly rods in hand casting to fat bream. With bucketfuls of fish, we return home to fillet and slice the bream, soak them in buttermilk, dredge them in cornmeal and fry them quickly in hot oil. This becomes the centerpiece of one of our favorite summertime meals, which we call "swimming French fries." Along with an assortment of vegetables from local farmers, this dish makes the perfect, Southern summer meal.

FRIED BREAM "SWIMMING FRENCH FRIES"
WITH LEMON MAYONNAISE

—◆—

CREAMED FIELD PEA AND
SUMMER SQUASH SALAD

—◆—

GRILLED CORN ON THE COB

—◆—

FRIED OKRA

—◆—

SLICED RUSKIN TOMATOES
WITH BASIL AND GOAT CHEESE

- WINE PAIRINGS -

We like to pair this menu with a refreshing white wine such as a Grüner Veltliner. The Nikolaihof estate makes a wonderfully balanced Grüner Veltliner with notes of lemon, herbs, and white peppercorn. Its steely acidity is a nice match for the tomato and goat cheese salad while the herbal qualities in this wine pair nicely with the fried okra and creamed field pea and squash salad. The nice long finish complements the richness of the fried seafood.

Fried Bream "Swimming French Fries" with Lemon Mayonnaise

Since our boys were young we have been on family fly-fishing trips for bream. The bream that are caught this time of year are generally small, between one-half and one pound each. Once they are filleted, skinned, and the bones are removed, the fillets are thin and small, about the size of thick-cut French fries. When our sons were little they would watch Chris fry the bream and called them "Swimming French Fries." The name stuck and when you try this dish you will find that, just like with French fries, it is hard to eat just one.

YIELD: 8 SERVINGS

1 cup buttermilk

1 tablespoon cayenne pepper, divided

1 tablespoon freshly ground black pepper, divided

16 small (2 to 3-ounce) bream fillets or catfish fillets

1 quart peanut oil, for frying

1 cup store-bought mayonnaise or Basic Aïoli (page 342)

2 tablespoons plus ½ teaspoon fresh lemon juice

1½ teaspoons freshly grated lemon zest

2 tablespoons plus ¼ teaspoon kosher salt, divided

1 cup cornmeal

1 cup corn flour

1 cup all-purpose flour

Whisk together the buttermilk, 1½ teaspoons of the cayenne, and 1½ teaspoons of the black pepper. Arrange the bream fillets in a wide bowl or baking dish, cover with the buttermilk mixture, and chill for 1 hour.

Pour the oil into a deep-sided skillet to a depth of 2 inches. (Alternately, a deep fryer can be filled with peanut oil.) Preheat the oil to 365°F.

Stir together the mayonnaise, lemon juice, zest, ¼ teaspoon of the salt, and a pinch of pepper in a small bowl. Refrigerate until ready to serve.

Stir together the cornmeal, corn flour, all-purpose flour, remaining 2 tablespoons of salt, remaining 1½ teaspoons cayenne, and the remaining 1½ teaspoons black pepper. Dredge the marinated fillets, one at a time, in the cornmeal mixture until evenly coated. Allow each fillet to sit in the cornmeal mixture for several minutes to soak up any excess liquid. Transfer the bream to a baking sheet, being careful not to shake off the excess cornmeal mixture.

Place the breaded bream in the preheated oil, two at a time. Fry for 2 minutes, or until crispy and golden brown. Arrange the bream on a paper towel–lined plate and keep warm until all of the bream have been cooked. Serve hot with a side of lemon mayonnaise, for dipping.

Creamed Field Pea and Summer Squash Salad

This recipe is our rendition of a classic southern pea salad and is perfect for all kinds of functions such as picnics or family reunions. Any type of fresh field pea can be used from butter beans to crowder peas.

YIELD: ABOUT 5 CUPS

DRESSING:

½ cup Basic Aïoli (page 342)

¼ cup Crème Fraîche (page 352)

2 tablespoons tarragon vinegar

1 tablespoon chopped fresh tarragon

1 tablespoon chopped fresh parsley

1 tablespoon chopped fresh chives

½ teaspoon kosher salt

⅛ teaspoon freshly ground black pepper

SALAD:

2 cups cooked field peas, such as black-eyed, pink-eyed, lady, or crowder peas

1 cup finely diced zucchini, about 1 small zucchini

1 cup finely diced yellow squash, about 1 small squash

1 cup freshly shaved, cooked corn, about 2 ears

1 cup chopped green onions

To Prepare the Dressing:

Whisk together the aïoli, crème fraîche, vinegar, tarragon, parsley, chives, salt, and pepper until combined. Refrigerate for 30 minutes before using.

To Prepare the Salad:

Combine the field peas, zucchini, squash, corn, and green onions in a large bowl. Toss with the chilled dressing until well coated and serve. This salad will keep, refrigerated for up to one day.

Grilled Corn on the Cob

For this recipe we purchase corn with the husks intact. The husks hold in moisture and keep the kernels from drying out. It is important to taste a kernel of fresh corn before purchasing a whole bushel. Since the sugars in corn begin to turn to starch as soon as the corn is picked, sweet, juicy corn is a sign of freshness.

YIELD: 8 SERVINGS

1 RED BELL PEPPER, ROASTED, PEELED, SEEDED, AND CHOPPED
1 POBLANO PEPPER, ROASTED, PEELED, SEEDED, AND CHOPPED
1 CUP (2 STICKS) UNSALTED BUTTER, AT ROOM TEMPERATURE
1½ TEASPOONS FRESH LEMON JUICE
2 TEASPOONS KOSHER SALT
1 TEASPOON FRESHLY GROUND BLACK PEPPER
8 EARS CORN ON THE COB WITH HUSKS ATTACHED
½ CUP WATER, DIVIDED

Combine the roasted peppers, butter, lemon juice, salt, and pepper in a food processor and process on high until smooth. Reserve half (about ¾ cup) of the roasted pepper butter for the grilled corn and chill the remaining half for another use. (The flavored butter will keep, refrigerated for up to two weeks and will keep frozen for up to two months.) Peel off and discard the outer husks of the corn, leaving 4 or 5 inner husks attached. Peel back inner husks and remove the corn silk from the cob. Rub 1½ tablespoons of the reserved butter evenly over each corn cob. Fold the corn husks over the corn cobs and place each cob on a 10 x 12-inch piece of aluminum foil. Pour 1 tablespoon of the water over each corn cob and tightly wrap aluminum foil around each cob. Refrigerate until ready to grill.

Preheat the grill to high heat (450°F to 500°F).

Place the foil-wrapped corn over the hottest part of the grill and cook, 10 minutes, turning occasionally. Remove from the heat and allow the corn to sit for 5 minutes before carefully unwrapping the aluminum foil. Peel back the corn husks and serve immediately.

Fried Okra

While we're already set up outside for a fish fry, we usually bread fresh summer okra to fry as a side dish. For traditional, sliced fried okra, try our recipe for Fried Okra Baskets with Chive Aïoli (page 342). If the small, whole fresh okra are available, try breading and frying them whole as in the Hot and Hot Tomato Salad recipe (page 85). Either way, fried okra is one of our favorite picnic foods.

Sliced Ruskin Tomatoes with Basil and Goat Cheese

Ruskin is an agricultural town in Florida, not far from Tampa. It is known for its first of the season tomatoes in May, which we purchase from our friend Mike at Sun-Up Produce. These tomatoes are worth the extra effort to source, but if they are unavailable in your area, any ripe, local or heirloom tomato can be substituted.

YIELD: 6 SERVINGS

6 large ripe red tomatoes, about 3 pounds
2 teaspoons kosher salt
1 teaspoon freshly ground black pepper
½ cup sliced basil leaves, about ¼-inch-thick slices
6 ounces fresh goat cheese
½ cup extra-virgin olive oil

Core the tomatoes and slice them into ½-inch-thick slices. Season the tomatoes on both sides with the salt and pepper. Arrange the tomatoes in a single layer on a large serving platter and sprinkle with the basil. Crumble the goat cheese over the tomatoes and drizzle with the extra-virgin olive oil. Serve at room temperature.

CHAPTER 2

JULY

&

AUGUST

SEVEN SUMMERS
WITH
GRANDMA MORANO

THE MOST VIVID SUMMERTIME MEMORIES OF IDIE'S CHILDHOOD REVOLVE AROUND LIFE WITH HER ITALIAN GRANDMA, ROSINA MARIA SCERBO. ROSINA MARRIED VINCENZO MORANO AND THE TWO SETTLED IN THE MINING TOWN OF CLYMER, PENNSYLVANIA, FAR FROM THEIR NATIVE HOME IN THE CALABRIA REGION OF SOUTHERN ITALY. VINCENZO AND ROSINA'S BROTHER, LOUIE, BUILT A DUPLEX HOUSE IN CLYMER WHERE THE TWO FAMILIES LIVED SIDE BY SIDE. UNCLE LOUIE AND AUNT THERESA SCERBO AND THEIR SIX GIRLS AND THREE BOYS LIVED ON ONE SIDE OF THE HOUSE WHILE GRANDPA AND GRANDMA MORANO LIVED IN THE OTHER WITH THEIR SIX BOYS AND THREE GIRLS. IDIE'S FATHER, JIM, WAS RAISED IN THIS FAMILY HOME UNTIL HIS FATHER'S DEATH WHEN ROSINA MOVED THE FAMILY TO CLEVELAND, OHIO. THE SCERBOS REMAINED IN CLYMER.

Idie's summers always included at least one trip back to visit relatives in Clymer. Whether it was to attend a family wedding, birthday bash, anniversary, or just to visit the Scerbos, the Moranos maintained close ties with their relatives and always returned to the home built by Vincenzo and Louie. Idie marvels that the home held two families with a combined total of four adults and eighteen children—something unheard of today.

When Idie's Grandma Morano moved the family to Cleveland, Idie's dad, Jim, and his brothers and sisters were grown with young families of their own. Grandma Morano settled them in the Italian neighborhood on Cleveland's west side where she bought a duplex (this time upstairs and downstairs flats). She moved into the bottom half with her young granddaughter Idie, and son Jim. One of Idie's aunts, an uncle, and two cousins took the top flat. The rest of the Morano family found housing nearby. The first seven years of Idie's life were spent living in that flat with her dad and grandmother. Her many aunts acted liked mothers to her. Needless to say, those formative years, enveloped in the love of her large extended family, had the most powerful impact on her. She learned much from listening to the family talk around the dinner table. As one of the youngest cousins, Idie developed a keen ability to listen and observe her surroundings from an early age. She absorbed everything her grandmother taught her.

As the family matriarch, Grandma Morano held court. All of her children called her daily to check in and young Idie, in particular, adored, worshipped, and clung to her every word. Sundays were extra special because that was the day the Morano clan attended mass at St. Rocco's and someone from the family always stopped by to visit Grandma. For the most part, the Moranos did everything together. Hours were spent planning meals, cooking, and gathering at the table. Idie grew up imagining all families were as close. She even attended elementary school with her many cousins. Through these early experiences, Idie grasped that family was everything and friends came second.

As much as Grandma Morano loved to eat, she had a passion for cooking. Her whole day focused on preparing the next meal—a labor of love for her. As soon as lunch was finished she would turn to Idie and ask, "What shall we have for dinner?" Cooking was an expression of love and comfort. Shopping for food was equally exciting and Grandma Morano often let Idie tag along. Cleveland's West Side Market was where the two would go to purchase the best sausages, Italian salamis, mortadella, prosciutto, cheeses, and olive oil. Zannoni's was another family-owned Italian market nearby. There, Idie looked forward to the special treat she would get at the candy counter—a piece of imported Italian nougat. The candy was sweet with dried fruits, nuts, and egg whites and it didn't matter to Idie that it stuck to her teeth, she was too busy admiring the beautiful box and parchment paper wrapping in which the special treat had come packaged.

Idie's dad, Jim, was an avid shopper too. Whether on the hunt for a new specialty store or simply browsing familiar grocery aisles, reading the ingredients on packages, comparing prices, tasting samples, or talking to the butcher, these were daily rituals he relished. Perhaps his excitement stemmed from his days working in the meat department of the Sgreccia Grocery Store back in Clymer. Regardless, Jim and Grandma Morano showed Idie that trips to the market were an adventure, not a chore.

Grandma Morano, Aunt Mary, and Aunt Emma often prepared meals for the priests at St. Rocco's and volunteered at the church preparing food for those in need. Then there were numerous festivals for which the community prepared throughout the year. Every Labor Day St. Rocco's held a celebration that included parades, races, and a famous "grease pole" contest where those who made it to the top of a greased telephone pole won a prize. Spectators were warned to stand back because it could get quite messy. Idie's favorite festival was the procession of the Blessed Mary, celebrated with a parade down the street in front of the Morano house, a memory that now conjures visions of the scene in *The Godfather* with the crowd following and sounds of music and the banging of pots and pans.

The Fourth of July was when the Moranos celebrated Idie's father and Aunt Jenny's (Jim's sister) birthday. Everyone was expected to bring a dish and with Grandma Morano, six uncles, three aunts, their spouses and cousins that meant a lot of food. The spread was more or less the same each year and served buffet style. The Moranos gathered at a long harvest table, really two tables end-to-end that were set up in an aunt and uncle's backyard. Though the day culminated with an actual dinner around the table, Idie remembers literally grazing all day long. As guests arrived, the grills were already smoking hot with the juices of the Italian sausages dripping and sputtering into the coals, chicken was basting in a lemon butter sauce, and an uncle could be found unwrapping the choice cuts of meat he'd procured from the West Side Market. Idie looked forward to her favorite side dish, an Italian rice salad that was an amalgam of cooked rice, fresh lemon, ground beef, tomato sauce, and Romano cheese. It was her Aunt Emma's specialty. Grilled, seasoned eggplant was another family favorite. And no Morano meal was complete

without Italian rolls on the table. Dessert was Jim and Jenny's birthday cake and fresh watermelon. The massive cake covered a full baking sheet and was decorated with a Fourth of July theme complete with sparklers for candles. When everyone was on their way home, Uncle Joe would say "summer's over, that's it."

The Moranos are a competitive bunch, so these family celebrations inevitably were filled with net games such as badminton and volleyball. The men also played horseshoes and bocce after dinner. Idie's father, Jim, quite possibly, remains the reigning king of horseshoes. The younger children played water sports in the pool, which often ended with water balloon fights. At the end of the evening, it was not uncommon for an unruly older child to throw one of the aunts into the pool. Even now, many years later, memories of these early Fourth of Julys embody the essence of summertime for Idie. After all, the first few years of a child's life are said to be some of the most pro-

found and certainly all of Idie's senses were honed during those seven years she lived with her dad and grandmother. When she closes her eyes, she can hear her Grandma Morano's voice, recall the comfort of her warm hugs, and the smell of her loaves of baking bread. Grandma Morano's legacy lives on in Idie and three generations of Moranos.

On Sundays, as Idie stirs a pot of homemade soup on the stove at home or rolls out handmade pasta for her boys, she feels the presence of her dad, Jim, who was so often found in their kitchen doing the exact same thing. And at the restaurant, when the lights are dimmed and the dining room hums with activity, it is almost as if her dad, aunts, and uncles are right there, sitting at their favorite spot, table 14, discussing the menu and the reminiscing about meals they shared back home. These warm memories of family and food nurture Idie's soul.

SUMMERS WITH OUR BOYS

Every year as school ended, we sought ways to keep our very active boys occupied. Our general rule was to spend time doing daily activities that fed them in a variety of ways, stimulating their minds and tuckering them out. Idie spent countless hours with them, weaving the paths of the Birmingham Zoo and the Botanical Gardens. Our oldest, Zeb, could easily have been a tour guide because he knew each place like his own backyard. He has always been the type to get down on his hands and knees to inspect the smallest plant, lizard, or stone and become familiar with the details. He took it all in.

When the boys tired or pleaded for a snack or lunch, Idie would guide them to the big tree just to the right of the metal-and-glass arboretum. There they would share a picnic lunch that might consist of fried chicken and okra or homemade mini cheese sandwiches, a selection of fruit and just-baked chocolate chip cookies. Idie never sets an ordinary picnic, she comes armed with a blanket and picnic basket filled with plates, silver, and cloth napkins. She relishes eating outside with cloth napkins and all the accoutrements. The boys saw this as perfectly normal. She spread everything out under the shade of that tree and they would devour their lunches, fighting over the last cookie before announcing at last that they were ready to go home and get out of the hot Alabama sunshine.

As they got older, they regularly wanted to set up their own lemonade stand. Their lemonade was not of the reconstituted powdered variety. Nope, that would never do! We took them to the store to touch and feel the lemons to select those that were soft, supple, and perfect for juicing. Our boys learned what to look for. We even bought them a juicer—certainly they were the only kids in the neighborhood with their very own kitchen appliance. We taught them how to make real, old-fashioned lemonade—adding sugar to the freshly squeezed juice, tasting and tasting along the way, until they agreed that a batch was ready for the front lines. At the edge of the yard where it meets the street, they set up their stand offering their very own "homemade" lemonade. It was an endeavor that taught them the importance of teamwork, great communication skills, and about the business of making money and dividing their earnings. We believe this early experience might have planted the seed that got Zeb dreaming about owning his own business someday and wanting to pursue a business degree to make it happen. Now in boarding school, when Idie sends him the homemade pecan pies he loves, we find that he has been selling them to his classmates . . . and for a sizeable profit!

Our boys also learned how to crank an old-fashioned ice cream machine. They learned to make the custard from scratch and patiently churn it into the most amazing ice creams. Looking forward with anticipation to licking the bowls and spoons in the same way we all feel compelled to lick cake batter from a spatula kept them focused on their task.

Reflecting on these family summers at home, we realize our boys ate everything we did. We never had a "children's" menu. We shared the same foods together at the communal table. Sadly, that's something so rare these days. Now away at boarding school, they call to request shipments of ribs, crawfish, oysters, pecan pie, lemon buttermilk tarts, and any type of cookie. We send them crawfish and they put on large crawfish boils up at their northeastern school and also teach their classmates how to suck down oysters topped with lemon and freshly grated horseradish, and to do so with gusto. We are proud that our love and appreciation of food—of procuring perfect ingredients, preparing them patiently, and then sharing the fruits of their labor—has rubbed off on them and they are passing it along.

JP'S POMERITA

This is bartender JP's take on a classic margarita. The pomegranate juice adds a bright tartness to this drink. While pomegranates are typically hard to find fresh this time of year, the juice is more commonly found in the refrigerator or freezer section of most stores. For best results, look for one that is made from 100 percent pomegranate juice.

YIELD: 1 SERVING

2 LIME WEDGES, DIVIDED
⅓ CUP MARGARITA SALT (OPTIONAL)
4 OUNCES (½ CUP) PURE POMEGRANATE JUICE
1½ OUNCES (3 TABLESPOONS) GOLD TEQUILA
½ OUNCE (1 TABLESPOON) LIME JUICE
1 OUNCE (2 TABLESPOONS) SIMPLE SYRUP (PAGE 362)

Rub the rim of a margarita glass with one of the lime wedges. Pour the margarita salt (if using) into a shallow dish and dip the top of the margarita glass into the salt. Set the glass aside.

Combine the pomegranate juice, tequila, lime juice, and syrup in a martini shaker filled halfway with ice. Shake until well chilled. Fill the prepared margarita glass with ice and strain the pomegranate mixture into the glass. Garnish the glass with the remaining lime wedge and serve immediately.

IN MEMORY OF BARTENDER JP

John Patterson, affectionately known as "JP" served on the Hot and Hot wait staff for many years. JP's passion for food, Auburn football, his close friends, and his work is his legacy. As a dedicated mixologist he created his signature drink, "JP's Pomerita" years ago and it will remain on our menu as long as we are open in memory of our dear friend. Several years ago, JP. passed away after a long battle with cancer. Customers fondly remember JP and toast to him many an evening at the restaurant. "Here's to JP a gentle, kind soul who lived life to the fullest."

NORMAN DRIVE LEMONADE

Whenever we see a bowl of lemons either in a photograph or a painting, we think of our boys making lemonade as children. It is interesting that traditionally in the South iced tea is served in the summer, but how often do you see children with iced tea stands? There are many lemonade stands throughout the neighborhoods but when you come upon one with fresh lemons and a commercial juicer on the table, you know you just have to stop and try a taste. The Norman Drive lemonade stand was that kind of stand.

YIELD: ABOUT 3 CUPS OR 4 SERVINGS

1 CUP FRESHLY SQUEEZED LEMON JUICE
1½ CUPS WATER
½ CUP GRANULATED SUGAR
⅛ TEASPOON PURE VANILLA EXTRACT

Fill four glasses or cups with ice and set aside.

Combine the lemon juice, water, sugar, and vanilla in a pitcher and stir with a wooden spoon until most of the sugar is dissolved. Pour ¾ cup of lemonade over each glass of ice and serve.

BLOND MARY

THIS DRINK IS OUR ANSWER TO A SURPLUS OF HEIRLOOM TOMATOES. THE YELLOW TOMATOES ARE LOWER IN ACIDITY THAN RED TOMATOES AND MAKE AN EXCEPTIONALLY REFRESHING BLOODY MARY. SINCE FRESH HORSERADISH CAN VARY IN INTENSITY, YOU MAY NEED TO TASTE AND ADJUST THE AMOUNT TO SUIT YOUR NEEDS. ANY PICKLED VEGETABLE WILL MAKE A GREAT GARNISH FOR THIS COCKTAIL. WE ALWAYS HAVE PICKLED OKRA ON HAND IN THE SUMMERTIME, BUT PICKLED GREEN BEANS, ONIONS, OR CARROTS ARE ALL GOOD ACCOMPANIMENTS.

YIELD: 1 SERVING

10 OUNCES (ABOUT 2 MEDIUM) YELLOW TOMATOES,
QUARTERED
1½ OUNCES (3 TABLESPOONS) HOUSE-INFUSED PEPPER
VODKA (PAGE 277)
½ OUNCE (1 TABLESPOON) OLIVE JUICE
½ OUNCE (1 TABLESPOON) FRESH LEMON JUICE
½ OUNCE (1 TABLESPOON) FRESH LIME JUICE
2 TEASPOONS FRESHLY GRATED HORSERADISH
½ TEASPOON TAMARIND SAUCE (PAGE 338)
½ TEASPOON KOSHER SALT
¼ TEASPOON FRESHLY GROUND BLACK PEPPER
1 TABLESPOON CHIFFONADE OF FRESH BASIL
1 PIECE IDA MAE'S PICKLED OKRA (PAGE 78),
FOR GARNISH
1 CELERY STALK, FOR GARNISH
1 LARGE GREEN OLIVE, FOR GARNISH

Place the quartered tomatoes in a food mill set over a bowl and turn until all of the liquid is extracted. Discard the peel and solids. Strain the tomato liquid through a China cap or fine-meshed colander to remove any seeds. (You will need about ⅔ cup of strained yellow tomato juice.)

Combine the yellow tomato juice, vodka, olive juice, lemon juice, lime juice, horseradish, tamarind sauce, salt, and pepper in a martini shaker filled halfway with ice. Shake until well chilled. Strain into a 16-ounce pint glass filled with ice. Add the basil and stir until combined. Garnish the glass with pickled okra, celery stalk, and olive. Serve immediately.

SHRIMP GAZPACHO WITH LEMON OIL

THIS IS OUR SOUTHERN TAKE ON A CLASSIC SPANISH SOUP. BECAUSE IT IS ALWAYS SERVED COLD, IT IS A LIGHT AND REFRESHING MEAL FOR A SULTRY SOUTHERN DAY. YOU CAN SUBSTITUTE JUMBO LUMP BLUE CRABMEAT FOR THE SHRIMP, IF YOU PREFER. MANY GOOD OLIVE OIL COMPANIES ALSO PRODUCE LEMON OIL IN WHICH THE OLIVES ARE PRESSED WITH FRESH LEMONS, CREATING A FRAGRANT, FLAVORFUL OIL. LEMON OIL ADDS A BRIGHT, RICH QUALITY TO THIS SOUP.

YIELD: ABOUT 6 CUPS OR 6 SERVINGS

1½ POUNDS RIPE TOMATOES, CORED, ABOUT 3 TO 4 MEDIUM TOMATOES

½ CUP PEELED, SEEDED, AND FINELY DICED CUCUMBER

½ CUP FINELY DICED ZUCCHINI

½ CUP FINELY DICED YELLOW SQUASH

½ CUP PEELED, SEEDED, AND FINELY DICED TOMATO

½ CUP SEEDED AND FINELY DICED RED BELL PEPPER

½ CUP SEEDED AND FINELY DICED YELLOW BELL PEPPER

½ CUP FINELY DICED POBLANO PEPPER

½ CUP EXTRA-VIRGIN OLIVE OIL

¼ CUP BALSAMIC VINEGAR

¾ TEASPOON KOSHER SALT

¼ TEASPOON FRESHLY GROUND BLACK PEPPER

26 LARGE (21 TO 25 COUNT) COOKED, PEELED, AND DICED FRESH SHRIMP, ABOUT 1 POUND

12 FRESH BASIL LEAVES, THINLY SLICED

3 TABLESPOONS LEMON OIL (PAGE 382)

Slice each of the tomatoes into quarters. Place the tomatoes in a food mill set over a bowl and turn until all of the juice is extracted. You will need about 2 cups of fresh tomato juice. Discard the tomato seeds and peel. Alternatively, the tomatoes can be seeded, roughly chopped, and puréed in a food processor or blender. Strain through a fine-meshed sieve and discard any solids.

Combine the tomato juice and the next 9 ingredients (cucumber through vinegar) in a large bowl, stirring well to combine. Season the soup with the salt and pepper and stir in the diced shrimp. Refrigerate for at least 2 hours or until the soup is well chilled. Ladle the soup into six serving bowls and garnish each serving with 1 teaspoon of the chopped basil and ½ tablespoon of lemon oil. Serve chilled.

IDA MAE'S PICKLED OKRA

THIS TIME OF YEAR IDA MAE, OR "IDIE" AS WE LOVINGLY CALL HER, AND I VISIT THE FARMERS' MARKET ABOUT THREE MORNINGS A WEEK. YEARS AGO IDIE DEVELOPED THIS PICKLING BRINE TO PRESERVE THOSE SMALL CUCUMBERS WE WOULD FIND AT THE MARKET. AT THE RESTAURANT WE USE THIS SAME BRINE TO PREPARE PICKLED OKRA THAT WE OFFER TO GUESTS AT OUR COCKTAIL BAR. THE LONGER THE OKRA SITS IN THE PICKLING BRINE, THE BETTER. THEY ARE THE PERFECT ACCOMPANIMENT FOR YOUR NEXT COCKTAIL HOUR OR SUNDAY BRUNCH BLOND MARY (PAGE 76).

YIELD: ABOUT 2 POUNDS PICKLED OKRA

6 CUPS WATER

3 CUPS CIDER VINEGAR

1 TABLESPOON PICKLING SPICE

2 TABLESPOONS IODIZED SALT

1½ TEASPOONS SEA SALT

1 TEASPOON GRANULATED SUGAR

1½ TEASPOONS BLACK PEPPERCORNS

8 LARGE GARLIC CLOVES, PEELED AND CRUSHED

12 FRESH THYME SPRIGS

9 DRIED ARBOL CHILE PEPPERS

6 FRESH DILL WEED SPRIGS

2 POUNDS FRESH OKRA

Combine the first 11 ingredients (water through dill weed) in a large stockpot and bring to a boil, stirring until the salt is dissolved. Reduce the heat to low and simmer for 15 to 20 minutes.

While the brine is simmering, rinse the okra with cold running water and pick through to remove any bad okra, tough stems, and leaves. Place the okra in a large stockpot or heavy-duty, heat-proof container. Remove the hot brine from the heat and pour over the raw okra. Weigh down the okra with a heat-proof plate to make sure they stay completely submerged. Allow the okra to steep at room temperature for 1 hour. Chill the okra and the brine for at least 48 hours but preferably up to 1 week. The pickled okra will keep, refrigerated, for up to one month.

CANNED VERSION:

For canning the pickled okra, place the fresh okra in pint-size sterilized jars. Pour the hot brine mixture over the okra into each jar, leaving ¼-inch headspace at the top of each jar. Divide the garlic cloves, dill sprigs, and chile peppers (from the brine) into each jar. Place the two-piece lids on each jar and turn just until the lids are tight. Submerge the jars in boiling water for 15 minutes. Carefully remove the jars from the boiling water and allow the jars to sit at room temperature until cool enough to handle. Check to ensure that there is an indention in the top of the lid on each jar before storing. Allow pickles to sit in a cool, dry place at room temperature for at least 2 weeks before using.

JEFFERSON COUNTY FARMERS' MARKET – OKRA AND TOMATOES

In most relatively large American cities there is some type of regional or county farmers' market and Birmingham is no exception. These markets not only provide small growers opportunities to sell their annual crops out of the back of their trucks but often they serve as a hub for receiving and distributing produce from larger farms. These markets are the life blood of agriculture in America—where farmers and buyers large and small can gather and conduct business. Farmers' markets give growers and distributors the opportunity to exchange information on growing, seeds, infestations, weather, and a multitude of things surrounding farming. They also provide the general public with a greater understanding about their towns and surrounding farms, local food history, and farming traditions. By visiting the Jefferson County Farmers' Market in Birmingham, one can experience why Chilton County peaches are so popular and why Sand Mountain tomatoes from the Northern part of Alabama or tomatoes from the small South Alabama town of Slocum are some of the most sought after tomatoes in the region. Local markets connect people to an intimate knowledge about their communities, the people and the products that bring such regional pride. At the core of these markets of course are the people. We would like to highlight a few unique people whom we have done business with for many, many years. They are what make our local market so amazing. Their love for their land, their disproportionate passion for farming, and their infectious energy for selling produce are what bring us back to the market year after year.

Edna Lenior and her husband Vernon began farming seventy-five acres of okra in 1962. On any given week during the height of okra season (June through the first fall frost), the Leniors employ one hundred pickers to harvest the okra. With that kind of manpower, Edna has about twelve hundred eight-quart basketfuls of okra to sell at the market each week. In the early days, the pickers were paid about 20¢ per basket while today they receive $3.50 for each basket of okra they pick. Edna and Vernon have been vendors at the Birmingham Farmers' Market for the past forty-six years and are known for providing the very best okra in three different sizes. They sell jumbo size, which is perfect for soups, gumbos, and the like, choice size, which is ideal for frying, and fancy size, which is often best for pickling and occasionally frying. Not all okra is created equal. Over the years we have traveled to markets all over the country in search of amazing okra and nobody anywhere has quality okra like Edna produces. Sadly, Vernon died in 2003 but Edna's two sons, George and Gregory, have stepped in to help her continue the tradition. The sons are not okra farmers by trade but are happy to help their mother harvest okra each week so that she can provide our community with her wonderful okra. Occasionally Chris has sat with Edna on the back of her truck and watched the buyers come and go. As he's listened to her conversations with the shoppers and seen the crowds that gravitate to her truck he's come to understand the magnitude of Edna's impact on our community. Other farmers, friends, and customers genuinely love Edna and her okra. Our entire community benefits from Edna and Vernon's lifetime of growing their very special okra.

We have another friend at the market who is not a farmer but a distributor. Mike Arnold of Sun-Up Produce runs a small operation by distributor standards, but his is a very important one. Purchasing produce from Sun-Up Produce allows us access to an even larger number of high-quality farms throughout our region. Mike travels all around the southeast from farm to farm buying only the best seasonal produce available. He has a vast knowledge of produce and a distinct memory for the farmers and field hands that he meets. We consider Mike our "non heirloom" tomato guru. Beginning on May 1 we depend on Mike to source the best first of the season tomatoes, which usually come out of Ruskin, Florida. He then tracks the tomatoes through their growing seasons into south Georgia, south Alabama, north Alabama, the Carolinas, and into Tennessee by the end of the season in late August to mid-September. Mike can tell us which specific field the tomatoes are grown in and which farm hand picked and packed them. He makes sure the perfectly ripe tomatoes are treated carefully, like children, and are cautiously packed into each box. Wow! Few people realize that sourcing and transporting quality produce can be an art. Because Mike is familiar with our tomato quality standards we continue to purchase tomatoes from Sun-Up Produce each year. He is one reason our legendary Hot and Hot Tomato Salad (page 85) is what it is today.

With people like Edna and Mike, who we consider extensions of our restaurant family, we can create dishes that are worthy of their produce. It is important to us that their stories are told and documented for future generations. We feel that if we as a community and a society at large do not support these people then there may come a day when they will no longer exist. The thought of the small American farm, like Edna's or the farms Mike buys from, disappearing brings tears to our eyes. We want to make it a point to find and support these people who keep the traditions and food lore of our state and region alive. We encourage our customers, who enjoy the regional produce at our restaurant, to find local markets of all kinds, ask questions, learn, get to know the vendors, and most importantly support the community farmers. It is a practice that will benefit our community for generations to come.

HOT AND HOT FRIED OKRA BASKET
with Chive Aïoli

At the restaurant we often serve small basket-size portions of fried okra with chive aïoli to our customers. Since it's popular with adults and kids alike, it also tends to be one of our family's favorite side dishes for summer dinners and fish fries. One of the keys to preparing crispy, fried okra is making sure each piece is breaded well. We like to gently sift the okra in a colander to keep any excess breading from clinging to the okra. Spreading the breaded okra evenly on a baking sheet allows the breading to soak up any excess moisture before frying.

YIELD: 4 SERVINGS

CHIVE AÏOLI:
1½ cups Basic Aïoli (page 342)
¼ cup finely chopped fresh chives
¼ teaspoon kosher salt
¼ teaspoon freshly ground black pepper

OKRA:
30 pieces fresh okra
¾ teaspoon kosher salt
¼ teaspoon freshly ground black pepper
¼ cup buttermilk
1 to 1½ quarts peanut oil, for frying
¼ cup all-purpose flour
¼ cup finely ground yellow cornmeal
¼ cup corn flour
Pinch of cayenne pepper

TO PREPARE THE CHIVE AÏOLI:
Whisk together the aïoli and chives until well combined. Season with the salt and pepper and refrigerate for at least 20 minutes before serving. This sauce will keep, refrigerated for up to one day.

TO PREPARE THE FRIED OKRA:
Wash the okra to remove any dirt and grit. Discard any bad or dark brown okra. Trim the tops off the okra and cut the pods into ½-inch slices. Place the sliced okra in a large bowl and season lightly with the salt and pepper. Cover the okra with buttermilk and soak for 5 minutes, stirring frequently.

Pour the oil into a deep-sided skillet to a depth of 3 inches. (Alternately, a deep fryer can be filled with peanut oil.) Preheat the oil to 350°F.

Combine the all-purpose flour, cornmeal, corn flour, and a pinch of cayenne in a large bowl. Drain the okra as much as possible and toss in the flour mixture, in small batches, until each piece is well coated. Place the okra in a dry sieve or colander and shake gently to sift out any excess breading. Spread the breaded okra out in an even layer on a baking sheet for at least 10 minutes before frying.

Fry the okra, in batches until crisp and golden, 1½ to 2 minutes per batch. Using a slotted spoon, transfer the okra to a paper towel–lined plate and season with additional salt to taste, if needed. Serve immediately alongside a small bowl of the chive aïoli.

ORIGIN OF THE HOT AND HOT TOMATO SALAD

In the early nineties, upon our return to the South from California, we began thinking about our future. It was either time to make plans for our own restaurant or to move on to another big city to take a job as a chef at an established restaurant. The quality of life Birmingham affords made our decision to stay here to start our own restaurant a relatively easy choice. With that decided, we still had to figure out exactly what we wanted our restaurant to be. Obviously, our focus would be on southern ingredients but we had to differentiate ourselves.

One of the great lessons we learned out in California was the importance of ingredients going straight from the farm to the table without missing a beat. Ingredients appeared on menus only when seasonally fresh and absolutely of-the-moment. But, beyond that, from a culinary standpoint, chefs there also adapted their techniques in the kitchen to the seasons at hand. During hot months, they would keep some things raw, serve cooked things chilled or at room temperature, and omit the big heavy sauces often served over meat, fish and game during cooler months. Chris became enamored by the plates of incomparably fresh vegetables and tender greens tossed to order with a flavorful vinaigrette and served at room temperature with a small portion of warm meat or seafood on top. This warm-cool contrast really showcased flavors in a way that was bright and refreshing. He knew that if he applied that same concept to southern ingredients it could have awesome results.

Deconstructing succotash (blasphemy!), something Southerners eat their entire lives, by preparing the ingredients individually and then recombining them to serve in a new way was our first experiment. The goal was to create the quintessential southern salad, truly summer-on-a-plate, but, instead of following the traditional method of cooking the tomatoes, okra, corn, field peas, bacon, and onions together in the usual fashion, Chris decided to reinvent the technique. Alabama is tomato heaven, so building a tomato salad around classic succotash components made sense. The recipe went through several derivations with okra fried or not fried, corn on the cob or off the cob, field peas of every variety available, and so on. Everything was to be cooked separately and served at room temperature with the exception of the hot okra and the crisp bacon just out of the pan to provide the pleasing temperature contrast. Vinaigrette made with fresh basil, balsamic vinegar, and scallions is a tomato's best friend and an absolutely harmonious mix, plus you can't beat balsamic with tomatoes.

We start receiving calls in April asking when the tomatoes will arrive at the restaurant, signaling the beginning of tomato salad season. We are stopped on our days off and field phone calls at home asking about the availability of tomatoes. There is a tomato frenzy at the farmers' market. In May, Chris calls Mike at the market asking about the status of first of the season tomatoes. Occasionally he receives a call from the market to come out and look at the tomatoes, but returns empty handed when the quality is not up to our standards. Meanwhile, customers are arriving at the restaurant to ask if the tomato salad will be served that evening. Usually when people run into us outside of the restaurant, they ask us how our boys are, but during April and May we're asked only about tomatoes. When we finally send out a newsletter announcing the much anticipated news, our restaurant phone lines are ringing constantly with reservations. Once the tomatoes arrive, the floodgates open. We have one line cook that is solely dedicated to preparing tomato salads night after night. At the end of the season, he or she is usually still dreaming about tomatoes. We display the tomatoes on the chef's counter and educate the customers on the heirloom names such as Pink Beauty, Brandywine, Ida Gold, and Cherokee Purple, to name a few. Yes, life is good but busy during tomato season!

Our approach to this tomato salad illustrates how we take a dish we've grown up with and then over time and through our travels, training, and experience, apply what we've learned to those very same ingredients to make something brand new and uniquely Hot and Hot. That tomato salad is probably the single menu item that best exemplifies our style of creativity in the kitchen. We know we've gotten it right when our guests return year after year when it reappears on our menu and every single time, without exception, they are awed all over again. The Hot and Hot Tomato Salad, like shad roe, is memory cuisine for many of our patrons now. To know we have created a dish that has developed an almost cultlike following and creates such an excitement makes us proud. This is really what the food industry is all about; making people happy through food. We are very fortunate.

HOT AND HOT TOMATO SALAD

We always look for a variety of locally grown, heirloom tomatoes at our farmers' market. If heirlooms are not available, we opt for ripe red tomatoes that are grown locally. The whole baby okra make for a beautiful presentation but if they are unavailable substitute the larger-size okra and cut them into one-half-inch pieces before breading and frying.

YIELD: 6 SERVINGS

SALAD:

6 large beefsteak tomatoes

2 large golden delight tomatoes

2 large rainbow tomatoes

½ pint Sweet 100 tomatoes (tiny cherry tomatoes can be substituted)

¾ cup plus 3 tablespoons Balsamic Vinaigrette (page 346), divided

1½ teaspoons kosher salt

¾ teaspoon freshly ground black pepper

1 smoked ham hock

1 large onion, peeled and quartered

1 fresh thyme sprig

6 ounces (1 cup) fresh field peas, such as black-eyed, pink-eyed, or butter beans

2 tablespoons peanut oil

3 ears of yellow corn, husked

6 slices Applewood smoked bacon, cooked until crisp

¾ cup Chive Dressing (page 347)

6 tablespoons chiffonade of fresh basil

OKRA:

4 cups vegetable oil

30 pieces whole baby okra

¼ cup buttermilk

¼ cup corn flour

¼ cup cornmeal

¼ cup all-purpose flour

1 teaspoon kosher salt, divided

½ teaspoon freshly ground black pepper, divided

FOR SERVING:

¾ cup Chive Dressing (page 347)

6 tablespoons chiffonade of fresh basil

(CONTINUED ON NEXT PAGE)

To Prepare the Salad:

Core and slice the beefsteak, golden delight, and rainbow tomatoes into ¼-inch-thick slices. Toss the sliced tomatoes and the Sweet 100 tomatoes with ¾ cup of the vinaigrette. Season the tomatoes with the salt and pepper and set aside at room temperature to marinate until ready to serve.

Combine the ham hock, onion, thyme sprig, and field peas in a medium stockpot with enough cold water to cover the beans. Bring the peas to a simmer and cook until just tender, 12 to 15 minutes, stirring occasionally. Remove from the heat, drain, and cool. Remove and discard the ham hock, onion quarters, and thyme sprig. Place the cooled peas in a mixing bowl and set aside.

Shave the kernels off the corn cobs, discarding the silk hairs. Heat the peanut oil in a large skillet over medium-high heat. Add the corn kernels and cook until tender, 8 to 10 minutes. Season the corn with salt and pepper to taste, and remove from the heat and cool slightly. Toss the corn kernels with the cooked field peas and the remaining 3 tablespoons of vinaigrette. Set the pea mixture aside to marinate at room temperature until ready to serve.

To Prepare the Okra:

Pour the vegetable oil into a deep-sided skillet to a depth of 3 inches. (Alternately, a deep fryer can be filled with vegetable oil.) Preheat the oil to 350°F.

Trim the okra stems and place okra pods in a small bowl with the buttermilk. Toss until well coated.

Combine the corn flour, cornmeal, all-purpose flour, salt, and pepper in medium bowl. Drain the okra from the buttermilk and toss in the cornmeal mixture. Shake off any excess cornmeal mixture. Place the okra in the preheated vegetable oil and fry for 2 to 3 minutes, or until golden. Remove okra from the hot oil with a slotted spoon and drain on a paper towel–lined plate. Season the okra with the remaining salt and pepper, if needed. Keep warm until ready to serve.

To Serve:

Arrange each of the different types of sliced tomatoes on six plates. Place the whole Sweet 100 tomatoes around the sliced tomatoes. Divide the pea and corn mixture evenly among plates on top of the tomatoes. Arrange 5 pieces of fried okra around each plate and place 1 slice of crispy bacon on the top of each salad. Drizzle 1 to 2 tablespoons of the chive dressing over the top of each salad and garnish each with 1 tablespoon of basil chiffonade. Serve immediately.

DAVE GARFRERICK

It was pure serendipity when a stranger appeared at our kitchen door one day eleven years ago offering us goods from his farm. Laden with the most beautiful tomatoes, peppers, eggplants, and squash blossoms, to name a few, Dave Garfrerick brought them asking nothing in return. He had heard that we were a restaurant with a reputation for using only the freshest, local, and seasonal foods and knew we would like what he was producing. What he brought that first day was the beginning of the stream of quality produce that we count on today to create the dishes our customers come back for again and again. That day was the beginning of a long-standing relationship, friendship, and kinship—the kind chef-owners dream about having with local farmers. Our famous Hot and Hot Tomato Salad became even more outstanding because of the ripe perfection of Dave's tomatoes. He simply grows the very best Sweet 100's, Cherokee Purples, Evergreens, Great Whites, Mr. Stripeys, Nebraska Weddings, and Yellow Taxis that you've ever seen (if you've even heard of these delicious heirlooms). Their subtle differences in flavor and more pronounced differences in color and texture enable us to create an array of tomato-based dishes that elevate our thinking about our craft and therefore enhance our cuisine.

Ours is a reciprocal relationship; we love and appreciate his backdoor visits in the same way one anticipates the arrival of an old friend. The staff gathers, wide-eyed, ready to see what Dave's boxes of produce hold. In return, he loves to eat at our chef's counter—the long curved bar that gives diners a bird's-eye view of the theatre of the kitchen—and learn about our menu. He discusses the fish and seafood offerings, talks techniques, and hears about other local fresh products by conversing with the chefs and servers. Chefs all over the world search for "Daves" but we just got exceedingly lucky when he appeared that day at our kitchen door. Today he continues to operate his farm, but has plans to open his own restaurant one day. And when that day comes, we will be there to support him just as the fruits of his hard work have been one of the backbones of our business.

DAVE'S SUMMER SALAD

THIS SALAD WAS BORN OUT OF AVAILABILITY. ALMOST ALL OF THE INGREDIENTS ARE GROWN BY FARMER DAVE GARFRERICK DURING THE SUMMER MONTHS. FEEL FREE TO SUBSTITUTE OTHER PRODUCE IF SOME OF THE INGREDIENTS ARE NOT AVAILABLE IN YOUR AREA. IF GOOD-QUALITY EGGPLANT IS HARD TO FIND, BUT BEAUTIFUL BABY SQUASH ARE PLENTIFUL, USE THEM INSTEAD. WE BELIEVE THAT COOKING IS DEPENDANT UPON GREAT INGREDIENTS. IT'S AN ART, NOT A SCIENCE. HAVE FUN, BE FLEXIBLE, AND ALLOW THE QUALITY OF THE PRODUCT TO RULE YOUR PURCHASING DECISIONS.

YIELD: 4 SERVINGS

1 LARGE HEIRLOOM TOMATO, SLICED INTO 8 (½-INCH-THICK) ROUNDS

¼ CUP BALSAMIC VINEGAR

2 TABLESPOONS CHOPPED FRESH BASIL

2 TABLESPOONS CHOPPED GREEN ONIONS

8 (¾-INCH-THICK) EGGPLANT SLICES

1¼ TEASPOONS KOSHER SALT

½ TEASPOON FRESHLY GROUND BLACK PEPPER

2 SMALL HEIRLOOM PEPPERS, SUCH AS ANAHEIM, BANANA, OR POBLANO PEPPERS, ROASTED, SEEDED, AND PEELED

2 TABLESPOONS EXTRA-VIRGIN OLIVE OIL

½ CUP FRESH GOAT CHEESE

½ CUP **BASIL PESTO (PAGE 350)**

¼ CUP FRESH MICROGREENS, FOR GARNISH (OPTIONAL)

Arrange the tomatoes in an 11 x 7-inch baking dish. Pour the vinegar over the tomatoes and add the basil and green onions. Allow the tomatoes to marinate at room temperature for at least 20 minutes.

While the tomatoes are marinating, preheat the grill to medium-high heat (350°F to 400°F).

Sprinkle the eggplant slices with salt and pepper and set aside for 10 minutes. Cut the roasted peppers into 8 equal squares and set aside until ready to serve.

Lightly brush the salted eggplant slices on both sides with the olive oil. Grill the eggplant slices for 2 minutes on each side, or until lightly browned and softened. Remove the slices from the grill and top each slice with 1 tablespoon of the goat cheese. Spoon 1 tablespoon of the pesto on each of four salad plates. Place a goat cheese–topped eggplant slice on each plate. Arrange a roasted pepper square over each eggplant and top each pepper with a tomato slice. Repeat layers with remaining eggplant, pepper, and tomato slices, until all of the vegetables have been used. Drizzle 1 tablespoon of the remaining pesto around each vegetable stack. Arrange 1 tablespoon of microgreens on top of each salad, if desired. Serve immediately.

STUDY OF HEIRLOOM TOMATOES
with Eggplant and Sweet Grass Dairy Goat Cheese

THIS SIMPLE APPETIZER IS MADE SPECTACULAR WHEN AN ARRAY OF LOCAL, HEIRLOOM TOMATOES AND EGGPLANT IS USED. FARMER DAVE GARFRERICK BRINGS US AN ASSORTMENT OF HEIRLOOM TOMATOES THAT COMES IN A RAINBOW OF COLORS. HIS COLORFUL CROP OF TOMATOES GIVES THIS DISH ITS STUNNING PRESENTATION. WE ENCOURAGE YOU TO TAKE THE EXTRA TIME TO SOURCE QUALITY INGREDIENTS FOR THIS SALAD, SUCH AS LOCAL CHEESE, COARSE SEA SALT, AND RIPE, JUICY TOMATOES.

YIELD: 4 SERVINGS

1 (16-OUNCE) HEIRLOOM EGGPLANT
1¼ TEASPOONS KOSHER SALT, DIVIDED
2 TABLESPOONS EXTRA-VIRGIN OLIVE OIL, DIVIDED
¾ TEASPOON FRESHLY GROUND BLACK PEPPER, DIVIDED
¼ CUP ROUGHLY TORN FRESH BASIL, DIVIDED
1 LARGE RED HEIRLOOM TOMATO
1 MEDIUM ORANGE HEIRLOOM TOMATO
1 MEDIUM GREEN HEIRLOOM TOMATO
1 MEDIUM YELLOW HEIRLOOM TOMATO
1 TEASPOON COARSE RED HAWAIIAN SEA SALT OR
    COARSE SEA SALT
½ CUP FRESH CHÈVRE FROM SWEET GRASS DAIRY (PAGE 290)
2 TABLESPOONS FRESH PARSLEY LEAVES

Preheat the grill to medium-high heat (350°F to 400°F).

Slice the eggplant into 1-inch-thick slices and arrange in an even layer on a baking sheet. Sprinkle ¾ teaspoon of the salt over the eggplant and set aside at room temperature for 30 minutes. Pat the eggplant slices with a dry paper towel and toss with 1 tablespoon of the extra-virgin olive oil and the remaining ½ teaspoon of salt and ½ teaspoon of the pepper. Grill the eggplant for about 2 minutes on each side or until tender and cooked through. Allow the eggplant to cool to room temperature and chop into ¼-inch-thick pieces. Toss the diced eggplant with the remaining tablespoon of extra-virgin olive oil and 2 tablespoons of the torn basil.

Slice the tomatoes into paper-thin horizontal slices. Arrange the slices in a single layer among four large plates, slightly overlapping the tomatoes and alternating colors. Season the tops of the tomatoes with the coarse red sea salt and the remaining ¼ teaspoon of the black pepper. Spoon 2 tablespoons of the goat cheese into a large spoon and shape into a quenelle (torpedo shape). Repeat with the remaining goat cheese. Arrange 2 quenelles of cheese on each plate. Spoon 2 tablespoons of the diced eggplant into a quenelle shape and repeat with remaining eggplant. Arrange 2 quenelles of eggplant on each plate. Gently tear the parsley into small pieces and sprinkle evenly over the tops of the salads along with the remaining torn basil. Serve immediately.

RED ALAE SEA SALT FROM HAWAII

Lava from Kauai's volcanoes falls into the sea and form red clay beds. Over time as the salt water washes over these iron-rich lava beds, salt crystals form. Some of the clay is left in the salt when harvested, which imparts a pink tint and an earthy, mineral flavor to the salt crystals. Alae is the Hawaiian term for clay or dirt. This salt is best used when sprinkled lightly over the top of a finished dish. It will add an interesting texture as well as enhance the basic flavors of the dish.

ARUGULA SALAD
with Pancetta-Wrapped Goat Cheese

FOR THIS SALAD, IT'S BEST TO HAVE THE PERSON AT YOUR LOCAL DELI COUNTER SLICE THE PANCETTA AS THINLY AS POSSIBLE. THIS ENSURES THAT THE PANCETTA WILL BROWN QUICKLY WITHOUT MELTING THE GOAT CHEESE. PREPACKAGED PANCETTA IS OFTEN THICKER AND MAY TAKE LONGER TO COOK. THE REDUCED BALSAMIC GLAZE GIVES A RICH SWEETNESS TO THIS SALAD THAT HELPS TO SOFTEN THE PEPPERY ARUGULA AND ACIDIC GOAT CHEESE. AT THE RESTAURANT WE OFTEN USE SABA, AN ITALIAN CONDIMENT MADE FROM THE SAME GRAPES USED TO MAKE BALSAMIC VINEGAR. SABA IS NOT FERMENTED OR AGED LIKE BALSAMICO; RATHER IT IS SLOWLY CARAMELIZED OVER AN OPEN FIRE. OFTEN FOUND AT SPECIALTY SUPERMARKETS OR INTERNET STORES, SABA IS A GREAT SUBSTITUTE FOR THE REDUCED BALSAMIC IN THIS DISH.

YIELD: 6 SERVINGS

2 CUPS BALSAMIC VINEGAR
12 VERY THIN SLICES PANCETTA (ABOUT 3 OUNCES)
6 (2-OUNCE) SLICES CHÈVRE OR GOAT CHEESE
2 TABLESPOONS VEGETABLE OIL
9 CUPS FRESH ARUGULA
½ CUP LEMON DIJON VINAIGRETTE (PAGE 346)
½ TEASPOON KOSHER SALT
¼ TEASPOON FRESHLY GROUND BLACK PEPPER
6 SLICES TOASTED FRENCH BAGUETTE, RUBBED WITH 1 PEELED AND SMASHED GARLIC CLOVE

Pour the vinegar into a stainless steel saucepan and bring to a boil over high heat. Allow the vinegar to boil until the mixture is reduced to ¼ cup, 20 to 22 minutes. Remove from the heat and set aside to cool completely.

While the vinegar is reducing arrange 2 pancetta slices on a clean work space in an X pattern. Place 1 round of goat cheese in the center of the X and wrap the pancetta around the goat cheese, trying to cover as much of the cheese as possible. Repeat with the remaining pancetta and goat cheese. Arrange the wrapped goat cheese on a parchment-lined baking sheet and refrigerate for at least 30 minutes.

Heat the oil in a large nonstick skillet over high heat. Add the chilled cheese to the skillet and cook for 1½ minutes on the first side, turn, and cook 1 to 1½ minutes on the second side or until the pancetta is golden brown and crispy. Transfer the goat cheese to a plate and keep warm until ready to serve.

Combine the arugula, vinaigrette, salt, and pepper in a large mixing bowl and toss gently. Divide the arugula evenly among six salad plates (about 1½ cups per serving). Place 1 warmed goat cheese in the center of each mound of greens and drizzle 1 to 2 teaspoons of the reduced balsamic over each salad. Place a baguette slice next to each salad and serve immediately.

HOUSE-CURED BACON-WRAPPED FIGS

with Bitter Greens and Walnuts

JUST LIKE THE PANCETTA USED FOR WRAPPING GOAT CHEESE IN THE ARUGULA SALAD (PAGE 91), SLAB BACON NEEDS TO BE SLICED PAPER THIN BY A BUTCHER FOR THIS APPETIZER. IF THE BACON IS TOO THICK, THE FIGS WILL BECOME MUSHY BEFORE THE BACON IS COOKED THROUGH AND CRISP. MOST SPECIALTY MARKETS AND FINE BUTCHERS WILL SELL BACON BY THE SLAB THAT CAN THEN BE SLICED TO CERTAIN SPECIFICATIONS.

YIELD: 6 SERVINGS

2 TABLESPOONS BALSAMIC VINEGAR

2 TABLESPOONS EXTRA-VIRGIN OLIVE OIL

12 FRESH RIPE FIGS (ABOUT 12 OUNCES) SLICED
    IN HALF LENGTHWISE

4 OUNCES SLAB BACON, THINLY SLICED INTO 24
    (8-INCH) LONG STRIPS

2 TABLESPOONS VEGETABLE OIL

1 CUP FRISÉE LETTUCE

1 CUP ARUGULA

1 CUP WATERCRESS

1 CUP SPINACH, STEMS TRIMMED

1 CUP THINLY SLICED ENDIVE

1 CUP ESCAROLE HEARTS, ROUGHLY TORN

¾ CUP WALNUT VINAIGRETTE (PAGE 345)

¼ TEASPOON KOSHER SALT

⅛ TEASPOON FRESHLY GROUND BLACK PEPPER

1 CUP PLUS ¼ CUP TOASTED WALNUT HALVES

Combine the balsamic vinegar and extra-virgin olive oil in a small baking dish and add the figs. Allow the figs to marinate at room temperature for 30 minutes, turning occasionally to coat evenly with the marinade. Drain and discard the excess marinade. Wrap one slice of bacon around each fig half, making sure to cover as much of the fig as possible without overlapping the bacon too many times.

Heat the vegetable oil in a large nonstick skillet over medium-high heat. Add the figs and cook for 1½ to 2 minutes on each side or until the bacon is crispy. Transfer the figs to a paper towel–lined plate and keep warm until ready to serve.

Combine the frisée, arugula, watercress, spinach, endive, and escarole in a large bowl. Add the vinaigrette, salt, and pepper and toss until well seasoned. Add the walnuts and toss gently until incorporated. Divide the lettuce and walnuts evenly among six salad plates, placing about 1 cup of lettuces and about 3 tablespoons of walnuts on each plate. Arrange 4 warm fig halves around each salad. Serve immediately.

TOMATO GUANCIALE PASTA

Many tomato sauces are prepared with canned tomatoes and any number of pork, beef, or veal components. This type of sauce is usually cooked for long periods of time in order to develop the flavors. This dish includes a light, summer tomato sauce that is made with fresh tomatoes and no meat products. The result is a clean, intense, fresh sauce that can stand on its own with the addition of a few herbs and cheese. For this dish we've added guanciale to the summer sauce which imparts a rich, depth of flavor to the dish. We really love this recipe.

YIELD: 6 SERVINGS

2 tablespoons olive oil

1¼ ounces (¼-inch-thick) diced guanciale, about ¼ cup

1 dried Arbol chile pepper

3 cups Summer Tomato Sauce (page 339)

6 cups cooked pasta, such as garganelli

2 cups freshly grated Parmesan cheese, divided

1 cup julienned fresh basil

¼ teaspoon kosher salt

⅛ teaspoon freshly ground black pepper

Heat the olive oil in a medium saucepan over medium-low heat. Add the guanciale and cook, stirring occasionally, for 15 to 17 minutes, or until golden brown and crispy. Add the chile pepper and cook, stirring, for 30 seconds. Stir in the tomato sauce and increase the heat to medium. Cook for 5 minutes, stirring occasionally, until the sauce has thickened slightly. Add the pasta, 1 cup of the Parmesan cheese, the basil, salt, and pepper and cook for 1 minute, stirring frequently. Remove from the heat and discard the chile pepper. Evenly divide the pasta among six appetizer plates or pasta bowls. Sprinkle the remaining cup of Parmesan over the top of each portion and serve immediately.

GUANCIALE

Guanciale is cured pork jowl or cheeks. It is similar to pancetta but has a richer, meaty, pork flavor. We first tasted guanciale on a trip to Rome years ago and have been addicted ever since. Now we either make our own guanciale for the restaurant or purchase it at specialty stores for use at home. If guanciale cannot be found, pancetta can be used with similar results.

HOT AND HOT VEGETABLE PLATE

In a region saturated with great meat-and-three restaurants that feature wonderful Southern vegetable plates, the Hot and Hot Vegetable Plate stands out as a popular tribute to our local bounty. Each night before dinner service begins at the restaurant we survey the menu and choose five vegetarian items from various dishes that would work well together on the vegetable plate for that evening. A typical summer vegetable plate might include the following recipes in a mini or half-size portion:

Items on the vegetable plate change daily and always incorporate a variety of the freshest vegetables available. We try to give a mixture of flavors and textures by incorporating soups, cold salads, warm salads, and vegetable medleys or purées on each plate. For the past fourteen years, the Hot and Hot Vegetable Plate has been and will continue to be local, organic, and our own.

RATATOUILLE (PAGE 370) | COOKED CAROLINA GOLD RICE (PAGE 353) TOSSED WITH GREEN GODDESS DRESSING (PAGE 347) | HOT AND HOT TOMATO SALAD (PAGE 85) SHRIMP GAZPACHO WITH LEMON OIL (PAGE 77) WITHOUT THE SHRIMP | THREE-BEAN SALAD (PAGE 94)

GRILLING TIPS FOR FISH: THREE BASIC RULES

First, it's important to start with a clean grill. A grill with leftover grit and grime on the food grates may give your food unwanted flavor. Use these simple steps to clean your grill before you start: Light the grill and get the food grates hot; brush and scrape the food grates well with a grill brush. Next, carefully remove the food grates from the grill and wipe them down with a damp cloth. This ensures that any dust created from scraping the grill is wiped away. Finally, place the food grate back on the grill and get it hot again. Brush peanut or vegetable oil over the food grate and you're ready to grill.

Second, make sure the grill is hot enough. Too often we see people trying to cook fish or protein on a less than hot grill. If fish fillets are placed on grill racks that aren't hot enough, you won't get a nice sear on the flesh and the fish will end up sticking to the grill.

Third, don't turn the fish too early or too frequently. If you start with a clean grill that's heated properly, you should have to turn your fish only one time, halfway through the cooking process. If your grill is hot enough and the fish is sticking when you try to turn it, it may not be time to turn it yet. Instead, allow the fillets a few extra minutes to cook before trying to turn them.

GROUPER WITH TOMATO, AVOCADO, AND GRILLED VIDALIA ONIONS

with Basil-Lime Vinaigrette

THIS DISH IS ALL ABOUT THE VINAIGRETTE. EXTRA LIMEY AND RICH FROM THE AVOCADO, IT MAKES A SIMPLE SUMMERTIME DISH THAT WILL IMPRESS ANY GUEST. GOOD OLIVE OIL AND A LOT OF FRESHLY PICKED BASIL ARE IMPORTANT, SO DON'T SKIMP ON THESE ITEMS.

YIELD: 6 SERVINGS

2 LARGE VIDALIA ONIONS, EACH SLICED INTO 1-INCH-THICK SLICES (ABOUT 5 OR 6 SLICES EACH)

¼ CUP OLIVE OIL

1 TABLESPOON KOSHER SALT, DIVIDED

2½ TEASPOONS FRESHLY GROUND BLACK PEPPER, DIVIDED

4 LARGE, RIPE HEIRLOOM TOMATOES, EACH CORED AND SLICED INTO 1-INCH-THICK SLICES

4 RIPE HAAS AVOCADOS, HALVED, PEELED, SEEDED, AND SLICED INTO ½-INCH-THICK SLICES

1 CUP FRESH LIME JUICE

1 CUP EXTRA-VIRGIN OLIVE OIL

⅔ CUP THINLY SLICED OR CHIFFONADE OF FRESH BASIL LEAVES

6 (6-OUNCE) GROUPER FILLETS

3 CUPS FRESH ARUGULA

Preheat the grill to high heat (400°F to 450° F).

Arrange the onion slices on a baking sheet and brush lightly with the olive oil. Season the onions lightly with ½ teaspoon of the salt and ½ teaspoon of the pepper. Grill the onion slices for 4 to 5 minutes on each side or until tender, sweet, and slightly charred. Transfer the grilled slices to a mixing bowl and separate the rings. Add the tomato and avocado slices to the onion rings and set aside.

In a separate bowl whisk together the lime juice, extra-virgin olive oil, and basil. Toss the vinaigrette with the grilled onion mixture and season the salad with 1 teaspoon of the salt and ½ teaspoon of the pepper. Allow the salad to marinate at room temperature for 10 to 15 minutes, tossing occasionally. (This allows the avocados to break down a little and slightly thicken the vinaigrette.)

Season the fish fillets on both sides with the remaining 1½ teaspoons of salt and 1½ teaspoons of pepper. Place the fillets on the hot grill and cook for 6 to 7 minutes or until the fillets begin to pull away and loosen from the grill rack. Turn and cook an additional 4 to 5 minutes or until the fillets are golden brown and cooked through. Remove the fillets from the heat and keep warm until ready to serve.

Arrange 1 marinated tomato slice in the center of each of six dinner plates. Using a slotted spoon, place onion and avocado slices on top of the tomatoes. Top each salad with a second marinated tomato slice. Spoon several tablespoons of the vinaigrette over and around each salad. Arrange the grilled grouper fillets on top of each salad. Toss the arugula in the mixing bowl with the remaining vinaigrette. Top each fish fillet with a small mound of the arugula. Serve immediately.

PAN-SEARED WILD SALMON ON THREE-BEAN SALAD

with Cherry Tomatoes and Basil Aïoli

FOR THE THREE-BEAN SALAD WE CHOOSE FROM A VARIETY OF FRESH BEANS SUCH AS DRAGON TONGUE, FIRE BEANS, YELLOW AND PURPLE ROMANO BEANS, WAX BEANS, POLE BEANS, OR GREEN AND PURPLE CARMELLINI BEANS. HARICOT VERTS OR FRENCH GREEN BEANS, WHICH CAN BE FOUND FRESH IN MANY LOCAL SUPERMARKETS, MAY BE A MORE PRACTICAL ADDITION.

YIELD: 6 SERVINGS

1½ POUNDS (ABOUT 6 CUPS) TENDER FRESH BEAN
    VARIETIES (CHOOSE AT LEAST 3 DIFFERENT COLOR
    VARIETIES, IF POSSIBLE)
¼ CUP FRESH LEMON JUICE
¼ CUP OLIVE OIL
¼ CUP EXTRA-VIRGIN OLIVE OIL
1 TEASPOON MINCED SHALLOTS
¼ CUP CHOPPED FRESH BASIL
2 TABLESPOONS CHOPPED FRESH PARSLEY
2 TABLESPOONS CHOPPED FRESH CHIVES
1 TEASPOON CHOPPED FRESH THYME
2 TEASPOONS KOSHER SALT, DIVIDED
2 TEASPOONS FRESHLY GROUND BLACK PEPPER, DIVIDED
6 (6-OUNCE) SKIN-ON WILD SALMON FILLETS
2 TABLESPOONS VEGETABLE OIL
1 CUP RED CHERRY TOMATOES
1 CUP YELLOW CHERRY TOMATOES
2 CUPS FRISÉE LETTUCE
2 CUPS WATERCRESS
2 CUPS ARUGULA
¾ CUP BASIL AÏOLI (PAGE 342)

Prepare a water bath by filling a large bowl with ice and a small amount of water. Bring a large pot of salted water to a boil.

Blanch each bean variety separately in the boiling water until tender, 2 to 3 minutes (cooking times may vary depending on the size and variety of bean). Plunge the beans into the ice water bath and stir until cool. Drain and pat the beans dry. Cut any larger beans to match the sizes of the smaller beans. Set the beans aside.

Preheat the oven to 400°F.

Whisk together the lemon juice, olive oils, shallots, basil, parsley, chives, and thyme in a medium bowl. Season the vinaigrette with ¼ teaspoon each of the salt and pepper. Set the vinaigrette aside.

Season the salmon fillets with 1½ teaspoons of the salt and 1½ teaspoons of the pepper, using about ¼ teaspoon of each on each fillet. Heat the vegetable oil in a large heavy skillet over medium-high heat. Add the salmon, skin side up, to the pan and cook for 3 minutes. Turn the salmon and place the skillet in the oven. Bake the salmon for 2 to 3 minutes (for medium) or until desired degree of doneness. Remove the salmon from the skillet and set aside to keep warm.

Combine the blanched beans, cherry tomatoes, frisée, watercress, and arugula in a large bowl with the vinaigrette. Season the salad with the remaining ¼ teaspoon of salt and ¼ teaspoon of pepper. Divide the salad evenly among six dinner plates and place 1 piece of salmon on each salad. Drizzle 2 tablespoons of the aïoli over each plate. Serve immediately.

BAKED SHOVEL NOSE LOBSTERS
with Cherry Tomato and Field Pea Salad

SHOVEL NOSE LOBSTERS ARE A RARE DELICACY FOUND IN THE GULF NEAR THE FLORIDA PANHANDLE. A CLOSE COUSIN TO THE AMERICAN LOBSTER, A SHOVEL NOSE LOBSTER HAS A FLATTENED HEAD THAT IS SHAPED LIKE A SHOVEL AND A COLOR THAT BLENDS WITH ITS SURROUNDINGS. THESE LOBSTERS ARE THE BY-CATCH OF SHRIMPERS AND ARE SOMETIMES SOLD OFF THEIR BOATS. COLD-WATER LOBSTERS CAN BE SUBSTITUTED FOR SHOVEL NOSE LOBSTERS. IF USING A COLD-WATER OR AMERICAN LOBSTER, TAKE OFF THE CLAWS FIRST AND COOK THEM SEPARATELY. CHOP THE COOKED CLAW MEAT AND TOSS WITH THE PEA SALAD MIXTURE BEFORE STUFFING THE LOBSTER HEAD, FOR ADDED FLAVOR.

YIELD: 6 SERVINGS

6 (1-POUND) LIVE SHOVEL NOSE LOBSTERS
1 TABLESPOON KOSHER SALT
1½ TEASPOONS FRESHLY GROUND BLACK PEPPER
3 CUPS HERB BREADCRUMBS (PAGE 356)
¾ CUP (1½ STICKS) UNSALTED BUTTER, MELTED
1¼ CUPS CREAMED FIELD PEA AND SUMMER SQUASH SALAD (PAGE 64)
1/3 CUP QUARTERED CHERRY TOMATOES

Preheat the oven to 375°F.

Split the lobsters down the middle and clean out both halves of the head cavity. Season the tail meat with the salt and pepper, using about ¼ teaspoon salt and ⅛ teaspoon pepper per tail half.

Toss the breadcrumbs and melted butter together in a small bowl until combined. Arrange the lobster halves on a jelly roll pan or rimmed baking sheet and pack ¼ cup of the breadcrumb mixture onto each tail half. Bake for 8 to 10 minutes or until the meat is cooked through and the crumbs are golden brown on top.

While the lobsters are cooking, stir together the pea salad and the tomatoes. Place ¼ cup of the salad into each lobster head. Arrange two lobster halves on each of six dinner plates Serve immediately.

DAD'S GRILLED CHICKEN
with *Summer Vegetables*

As a kid, this was one of Chris' favorite meals. Today his boys love and enjoy it too. The key to his dad's recipe is to really char the outside of the chicken. The cooked skin should be very dark brown and almost black in color. The butter in the marinade will caramelize and brown on the chicken when grilled. You will see, it's awesome.

YIELD: 8 SERVINGS

1 CUP (2 STICKS) UNSALTED BUTTER

1 CUP WORCESTERSHIRE SAUCE

1 CUP FRESH LEMON JUICE

4 GARLIC CLOVES, SMASHED AND PEELED

1 DRIED ARBOL CHILE PEPPER

1 TABLESPOON PLUS 2 TEASPOONS KOSHER SALT, DIVIDED

2 (4-POUND) CHICKENS, EACH CUT INTO 8 PIECES (2 WINGS, 2 DRUMSTICKS, 2 THIGHS, 2 BREAST HALVES)

6 JUMBO ASPARAGUS SPEARS, PEELED AND BLANCHED UNTIL TENDER

1 LARGE RED BELL PEPPER, STEM AND SEEDS REMOVED AND SLICED INTO 1-INCH STRIPS

1 LARGE YELLOW BELL PEPPER, STEM AND SEEDS REMOVED AND SLICED INTO 1-INCH STRIPS

2 LARGE VIDALIA ONIONS, CUT INTO 1-INCH-THICK SLICES

3 JAPANESE EGGPLANTS, DIAGONALLY SLICED INTO ½-INCH-THICK AND 4-INCH-LONG PIECES

2 LARGE FENNEL BULBS, SLICED INTO 1-INCH-THICK PIECES

3 BABY BOK CHOY, HALVED LENGTHWISE AND BLANCHED UNTIL TENDER

½ CUP OLIVE OIL

1 TEASPOON FRESHLY GROUND BLACK PEPPER

½ CUP FINELY SLICED FRESH BASIL

Combine the butter, Worcestershire, lemon juice, garlic, chile pepper, and 2 teaspoons of the salt in a small saucepan and cook over medium-low heat until melted. Pour 1 cup of the butter mixture over the chicken pieces and refrigerate for 1 hour. Reserve the remaining marinade for basting the chicken.

Preheat the grill to high heat (400°F to 450°F).

Grill the marinated chicken, basting frequently with the remaining marinade and turning occasionally until the chicken is dark brown and cooked through. (The chicken will take about 20 minutes for the wings, 25 minutes for the drumsticks, and 30 minutes for the thighs and breast halves to cook.) Set the chicken aside on a warm platter and cover loosely with aluminum foil until ready to serve.

Allow the grill to cool down slightly to medium-high heat (350°F to 400°F).

Combine the remaining vegetables (asparagus through bok choy) in a large mixing bowl and toss with the olive oil until well coated. Season the vegetables with the remaining tablespoon of salt and the pepper.

Grill the vegetables, in batches, until tender and slightly charred on both sides, 2 to 3 minutes per side for the asparagus, bell peppers, and bok choy and 3 to 4 minutes per side for the fennel, eggplant, and onions.

Arrange the grilled vegetables on a large serving platter and sprinkle with the sliced basil. Serve immediately alongside the grilled chicken.

GRILLED BEEF SIRLOIN ON POTATO GALETTE

with Mixed Baby Greens, Balsamic Onions, Blue Cheese, Tamarind Sauce, and Chive Aïoil

THIS PARTICULAR TYPE OF SIRLOIN IS CALLED A CULOTTE OR A TOP SIRLOIN CAP STEAK. MOST BUTCHERS ARE FAMILIAR WITH THIS CUT WHICH IS GRADUALLY BECOMING MORE POPULAR. A LONDON BROIL OR YOUR FAVORITE CUT OF STEAK CAN ALSO BE USED INSTEAD. THIS ENTRÉE HAS BEEN ON OUR RESTAURANT MENU FOR OVER THIRTEEN YEARS. EVERYONE LOVES A STEAK AND THIS PREPARATION FEATURES A FRESH, NEW APPROACH TO THE TRADITIONAL STEAK SIDES.

YIELD: 6 SERVINGS

1½ CUPS PEANUT OIL

2 LARGE, ABOUT 1⅓ POUNDS, BAKING POTATOES PEELED

1 TABLESPOON PLUS 1 TEASPOON KOSHER SALT, DIVIDED

2½ TEASPOONS FRESHLY GROUND BLACK PEPPER, DIVIDED

1 (2-POUND) TOP SIRLOIN CAP STEAK, TRIMMED OF ANY FAT

8 CUPS MIXED BABY GREEN LETTUCES

1 CUP SLICED BALSAMIC ROASTED RED ONIONS (PAGE 379)

1 CUP CRUMBLED BLUE CHEESE

¼ CUP LEMON DIJON VINAIGRETTE (PAGE 346)

¾ CUP TAMARIND SAUCE (PAGE 338)

¾ CUP CHIVE AÏOLI (PAGE 342)

Pour the oil into an 8-inch cast-iron skillet and heat over medium-low heat.

Using a mandoline, cut the potatoes into shoestring- or matchstick-style strips. Place the potato strips into a small bowl and season with 1 teaspoon of the salt and ½ teaspoon of the pepper. Test the oil with a small strip of potato to see if it sizzles. When the oil sizzles, add the seasoned potatoes to the skillet, pressing down gently with a wooden spoon until the potatoes form a circle about the size of the skillet. Cook the potatoes for 15 minutes or until they are golden brown on the bottom side. Using a slotted spatula, carefully turn the potatoes (which have now formed a thin cake called a galette) and increase the heat to medium. Cook the potatoes an additional 5 to 6 minutes or until golden brown and crispy. Remove the potatoes from the hot oil and drain on a paper towel–lined plate. Set aside until ready to serve.

Preheat the grill to medium-high heat (350°F to 400°F).

Season the sirloin on all sides with the remaining tablespoon of salt and 2 teaspoons of pepper. Allow the sirloin to sit at room temperature for 30 minutes while the grill preheats.

Grill the sirloin, turning occasionally, until well seared on the outside, about 30 minutes (for medium) or until desired degree of doneness. Allow the sirloin to rest for 5 minutes before slicing.

Combine the baby greens, onions, and blue cheese in a large mixing bowl. Break the crispy potato galette into large chunks into the salad mixture. Add the vinaigrette and toss until well combined. Divide the salad mixture evenly among six dinner plates. Slice the sirloin across the grain into thin (¼-inch-thick) slices. Arrange 3 to 4 slices over each salad. Drizzle 2 tablespoons of the tamarind sauce over each portion of meat. Spoon 2 tablespoons of the aïoli over and around each salad. Serve immediately.

BBQ BEEF SHORT RIBS
ON SWEET CORN SUCCOTASH

with *Cracklin' Cornbread*

We make several references to San Francisco and Bradley Ogden in this book as he is a long-time friend and a mentor to Chris. Though Brad is by no means a Southerner we have always been impressed by his knowledge, skill, and creativity with Southern cuisine. It was our Yankee friend, Brad, who taught Chris how to braise meats using a combination of beef stock and barbecue sauce. The richness of the ribs and stock combined with the sweet, hot barbecue sauce are a brilliant balance of flavors. Combine these barbecue ribs with one of your favorite vegetable dishes, some Creamy Coleslaw (page 369) and our Cracklin' Cornbread (page 171) and try not to eat your hands while enjoying this dish!

YIELD: 8 SERVINGS

SHORT RIBS:

½ cup peanut oil

8 (2-inch thick) bone-in beef short ribs,
  3 bones per piece

2 teaspoons kosher salt

1 teaspoon freshly ground black pepper

2 tablespoons unsalted butter

4 cups equal parts roughly chopped onions,
  celery, and carrots (mirepoix)

6 fresh thyme sprigs

3 garlic cloves, smashed and peeled

1 bay leaf

6 cups store-bought beef broth or Veal Stock
  (page 335)

4 cups BBQ Sauce (page 336)

SUCCOTASH:

1½ tablespoons peanut oil

3 tablespoons finely diced Applewood smoked
  bacon, such as Nueske's brand

¾ cup finely diced yellow onion

3 cups diced fresh okra, about ½ inch thick

3 cup peeled, seeded, and diced tomatoes

3 cups freshly shaved sweet yellow corn

3 cups cooked Field Peas (page 372)

1¼ cups reserved Field Pea Liquor (page 372)

3 tablespoons unsalted butter

1 tablespoon kosher salt

2 teaspoons freshly ground black pepper

¼ cup plus 2 tablespoons chiffonade of sweet basil

FOR SERVING:

16 Cracklin' Cornbread Sticks (page 171)

(CONTINUED ON NEXT PAGE)

To Prepare the Short Ribs:

Heat the peanut oil in a large cast-iron skillet or other heavy-bottomed skillet over high heat. Season the short ribs on all sides with the salt and pepper. Sear the ribs in the hot oil until well browned on all sides, about 8 minutes. Remove the ribs from the skillet and arrange in a single layer in a 14 x 11-inch roasting pan. Carefully discard the peanut oil from the skillet, reserving any browned bits in the bottom.

Preheat the oven to 325°F.

Scrape the browned bits into a medium stockpot and place over high heat. Add the butter and stir until melted. Add the mirepoix and cook, stirring frequently, until golden brown, about 5 minutes. Stir in the thyme, garlic, and bay leaf and continue cooking for 2 minutes. Add the stock and barbecue sauce to the stockpot and bring the mixture to a boil. Once it begins to boil, pour the liquid over the short ribs and cover the roasting pan with a tight-fitting lid or aluminum foil.

Place the roasting pan in the oven and roast for 2½ hours or until the rib meat is tender and pulls away easily from the bones. Carefully remove the ribs from the braising liquid with a slotted spoon. Cover the ribs and keep warm until ready to serve.

Strain the braising liquid through a fine-meshed strainer into a saucepan; discard the vegetables. Bring the braising liquid to a boil, reduce the heat to medium low, and simmer until the liquid has reduced by one-third, about 5 minutes. Set the sauce aside until ready to serve.

To Prepare the Succotash:

Heat the peanut oil in a large cast-iron skillet over medium-high heat. Add the bacon and cook until brown and crispy, about 3 minutes. Add the onion and cook, stirring frequently, until softened and translucent but not brown, about 3 minutes. Increase the heat to high, add the okra and cook for 8 to 10 minutes, stirring frequently. Add the tomatoes and corn and cook an additional 3 minutes. Stir in the field peas and field pea liquor and bring the mixture to a boil. Cook until the peas are heated through, about 1 minute. Remove from the heat, add the butter, and stir until melted. Season the succotash with the salt and pepper and add the basil. For best results, serve warm within 30 minutes of preparing.

To Serve:

Spoon ½ cup of the succotash onto each of eight plates. Submerge each portion of the short ribs (3 bones each) into the reduced braising liquid and place on each plate. Arrange two warm cornbread sticks on each plate. Serve immediately.

WARM JOHNNY CAKES
with Blackberries and Buttermilk Ice Cream

JOHNNY CAKES, ALSO KNOWN AS HOE CAKES, ARE GENERALLY MADE FROM A SIMPLE BATTER OF CORNMEAL, WATER, AND PORK FAT. THEY WERE A STAPLE AMONG POOR SOUTHERNERS WHO COOKED THE CAKES ON THEIR HOES OVER OPEN FIRES WHILE WORKING THE FIELDS. THIS RECIPE IS OUR RENDITION OF THE ORIGINAL JOHNNY CAKE WITH THE ADDITION OF YEAST AND HONEY TO TAKE IT FROM THE BACKS OF HOES TO A DESSERT WORTHY OF YOUR MOST IMPORTANT DINNER GUEST.

YIELD: 6 SERVINGS

⅔ CUP WHOLE MILK
¼ CUP HONEY
1 TEASPOON GRATED LEMON ZEST, DIVIDED
½ TEASPOON DRY YEAST
1½ CUPS FINELY GROUND YELLOW CORNMEAL
3 CUPS FRESH BLACKBERRIES
¼ CUP PLUS 1 TABLESPOON GRANULATED SUGAR
3 TABLESPOONS LEMON JUICE
2 LARGE EGG WHITES
¼ CUP (½ STICK) UNSALTED BUTTER
3 CUPS BUTTERMILK ICE CREAM (PAGE 366)

Combine the milk, honey, and ¼ teaspoon of the lemon zest in a small saucepan over low heat. Stir occasionally until the honey is dissolved and the mixture is heated to 110°F.

Remove the pan from the heat, add the yeast, cover, and steep for 15 minutes or until the yeast begins to foam.

Stir together the cornmeal and milk mixture in a mixing bowl and whisk until smooth. Cover the bowl with plastic wrap and set aside in a warm place to rise for 30 minutes.

Place the blackberries in a medium bowl and sprinkle with 3 tablespoons of the sugar. Stir in the lemon juice and remaining ¾ teaspoon of lemon zest and allow the berries to sit, at room temperature, for 30 minutes, stirring occasionally.

Place the egg whites in the bowl of a standing mixer. Whisk the egg whites on low until foamy. With the machine running on low, add the remaining 2 tablespoons of sugar, ½ tablespoon at a time until all of the sugar has been added. Increase the speed to medium and whisk until the egg whites form medium-stiff peaks. Set aside.

Once the dough has risen and soaked up most of the liquid, fold one-third of the egg whites into the batter mixture. Add a second third of the egg white mixture to the batter and fold until well incorporated. Fold in the remaining egg whites, being careful not to overmix or deflate the batter.

Heat 1 tablespoon of the butter in a cast-iron skillet over medium-high heat. Add the batter 2 rounded tablespoonfuls at a time, to form cakes about the size of a silver dollar. Cook the cakes for 1½ minutes on each side or until golden brown and cooked through. Transfer the cakes to a plate and keep warm until ready to serve. Repeat with the remaining butter and batter.

Arrange 3 cooked cakes on each of six dessert plates. Evenly divide the macerated blackberries and their juices over each serving of cakes. Top each plate with ½ cup of the ice cream. Serve immediately.

RED MOUNTAIN HONEY FROM BIRMINGHAM'S CARTER-HOLCOMB APIARY

The crest of Red Mountain rises up through the middle of Birmingham, overlooking downtown on one side and the Birmingham Botanical Gardens on the other. Tina Holcomb and Carol Carter are two moms who are avid gardeners in their spare time. Interested in introducing more honeybees into their yards, they decided to learn more about bees and their habits. They situated beehives in their backyards along the Red Mountain crest, giving the bees access to the flowers in their yard, the trees, and the uncommon diversity of plants that the Botanical Gardens has to offer during their daily two-mile flight path. When we first tasted the rich, amber-colored honey, robbed from Tina and Carol's beehives, we were knocked out by just how delicious it was and wanted to know more about the story behind the product.

Most honeybees are released by beekeepers to pollinate particular crops or come from hives placed in areas close to a specific type of flora—lavender, clover, tupelo trees, and so forth. It's the prominence of local tree pollen that Tina and Carol's bees have access to that gives Red Mountain Honey its unique, truly complex flavor that cannot be quantified as any one particular honey variety. The Carter-Holcomb Apiary is a small, family business that provides top-quality honey right from our city center. We prize their product for its superior quality and flavor profile.

At the restaurant, we buy honey mostly on the comb. To serve it, we pull the comb out, let it drain a bit, then cut it into small pieces and include it with the honey on our cheese plate. We also drizzle a little over sorbets or fresh berries, add it to vinaigrettes or mix some into crème fraîche, but for all intents and purposes, we serve it as unadulterated as possible. Our customers have been so excited by this local honey that we now sell it at the restaurant and from our online store.

Red Mountain Honey is yet another example of our philosophy of finding amazing products that are of this place—our home. We are proud to introduce and serve the honey to our guests, plus it makes a great story.

PLUM AND NECTARINE GALETTE
with Vanilla Ice Cream

Idie learned to make galettes at a French bakery where she worked during her externship in culinary school. Galettes can be made with flaky pastry dough, as in this recipe, or with a yeast dough. The plum and nectarines release a lot of juice, so your parchment paper may look a bit messy when you remove the tart from the oven. Don't worry, once you take the galette off the paper, you will find a perfectly cooked tart with plenty of juice left inside. The warm fruit compliments the chill of the vanilla ice cream.

YIELD: 6 TO 8 SERVINGS

1 POUND (ABOUT 3) LARGE FRESH NECTARINES, PEELED AND CUT INTO 1-INCH-THICK WEDGES
1 POUND (ABOUT 4) LARGE FRESH PURPLE PLUMS, PEELED AND CUT INTO 1-INCH-THICK WEDGES
3 TABLESPOONS LEMON SUGAR (PAGE 367)
½ CUP GRANULATED SUGAR
3 TABLESPOONS ALL-PURPOSE FLOUR
PINCH OF SALT
1 POUND SWEET PASTRY DOUGH (PAGE 358), ABOUT 1¼ RECIPES
2 TABLESPOONS FINELY GROUND YELLOW CORNMEAL
1 LARGE EGG
1 TABLESPOON HEAVY CREAM
1 TABLESPOON COARSE RAW SUGAR
1½ TABLESPOONS UNSALTED BUTTER
1 QUART (4 CUPS) VANILLA ICE CREAM, FOR SERVING

Combine the nectarines and plums in a large mixing bowl and sprinkle with the lemon sugar and granulated sugar. Stir in the flour and salt and toss until well combined. Allow the fruit to macerate at room temperature for 20 minutes.

Preheat the oven to 400°F. Line a jelly roll pan or rimmed baking sheet with parchment paper and set aside.

Place the dough on a lightly floured surface and roll out into a 16-inch circle, about ¼ inch thick. Trim any rough edges of the circle to create a round 15-inch pastry. Cut 9 evenly spaced (2-inch-deep) slits around the edge of the pastry, perpendicular to the edge. Transfer the pastry round to the prepared jelly roll pan and sprinkle the cornmeal over the top of the pastry.

Whisk together the egg and heavy cream. Brush the top edges of the pastry round with the egg wash. Mound the fruit mixture in the center of the pastry dough, keeping the juices from running through the slits as much as possible. Fold the pastry around the fruit, overlapping the pastry at the slits and pressing to seal. (There will be a 4 to 5-inch opening in the center of the tart.) Brush the outside of the pastry with the remaining egg wash and sprinkle the raw sugar evenly over the top. Dice the butter and arrange evenly on top of the tart opening.

Loosely cover the top of the galette with aluminum foil and bake for 20 minutes. Remove the foil and bake an additional 15 to 20 minutes or until the top is golden brown and crispy. Allow the galette to cool for 10 minutes before slicing. Serve each slice warm with ½ cup scoop of vanilla ice cream.

FOUR FIG TARTS

with *Lemon Verbena Ice Cream*

At any given time during fig season, we have up to eight different fig varieties in the restaurant. If you have never tried a fresh fig, this is the recipe that can bring you around. Fig season is very short and the figs ripen quickly. At their peak, fresh figs have a variety of textures and flavors ranging from sweet, preserve-like, to firm and "green" tasting. When these tarts are being made, you can bet we are walking by to grab a fresh fig before it goes into the tarts. The lemon verbena ice cream gives the tarts a bright, zingy, and slightly herbal flavor.

YIELD: 6 SERVINGS

11 to 12 ounces Sweet Pastry Dough (page 358), about 1 recipe

1¾ cups Fig Preserves (page 116), divided

½ cup water, divided

¾ cup mascarpone

2 teaspoons grated lemon zest

2 tablespoons honey

8 assorted ripe fresh figs, such as LSU Purple, Green Ischia, Alma, Mission, or Black Italian, sliced into ⅛-inch slices

1½ cups Lemon Verbena Ice Cream (page 366)

Preheat the oven to 375°F.

Place the chilled pastry dough on a lightly floured surface. Roll the dough out into a circle, about ⅛ inch thick. Cut 6 (5½-inch) circles out of the dough. Fit the circles into 6 (4-inch) round fluted tart pans, and gently press the dough into the sides and bottom of the pan. Trim off and discard any excess pastry. Line each tart shell with a piece of parchment paper and fill with pie weights or baking beans. Place the tart shells on a baking sheet and bake for 10 to 12 minutes or until golden brown. Cool the shells completely before removing parchment paper and pie weights.

Heat ¼ cup of the fig preserves and ¼ cup of the water over low heat just until warm. Transfer the fig mixture to a blender and process on low, adding the remaining ¼ cup of water, 1 tablespoon at a time, until a smooth glaze is formed. Reserve 6 tablespoons of the glaze for the fig tarts and refrigerate the remaining glaze for another use.

Whisk together the mascarpone, lemon zest, and honey in a small bowl until smooth. Chill the mixture for at least 30 minutes before assembling the tarts.

Spread 2 tablespoons of the chilled mascarpone mixture in each tart shell. Spread ¼ cup of the remaining fig preserves in each tart over the mascarpone. Arrange the sliced figs over the top of each tart, alternating colors and slightly overlapping. Brush 1 tablespoon of the reserved fig glaze over the top of each tart. Just before serving spoon a small (¼ cup size) scoop of lemon verbena ice cream in the center of each tart.

LATTICE-TOP CHERRY PIE

WHO DOESN'T LOVE A CHERRY PIE? BUT THE QUESTION REMAINS, WHAT'S THE BEST WAY TO PIT FRESH CHERRIES? THERE ARE VARIOUS CHERRY PITTERS THAT CAN BE PURCHASED AT KITCHEN STORES OR YOU CAN TRY OUR WAY. PLACE A PIPING TIP ON A FLAT SURFACE (SUCH AS AN UPSIDE-DOWN RAMEKIN) PLACED INSIDE A LARGE MIXING BOWL. POP THE CHERRY ON TOP OF THE TIP AND PRESS DOWN UNTIL THE STONE COMES OUT. THIS METHOD IS EASY AND NOT TOO MESSY. WE HAVE FOUND THAT WHEN THIS PIE SITS FOR A DAY, THE FLAVORS BECOME BETTER AND MORE INTENSE. IN THE MORNING, WE OFTEN GO TO THE REFRIGERATOR AND SEE THAT OUR BOYS HAVE LEFT THE FORK IN THE PIE PLATE FROM THE EVENING BEFORE!

YIELD: 1 (9-INCH) PIE OR 8 TO 10 SERVINGS

5 CUPS FRESH, PITTED, DARK SWEET CHERRIES, ABOUT 2 POUNDS
¼ CUP PLUS 3 TABLESPOONS ALL-PURPOSE FLOUR
1¼ CUPS GRANULATED SUGAR
½ CUP PLUS 2 TABLESPOONS FRESH LEMON JUICE
⅛ TEASPOON PURE VANILLA EXTRACT
1 POUND PLUS 2 OUNCES SWEET PASTRY DOUGH (PAGE 358), ABOUT 1½ RECIPES

Preheat the oven to 375°F.

Combine the cherries, flour, sugar, lemon juice, and vanilla in a large bowl. Allow the cherry mixture to sit at room temperature, stirring occasionally for at least 30 minutes.

While the cherries are macerating, roll two-thirds (about 12 ounces) of the pastry dough out on a lightly floured surface into a 12-inch circle. Fit the pastry round into a 9-inch round pie pan, allowing the excess dough to drape over the edge of the pan. Using a rubber spatula, scrape the cherries and their juices into the pastry shell, spreading them in an even layer; set aside.

Roll the remaining one-third (about 6 ounces) of the pastry dough out on a lightly floured surface into a 12 x 8-inch rectangle. Using a ruler, cut the dough into even strips, each about ½ inch wide. Arrange the strips into a lattice pattern over the top of the cherry mixture and trim the edges of the strips. Fold the edge of the pastry dough under and crimp.

Place the pie on a baking sheet and loosely cover with aluminum foil. Bake for 40 minutes, remove the foil and bake an additional 20 minutes or until the top is golden brown and bubbling. Allow the pie to cool for 10 minutes before slicing.

CRABBING AS A BOY ON PAWLEYS ISLAND

Few things in life have meant more to Chris than the times spent as a child in the salt marsh of Pawleys Island. As a kid who simply loved being on the water, he was drawn to the salt marsh daily and spent all his waking time there. Back in the mid-sixties and seventies, Pawleys Island had lots and lots of blue crabs and catching them was as simple as tying chicken necks to some string from a stick, dropping the bait in the shallows, and waiting for crabs to grab hold. A tug on the line meant it was time to gently pull up your catch and scoop up the feasting crab with a net. In those days, you could go out on the salt marsh and get a bushel of crabs for supper in no time. The sheer fun of the activity was so addictive that returning day after day never got old and the place continues to be a powerful draw for Chris even as an adult.

Think of the salt marsh as the incubator of the ocean. Such a huge array of sea life passes through it, is born there, and then goes back out to the sea only to return again to spawn. Crabbing is just one pastime that provides a window into the magical cycles of life in this body of water. Patiently waiting for a crab to tug your line, surrounded by the beauty of a natural place teeming with life, it's impossible not to grow attached.

Of all seafood, blue crab is perhaps Chris' favorite and he continues to crab with the enthusiasm of a child. The multigenerational "creek boy" tradition of his family came to him quite naturally, so it's no surprise that when Chris and Idie took their oldest son, Zeb, to Pawleys Island it was like a walk back in time. Zeb took to crabbing just as his father had done. Zeb was photographed while crabbing off the very same dock Chris had been photographed on forty years before. Other than one photo being in color and the older one black-and-white, they were eerily the same. There is a similar intensity in their task. It's as if the passion for the salt marsh is imprinted in the family genes, and surely it is. Only nowadays, it is the Gulf Coast of Florida where the Hastings spend most of their time vacationing with their boys. The Florida Panhandle is Zeb and Vincent's Pawleys Island.

The lessons learned on the salt marsh, catching crabs and then cooking and eating them for dinner, molded Chris. He is compelled to talk about the magic of the place so that others will understand the value in such experiences and make choices to preserve these special places that are slowly disappearing, so that the next generation . . . and the next and the next . . . can experience a similar connection shared by his own family for almost two hundred years.

FIG PRESERVES

We use brown turkey figs to make our preserves, but any type of fresh fig will work. You may need to adapt the amount of sugar depending on the sweetness of the variety you choose. We use this fig preserve in our fig tart but there are many other uses. You can spread the preserves on toasted brioche, use in peanut butter and fig preserve sandwiches, pour warm over vanilla ice cream, or serve as an accompaniment to cheese and crackers or with seared foie gras. If you have time you can seal the preserves in jars which make great gifts.

YIELD: ABOUT 1 ¾ CUPS

16 ounces fresh, ripe brown turkey figs, stems removed
½ cup firmly packed dark brown sugar
1 (2-inch) strip fresh orange peel
1 tablespoon fresh orange juice
1 (1-inch) strip lemon peel

Fill a large saucepan halfway with water and bring to a boil. Add the figs to the boiling water and remove from the heat. Cover and steep the figs for 3 to 4 minutes or until the skins are slightly softened; drain, reserving the figs.

Finely chop the softened figs and place in a medium saucepan. Add the remaining ingredients (brown sugar through lemon peel) and stir until the sugar has begun to melt and everything is well combined.

Bring the fig mixture to a simmer over low heat. Cook, stirring occasionally, for 30 to 35 minutes or until the preserves are reduced and slightly thickened. The preserves can be placed immediately into sterilized jars and canned, or chilled and refrigerated for up to two weeks.

BEACH DINNER AT THE "HAPPY HOUSE"

Always the creek boy, Chris has taught our sons how to catch all of our own seafood for dinner. Along with a few local organic produce we pick up at roadside stands, we are able to create simple meals that are of that moment and place. It's really not about a specific place, but it's a way of life for us. To eat locally and seasonally, no matter where we are, is what we strive to accomplish. This menu is a perfect example. Most of our summers were spent at the "Happy House," a house that my mother's mother, mama (pronounced mãmã), rented each summer. My fondest memories of gathering at that table are in that house, sharing a meal that we gathered locally.

DEVILED CRAB

—◆—

MAMA'S TOMATO SALAD

—◆—

WHOLE ROASTED SPECKLED
TROUT WITH PEPPERS, SQUASH,
TOMATO, AND BASIL

—◆—

CHILLED RED AND
YELLOW SUGAR BABIES

- WINE PAIRINGS -

A DAY OF FISHING AND CRABBING AT THE BEACH BEGS FOR A CRISP, REFRESHING GLASS OF WINE.
THE CATALINA SOUNDS SAUVIGNON BLANC FROM NEW ZEALAND IS ONE OF OUR TOP PICKS. ITS
CITRUS AND HERBACEOUS QUALITIES STAND UP WELL TO THE TOMATO SALAD AND THE CHILLED
WATERMELON. THIS CRISP, LIGHT WINE HAS A NOSE OF FRESH FRUIT, FLORAL SPICE, AND PAS-
SION FRUIT WITH A GOOD MOUTHFEEL AND A CLEAN FINISH. IT IS A PERFECT MATCH TO THE
FRESH SEAFOOD IN THIS MENU.

Deviled Crab

Chris' parents showed all of the children in his family from a very early age how to clean crabs. They were taught the importance of getting all of the meat from the shell so that nothing went to waste—even the shells were utilized as baking dishes. If you have access to whole steamed crabs, clean the top of the shell and fill it with the crabmeat mixture. It not only cuts down on dish cleanup, it adds a richer crab flavor to the filling and looks impressive.

YIELD: 10 TO 12 SERVINGS

6 large eggs
1½ cups chopped green onions, about 2 bunches
⅓ cup fresh lemon juice
¼ teaspoon ground nutmeg
2 tablespoons grated lemon rind
1 pound fresh, lump crabmeat, drained and picked through for shells and cartilage
1½ cups (3 sticks) unsalted butter, melted and divided
5½ cups fresh breadcrumbs, divided
1 cup chopped fresh parsley
¾ teaspoon kosher salt
¼ teaspoon freshly ground black pepper

Preheat the oven to 400°F.

Combine the first 6 ingredients (eggs through crabmeat) in a large bowl. Add 1 cup of the melted butter, 4 cups of the breadcrumbs, and the next 3 ingredients (parsley through pepper) and stir just until combined. Spoon the crabmeat mixture into ten cleaned crab shells or twelve individual baking dishes, such as 6-ounce (¾-cup) shallow ramekins.

Top each portion evenly with 2 tablespoons of the remaining breadcrumbs and drizzle each with 2 teaspoons of the remaining butter. Bake, uncovered, for 20 minutes, or until the crab stuffing is golden brown and heated through. Serve immediately.

Mama's Tomato Salad

The beauty of this salad is its simplicity. It's made with only four ingredients (plus salt and pepper), is well balanced, and is perfect for a summer dinner. Chris' mom made this salad often and now it's a staple for our boys. Because of the subtle sweetness, it's kid-friendly, even with the onions!

YIELD: 6 SERVINGS

6 large, locally-grown vine-ripe tomatoes, about 3 pounds
½ large Vidalia onion, peeled and thinly sliced
1 cup champagne vinegar
½ cup granulated sugar
2¼ teaspoons kosher salt
½ teaspoon freshly ground black pepper

Slice the tomatoes horizontally into ½-inch-thick slices. Arrange the tomato and onion slices in an even layer on a rimmed serving platter. Whisk together the remaining ingredients until the sugar begins to dissolve. Spoon the vinegar mixture over the tomatoes and refrigerate for at least 1 hour, turning the tomatoes halfway through to coat with the marinade. Allow tomatoes to sit at room temperature for about 20 minutes before serving.

....

Chilled Red and Yellow Sugar Babies

Sugar babies are the small, round, dark green watermelons often seen on roadside stands throughout the South in the height of summer. As a kid, this was one of Chris' favorite treats and was served as a dessert more often than not. Now it's a summertime food tradition that our boys enjoy. The easiest way to chill the melons is to fill a large cooler with ice and submerge the melons until they are cold all the way through. Slice the melons into wedges or triangles and serve with plenty of napkins.

Whole-Roasted Speckled Trout

WHOLE ROASTING A FISH IS THE BEST WAY TO FULLY EXTRACT THE FLAVOR. THIS RECIPE CAN BE APPLIED TO ANY ROASTING-SIZE (TWO TO FOUR POUND) FISH. IF YOU HAVE NEVER ROASTED A WHOLE FISH BEFORE, THIS RECIPE IS A GOOD PLACE TO START. CHRIS TAUGHT HIS BROTHER, STEVEN, HOW TO ROAST A WHOLE FISH SEVERAL SUMMERS AGO. HE HAS NOT FORGOTTEN THAT EXPERIENCE AND NOW PREPARES IT WITH EASE AT HOME.

YIELD: 6 SERVINGS

3 (1½ TO 2-POUND) WHOLE SPECKLED TROUT, SCALED AND INTERNAL CAVITY CLEANED

1 TABLESPOON PLUS ½ TEASPOON KOSHER SALT, DIVIDED

1¾ TEASPOONS FRESHLY GROUND BLACK PEPPER, DIVIDED

1½ LEMONS, THINLY SLICED

1½ CUPS ROUGHLY CHOPPED FRESH BASIL, ABOUT 3 LARGE SPRIGS

2 LARGE ONIONS, PEELED AND EACH CUT INTO 3 (¾-INCH-THICK) SLICES

1 LARGE RED BELL PEPPER, SEEDED AND CUT INTO ½-INCH-WIDE STRIPS

1 LARGE YELLOW BELL PEPPER, SEEDED AND CUT INTO ½-INCH-WIDE STRIPS

2 LARGE ZUCCHINI, HALVED LENGTHWISE

2 LARGE YELLOW SQUASH, HALVED LENGTHWISE

2 LARGE RIPE TOMATOES, EACH CUT INTO 3 (¾-INCH-THICK) SLICES

½ CUP EXTRA-VIRGIN OLIVE OIL

3 LARGE FRESH BASIL SPRIGS

12 FRESH THYME SPRIGS

Preheat the oven to 400°F.

Pat the inside cavities of the trout dry and season each with ½ teaspoon of the salt and ¼ teaspoon of the pepper. Stuff each cavity with lemon slices (about ½ lemon per trout) and the chopped basil (about ½ cup of the basil per trout). Set aside.

Arrange the onion slices, bell peppers, zucchini, squash, and tomatoes in an even layer in a large roasting pan. Drizzle the olive oil over the vegetables and season with ½ teaspoon of the salt and ¼ teaspoon of the pepper, tossing until well coated. Top the vegetables with the basil and thyme sprigs. Place the trout in a single layer over the vegetables and herbs. Season the tops of the trout with the remaining 1½ teaspoons of salt and ¾ teaspoon of pepper.

Bake the trout at 400°F for 30 to 35 minutes or until cooked through and the flesh flakes easily when tested with a fork. Allow the fish to rest for 5 minutes before serving. To serve, arrange 1 onion slice and 1 tomato slice on each of six dinner plates. Evenly divide the peppers and squash among the plates. Arrange half of a roasted trout on each plate over the vegetables. Serve immediately.

CHAPTER 3

SEPTEMBER

&

OCTOBER

HARVEST MOON, PUMPKINS, AND LESSONS ON GROWING UP

IF HEIRLOOM TOMATOES USHER IN SUMMER FOR US, THE APPEARANCE OF SCUPPERNONGS AND MUSCADINES SIGNAL AUTUMN IS ON THE HORIZON AND IT IS AGAIN TIME TO ADJUST OUR FOCUS AND FINE-TUNE OUR THINKING IN THE KITCHEN. THE SEASON IS HOST TO SO MANY WONDERS BOTH ON THE TABLE AND IN OUR LIVES. THE HARVEST MOON IS PERHAPS THE MOST SIGNIFICANT MARKER OF THE SEASONAL SHIFT FOR US. FROM A CULINARY STANDPOINT, ITS APPEARANCE REPRESENTS THE END OF SUMMER'S BOUNTIFUL HARVEST AND THE NEED TO HUSTLE TO PUT UP THE LAST OF THE WARM SEASON VEGETABLES FOR THE MONTHS AHEAD, YET THIS BIG SAUCER MOON ALSO USHERS IN CROPS LIKE PUMPKINS, SQUASH, AND WILD-FORAGED MUSHROOMS. AT THE RESTAURANT, WITH COOLER DAYS WE RETURN TO CURING MEATS IN THE MANNER OF TRADITIONAL SOUTHERN SMOKEHOUSES AND OLD WORLD CHARCUTERIE.

The harvest moon is also called the "woodcock moon" because with its rise begins the migration of woodcock from Canada to Louisiana and the start of the fall hunting season. Woodcock hunting has become an annual tradition shared with friend and author, Charles Gaines, who wrote the foreword for this book. We gather each autumn to hunt woodcock and grouse and fish for wild Atlantic salmon in Canada. This experience is an opportunity for Chris to reconnect to the land and the changing of the seasons beyond the confines of the kitchen. In a powerful way woodcock hunting renews his passion for his craft and inspires his approach to a new season of cooking and living. The meals prepared on that trip—the wild and foraged foods shot or gathered that very day that are of that place and of that moment reaffirm Chris' commitment to the land, seasonality, and his craft in the most elemental way. Some close friends, a bottle or two of Hermitage and you can feel the restorative, magical effect food can have on one's life.

Likewise, the yearly father-son dove shoot has been an event of great significance in the lives of sons, Zeb and Vincent. As young dove hunters, they have garnered an appreciation for game limits and an understanding of the imperative of gun safety. Equally important, as young men, they have learned the social power of proper manners, respecting age-old traditions, and their elders.

Chris' father is a man of a creative bent—architect, artist, sculptor, and master pumpkin carver—and Chris has inherited an artistic streak of his own. The childhood fun of carving jack-o-lanterns and awe of admiring his father's handiwork have spilled over into his Chris' adulthood. For several days each October, he is consumed by the craft of carving pumpkins while the neighborhood children wait in anticipation for their appearance on the front stoop of the Hastings' home. The ritual has become a seasonal art form admired by the entire neighborhood during the annual Halloween parade and night of trick-or-treating that follows. Chris has vowed to carve pumpkins for as long as he is able for all those who have come to count on them so that the Hastings' tradition endures.

As the heat wanes, so does our summer approach to ingredients at the restaurant. With the transition from peas, corn, okra, and tomatoes to squash, pumpkins, and wild mushrooms we turn to different styles of cooking—smoking, braising, curing, pickling, and preserving. Each season provides us with opportunities anew to get reinvigorated and passionate about what we do. Seasonal shifts are much like finding a new purveyor—only in this case it's Mother Nature bringing us new gems from forest and field. New ingredients are an opportunity to refine our cooking. When we cook by a seasonal compass we are truly keepers of our craft and our menu stays diverse and interesting. Ironically, it seems that just as we are ready for summer to move along, fall arrives and with it loads of new inspiration and opportunities for creativity.

BOG SUCKER

Chris first experienced a Bog Sucker on a trip with good friend Ben Johnson to Frank Harris' hunting camp in Louisiana. After hunting woodcock all day, the group of hunting buddies retired to Frank's house to sip Bogg Suckers and enjoy a meal of grits and grillades prepared by their host. The next morning they were awakened to the VMI choir singing the "Bonny Blue Flag," which made reference to the secessionist flag. Bog Sucker is also another name for the woodcock. Occasionally hunters will tie a woodcock feather to a hawthorn before skewering an olive for the garnish. Our favorite variety of olive used in this cocktail is Miss Scarlett's Fiery Hot Devils (page 382).

YIELD: 5 SERVINGS

3 cups gin
½ cup dry sherry
5 green olives, each skewered with a hawthorn or
    toothpick for garnish

Combine the gin and sherry in a mason jar and freeze until well chilled, at least 4 hours. Pour the chilled liquor into five old-fashioned glasses filled with ice and garnish each with an olive-skewered hawthorn. Serve immediately.

FIG-INFUSED SMALL-BATCH BOURBON

In years when we have a bumper crop of summer figs, we always put up a case of Basil Hayden bourbon with figs. Try it! On a cold winter night by a crackling fire, one sip will make you thankful that you took time during the dog days of summer to make this bourbon infusion.

YIELD: 1 (750ML) BOTTLE

1 POUND FRESH RIPE FIGS, SUCH AS BROWN TURKEY, MISSION, OR CELESTE

1 (750ML) BOTTLE GOOD-QUALITY SMALL-BATCH BOURBON, SUCH AS BASIL HAYDEN

Wash the figs well under warm running water and pat dry. Remove the stems and cut into quarters. Place the quartered figs into a 3-quart sterilized jar. Add the bourbon to the jar, reserving the original bourbon bottle, and secure the top of the jar. Allow the bourbon to sit in a cool, dry place for at least two weeks or until the bourbon has a distinct fig aroma and flavor.

Strain the infusion through a fine-meshed sieve into a clean container. Place the bourbon-soaked figs into an airtight container in the refrigerator and reserve for the Fig-Infused Bourbon "Toddy" (next column). Pour the infused bourbon back into the reserved bourbon bottle. The bourbon is ready to use and will keep, at room temperature for up to one year.

FIG-INFUSED BOURBON "TODDY"

A toddy, by definition, is a drink made from brandy or whiskey, mixed with hot water and sugar. Idie's father, Jim, was fond of his toddy made from part whiskey and part ginger ale over ice cubes. This toddy is our tribute to Jim, and is updated with fig-infused bourbon rather than plain whiskey.

YIELD: 1 SERVING

3 TABLESPOONS FIG-INFUSED BOURBON ½ BOURBON-SOAKED FIG, CUT INTO QUARTERS

1 CUP ICE

1 WHOLE PRESERVED FIG OR MARASCHINO CHERRY, FOR GARNISH

Combine the bourbon, bourbon-soaked fig, and the ice in a martini shaker and muddle until the fig is well mashed and the ice is crushed. Pour the mixture into a rocks glass and garnish with the preserved fig or cherry. Serve immediately.

HOT MULLED APPLE CIDER

FORTUNATELY, FRESH SQUEEZED APPLE CIDER IS READILY AVAILABLE IN THE FALL AND WINTER MONTHS, BUT IF YOU HAVE TROUBLE FINDING A GOOD-QUALITY CIDER, TRY ONE OF OUR FAVORITE ONES (PAGE 381). THIS RECIPE IS GREAT WITH OR WITHOUT THE RUM AND FILLS YOUR HOUSE WITH THE FRAGRANT AROMAS OF APPLES, CITRUS, AND SPICE. BECAUSE WE USE A FULL-FLAVORED APPLE CIDER, WE DON'T LIKE TO ADD TOO MUCH SPICE TO THIS RECIPE, BUT FEEL FREE TO ADJUST THE AMOUNTS TO YOUR LIKING.

YIELD: 6 SERVINGS

3 CUPS FRESH APPLE CIDER
5 WHOLE CLOVES
1 CINNAMON STICK, BROKEN IN HALF
2 LEMONS, CUT INTO ½-INCH-THICK SLICES, DIVIDED
2 SMALL ORANGES, CUT INTO ½-INCH-THICK SLICES
⅓ CUP DARK SPICED RUM (OPTIONAL)
6 WHOLE CINNAMON STICKS, FOR GARNISH

Combine the cider, cloves, cinnamon, half of the lemon slices, and the orange slices in a medium saucepan. Bring to a simmer over low heat, being careful not to allow the mixture to boil. Stir in the rum (if using) and cook just until heated through. Remove and discard the cinnamon stick and citrus slices.

Transfer the cider into six warmed mugs and garnish each with a lemon slice and a cinnamon stick. Serve immediately.

CINDERELLA PUMPKIN SOUP

with Fried Sage and Lemon Oil

THERE ARE AS MANY NAMES FOR THIS PARTICULAR PUMPKIN AS THERE ARE REGIONS GROWING IT, SO LOOK FOR SQUATTY, SMOOTH-SKINNED VARIETIES WITH A KHAKI HUE. THE PUMPKIN'S FLESH IS A DEEP, RICH ORANGE AND HAS A SWEET, MELONLIKE AROMA.

YIELD: 2 QUARTS OR 8 SERVINGS

2 TABLESPOONS UNSALTED BUTTER
2 CUPS THINLY SLICED LEEKS (WHITE PART ONLY)
2 TEASPOONS CHOPPED FRESH THYME
8 CUPS PEELED AND MEDIUM DICED CINDERELLA PUMPKINS
2 TEASPOONS KOSHER SALT
2 TEASPOONS GRANULATED SUGAR
½ CUP CHICKEN STOCK (PAGE 335)
4 CUPS WATER (OR JUST ENOUGH TO COVER)
¼ TEASPOON FRESHLY GROUND BLACK PEPPER
8 FRIED SAGE LEAVES (PAGE 376), OPTIONAL
1 TABLESPOON PLUS 1 TEASPOON LEMON OIL

Melt the butter in a heavy stockpot over medium heat. Add the leeks and thyme and cook until tender but not brown, about 5 minutes. Add the pumpkin, salt, sugar, chicken stock, water (only enough to barely cover the diced pumpkin), and pepper and bring to a boil; cover and reduce the heat to low. Allow the mixture to cook, covered, at a simmer for 10 minutes or until the pumpkins are fully cooked through and tender. Remove the stockpot from the heat and allow the mixture to cool slightly.

Transfer the pumpkin mixture to a blender in small batches and purée until smooth. Adjust the seasonings with additional salt and pepper, if needed. Ladle the soup equally into eight warm soup bowls. Garnish each bowl with a fried sage leave, if using, and drizzle ½ teaspoon of the lemon oil over each. Serve immediately.

ANNUAL PUMPKIN CARVING

One of Chris' passions each autumn is pumpkin carving. Growing up, he carved pumpkins with his family each Halloween like most kids on the block. Only at his house, the creations were more fanciful. Chris' dad, Charlie, an architect and an artist in his own right, created pumpkins that turned the heads of passersby. Charlie always sketched his vision on the pumpkin in advance and his creations went way beyond your run-of-the-mill jack-o-lanterns. As an adult, Chris has carried on this family tradition.

While Chris' creative bent is most often expressed as a chef through food, the other major opportunity comes as Halloween approaches and there are pumpkins to be carved. Certainly his well-honed knife skills are an asset, but he also relies on his ability to draw freehand. Beyond tradition, carving pumpkins provides the chance to relive his own childhood through the eyes of the boys. All the cool things he enjoyed as kid—crabbing, fishing, hunting, and carving pumpkins—have taken on a richer meaning with fatherhood. When the first pumpkins begin to show up in the markets, they will begin to catch his eye and so begins the fun associated with procurement of the many shapes, sizes, and varieties that make up a full complement of jack-o-lanterns for the stoop. And what started decades ago with just a few pumpkins soon morphed into six, eight, and then ten. Zeb and Vincent would carve one or two while Chris enthusiastically churned out twenty pumpkins at one sitting.

Though the boys are grown and away at school, Chris remains compelled to take on the monumental task of carving two dozen or so pumpkins each and every year. Idie thinks he's a bit crazy, but realizes it is an obsession. It starts a couple of weeks before Halloween each year when Chris embarks on a mission for the perfect assortment of pumpkins. He demands tall, fat, squatty, jack-o-lantern style, white ones, green ones—a varied palette—for balance on the porch. All of them must have good stems. He has developed a relationship with four or five pumpkin growers over the years and makes rounds to select his favorites.

Once the pumpkins are all in the house, lined up in the back room where the carving will take place, Chris spends a day removing the seeds and flesh from the cavities and putting the pumpkin tops back on. The next day, stationed in a chair with a pumpkin in front of him, he sketches a design freehand then carves until each pumpkin's unique personality is realized. He will carve one after another until there is a crowd of pumpkin faces perched on the worktable. The pumpkins are then ceremoniously placed on our stoop as the neighborhood begins to gather for the annual Halloween parade. Neighbor kids anticipate each year's efforts. If for no other reason, Chris carves pumpkins for the kids. His handiwork survives at most only a day on the stoop in the Alabama sun at which point we take the festive assortment to the restaurant to be enjoyed for a few days more.

Like cooking, his pumpkins are transient art and yet a perfect reflection of the seasonal, of-the-moment life we live by. Chris compares the transitory nature of his pumpkin project to a turkey hunt. After all, he doesn't hunt turkeys simply because he wants to, rather when the season comes around he is driven to participate. It is a compulsion. When he wakes up, turkeys are what he thinks about. And, when the season ends, turkeys no longer occupy his thoughts. The annual pumpkin carving is the same. It provides yet another opportunity to celebrate the season at hand, savor it, and move on.

The smaller pumpkins have seeds that are perfect for slow roasting. We use the flesh of the "Cinderella" pumpkins in any number of dishes that exemplify this moment in the growing season, when pumpkins can be celebrated in their full glory on the stoop and on the table.

APPLE, ALMOND, AND ENDIVE SALAD
with *Creamy Herb Dressing*

THIS IS A SIGNATURE SALAD ON OUR RESTAURANT MENU EACH FALL AND HAS BECOME VERY POPULAR WITH OUR CUS-TOMERS. IT'S A BEAUTIFULLY PRESENTED ALTERNATIVE TO A BASIC GREEN SALAD. IF RED OR GREEN ENDIVE IS UNAVAILABLE, USE DOUBLE THE AMOUNT OF WHATEVER ENDIVE YOU CAN FIND—THE DIFFERENT TYPES ARE MAINLY FOR COLOR. WE PREFER SWEET, CRISP, SLIGHTLY TART APPLES FOR THIS SALAD, SUCH AS ALABAMA'S NATIVE CUMBERLAND SPUR APPLE, BUT FUJI, JONATHAN, OR MCINTOSH ARE WORTHY STAND-INS.

YIELD: 6 SERVINGS

2 MEDIUM CUMBERLAND SPUR APPLES, CORED AND THINLY SLICED
4 HEADS RED ENDIVE, STEMS REMOVED, LEAVES SEPARATED AND WASHED
4 HEADS GREEN ENDIVE, STEMS REMOVED, LEAVES SEPARATED AND WASHED
1 CUP CREAMY HERB DRESSING (PAGE 346)
¼ TEASPOON KOSHER SALT
¼ TEASPOON FRESHLY GROUND BLACK PEPPER
⅓ CUP LIGHTLY TOASTED SLICED ALMONDS
3 TABLESPOONS FRESH PARSLEY LEAVES

Combine the apple slices, endive leaves, and the dressing in a large bowl. Toss gently until the leaves are well coated with dressing. Season the salad with the salt and pepper.

Arrange the endive leaves and apple slices in a crisscross pattern, alternating the red and green endive leaves, on each of six plates. Divide the almonds evenly over each salad and garnish each with a few fresh parsley leaves. Serve immediately.

PANCETTA-WRAPPED LOCAL KIEFER PEAR SALAD
with Saba and Arugula

GOOD-QUALITY PANCETTA CAN BE FOUND IN MOST SPECIALTY GROCERIES. THE SAME IS TRUE FOR ITALIAN SABA, A REDUCED GRAPE JUICE CONDIMENT ALSO CALLED "VIN COTTO" THAT IS USED TO SWEETEN AND FLAVOR A VARIETY OF DISHES. SABA IS A VERSATILE ADDITION TO ANY PANTRY, SO LOOK FOR IT IN STORES OR PURCHASE IT ONLINE.

YIELD: 4 SERVINGS

2 LARGE **K**EIFER PEARS OR OTHER FIRM BAKING PEAR, ABOUT ¾ POUND
10 PAPER-THIN SLICES PANCETTA, ABOUT **5** OUNCES, UNROLLED INTO STRIPS
5 CUPS (**3** OUNCES) LOOSELY PACKED FRESH ARUGULA
1 TEASPOON EXTRA-VIRGIN OLIVE OIL
¼ TEASPOON KOSHER SALT
PINCH OF FRESHLY GROUND BLACK PEPPER
1 TEASPOON SABA

Preheat the oven to 425°F.

Core and slice the pears into wedges, about 10 wedges per pear. Cut the pancetta crosswise, to create 5-inch-long strips. Wrap each pear wedge in a strip of pancetta, slightly overlapping the pancetta and tucking the ends under to secure. (When wrapped, the pear wedges will not be completely covered by the pancetta.) Arrange the pear wedges in an even layer in a large cast-iron skillet. Place the skillet in the oven and bake for 13 to 15 minutes or until the bottoms are brown and crispy. Turn the pears and bake an additional 5 minutes or until the pancetta is browned and crispy and the pears are tender. Set the pears aside to cool slightly.

Toss the arugula in a large mixing bowl with the olive oil, salt, and pepper. Evenly divide the arugula among four salad plates. Arrange five warm pear wedges around each salad. Drizzle ¼ teaspoon of the saba over and around each salad and serve immediately.

LEE JONES – THE CHEF'S GARDEN®

Lee Jones' dad, Bob, grew up in the commercial wholesale farming business. In the late seventies and early eighties, as interest rates hit 21 percent for a period of time, a massive hailstorm decimated the Jones family farm in a matter of minutes. Lee's parents reinvested every last penny to save their farm. Like most farmers, they borrowed their operating money in spring or winter and paid it back once the crops came in, but because of the storm and the hasty reinvestment, they were mired in debt at a time of historically high interest rates and couldn't hang on. They were forced to sell.

Bob Jones had crossed paths with chefs from time to time. The famous chef, Jean-Louis Palladin, one of the first French chefs in America, sought out quality produce for his New York restaurant while most farmers were just growing to meet consumer demand for the cheapest products. Desperate for a way to survive in agriculture, the Jones family took a gamble to grow the way these chefs wanted. Lee recalls that if a chef told them to grow a specific variety with the best flavor and harvest it just as it reached a specific size (in other words, "Do it the way we tell you!") then the Joneses responded with a salute, "OK, we hear you. Teach us."

Lee met Chris while he was working under Bradley Ogden at the Lark Creek Inn. The farmer and the young chef immediately connected because it was apparent to Lee that Chris had the training, roots, and fundamental understanding of quality that the group of close-knit chefs associated with The Chef's Garden all came to the table with. Lee credits Chris as one of the original chefs who focused The Chef's Garden vision with others like Jean-Louis Palladin, Alain Ducasse, Thomas Keller, Charlie Trotter, and Bob Waggoner.

It might seem strange that it was Bob Jones and not his young sons, Lee and Bobby, who recognized the possibility in what those chefs were seeking. Though it didn't exist at the time, such quality had existed on farms fifty years before when Bob was just a boy. The chefs' desire for such uncommon quality resonated with him in an almost nostalgic way. Five years after starting over, with 98½ percent of the Jones family business linked to farmers' markets and only one-and-a-half percent to "these pain-in-the-ass chefs," Lee says endearingly, Bob declared, "We are jack of all and master of none" because the family business was trying to serve two masters—the handful of chefs looking for artisan production and the rest of the world just looking for cheap. It was decided a family vote would be taken. Everyone at the table voted to stay in the farmers' market business. Nonetheless, the patriarch stood up and exclaimed, "Nope, there's more potential with the chefs so we're going to abandon the farmers' markets . . . my vote counts as five, your votes count as one. End of discussion!" That was that. The Chef's Garden was born.

Chris takes great pride in being right there from the very beginning to help steer the direction of the farm by serving on its advisory board. The fact that this farm has an "advisory board" is a testament to its success. Lee Jones humbly says, "It's not really about us. We're really just tenants for the chef. We exist because they've allowed our existence. It is a privilege to work with these chefs. They are why we are still farming."

CHEF'S GARDEN BEET SALAD
with Goat Cheese and Citrus Vinaigrette

BEETS ARE OUR ALL-TIME FAVORITE ROOT VEGETABLE AND WITH THEIR EARTHY, NATURALLY SWEET FLAVOR AND TREMENDOUS VARIETY IN COLOR AND SIZE, WE INCORPORATE THEM INTO DISHES ON OUR MENU EVERY CHANCE WE GET. WE FIND THAT PEOPLE EITHER LOVE OR DISLIKE BEETS. ROASTING THE BEETS, AS IN THIS RECIPE, BRINGS OUT THE NATURAL SWEETNESS OF THE VEGETABLE AND OFTEN CONVINCES CRITICS TO RETHINK THEIR STANCE ON BEETS. WE PURCHASE A VARIETY OF SMALL, BABY BEETS FROM THE CHEF'S GARDEN, BUT LARGER BEETS CAN BE SUBSTITUTED IF THEY'RE CUT INTO SMALL WEDGES.

YIELD: 4 SERVINGS

- 4 TO 5 BABY YELLOW BEETS, ROASTED AND PEELED (PAGE 378)
- 4 TO 5 BABY RED BEETS, ROASTED AND PEELED (PAGE 378)
- 4 TO 5 BABY CHIOGGIA (CANDY-STRIPED) BEETS, ROASTED AND PEELED (PAGE 378)
- ½ CUP CITRUS VINAIGRETTE (PAGE 344), DIVIDED
- 6 OUNCES (ABOUT 1 CUP LIGHTLY PACKED) FRESH GOAT CHEESE
- ¾ CUP TOASTED WALNUTS
- 4 CUPS LOOSELY PACKED BABY ARUGULA
- 2 CUPS TRIMMED FRISÉE LETTUCE
- ¼ TEASPOON KOSHER SALT
- PINCH OF FRESHLY GROUND BLACK PEPPER

Cut the beets into halves (or quarters, depending on their size). Place the beets in a small bowl and add 1 tablespoon of the vinaigrette. Toss the beets in the vinaigrette until well coated.

Divide the goat cheese into twelve equal portions and arrange three portions on each of four salad plates. Sprinkle 3 tablespoons of the walnuts evenly over each plate. Arrange about six beet halves on each plate.

Combine the arugula and frisée in a large bowl and season the lettuce lightly with the salt and pepper. Drizzle the remaining 7 tablespoons of vinaigrette into the bowl and toss until the greens are well dressed. Evenly divide the lettuce into four portions and arrange each portion in the center of each plate. Serve immediately.

FRISÉE LETTUCE

Frisée is a member of the chicory family of lettuces most commonly noted for their slightly bitter flavor and sturdy leaves. This type of lettuce has slender, curly leaves with a mildly bitter flavor and a crispy texture. We are fans of all of the chicory lettuces, especially frisée. By incorporating this lettuce into salads, we add a crunchy, bitter flavor contrast to sweet lettuces that gives a dish both depth of flavor and texture.

HOT AND HOT SEAFOOD SPRING ROLLS
with Coconut Curry Dipping Sauce

THIS IS A VERY VERSATILE RECIPE THAT CAN BE WIDELY ADAPTED BASED ON THE AVAILABILITY OF INGREDIENTS. ALMOST ANY VARIETY OF FISH OR SEAFOOD CAN BE USED OR YOU CAN MAKE A VEGETARIAN VERSION, USING FRESH SLICED BELL PEPPERS, BEAN SPROUTS, OR SLICED DAIKON RADISHES. AT THE RESTAURANT, WE SERVE THESE SPRING ROLLS AS AN APPETIZER ON A BED OF ASIAN VEGETABLE SLAW (PAGE 38) THAT IS DRESSED WITH SOY SAUCE, SESAME OIL, SALT, AND PEPPER.

YIELD: ABOUT 25 ROLLS OR 12 SERVINGS

1½ OUNCES VERMICELLI NOODLES, SOFTENED ACCORDING TO PACKAGE DIRECTIONS
3 CUPS CHOPPED FISH FILLETS (ABOUT ½-INCH PIECES), SUCH AS SNAPPER, SCAMP, FLOUNDER, TUNA, OR SALMON
1 TEASPOON PEELED AND FINELY CHOPPED FRESH GINGER
2 TABLESPOONS CHOPPED FRESH CILANTRO
2 TABLESPOONS FISH SAUCE
3 TABLESPOONS HOISIN SAUCE
2 TABLESPOONS GROUND CHILI PASTE, SUCH AS SAMBAL
1 (12-OUNCE) PACKAGE SQUARE SPRING ROLL WRAPPERS, ABOUT 25 WRAPPERS
2 QUARTS PEANUT OIL, FOR FRYING
3 TABLESPOONS CORNSTARCH
2 LARGE EGGS, LIGHTLY BEATEN
3 CUPS COCONUT CURRY DIPPING SAUCE (PAGE 338)
12 FRESH CILANTRO SPRIGS, FOR GARNISH

Gently squeeze the excess water out of the prepared noodles and place in a large mixing bowl. Add the diced fish, ginger, cilantro, fish sauce, hoisin sauce, and chili paste and mix until well combined.

Lay several spring roll wrappers in an even layer on a clean, dry work surface. Keep the remaining wrappers covered until ready to use. Spoon about 3 tablespoons of the fish and noodle mixture in one corner of each wrapper. Roll the pastry over the fish mixture to the center of the wrapper. Fold the two side corners to the center of the wrapper, over the fish bundle and continue rolling towards the top corner. Stop rolling 1-inch from the top corner and set bundles aside. Repeat with remaining wrappers and filling.

Pour the peanut oil into deep-sided skillet to a depth of 3 inches. (Alternately, a deep fryer can be filled with peanut oil.) Preheat the oil to 350°F.

Lightly dust a clean, dry work surface with the cornstarch. Brush the inside of the open wrapper corners with the eggs and fold the corners over the spring rolls to seal. Roll the spring rolls in the cornstarch to keep from sticking. At this point the spring rolls can be refrigerated for up to 1 day before frying.

Fry the spring rolls, in batches in the preheated oil for 2 to 3 minutes, turning occasionally, until golden brown on all sides. Remove the spring rolls from the fryer and drain on a paper towel–lined plate. Allow the spring rolls to cool for 1 to 2 minutes before serving. Arrange two spring rolls on each small plate with several tablespoons of coconut curry dipping sauce. Garnish each plate with a sprig of fresh cilantro and serve warm.

STEAMED MUSSELS

with Fennel, Leeks, and Winter Savory

As a rule, the best mussels served in the lower forty-eight states come from Prince Edward Island Sound, in Canada. Also known as PEIs, these mussels can be purchased from almost any fishmonger if you ask for them by name. Since every bag of mussels harvested is tagged with a harvest date, it is a good idea to ask your fishmonger to see the tag from the bag your mussels came from. If the harvest date is older than one week, you may want to hold off on purchasing the mussels. To check for freshness, gently squeeze the shell of an open mussel to see if it closes. If it does not shut, the mussel is probably dead and should not be used. Alternately, mussels that do not open after being steamed are also dead and should be thrown out before the dish is served.

YIELD: 6 SERVINGS

½ cup extra-virgin olive oil, divided
¾ cup (1½ sticks) unsalted butter, divided
6 fresh winter savory sprigs
1 bay leaf
1 teaspoon chopped fresh garlic
2 large fennel bulbs, cored and cut into ¼-inch-thick slices (about 4 cups)
2 large leeks, cut in half lengthwise, and cut into ½-inch-thick pieces (white part only, about 3½ cups)
2 cups dry white wine
2 cups Shrimp Stock (page 334)
4 (2-inch-long) strips lemon peels
2 pounds (about 72) fresh Prince Edward Island mussels, scrubbed and debearded
1 teaspoon kosher salt
½ teaspoon freshly ground black pepper
2 tablespoons chopped fresh parsley

Heat ¼ cup of the olive oil and 6 tablespoons of the butter in a large rondeau or wide sauté pan with 3-inch-deep sides over medium-high heat until the butter is melted. Add the savory, bay leaf, and garlic and cook, stirring constantly, for 30 seconds. Add the fennel and leeks, reduce the heat to medium, and cook, stirring occasionally, for 10 minutes or until the vegetables are tender. Add the white wine, bring the mixture to a simmer and allow the wine to reduce slightly, 5 to 7 minutes. Increase the heat to high, add the shrimp stock and lemon peels and return the mixture to a simmer. Add the mussels, stir well, cover, and allow the mixture to cook for 3 to 4 minutes or until the mussels have opened. Discard any unopened mussels. Evenly divide the open mussels among six wide soup bowls.

Return the broth mixture to a boil over high heat, season with the salt and pepper, and allow the liquid to reduce by half, about 8 minutes. Remove the broth mixture from the heat and stir in the remaining ¼ cup of olive oil, 6 tablespoons of butter, and the parsley. Discard the bay leaf, savory sprigs, and lemon peels before serving. Spoon the broth and vegetable mixture evenly over the mussels and serve immediately.

SEARED FOIE GRAS

with Brioche Bread and Wild Persimmon Jam

WE REALIZE THAT MOST FOLKS DON'T HAVE ACCESS TO WILD PERSIM-
MONS LIKE THOSE WE GET FROM PURVEYOR AND FORAGER CHRIS
BENNETT, SO USE CULTIVATED PERSIMMONS OR THE HIGHEST QUALITY
PERSIMMON JAM YOU CAN FIND IN STORES. THE TART-SWEET, AUTUM-
NAL JAM IS A DELICIOUS FOIL FOR THE RICHNESS OF BUTTERY FOIE GRAS.

YIELD: 6 SERVINGS

1 (1-POUND) LOBE FRESH FOIE GRAS

6 (¼-INCH-THICK) SLICES BRIOCHE BREAD, CRUSTS
    REMOVED

1 TABLESPOON KOSHER SALT

¾ TEASPOON FRESHLY GROUND BLACK PEPPER

1 TABLESPOON MINCED SHALLOTS

1 CUP LATE HARVEST RIESLING

1 TABLESPOON UNSALTED BUTTER

1 TEASPOON CHOPPED FRESH CHIVES

½ TEASPOON FRESH LEMON JUICE

¼ CUP PLUS 2 TABLESPOONS WILD PERSIMMON JAM
    (PAGE 361)

Remove any white fat or slightly greenish veins from the foie gras. Dip a sharp chef's knife in hot water, pat dry, and slice the foie gras into 2½ to 3-ounce portions, about ¾ inch thick. Reheat the knife before cutting each slice. Score the top and bottom sides of each portion with ¼-inch squares. Refrigerate the foie gras portions until well chilled, at least 30 minutes.

Preheat the oven to 400°F.

Cut each brioche slice into 4 triangles. Arrange the triangles in an even layer on a baking sheet and bake for 4 to 5 minutes or until lightly golden and toasted. Set aside to cool completely.

Season the foie gras portions on all sides with the salt and pepper, using about ½ teaspoon salt and ⅛ teaspoon pepper per serving. Heat a large cast-iron skillet over medium-high heat until it almost begins to smoke. Add half of the foie gras portions to the skillet and cook for 30 to 45 seconds or until well browned. Turn the foie gras and cook an additional minute or until golden brown and heated through. Transfer the foie gras to a serving platter to keep warm. Discard any fat from the skillet and repeat with remaining foie gras.

After all of the foie gras has been seared, discard all but ½ teaspoon of the fat from the skillet. Add the shallots and Riesling to the hot fat and bring to a boil. Allow the mixture to boil for 1½ to 2 minutes or until reduced by half. Remove the skillet from the heat and whisk in the butter, chives, and lemon juice.

Arrange four brioche triangles on each of six appetizer plates. Arrange a seared foie gras on each plate and drizzle 1½ teaspoons of the sauce over each foie gras portion. Spoon 1 tablespoon of the jam over each piece of foie gras and serve immediately.

SMOKING: SOUTHERN HISTORY AND PAYING HOMAGE TO THE PIG

Smoking is a tradition born of the days before refrigeration. The approach of cooler months signaled the time to slaughter animals and preserve the meat for use throughout the year. Animals that had been fattened all summer would be butchered and "put up" for the leaner days ahead.

It is not that the Southern method of curing and smoking is that much different from the Old World methods of Italy or France. Our tradition simply centers on the pig. *Charcuterie* is the French term for the processing of fresh cuts of pork into sausages, hams, pâtés and the like. And while we share similar techniques for curing, smoking, and preserving with those across the Atlantic, the end result is often quite different.

In the South, methods for slaughtering hogs to make souse meat or headcheese, smoked ham and homemade sausages have developed into regional art forms that are as unique to areas as dialects. Cured and smoked pork products are an intrinsic part of Southern culture and pride. What the Virginians do with their hams is different from what those in the Carolinas do. And citizens of both states will argue tooth and nail that their ham is best. It is an age-old, passionate debate centered on methods that are as distinctive and as numerous as the nuanced techniques of barbecuing throughout the South.

For instance, Conecuh County in Alabama produces an amazing and distinctive sausage. It's the only sausage on our menu that we don't produce ourselves because it is simply beyond compare. It is a product born out of the humble tradition of Southern family farms butchering their hogs and putting up the leaf fat for baking, setting aside the meat to be cured, smoked, or cooked, and then taking all the leftover bits and churning out sausages so that not a scrap is wasted. There is an old saying that you must use everything from "the rooter to the tooter." And Conecuh County sausage is a great example of something born out of frugality that has ended up becoming a regional delicacy. American culture, by and large, has become one that just eats the chop and shoulder. Few people eat or understand how to cook the belly, jowls, ears, or trotters (portion from the knee to hoof) anymore. At Hot and Hot we use all of these cuts in our cooking, yet we do so in creative enough ways to get people to try them. One taste and most people either gain renewed appreciation for the inexpensive cuts of their childhood tables or find themselves appreciating something they have never tasted before or thought they would ever try. That's success.

SMOKED AND GRILLED QUAIL
with Winter Vegetables and White BBQ Sauce

THIS RECIPE WAS CREATED ONE DAY AFTER OUR GOOD FRIEND AND SOUS CHEF AT THE TIME, GEORGE McMILLAN, BROUGHT IN SMOKED CHICKEN WITH WHITE BARBEQUE SAUCE FOR LUNCH TO SHARE WITH THE COOKS. THE CHICKEN WAS PERFECTLY MOIST AND SMOKY, BUT IT WAS THE WHITE BARBEQUE SAUCE THAT GARNERED RAVES. WE KNEW WE HAD TO CREATE OUR OWN VERSION OF THAT TANGY, ALABAMA-STYLE WHITE SAUCE AND THIS IS THE RESULT.

YIELD: 8 SERVINGS

8 (6-OUNCE) SEMI-BONELESS QUAIL

4 CUPS BROWN SUGAR CURE (PAGE 374)

1 TABLESPOON UNSALTED BUTTER

1 TABLESPOON MINCED SHALLOTS

1 TEASPOON CHOPPED FRESH THYME

1 PARSNIP, PEELED, BLANCHED, AND CUT INTO 1-INCH PIECES

4 BABY BEETS, ROASTED, PEELED, AND QUARTERED

16 BABY CARROTS, PEELED AND BLANCHED, OR ABOUT 4 LARGE CARROTS, PEELED, BLANCHED, AND CUT INTO 1-INCH PIECES

8 CIPOLLINI ONIONS, ROASTED, PEELED, AND HALVED

4 FINGERLING POTATOES, ROASTED AND HALVED LENGTHWISE

¼ TEASPOON KOSHER SALT

⅛ TEASPOON FRESHLY GROUND BLACK PEPPER

¾ CUP WHITE BARBECUE SAUCE (PAGE 337)

Rinse the quail under cold running water and pat dry. Arrange the quail in an even layer in a large baking dish and cover completely with the brown sugar cure. Cover and refrigerate the quail for 4 hours. Remove the quail from the cure, rinse under cold running water, and pat dry.

Preheat a smoker to 120°F. Arrange the quail in the preheated smoker over indirect heat and smoke for 2 hours. Remove the quail and set aside until ready to grill.

Preheat the grill to medium heat (300°F to 350°F). It is important not to add the quail to a hot grill, as the cured quail will burn more easily because of the higher sugar content.

Preheat the oven to 400°F. Add the quail, skin side down, to the preheated grill and cook for about 6 minutes. Turn the quail and grill, with the grill covered, an additional 5 to 6 minutes. Transfer the quail to a platter and cover to keep warm.

Melt the butter in a medium ovenproof skillet over medium heat. Add the shallots and thyme and cook until softened, about 1 minute. Add the parsnips, beets, carrots, onions, and potatoes and toss until well coated with the butter mixture. Season the vegetables lightly with the salt and pepper and place in the oven. Roast the vegetables at 400°F for 5 minutes or until tender and heated through.

Divide the vegetables evenly among eight dinner plates. Cut each quail in half and place two halves over each portion of vegetables. Drizzle 1 to 2 tablespoons of the white barbecue sauce over each plate and serve immediately.

HENRY FUDGE – FUDGE FAMILY FARMS PORK

Henry Fudge is the master of pork and a shining example of why we are committed to seeking out the best purveyors and ingredients. Henry is a hog farmer and champion of the perfect pig. Achieving it has been a decade-long endeavor of fine-tuning genetics and the singular task to which he has dedicated himself. His efforts are finally paying off. What started as a hobby to raise the original, mother breed of pigs and move away from hogs so hybridized that they looked more like missiles than swine has turned into a happy accident of a culinary kind. Henry found that the meat of his Berkshire-Duroc cross has the perfect ratio of fat to lean muscle. It is this intramuscular fat that gives his pork its incomparable flavor. He has also created a network of dedicated Amish farmers who provide his hogs with an organic corn diet and wild foraged acorns. The result is pork as good as any we've eaten.

All of this is thanks to Henry's devotion to that singular thing—raising pigs. At Hot and Hot Fish Club, he has given us an opportunity to move beyond traditional thinking about pork preparation because we now have access to the whole hog. We use the head, leaf fat, liver, trotters, belly, and other parts of the freshest, most exceptional quality. We get to play with ideas and experiment and, in doing so, gain renewed creativity simply through access to these new, top-quality cuts. For instance, pure white leaf fat is worked into our pastry dough and we also make souse meat, a southern version of headcheese. We make pancetta from the belly and guanciale from the jowls. Those are things we simply couldn't do before we met Henry Fudge. Access to the whole pig is key and what has allowed us to move beyond the shoulder, loin, and chop.

It was pure serendipity when Henry walked in our back door eight years ago saying he'd heard that we were the guys in town who would really be interested in his whole pigs. We jumped at the opportunity. He was equally excited to find that we truly understood and appreciated the concept of using the whole hog. Certainly nothing needs to be wasted and those hogs have opened a world of possibilities for our cooking. The head has value, the trotter has value, the belly has value—it is the value of expanding our thinking. Our relationship with Henry Fudge has allowed us to appreciate everything from the rooter to the tooter, as Southerners like to say. Quite frankly, Henry Fudge has been one of our most recent heroes of purveying. Like Chris Bennett and his wild-foraged products, Henry has brought us a product that gets us outside the box in terms of our thinking. Products that move us beyond the confines and routine of everyday cooking are true gifts to chefs.

ROASTED PORCINI MUSHROOMS

with Bresaola, Mustard Greens, and Lemon Oil

To purchase fresh porcini mushrooms, see our sources guide (page 380). If fresh porcinis are unavailable, substitute whole portobello mushroom tops and follow the same cooking instructions below for similar results.

YIELD: 6 SERVINGS

3 TABLESPOONS OLIVE OIL

3 TABLESPOONS UNSALTED BUTTER

1 TEASPOON CHOPPED FRESH THYME

¾ TEASPOON KOSHER SALT, DIVIDED

½ TEASPOON FRESHLY GROUND BLACK PEPPER, DIVIDED

6 MEDIUM FRESH PORCINI MUSHROOMS, ABOUT ½ POUND, OR PORTOBELLO MUSHROOMS TOPS

12 THIN SLICES (6 OUNCES) BRESAOLA OR ANY THINLY SLICED CURED MEAT, SUCH AS PROSCIUTTO

3 CUPS FRESH BABY MUSTARD GREENS OR OTHER HEARTY FALL GREENS, SUCH AS ARUGULA OR SPINACH

1 TABLESPOON FRESH LEMON JUICE

2 TABLESPOONS EXTRA-VIRGIN OLIVE OIL

24 THIN SLICES PECORINO ROMANO CHEESE

2 TABLESPOONS LEMON OIL (OPTIONAL)

Preheat the oven to 400°F.

Heat the olive oil, butter, and thyme in a large, ovenproof skillet over medium heat until the butter is melted. Add ½ teaspoon of the salt and ¼ teaspoon of the pepper and stir until combined. Add the mushrooms and turn until well coated with the butter. Place the skillet in the oven and roast the mushrooms at 400°F for 25 minutes, turning the mushrooms halfway through the cooking time. Remove from the oven and allow the mushrooms to cool slightly about 10 minutes. Slice the mushrooms into ½-inch-thick slices.

Arrange two thin slices of the bresaola in an even layer on each of six salad plates.

Combine the greens, lemon juice, and olive oil in a mixing bowl and toss until well dressed. Season the greens with the remaining ¼ teaspoon each of the salt and pepper. Arrange an even amount of greens on top of each portion of bresaola. Place an equal amount of sliced porcinis on each salad and top with four slices of pecorino. Drizzle 1 teaspoon of the lemon oil over and around each salad, if using, and serve immediately.

BIBB LETTUCE SALAD

with Candied Pecans, Cambozola, and Pomegranate Vinaigrette

THERE ARE A NUMBER OF COMMONLY AVAILABLE VARIETIES OF BIBB LETTUCE IN MOST GROCERY STORES. WHILE THE HYDROPONICALLY GROWN LETTUCES ARE GOOD, WE PREFER THE BIBB VARIETIES THAT ARE GROWN IN THE GROUND. THIS TYPE OF LETTUCE HAS MORE FLAVOR AND TENDS TO BE HEARTIER THAN THOSE GROWN OUT OF THE SOIL.

YIELD: 6 SERVINGS

1 POUND (ABOUT 12 CUPS) FRESH BIBB LETTUCE,
    TORN INTO BITE-SIZE PIECES
¼ TEASPOON KOSHER SALT
⅛ TEASPOON FRESHLY GROUND BLACK PEPPER
⅓ CUP POMEGRANATE VINAIGRETTE (PAGE 343)
1½ CUPS CANDIED PECANS (PAGE 364)
¾ CUP FRESH POMEGRANATE SEEDS (OPTIONAL)
12 OUNCES CAMBOZOLA CHEESE, CUT INTO 6 (2-OUNCE) WEDGES

Combine the lettuce, salt, and pepper in large bowl. Drizzle the vinaigrette over the lettuce and toss until well combined. Evenly divide the salad among six plates. Top each serving with ¼ cup of the pecans and 2 tablespoons of the pomegranate seeds, if using. Arrange a wedge of Cambozola cheese on each salad and serve immediately.

LOW-COUNTRY PIRLOU AND INFLUENCES

The South Carolina Low Country refers to the coastal plain extending from the Savannah River at the Georgia state line northward to Pawleys Island and reaching about eighty miles inland. It is here that a creolized rice stew called "pirlou," prepared by the Gullah, descendants of African slaves, has become a regional mainstay. The dish is a veritable melting pot of influences—a tangle of Middle Eastern, Spanish, French, and African that most likely first appeared in Africa via the Arab spice trade and then made its way to the New World with those sold into slavery.

Wherever rice is prevalent, it becomes a backdrop or foil for other ingredients. Louisiana has its jambalayas, Italy its risottos, Spain its paellas, and the examples could go on and on. In the Low Country, in particular, pirlou is centered on seafood because of the proximity of the ocean and the salt marsh, teeming with a bounty of fresh fish and shellfish. A classic Low-Country pirlou will typically feature shrimp or oysters, but crab, fish, clams, crawfish, and even sausage are not uncommon.

Pirlou was traditionally made with long-grain Carolina Gold rice with its distinctive flavor. Beginning in the 1600s and continuing for some two hundred years, Carolina Gold rice was the cultivated King of the Low Country. Then, in the late 1800s, a spate of tropical storms flooded the rice paddies with salt water and ended the reign of this prized grain. Fortunately, some landowners continued to grow the rice on unspoiled higher ground in small batches, keeping it from extinction. Sadly, though, the Low Country could no longer compete with the budding Midwest rice industry and the heyday was over. Carolina Gold did not experience a commercial rebound until Dr. Richard Schulze, an eye surgeon and plantation owner from Savannah, collected stores of this heirloom rice from the USDA seed bank and planted it back along the coastal wetlands around Charleston during the mid-eighties. By 1986 Dr. Schulze had produced enough rice to sell, allowing companies like Anson Mills (page 380) to resume mass cultivation of the rice and make it commercially available once again.

Carolina Gold was so popular because it of its unique, nutty flavor and versatile texture (depending on how it is cooked) which worked in a wide array of dishes. Just as risotto requires short-grained, starchy Arborio or Carnaroli rice, Carolina Gold is the rice of choice for pirlou, which starts off much like a pilaf by sweating aromatics and herbs in butter and then toasting the dry rice in the pan. Big, fresh head-on shrimp might be added and sautéed just a bit before pouring in the broth. Once the broth simmers, the pan is covered and transferred to the oven to finish cooking for no more than twenty minutes. The shrimp used should be large so that they have the same cook time as the rice. Of course, there are many recipes and methods. At the restaurant, we quite often parboil the rice and then cool it. We then prepare pirlou to order by sautéing thyme with aromatics such as onion, leek, and garlic in butter before tossing in cooked seafood, sausage, and the parboiled rice. We moisten it with broth, then cover the pan and bake the rice a short time to finish and plate. It is imperative to taste a cooked pirlou and season it well for serving. We add a knob of butter for richness to carry flavor. It's that simple and that's the way it always has been. With a dish this good there is no need to veer too far from the classic.

LOW-COUNTRY PIRLOU

with Clams, Sausage, Shrimp, and Carolina Gold Rice

CAROLINA GOLD RICE (PAGE 353) CAN BE SUBSTITUTED FOR ANY LONG-GRAIN RICE OF SIMILAR COOKING TIME. HOWEVER, DO YOURSELF A FAVOR, AND TRY THIS PARTICULAR VARIETY OF RICE. ITS UNIQUE, NUTTY FLAVOR, DISTINCT TEXTURE, AND VERSATILITY WILL MAKE YOU A LIFELONG FAN.

YIELD: 6 SERVINGS

¼ CUP PLUS 1 TABLESPOON UNSALTED BUTTER

1 TEASPOON MINCED GARLIC

2 CUPS DICED SWEET ONION, ABOUT 1 LARGE ONION

½ CUP CHOPPED CELERY, ABOUT 1 STALK

½ CUP CHOPPED CARROT, ABOUT 2 MEDIUM CARROTS

1 BAY LEAF

1 TABLESPOON CHOPPED FRESH THYME

1 TEASPOON KOSHER SALT

½ TEASPOON FRESHLY GROUND BLACK PEPPER

1 POUND SMOKED SAUSAGE (SUCH AS CONECUH BRAND), SLICED IN HALF LENGTHWISE AND CUT INTO ½-INCH-THICK SLICES

2 CUPS UNCOOKED CAROLINA GOLD RICE, RINSED WELL UNDER COLD RUNNING WATER AND DRAINED

2 CUPS SEEDED AND DICED TOMATOES

3 CUPS CHICKEN STOCK (PAGE 335)

2 CUPS FISH STOCK (PAGE 334) OR SHRIMP STOCK (PAGE 334)

18 FRESH LITTLENECK CLAMS, SCRUBBED, ABOUT 1¼ POUNDS

18 FRESH MUSSELS, SCRUBBED AND DEBEARDED, ABOUT 1 POUND

19 FRESH MEDIUM (25 TO 30 COUNT) SHRIMP, ABOUT ½ POUND, PEELED AND DEVEINED, LEAVING THE LAST TAIL SEGMENT INTACT

½ POUND FRESH LUMP CRABMEAT, PICKED THROUGH FOR SHELLS AND CARTILAGE

1 CUP CHOPPED FRESH PARSLEY

Melt the butter in a Dutch oven over medium-high heat. Add the garlic and the next 7 ingredients (onion through pepper) and sauté 5 to 6 minutes or until the vegetables are tender. Add the sausage and cook 3 to 4 minutes, stirring frequently. Add the rice and tomatoes and cook, stirring until well moistened, about 1 minute. Add the chicken and fish stocks and bring the mixture to a boil. Cover, reduce the heat to low, and simmer 12 minutes. Add the clams, cover, and cook 5 minutes. Add the mussels, cover, and cook 3 minutes. Add the shrimp, stirring well to incorporate, cover, and remove the Dutch oven from the heat. Allow the mixture to steam, covered, for 7 to 8 minutes or until the clams and mussels have opened and the shrimp are cooked through. Discard any unopened shells and the bay leaf. Stir in the crabmeat and parsley. Evenly divide the pirlou among six dinner plates and serve immediately.

HOT AND HOT FISH FRY

with Fennel Slaw, Hushpuppies, and Spicy Rémoulade

THE KEY TO A GOOD FRY MIX IS THE RATIO OF FLOUR TO CORNMEAL TO CORN FLOUR. WE HAVE FOUND THAT A PERFECTLY BALANCED BLEND IS IDEAL, MIXED WITH AN AMPLE DOSE OF SEASONINGS. THE CORN FLOUR LENDS A DELICACY TO THE BREADING THAT CANNOT BE ACCOMPLISHED BY CORNMEAL AND WHEAT FLOUR ALONE.

YIELD: 12 SERVINGS

5 CUPS BUTTERMILK

2½ TEASPOONS CAYENNE PEPPER

2 TEASPOONS FRESHLY GROUND BLACK PEPPER

2 TEASPOONS KOSHER SALT

24 EXTRA-LARGE (16 TO 20 COUNT) SHRIMP, PEELED AND DEVEINED

2 POUNDS FRESH SQUID, CUT INTO 1-INCH RINGS

12 JUMBO SCALLOPS, CLEANED

24 (1-OUNCE) PIECES FRESH GROUPER OR OTHER FIRM, WHITE-FLESHED FISH

6 SOFT-SHELL CRABS, CLEANED AND SPLIT

2 QUARTS OF PEANUT OIL, FOR FRYING

12 CUPS FRY MIX (PAGE 353)

24 HUSHPUPPIES (PAGE 360)

4 CUPS FENNEL COLESLAW (PAGE 170)

3 CUPS SPICY RÉMOULADE SAUCE (PAGE 339)

12 LEMON WEDGES, FOR GARNISH

1 BUNCH FLAT-LEAF PARSLEY SPRIGS, FOR GARNISH

Combine the buttermilk, cayenne, black pepper, and salt in a large bowl and whisk to combine. Separate each variety of seafood into small bowls and pour 1 cup of the seasoned buttermilk mixture over each. Transfer the bowls to the refrigerator and marinate for up to 2 hours.

Pour the peanut oil into a deep-sided skillet to a depth of 3 inches. (Alternately a deep fryer can be filled with peanut oil.) Preheat the oil to 360°F. Each type of seafood should be fried separately, allowing the oil to return to 360°F after frying each batch and adding more oil if needed.

Remove the shrimp from the buttermilk and dredge in the fry mix, one at a time. Set aside on a baking sheet. Repeat with the remaining shrimp and seafood. Place the shrimp in the preheated oil and fry for 2 to 3 minutes, or until golden brown. Drain and set on a paper towel–lined baking sheet. Fry the squid for 1 to 2 minutes or until crispy and golden. Drain and set on the prepared baking sheet. Fry the scallops for 2 to 3 minutes. Drain and set on the prepared baking sheet. Fry the grouper for 2 to 3 minutes, or until golden brown and cooked through. Drain and set on the prepared baking sheet. Fry the soft-shell crabs for 2½ to 3 minutes, or until golden brown and cooked through. Season all of the seafood lightly with salt, if needed.

Arrange a mix of fried seafood on each of twelve plates. Place two hushpuppies and ⅓ cup of the fennel coleslaw on each plate. Serve the rémoulade sauce in individual ramekins on each plate. Garnish each serving with a lemon wedge and fresh parsley sprigs and serve immediately.

SAFFRON PAPPARDELLE
with Wild Oyster Mushrooms and Parmesan

Oyster mushrooms are fairly easy to find these days since they are now cultivated, but fresh portobello or good old button mushrooms work well in a pinch. We also list sourcing for wild mushrooms that can be shipped right to your door (page 381).

YIELD: 6 SERVINGS

¼ cup (½ stick) unsalted butter, divided
2 tablespoons minced shallots
1 tablespoon chopped fresh thyme
1 pound fresh oyster mushrooms, trimmed and cut into 2 to 3-inch pieces
1 teaspoon kosher salt
4 cups Chicken Stock (page 335)
20 ounces fresh saffron pappardelle (page 357), about 64 noodles or any store-bought pappardelle noodles
½ teaspoon freshly ground black pepper
1 cup (2 ounces) grated Parmesan cheese, divided
1 tablespoon chopped fresh parsley
1 tablespoon chopped fresh chives

Bring a large pot of salted water to a boil.

Melt 2 tablespoons of the butter in a large skillet over medium-high heat. Add the shallots and thyme and cook, stirring constantly, for 1 minute. Add the mushrooms and the salt and cook, stirring frequently, for 8 to 10 minutes or until the mushrooms are softened and lightly browned.

Pour the chicken stock into the skillet and stir to loosen any browned bits from the bottom of the skillet. Bring the mixture to a boil, reduce the heat to medium low, and simmer for 10 to 12 minutes. Towards the end of the simmering, add the pappardelle to the boiling water and cook for 2 minutes or until al dente. Drain and add the cooked noodles to the simmered sauce, tossing until well incorporated. Remove the skillet from the heat and add the pepper, half of the cheese, the parsley, and the chives. Evenly divide the pasta and mushrooms among six wide pasta bowls. Garnish the top of each serving with the remaining ½ cup of Parmesan cheese and serve immediately.

SAUTÉED HALIBUT ON PURPLE MASHED POTATOES

with Brown Butter Vinaigrette and Fried Capers

WHEN POSSIBLE, CHOOSE LINE-CAUGHT HALIBUT. NET-CAUGHT FISH THRASH ABOUT TRYING TO ESCAPE, RELEASING LACTIC ACID, WHICH CHANGES THE COLOR AND TEXTURE OF ITS FLESH. IF THE MEAT HAS A MILKY TINGE INSTEAD OF AN OPAQUE BLUE-GRAY HUE, ITS TEXTURE IS PROBABLY COMPROMISED. BE SURE TO ASK YOUR FISHMONGER NOT ONLY WHEN, BUT ALSO HOW, THE FISH WAS CAUGHT.

YIELD: 6 SERVINGS

6 (6-OUNCE) HALIBUT FILLETS, SKIN REMOVED

1½ TEASPOONS KOSHER SALT

¾ TEASPOON FRESHLY GROUND BLACK PEPPER

2 TABLESPOONS PEANUT OIL

6 CUPS PURPLE MASHED POTATOES (PAGE 368)

2 CUPS TRIMMED AND BLANCHED HARICOT VERT OR OTHER SMALL, FRESH GREEN BEAN

1½ CUPS BROWN BUTTER VINAIGRETTE (PAGE 341)

¼ CUP PLUS 2 TABLESPOONS FRIED CAPERS (PAGE 153)

Season the halibut on both sides with the salt and pepper, using about ¼ teaspoon of the salt and ⅛ teaspoon of the pepper per fillet. Heat the oil in a large heavy skillet over high heat, just until the oil begins to smoke. Add the fillets, flesh side down and reduce the heat to medium high. Cook the halibut for 3 to 4 minutes, turn, and cook an additional 2 to 3 minutes or until the fillets flake easily when tested with a fork and are golden brown on both sides. Set aside to keep warm.

Spoon 1 cup of the mashed potatoes and ⅓ cup of the green beans on each of six dinner plates. Place 1 halibut fillet over each portion of potatoes and spoon about ¼ cup of the vinaigrette on top and around the fish. Sprinkle each dish with 1 tablespoon of fried capers and serve immediately.

SCUPPERNONGS AND MUSCADINES

Muscadines are thick-skinned grapes native to the southeastern region of the United States where they have been cultivated for centuries, first by Native Americans who dried and preserved them for the colder months, then by settlers who found the grapes ideal for making homemade sweet wine. Muscadines come in hues ranging from bronze to deep burgundy, but over time "scuppernong" became the generic term for all light-skinned muscadines, named for the Carolina river region where they appeared so abundantly. The muskier, dark purple varieties are commonly referred to as "muscadines." Historically, both varieties were used in pies, jellies, and spirits.

When muscadines and scuppernongs arrive at the farmers' market, we know that summer is waning no matter the wilting heat. If it can be said that peaches herald summer then scuppernongs and muscadines signal the end of the season. Their appearance is a marker that indicates we soon will have one foot in summer and one in fall in terms of the way we think and cook.

We do all manner of things with these native grapes—juice them for seasonal cocktails and vinaigrettes, roast them with game and poultry, and use them as basis for incredible sorbets. When we roast the grapes with chicken, a bit of verjus (green grape juice), and chicken stock until they burst and release their juice, their musky sweetness mingles with the verjus and pan juices to create a slightly sweet sauce with perfectly balanced acidity—nothing more than a smattering of fresh herbs and bit of butter is needed to finish. On a bed of creamy Anson Mills white grits, it is a magical combination.

Beyond cocktail hour and main courses, we also incorporate muscadines and scuppernongs into desserts. Simmering and straining them yields juice with a high pectin content that lends sorbet, in particular, a creamy mouth feel.

The key to cooking and eating these grapes is to select them at their ripest. Light-skinned scuppernongs should have a golden speckled blush to the skin to be sweet and fabulous, while muscadines will be a deep, mottled purple at their prime. Taste them before they are ripe and you will have a mouth-puckering experience you won't soon forget. Savor them when they are ripe in all manners of recipes and you will come to appreciate the uniqueness of the indigenous fruits of the vine.

OVEN-ROASTED CHICKEN BREASTS ON ANSON MILLS GRITS

with *Local Scuppernongs, Muscadines, and Verjus*

WHILE WE LOVE TO SERVE THIS DISH WITH THE MUSCADINE AND SCUPPERNONG GRAPES, WHEN THEIR SEASON HAS PAST, WE SUBSTITUTE THE SMALL CHAMPAGNE GRAPES INSTEAD.

YIELD: 4 SERVINGS

- **4 (8-OUNCE) BONELESS CHICKEN BREAST HALVES, WITH THE FIRST WING JOINT BONE LEFT IN**
- **1¼ TEASPOONS KOSHER SALT, DIVIDED**
- **½ TEASPOON FRESHLY GROUND BLACK PEPPER, DIVIDED**
- **¼ CUP PEANUT OIL**
- **2 TABLESPOONS MINCED SHALLOTS**
- **2 TEASPOONS CHOPPED FRESH THYME**
- **24 FRESH MUSCADINE GRAPES (10½ OUNCES TOTAL), HALVED AND SEEDS REMOVED**
- **24 FRESH SCUPPERNONG GRAPES (10½ OUNCES TOTAL), HALVED AND SEEDS REMOVED**
- **1 CUP VERJUS OR CIDER VINEGAR**
- **1½ CUPS (3 STICKS) UNSALTED BUTTER, DICED**
- **2 TABLESPOONS FRESH LEMON JUICE**
- **2 TABLESPOONS CHOPPED FRESH PARSLEY**
- **6 CUPS COOKED ANSON MILLS WHITE ANTEBELLUM GRITS (PAGE 354)**

Preheat the oven to 400°F.

Season the chicken breast halves on all sides with ¾ teaspoon of the salt and ¼ teaspoon of the pepper. Heat the peanut oil in a large cast-iron skillet over medium-high heat. Add the chicken breasts, skin side down, to the skillet and cook for 5 minutes or until the skin is well browned. Turn the chicken and place the skillet in the oven. Roast the chicken for 10 to 12 minutes or until the chicken is cooked through. Transfer the chicken to a platter and cover to keep warm.

Drain all of the fat out of the skillet except for 1 tablespoon. Place the skillet over medium-high heat and add the shallots and thyme. Cook for 1 minute, stirring frequently, until the shallots are softened. Add the muscadines, scuppernongs, and verjus to the skillet, and bring the mixture to a boil. Allow the mixture to cook until it has reduced by three-fourths, about 15 minutes (about ¼ cup of liquid will be left). Reduce the heat to low and whisk the butter into the verjus mixture, a little at a time, until all of the butter has been added and the sauce is emulsified. Remove the sauce from the heat and stir in the lemon juice and parsley.

Spoon 1 cup of the grits onto each of six dinner plates. Arrange one chicken breast on each serving of grits and spoon ¼ cup of the sauce over each portion. Serve immediately.

FUDGE FARMS PORK AND BEANS

with Braised Greens, Cracklin' Cornbread, and Chowchow

We tried not to go too "chef-y" in this book, but this is one of those dishes worthy of the extra effort and more involved preparation. If you're strapped for time, you can serve the braised white bean mixture without the pork loin slices and purchase your favorite brand of chowchow relish.

YIELD: 6 SERVINGS

3 tablespoons olive oil
1 (3-pound) boneless pork loin
2 tablespoons Hastings Creations All-Purpose Herb Salt (page 381) or kosher salt
1 tablespoon freshly ground black pepper
¼ cup vegetable oil
3 cups warm Braised White Beans (page 369)
2 tablespoons chopped fresh parsley
6 warm Cracklin' Cornbread Sticks (page 171), sliced in half lengthwise
3 cups warm Braised Collard Greens (page 170)
¼ cup plus 2 tablespoons Chowchow Relish (page 349)
2 tablespoons fresh chopped chives

Preheat the oven to 400°F.

Rub the olive oil over the pork loin and season evenly with the herb salt and black pepper. In a heavy, cast-iron skillet, heat the vegetable oil until hot and almost smoking. Add the pork loin and sear on all sides until well browned, about 4 minutes per side. Place the loin on a cooking rack set inside a roasting pan and roast at 400°F for 20 minutes. Reduce the oven temperature to 325° and cook for an additional 20 to 30 minutes or until a thermometer inserted into the center of the pork loin registers 160°. Remove the pork from the oven and set aside to rest for 15 minutes in a warm spot. Slice the pork loin into about twelve slices, about ¾ inch thick each.

Combine the braised beans and parsley and spoon ½ cup of the beans into each of six wide serving bowls or dinner plates. Place the cornstick halves in an "x" position on top of the bean mixture. Spoon ½ cup of the collard greens over each serving. Arrange 2 slices of the pork loin over each serving. Spoon 1 tablespoon of the chowchow relish on top of each dish and garnish with 1 teaspoon each of fresh chives. Serve immediately.

GRILLED VEAL LIVER STEAK

with Fennel Mashed Potatoes, Onion Rings, and Tamarind Sauce

WHEN PURCHASING VEAL LIVERS, HAVE YOUR BUTCHER TAKE OFF THE SKIN AND REMOVE THE VEINS FOR YOU. AT THE RESTAURANT WE OFTEN SERVE THIS DISH WITH A MIXTURE OF CARAMELIZED ONIONS, GRILLED ONIONS, AND FRIED ONION RINGS. TO SIMPLIFY, JUST PREPARE YOUR FAVORITE STYLE OF ONION.

YIELD: 4 SERVINGS

2 TABLESPOONS PLUS 1 TEASPOON PEANUT OIL, DIVIDED

8 THICK-CUT SLICES APPLEWOOD SMOKED BACON

4 (6-OUNCE) VEAL LIVERS, CLEANED

2¼ TEASPOONS KOSHER SALT, DIVIDED

2⅛ TEASPOONS FRESHLY GROUND BLACK PEPPER, DIVIDED

1 TABLESPOON OLIVE OIL

2 TABLESPOONS UNSALTED BUTTER

¼ CUP MINCED SHALLOTS

½ POUND FRESH BABY SPINACH, STEMS REMOVED

4 CUPS FENNEL MASHED POTATOES (PAGE 368)

8 FRIED ONION RINGS (PAGE 373)

¼ CUP TAMARIND SAUCE (PAGE 338)

Preheat the grill to medium-high heat (350°F to 400°F).

Heat 1 teaspoon of the peanut oil in a large cast-iron skillet over medium heat. Add the bacon slices in an even layer and cook until well browned and crispy, 10 to 12 minutes. Transfer the bacon to a paper towel–lined plate to drain and reserve the rendered bacon grease in the skillet.

Rub the veal livers with the remaining 2 tablespoons of peanut oil. Season the livers on both sides with 2 teaspoons of the salt and 2 teaspoons of the pepper, using about ½ teaspoon of salt and ½ teaspoon of pepper on each liver.

Grill the veal livers for 3½ to 4 minutes on the first side, basting occasionally with the reserved bacon grease. Turn the livers and grill an additional 3½ to 4 minutes, basting occasionally with the reserved bacon grease. Remove the livers from the grill and brush with any remaining bacon grease. Transfer the livers to a serving platter and cover to keep warm until ready to serve.

Heat the olive oil and butter in a large saucepan or pot over medium-high heat until the butter is melted. Add the shallots and cook, stirring frequently, for 30 seconds. Add the spinach and cook until wilted but still bright green, about 3 minutes. Season the spinach with the remaining ¼ teaspoon of the salt and ⅛ teaspoon of the pepper.

Spoon 1 cup of the fennel mashed potatoes on each of four dinner plates. Evenly divide the wilted spinach among the dinner plates next to the potatoes. Arrange a veal liver on top of each portion of potatoes. Lay two slices of crispy bacon over the top of each liver in a crisscross pattern. Arrange two onion rings on top of each dish and drizzle each with 1 tablespoon of the tamarind sauce. Serve immediately.

MUSCADINE SORBET

An ideal sorbet is neither too tart nor too sweet; at its best, it showcases the essence of the main ingredient. We like to balance the sweetness with a touch of lemon juice, which brightens the flavor on the palate.

YIELD: 1½ QUARTS (6 CUPS)

4 quarts (about 5½ pounds) fresh muscadine grapes, washed
1½ cups Simple Syrup (page 362)
Dash of freshly squeezed lemon juice

Combine the muscadines and syrup in a large saucepan over medium-high heat. Cook, partially covered and stirring occasionally, until the grapes soften and begin to break open, about 30 minutes. Remove the mixture from the heat and cool slightly, about 30 minutes.

Place the grape and syrup mixture into a fine-meshed strainer or chinois set over a medium bowl. Gently press the grapes in the strainer with a rubber spatula to release as much juice as possible; discard the pulp mixture. You should have about 4½ cups of juice. Add the lemon juice. Refrigerate the muscadine juice until well chilled.

Pour the muscadine juice into the ice cream machine and freeze according to the manufacturer's directions. Remove the sorbet from the machine and transfer into a freezer-safe container. Freeze the sorbet for at least 4 hours, or until ready to serve. This sorbet is much softer than regular sorbets, even if frozen for the correct amount of time.

VARIATION: For 1½ quarts (6 cups) scuppernong sorbet, substitute 6 quarts (about 8¼ pounds) of fresh scuppernongs for the muscadines and proceed with the sorbet recipe as directed above.

BAKED CUMBERLAND SPUR APPLES

with Nutmeg Ice Cream

THIS RECIPE HANGS ITS HAT ON THREE FLAVORS—THE WARM SPICE OF NUTMEG, JUST-PICKED APPLES, AND A BUTTERY SWEET BASE. IF TIME DOES NOT PERMIT MAKING HOMEMADE ICE CREAM, USE QUALITY STORE-BOUGHT VANILLA ICE CREAM AND GARNISH WITH A SCRAPE OF FRESH NUTMEG.

YIELD: 6 SERVINGS

3 CUMBERLAND SPUR APPLES (ABOUT 1 POUND), CORED, OR OTHER RED DELICIOUS APPLE VARIETY
2 TABLESPOONS FIRMLY PACKED DARK BROWN SUGAR, DIVIDED
2 TABLESPOONS UNSALTED BUTTER, DIVIDED
1 CUP FRESH APPLE CIDER
PINCH OF SEA SALT
1½ CUPS NUTMEG ICE CREAM (PAGE 366)

Preheat the oven to 350°F.

Arrange the apples in a 11 x 7-inch baking dish. Pack 1 teaspoon of the brown sugar into the cavity of each apple. Arrange 1 teaspoon of the butter on top of each apple. Add the remaining brown sugar and the remaining butter to the bottom of the baking dish along with the apple cider and sea salt. Cover the baking dish tightly with aluminum foil and bake for 1 hour or until the apples are tender. Transfer the apples to a platter to cool slightly.

Pour the apple cider mixture from the baking dish into a small saucepan and bring to a boil over high heat. Allow the mixture to reduce until 6 tablespoons are remaining and the liquid is slightly thickened, 5 to 6 minutes.

Slice the baked apples in half crosswise and place one apple half in each of six dessert bowls. Top each warm apple with ¼ cup of the nutmeg ice cream. Drizzle 1 tablespoon of the cider syrup over the top of each and serve immediately.

SWEET POTATO FRIED PIES

with Cinnamon Ice Cream

DOWN SOUTH, FRIED PIES, LIKE POT LIQUOR AND PORK, ARE LIKE RELI-GION, SO GO TO THE TROUBLE AND GET SOME RELIGION, PRAISE THE LORD, AND PASS THE FRIED PIES! FOR THOSE LESS THAN COMFORTABLE WITH DEEP-FRYING, YOU CAN BAKE THESE PIES AT 350 DEGREES FOR ABOUT TWELVE MINUTES INSTEAD. TAKE CARE NOT TO OVER SEASON; THE FLAVOR OF THE FILLING—BE IT SWEET POTATO, PEACH, OR APPLE—SHOULD SHINE. WE LIKE TO USE PALE YELLOW SWEET POTATOES.

YIELD: 10 SERVINGS

1½ SWEET POTATOES (ABOUT 1 POUND), WASHED
    AND UNPEELED
1½ TABLESPOONS PEANUT OIL, PLUS MORE FOR FRYING
4 TABLESPOONS (½ STICK) UNSALTED BUTTER, MELTED
6 TABLESPOONS FIRMLY PACKED DARK BROWN SUGAR
¼ TEASPOON GROUND CINNAMON
¼ TEASPOON SALT
PINCH OF FRESHLY GRATED NUTMEG
1½ POUNDS (24 OUNCES) CHILLED SWEET PASTRY
    DOUGH (PAGE 358)
3 TABLESPOONS TURBINADO OR COARSE RAW SUGAR,
    FOR SPRINKLING
2½ CUPS CINNAMON ICE CREAM (PAGE 336)

Preheat the oven to 375°F.

Place the sweet potatoes on a baking sheet and pierce with a sharp knife in several places. Drizzle with the peanut oil and bake the potatoes for 1 hour and 20 minutes, or until very tender. Remove and cool completely.

Peel the potatoes, place the flesh in a food processor, and process until smooth. Add the butter, brown sugar, cinnamon, salt, and nutmeg. Purée until well combined. Set the filling aside.

Divide the chilled pastry dough into 10 equal portions. Place one portion on a lightly floured surface and roll into a 6-inch diameter, about ¼ inch thick. (Avoid rolling the pastry too thinly, as it will not hold up well to the filling and tear.) Place about 3 tablespoons of the sweet potato filling in the center of the pastry. Fold the pastry in half, over the filling and crimp the folded edges with a fork. Place the pie on a parchment-lined baking sheet and repeat the process with the remaining dough and filling. Chill the pies for at least 30 minutes before frying.

Pour the peanut oil into a deep-sided skillet to a depth of 2 inches. (Alternately, a deep fryer can be filled with peanut oil.) Preheat the oil to 375°F. Fry the pies, one at a time, for 2 to 4 minutes, turning occasionally, or until golden brown and crispy. Place the pies on a paper towel–lined plate to blot and sprinkle with the coarse sugar.

Place each pie on one of ten dessert plates and top with a small scoop (about ¼ cup) of the cinnamon ice cream. Serve immediately.

SAFFRON RICE PUDDING
with Sauternes Poached Persimmons

RICE PUDDINGS ARE NOT AS FASHIONABLE AS THEY ONCE WERE, BUT THIS ONE IS JUST LIKE GRANDMA USED TO MAKE.

SEEK OUT FRESH, LOCAL, FREE-RANGE EGGS WITH THEIR DEEP, YELLOW YOLKS FOR A DENSELY RICH CUSTARD.

YIELD: 6 SERVINGS

POACHED PERSIMMONS:

3 RIPE PERSIMMONS, PEELED, SEEDED, AND EACH CUT
   INTO 6 WEDGES (ABOUT 1¼ CUPS)

¾ CUP SAUTERNES WINE

2 TABLESPOONS HONEY

1 (2-INCH-LONG) STRIP FRESH ORANGE PEEL

1 CINNAMON STICK

½ TEASPOON PEELED AND MINCED FRESH GINGER

RICE PUDDING:

1 TABLESPOON CONFECTIONERS' SUGAR

½ CUP BROKEN CAROLINA GOLD RICE (PAGE 353) OR
   OTHER LONG-GRAIN VARIETY

4 CUPS WHOLE MILK

½ CUP GRANULATED SUGAR

¼ VANILLA BEAN, SPLIT IN HALF LENGTHWISE

½ CINNAMON STICK

½ TEASPOON CRUSHED SAFFRON THREADS

1 TABLESPOON UNSALTED BUTTER, AT ROOM TEMPERATURE

2 LARGE EGG YOLKS

To Prepare the Poached Persimmons:

Combine the persimmon wedges, wine, honey, orange peel, cinnamon stick, and ginger in a small saucepan and bring to a boil over high heat. Cover, reduce the heat to low, and simmer for 20 minutes, or until the persimmons are soft. Strain the persimmons out of the poaching liquid and set aside. Return the poaching liquid to the saucepan and bring to a boil. Cook, uncovered, for 2 to 3 minutes or until the liquid is slightly thickened. Pour the syrup mixture over the persimmons and cool to room temperature.

To Prepare the Rice Pudding:

Bring 1 quart of water and the confectioners' sugar to a boil over high heat. Add the rice and cook, stirring occasionally, for 5 minutes. Drain the rice and rinse well under cold running water.

Combine the blanched rice, milk, and sugar in a heavy-bottomed saucepan. Scrape the vanilla bean seeds into the rice mixture and add the vanilla bean pods, the cinnamon stick, and saffron. Bring to a boil over medium-high heat, reduce the heat to medium low, and simmer, uncovered and stirring frequently, for 1 hour or until the rice is tender and most of the liquid has been absorbed. Remove the rice mixture from the heat and cool for 5 minutes. Remove and discard the vanilla bean pods and the cinnamon stick.

Preheat the oven to 250°F. Using the softened butter, grease the bottom and sides of six ½-cup ramekins or baking dishes.

Whisk the egg yolks into the slightly cooled rice mixture. Divide the rice mixture evenly among the prepared ramekins. Arrange the ramekins inside a baking dish and fill the baking dish with enough water to come halfway up the sides of the ramekins. Cover the baking dish with aluminum foil and bake the puddings at 250°F for 30 to 35 minutes or just until set. Remove the baking dish from the oven and allow the puddings to cool to room temperature in the warm water.

Unmold the cooled puddings into six shallow dessert bowls. Evenly divide the poached persimmons and their liquid among each pudding and serve immediately.

FATHER-SON DOVE HUNT

LATE EACH SUMMER, SINCE OUR BOYS WERE ALL OF FIVE AND SEVEN YEARS OLD, WE HAVE PARTICIPATED IN A FATHER-SON DOVE SHOOT. WHILE THEY DIDN'T CARRY GUNS FROM THE START, ZEB AND VINCENT PARTICIPATED IN ALL SOCIAL ASPECTS OF THE DOVE SHOOT. DOVE SEASON OFFERS AN OPPORTUNITY TO EXPOSE CHILDREN TO A LOT OF UNIQUE SCENARIOS WHILE REINFORCING RESPONSIBILITY AND GOOD BEHAVIOR. ON THE DOVE FIELD, OUR BOYS LEARNED THE PROPER WAY TO INTERACT WITH THEIR ELDERS, TO HANDLE A GUN, RESPECT LICENSING AND BAG LIMITS, AND BE CONSERVATIONISTS, OUTDOORSMEN, AND HUNTERS ALIKE.

BECAUSE WE ARE THE PARENTS OF SONS, THE DOVE SHOOTS IN WHICH WE'VE PARTICIPATED HAVE BEEN PRIMARILY GATHERINGS OF YOUNG MEN AND THEIR FATHERS. IT IS FROM THE SOCIAL ASPECTS OF THE SHOOT THAT OUR BOYS HAVE GAINED THE MOST. AT SUCH GATHERINGS YOUNG MEN ARE EXPECTED TO LOOK A GROWN-UP IN THE EYE AND FIRMLY SHAKE HIS OUTSTRETCHED HAND. THEY ARE REQUIRED TO LISTEN CAREFULLY AND RESPECT ALL DIRECTIONS GIVEN, AND TO SAY, "YES, SIR," OR "NO, SIR," WITHOUT PRODDING. DOVE SHOOTS ARE ALSO OPPORTUNITIES TO TEACH KIDS ABOUT GUN SAFETY, THE RULES OF THE HUNT, AND THE SOCIAL NORMS OF ANY COMMUNAL GATHERING. FOR US, THESE EVENTS HAVE STRENGTHENED THE SOUTHERN VALUES WE REVERE AND WHICH WE BELIEVE ARE IMPERATIVE FOR OUR KIDS TO ADOPT. IN THIS SETTING, THE BOYS GET TO PROVE THEY ARE RESPONSIBLE, SAFE, WELL MANNERED, RESPECTFUL AND THEREFORE WORTHY OF THE PRIVILEGE. THEY HAVE GROWN UP IN THIS ENVIRONMENT AND HAVE COME TO LOVE IT.

THEY ARE THE FIRST TO ADMIT THAT IT IS A BIG DEAL AND QUITE COMPETITIVE BETWEEN THEM TO SEE WHO BAGS THE MAXIMUM NUMBER OF BIRDS, BUT WHAT THEY GET OUT OF THE DOVE SHOOT GOES SO FAR BEYOND THAT. PARTICIPATION IN THE HUNT DEMANDS A CERTAIN LEVEL OF MATURITY BECAUSE THERE IS A HEFTY DOSE OF RESPONSIBILITY LAID UPON A HUNTER'S SHOULDERS. WHEN HE SHOOTS A BIRD, HE DOES NOT SHOOT AGAIN UNTIL HE HAS FOUND THE BIRD HE HAS DOWNED. LEAVING IT WOULD BE A HORRIBLE LESSON TO PASS ALONG. HUNTER PROTOCOL DICTATES THAT YOU FIND WHAT YOU'VE SHOT. IT DOESN'T MATTER IF THERE ARE A ZILLION BIRDS FLYING AROUND AT THAT VERY MOMENT (TOUGH LUCK!); YOU HAVE A RESPONSIBILITY TO GO OUT THERE AND BAG THE BIRD YOU JUST SHOT FIRST. A GOOD HUNTER RESPECTS THE LIFE OF WHATEVER IT IS THAT HAS BEEN SACRIFICED FOR THE TABLE.

The responsibilities of a shoot don't end there. Once it is over and everybody is safe, you must clean your hulls, thank the landowner, and go back to the designated area to clean all your birds before paying proper respect to your host and companions. Without a doubt, the dove shoot has been a rite of passage for our kids. It has helped them grow from boys into men while reinforcing through real life experience all the lessons we've tried our best to instill. Out there they get to see other dads and granddads holding their own kids and grandkids to the same high standard we demand at home. Father-son dove shoots have made our boys realize that our lessons have been more than just talk; they are the rules for how a respectful and honorable life is to be lived.

DOVE BREASTS WRAPPED IN BENTON'S BACON

FENNEL COLESLAW

BRAISED MUSTARD GREENS

CRACKLIN' CORN BREAD

LADY PEAS

- WINE PAIRINGS -

The Maysara Jamsheed Pinot Noir from Oregon is a well representative blend of the entire Maysara estate. It is a medium-bodied pinot noir with aromas of dark fruits such as cherry, plum, and black current and nice brown spice. This wine has a balanced acidity and soft tannins with a long, soothing finish that pairs nicely with wild game. This wine is a great wine choice for the dove hunt menu or your next wild game dinner.

Dove Breasts Wrapped in Benton's Bacon

THERE ARE THREE KEYS TO PERFECTING THIS RECIPE. THE FIRST IS TO MAKE SURE YOUR BACON IS PAPER THIN, BY ALLOWING YOUR BUTCHER OR FAVORITE RESTAURANT CHEF TO SLICE SLAB BACON TO ABOUT ONE-THIRTY-SECOND OF AN INCH. NEXT IS TO TAKE CARE NOT TO OVERSEASON THE MEAT. TOO OFTEN DOVE BREASTS AND OTHER WILD GAME ARE HEAVILY SEASONED WITH ITEMS SUCH AS ITALIAN DRESSING OR STEAK SAUCE MARINADE, MAKING IT DIFFICULT TO TASTE THE PURE FLAVOR OF THE FRESH MEAT. LASTLY, DON'T OVER COOK THE DOVE BREASTS. THEY ARE BEST WHEN SERVED RARE TO MEDIUM RARE.

YIELD: 4 SERVINGS

24 DOVE BREAST HALVES (FROM 12 DOVE), ABOUT 14 OUNCES
¾ TEASPOON KOSHER SALT
¾ TEASPOON FRESHLY GROUND BLACK PEPPER
12 PAPER-THIN SLICES (ABOUT 3 OUNCES TOTAL) BENTON'S BACON
   OR OTHER LOCAL SMOKED SLAB BACON, CUT IN HALF CROSSWISE
2 TABLESPOONS PEANUT OIL, DIVIDED

Season the dove breast halves on both sides with the salt and pepper. Wrap each breast half in a half slice of bacon. (The bacon does not have to completely cover the dove breast.)

Heat 1 tablespoon of the peanut oil in an 8-inch cast-iron skillet over medium high heat just until the oil begins to smoke. Add half of the wrapped breasts, seam side down, and cook for 2 minutes. Turn the breasts and cook for 1 more minute (for medium rare) or until the bacon is golden and crispy on both sides. Transfer to a serving plate and keep warm until ready to serve. Add the remaining tablespoon of oil to the skillet, if needed, and preheat just until smoking. Repeat the cooking process with the remaining dove breasts. Serve immediately, using about six dove breasts per serving.

Fennel Coleslaw

WE HAVE FOUND THAT THE BEST WAY TO ACHIEVE A BALANCED SLAW IS TO PREPARE THE DRESSING FIRST. BY WHISKING TOGETHER THE MAYONNAISE, VINEGAR, AND SUGAR AT THE BEGINNING OF THE RECIPE, YOU CAN TASTE AND ADJUST THE TARTNESS OR SWEETNESS MUCH MORE EASILY. IT IS DIFFICULT TO FULLY INCORPORATE ADDITIONAL SUGAR OR VINEGAR ONCE THE CABBAGE AND FENNEL HAVE BEEN ADDED.

YIELD: ABOUT 2 QUARTS OR 6 TO 8 SERVINGS
3 TABLESPOONS GRANULATED SUGAR
¼ CUP PLUS ½ TABLESPOON APPLE CIDER VINEGAR
1 TEASPOON KOSHER SALT
¼ TEASPOON FRESHLY GROUND BLACK PEPPER
1½ CUPS BASIC AÏOLI (PAGE 342)
3 HEADS FENNEL, CORED AND THINLY SHAVED
1 SMALL (ABOUT 1 POUND) HEAD GREEN CABBAGE, HALVED, CORED, AND THINLY SHAVED
1 CARROT, PEELED AND GRATED

Whisk together the sugar, vinegar, salt, and pepper until well combined. Add the aïoli and whisk until smooth. Toss in the fennel, cabbage, and carrot. Adjust the seasonings with salt and pepper, if needed. Serve immediately or chill up to 1 hour before serving.

Braised Mustard Greens

MUSTARD GREENS GROW IN VERY SANDY SOIL AND TEND TO BE FULL OF GRIT AND SAND WHEN PURCHASED FRESH. MAKE SURE TO WASH THE GREENS THREE OR FOUR TIMES TO ENSURE THAT THEY ARE CLEANED PROPERLY. IF FRESH MUSTARD GREENS ARE UNAVAILABLE, FEEL FREE TO SUBSTITUTE TURNIP OR COLLARD GREENS AND INCREASE THE COOK TIME SLIGHTLY UNTIL THEY ARE TENDER.

YIELD: ABOUT 3 CUPS OR 6 SERVINGS
1 TEASPOON VEGETABLE OIL
2 SLICES THICK-CUT APPLEWOOD SMOKED BACON, DICED (ABOUT ¼ CUP)
1¾ CUPS FINELY CHOPPED SWEET ONION, ABOUT 2 SMALL
1 CUP SPICY HAM HOCK BROTH (PAGE 336) OR CHICKEN STOCK (PAGE 335)
1 POUND CLEANED AND ROUGHLY CHOPPED FRESH MUSTARD GREENS
1 TEASPOON KOSHER SALT
½ TEASPOON FRESHLY GROUND BLACK PEPPER

Heat the oil in a large, heavy stockpot over medium-high heat. Add the bacon and cook until the fat is rendered and the bacon is crispy, 5 to 8 minutes. Add the onion and cook until translucent and lightly browned, 4 to 5 minutes. Pour in the broth and bring the mixture to a boil.

Place the mustard greens into the boiling broth mixture, stirring until they begin to wilt. Season the greens with the salt and pepper, cover, and reduce the heat to medium low. Cook, covered, stirring occasionally for 15 to 20 minutes or until the greens are tender. Serve immediately.

Cracklin' Cornbread

This batter works well in any shaped cast-iron skillet or pan. For dove hunts and picnics, we use a large round cast-iron skillet and slice the bread into wedges. At the restaurant we like to use a corn-stick–shaped iron pan. Whatever pan you choose, it is important to make sure you start with one that is very hot and well greased with vegetable oil or bacon drippings. Listen for the sizzle when you add the batter to make sure the pan is at the proper temperature. This ensures a well-browned crust and a cornbread that removes easily from the pan.

YIELD: 1 (8-INCH) ROUND CORNBREAD OR 6 TO 8 SERVINGS

2 tablespoons vegetable oil, divided
¼ cup diced thick-cut Applewood smoked bacon
½ cup thinly sliced green onions, about 6 small
1 cup freshly shaved yellow corn
1 cup finely ground yellow cornmeal
⅓ cup corn flour
⅓ cup all-purpose flour
1 teaspoon baking powder
1 teaspoon kosher salt
¼ teaspoon freshly ground black pepper
1 large egg
1½ cups buttermilk

Heat 1½ teaspoons of the oil in a medium skillet over medium-low heat. Add the bacon and cook, stirring occasionally, until brown and crispy, 5 to 8 minutes. Add the green onions and corn and sauté for 1 minute. Remove the skillet from the heat and set aside to cool slightly.

Add the remaining 1½ tablespoons of the oil to an 8-inch cast-iron skillet. Place the skillet in the oven and preheat the oven to 400°F.

Combine the cornmeal, corn flour, all-purpose flour, baking powder, salt, and pepper in a large bowl. Whisk together the egg and buttermilk and add to the cornmeal mixture. Stir in the bacon and onion mixture, and stir just until combined.

Add the cornmeal mixture to the hot cast-iron skillet and bake for 22 to 25 minutes or until cooked through and golden brown. Remove the cornbread from the skillet and serve warm.

VARIATION:

To make two dozen Cracklin' Cornsticks, prepare the recipe as directed above, but replace the 8-inch cast-iron skillet with a cast-iron cornstick pan. Add 1 teaspoon of vegetable oil to each cornstick indention and fill each with 2 tablespoons of the Cracklin' Cornbread batter. Bake the cornsticks at 400°F for 15 to 17 minutes or until cooked through and golden brown.

Lady Peas

LADY PEAS ARE THE SMALLEST, MOST DELICATE OF ALL THE FIELD PEAS. THEY ARE NOT AS WIDELY GROWN AND CAN BE A LITTLE MORE DIFFICULT TO SOURCE. THE OLD-TIMERS KNOW WHERE TO LOOK AND, LIKE A GOOD FISHING HOLE, THEY MAY NOT TELL MANY FOLKS WHERE TO FIND THEM. IF LADY PEAS ARE UNAVAILABLE, ANY FRESH FIELD PEA SUCH AS BLACK-EYED, PINK-EYED, LIMA, OR CROWDER PEA CAN BE SUBSTITUTED. SINCE LADY PEAS ARE SMALLER, THEIR COOK TIME IS GENERALLY FIVE TO EIGHT MINUTES SHORTER THAN THE OTHER FIELD PEA VARIETIES.

YIELD: ABOUT 3 CUPS OR 6 SERVINGS

1 TABLESPOON OLIVE OIL

2 SLICES THICK-CUT APPLEWOOD SMOKED BACON, DICED (ABOUT ¼ CUP)

1 CUP FINELY CHOPPED SWEET ONION, ABOUT ½ SMALL ONION

1 BAY LEAF

2 FRESH THYME SPRIGS

3 CUPS FRESH LADY PEAS

4 CUPS COLD WATER

1 TEASPOON KOSHER SALT

½ TEASPOON FRESHLY GROUND BLACK PEPPER

Heat the olive oil in a medium saucepan over medium heat. Add the bacon and cook until lightly browned and crispy, 8 to 10 minutes. Add the onion, bay leaf, and thyme and cook, stirring occasionally, until the onions is soft and translucent, 6 to 8 minutes. Stir in the peas. Add the water and bring the mixture to a boil over high heat. Reduce the heat to medium low and simmer for 10 to 12 minutes or until the peas are just tender. Stir in the salt and pepper and remove from the heat. Serve warm or transfer the peas and their cooking liquid to a clean container to cool.

If you are reserving the cooked peas for later use, allow the peas to cool completely in their braising liquid. The peas should also be reheated in their braising liquid.

CHAPTER 4

NOVEMBER

&

DECEMBER

FAMILY MEMORIES AND FOOD TRADITIONS

AUTUMNAL THANKSGIVING FEASTS SPARK NOSTALGIA FOR MANY PEOPLE AS THEY TASTE THEIR MOTHER'S PECAN PIE OR GRANDMOTHER'S SWEET POTATO RECIPES. IT IS AS IF FOOD IS A TIME CAPSULE, TRANSPORTING THEM BACK TO THEIR YOUTH. THESE ARE THE FOOD MEMORIES OF WHICH WE SPEAK SO OFTEN THROUGHOUT THIS BOOK. FOOD CAN BE SO POWERFUL AND EMOTIONAL. CERTAINLY COMFORT CAN BE FOUND IN THE ENJOYMENT OF DISHES MADE FROM RECIPES OF RELATIVES NOW LONG GONE. THE EXPERIENCE BRINGS THE LOVED ONES AND TIMES SPENT TOGETHER BACK TO MIND IN SUCH AN EXPERIENTIAL WAY.

This is quite true for Idie. Christmas is certainly the most significant holiday in her life because, as a Catholic, she appreciates the significance of Christmas Eve. While all holidays, birthdays, and Sunday gatherings were celebrated at Grandma Morano's house, much more energy, time, planning, and work were put into Christmas Eve dinner than any other occasion. As a young girl, Idie got to see the bustle of activity firsthand, but after she moved out, at just seven and a half years of age, she would sit at home with her dad and wonder what her grandmother might be busy doing. She could hardly wait to visit Grandma Morano and all her aunts, uncles, and cousins.

In those days, the Christmas Eve festivities always began at 6:00 p.m. sharp. The family arrived at the Trent Avenue house, knowing it would be a very late night due to Midnight Mass. It was magical to Idie to arrive at a packed church in the middle of the night with the choir singing, the church decorated, the aroma of incense, and the anticipation of presents in the morning. Christmas Eve had that dreamlike quality of childhood.

Everyone pitched in to help with Christmas Eve dinner. All the aunts helped with the cooking because the Moranos were a big family to feed. Much like a restaurant, Grandma Morano had her prep list organized, a plan on the timing of things, and spent days prepping and storing ingredients for cooking later. Each aunt was given an assignment to complete.

Fulfilling her shopping list for the celebration often meant going on a mission for the best ricotta cheese, honey, walnuts, hazelnuts, and pistachios. When chestnuts appeared, Idie knew Christmas was around the corner. Grandma Morano and the aunts could be found in the kitchen baking, the scent of roasting chestnuts filling the whole house. Christmas always included bowls of fresh fruit and nuts on the dinner table. An unabashed sweet tooth, Idie would head straight to the almond-orange biscotti and her Aunt Mary's pizzelles (a crisp, Italian cookie made with sugar, flour, butter, and eggs, flavored with anise and baked in a pizzelle iron).

The aroma of baking bread was a constant in Grandma Morano's home. In Italy, bakers are revered and their handiwork is prized. There are names and specific shapes of bread for every region in Italy. Idie was taught that bread was not to be wasted. Grandma Morano made so many types of bread and rolls that it was hard to keep up with their names. Idie does remember the grand "elephant ears," made from yeast dough that gets fried and rolled in sugar. Occasionally, Grandma Morano would fill bread dough with tuna for a savory snack. Year after year she would have variations on her yeast dough, but she stayed true to her standard Christmas Eve menu of a pasta dish with homemade meatballs, a platter of breaded shrimp, a basket of fried celery greens, Aunt Mary's cheese pizza, tuna marinara with rigatoni, and grilled Italian sausages.

After dinner, Idie's uncles would play the card game pinochle, drink grappa, and smoke cigars. The aunts would make coffee and bring out an assortment of Italian cookies for dessert. They would all sit and talk while Christmas music played in the background, until it was time to attend Midnight Mass.

With the passing of Grandma Morano, the festivities moved to a cousin's home then eventually to that of an aunt and uncle. Idie spent her teenage years observing the passing of the tradition from home to home until, eventually, the family stopped going to Midnight Mass and attended services on Christmas Day instead with their individual families. This is the tradition that continues today.

It is a real treat for Idie and Chris to be back in Cleveland for the Christmas holiday with their boys, sharing in the traditions of Idie's childhood. She honors those traditions with her own family during holidays spent in Birmingham. After Christmas Eve Mass at 6:00 p.m., Chris, Idie, Zeb, and Vincent return home to an Italian meal, inspired by the food memories of Idie's youth at Grandma Morano's Christmas Eve table. Even today, Idie views the Christmas season through the lens of her childhood and feels the presence of her large extended family by her side in spirit.

BLOOD ORANGE MARTINI

BLOOD ORANGES ARE AVAILABLE FROM NOVEMBER THROUGH FEBRUARY IN HIGH-END GROCERY STORES AND LATIN MARKETS.

YIELD: 1 SERVING

3½ TABLESPOONS VODKA
¼ CUP FRESHLY SQUEEZED BLOOD ORANGE JUICE
1 THIN SLICE BLOOD ORANGE, FOR GARNISH

Chill a martini glass for at least 20 minutes before serving. Combine the vodka and blood orange juice in a martini shaker filled halfway with ice. Shake until the mixture is well chilled. Strain into a martini glass, garnish with a blood orange slice, and serve immediately.

THE HASTINGS' CHRISTMAS PARTY AND BLOOD ORANGE MARTINIS

Each year we enjoy hosting a holiday Christmas party for our neighborhood. Our friends and family agree that the Blood Orange Martinis are the highlight of this festive affair. The beautiful red-orange color of this drink in a simple martini glass is an elegant reminder of the holiday season. While bottled blood orange juice can be purchased in specialty markets, nothing compares to the freshly squeezed orange juice. To make a large batch, you can juice the blood oranges ahead of time, up to four hours before serving.

HOT AND HOT
POMEGRANATE COCKTAIL

POMEGRANATE JUICE IS READILY AVAILABLE IN THE REFRIGERATED SECTION OF PRODUCE AISLES IN MAIN-
STREAM GROCERY STORES THESE DAYS. USE EITHER SWEETENED OR UNSWEETENED VARIETIES TO SUIT YOUR
TASTE. IF YOU HAVE THE TIME, YOU CAN JUICE FRESH POMEGRANATE SEEDS (PAGE 343).

YIELD: 1 SERVING

½ CUP CHILLED PROSECCO
2 TABLESPOONS FRESH POMEGRANATE JUICE
1 TABLESPOON SIMPLE SYRUP (PAGE 362)
4 TO 5 POMEGRANATE SEEDS, FOR GARNISH
1 LEMON TWIST, FOR GARNISH

Combine the Prosecco, pomegranate juice, and syrup in a martini shaker and swirl gently until
combined. Slowly pour the mixture into a 6-ounce champagne flute. Drop the pomegranate
seeds into the bottom of the glass and garnish with a lemon twist. Serve immediately.

AUNT EMMA'S ITALIAN WEDDING SOUP (ZUPPA MARITATA)

This soup is very simple to make. Idie's Aunt Emma and Aunt Ida served this soup every Thanksgiving for the Morano family. She remembers it being served in small soup bowls, always thankful that is was that time of year again. It is amazing that a chicken broth soup can become something outstanding with the addition of a few simple ingredients like meatballs, spinach, egg, and cheese. You can make the meatballs ahead of time and freeze them until needed. Feel free to vary the ingredients to suit your tastes.

YIELD: ABOUT 3 QUARTS OR 12 SERVINGS

3 quarts Chicken Stock (page **335**)
60 cooked Homemade Small ½-inch Meatballs
   (page **375**), cooked
2 cups roughly chopped, tightly packed, fresh spinach
2 large eggs
1 cup freshly grated Pecorino Romano cheese
1½ teaspoons kosher salt
½ teaspoon freshly ground black pepper

Bring the chicken stock to a boil in a large stockpot over medium-high heat. Add the meatballs, reduce the heat to medium low, and simmer for 15 to 20 minutes. Add the spinach and cook 2 minutes or until tender.

Whisk together the eggs and cheese. Stir the soup in a circular motion with a large whisk while gradually drizzling in the egg mixture. Stir the broth gently with a fork to form thin strands of egg, about 1 minute. Season the soup with the salt and pepper and serve immediately.

OYSTER SHOOTERS

With cocktails or as an appetizer, this is a crowd pleaser. When sourcing oysters for this dish, work with your local fishmonger to make certain you are getting oysters that have been out of the water no longer than three to four days and select only those that are tightly closed. Tap on the shell and if it sounds hollow, it is no good. The oysters should feel heavy in the hand. If fresh oysters in the shells are unavailable, you can substitute a pint of shucked oysters instead.

YIELD: 12 SERVINGS

2 MEDIUM (ABOUT ¾ POUND) RIPE RED TOMATOES, CUT INTO QUARTERS
3 TABLESPOONS FRESHLY GRATED HORSERADISH
2 TABLESPOONS FRESH LEMON JUICE
2 TABLESPOONS FRESH LIME JUICE
2 TABLESPOONS CHOPPED FRESH CILANTRO
¼ CUP ROASTED, PEELED, SEEDED, AND DICED POBLANO PEPPERS
¼ CUP PEELED, SEEDED, AND DICED TOMATOES
2 TEASPOONS KOSHER SALT
1 TEASPOON FRESHLY GROUND BLACK PEPPER
24 FRESHLY SHUCKED OYSTERS AND THEIR LIQUOR
1½ CUPS TEQUILA, WELL CHILLED
12 FRESH CILANTRO LEAVES, FOR GARNISH

Place twelve 2-ounce shot glasses in the freezer for at least 30 minutes or until well chilled.

Place the tomato quarters into a food mill set over a clean bowl. Process until all the liquid is extracted from the tomatoes and discard the solids. Strain the tomato liquid through a fine-mesh sieve. You should have about ¾ cup fresh tomato juice.

Combine the tomato juice and the next 8 ingredients (horseradish through black pepper). Chill the mixture for at least 30 minutes before serving. Arrange 1 tablespoon of the mixture in each prepared shot glass and top each with one oyster and 1 tablespoon of the tequila. Repeat the layers one more time and garnish with cilantro leaves. Serve immediately.

OYSTER STEW

with Homemade Oyster Crackers

THE VERY BEST WARM WATER OYSTERS ARE FROM BUDDY WARD AND
SONS 13-MILE SEAFOOD COMPANY IN APALACHICOLA (PAGE 380).
YOU NEED LOOK NO FURTHER!

YIELD: ABOUT 12 CUPS OR 8 TO 10 SERVINGS

SAFFRON CREAM:

¼ CUP WHITE WINE

PINCH OF SAFFRON THREADS

1 CUP CRÈME FRAÎCHE (PAGE 352)

¼ TEASPOON KOSHER SALT

PINCH OF FRESHLY GROUND BLACK PEPPER

OYSTER STEW:

¼ CUP PEANUT OIL

¼ CUP FINELY DICED BACON

6 TABLESPOONS ALL-PURPOSE FLOUR

1 CUP FINELY CHOPPED ONION

1 CUP FINELY CHOPPED CARROTS

1 CUP FINELY CHOPPED CELERY

1 CUP FINELY CHOPPED LEEKS (WHITE PART ONLY)

1 TABLESPOON CHOPPED FRESH THYME

4 CUPS BOTTLED CLAM JUICE OR FISH STOCK (PAGE 334)

2 CUPS HEAVY CREAM

1½ CUPS PEELED AND FINELY CHOPPED POTATOES

1 TABLESPOON KOSHER SALT

1 TEASPOON FRESHLY GROUND BLACK PEPPER

2 PINTS FRESHLY SHUCKED OYSTERS AND THEIR LIQUOR

4 TABLESPOONS CHOPPED FRESH CHIVES, FOR GARNISH

HOMEMADE OYSTER CRACKERS (PAGE 358)

TO PREPARE THE SAFFRON CREAM:

Heat the white wine and saffron in a small saucepan over medium heat. Simmer until the mixture is reduced by half, about 2 tablespoons. Remove the pan from the heat and cool completely. Remove and discard the saffron threads. Whisk the reduced wine in the crème fraîche and season with the salt and pepper. Refrigerate the saffron cream for at least 20 minutes or until ready to serve.

TO PREPARE THE OYSTER STEW:

Heat the peanut oil in a medium stockpot over medium-low heat. Add the bacon and cook, stirring occasionally, until browned and crispy, 5 to 8 minutes. Add the flour and cook, stirring constantly, just until the mixture begins to turn a light golden color, about 5 minutes. (Be careful not to let the flour mixture burn or get too dark.)

Add the onion, carrots, celery, leeks, and thyme and cook, stirring frequently, 5 to 7 minutes. Stir in the clam juice or fish stock and bring to a boil over medium-high heat. Reduce the heat to medium low and simmer for 10 minutes. Add the cream, potatoes, salt, and pepper and cook for 5 to 7 minutes or until potatoes are tender. Stir in oysters and their liquor and cook, stirring, for about 30 seconds, just until the oysters are heated through. Remove the stew from the heat.

Ladle the stew evenly into warmed soup bowls and garnish each serving with 1 to 2 tablespoons of the saffron cream and about 1 teaspoon of the chives. Serve warm with homemade oyster crackers.

CAULIFLOWER SOUP

with White Truffle Oil

DON'T TELL ANYONE WHAT SOUP YOU ARE SERVING UNTIL AFTER THE FIRST SPOONFUL BECAUSE, SADLY, CAU-LIFLOWER GETS A BAD RAP AND YOU MIGHT JUST LOSE THE CHANCE TO IMPRESS YOUR GUESTS IF YOU TIP YOUR HAND. THIS SOUP IS SIMPLE TO MAKE AND A PLEASANT SURPRISE TO THOSE WHO MIGHT NORMALLY TURN UP THEIR NOSES AT THE THOUGHT OF CAULIFLOWER.

YIELD: ABOUT 5 CUPS OR 6 SERVINGS

2 TABLESPOONS UNSALTED BUTTER

1½ CUPS SLICED YELLOW ONION, ABOUT 1 MEDIUM

2 TEASPOONS CHOPPED FRESH THYME

1 POUND WHITE CAULIFLOWER FLORETS

2 CUPS VEGETABLE STOCK (PAGE 334)

1 CUP HEAVY CREAM

1 TEASPOON KOSHER SALT

¼ TEASPOON FRESHLY GROUND BLACK PEPPER

WHITE TRUFFLE OIL (OPTIONAL)

Melt the butter in a medium stockpot over medium-low heat. Add the onion and thyme and cook, stirring occasionally, for 10 minutes or until the onion is softened and translucent. Add the cauliflower and stock and bring the mixture to a boil; reduce the heat to medium low and simmer for 20 minutes. Add the cream and cook for an additional 15 minutes or until the cauliflower is tender and the mixture is slightly reduced.

Transfer the cauliflower mixture to a blender and process until puréed. Season the soup with the salt and pepper. Ladle ¾ cup of the soup into six bowls and drizzle each serving with 1 to 2 drops of the truffle oil, if using. Serve immediately.

HEARTS OF PALM SALAD
with Pink Grapefruit and Avocado

CHRIS' FATHER'S MOTHER, FONDLY CALLED GRANZIE, ALWAYS VISITED AT THANKSGIVING AND CHRISTMAS AND SHE MADE A SALAD WITH PINK GRAPEFRUIT, AVOCADO, AND BOTTLED ITALIAN DRESSING. HE REMEMBERS THE GREAT TART FLAVORS OF THE GRAPEFRUIT AND SALAD DRESSING PAIRED WITH THE CREAMINESS OF THE AVOCADO. ONE PARTICULAR AFTERNOON, THEY STOOD OVER THE KITCHEN SINK PEELING GRAPEFRUITS AND SHE TOLD CHRIS HOW MUCH SHE LOVED THOSE SEASONAL, PINK GRAPEFRUITS. SHE DESCRIBED THE SWEETNESS IN THE RUBY RED GRAPEFRUITS THAT WERE SO UNLIKE THE REGULAR GRAPEFRUITS THAT YOU CAN FIND YEAR-ROUND. TOGETHER THEY WOULD PEEL AND CUT THE GRAPEFRUITS INTO SEGMENTS AND SHE WOULD GIVE HIM THE LEFTOVER PITHS TO SUCK OUT THE REMAINING JUICE. TODAY, WE'VE UPGRADED THE SAME SALAD BY ADDING HEARTS OF PALM AND OUR OWN HOMEMADE VINAIGRETTE. THIS SALAD ALWAYS REMINDS CHRIS OF BEING A KID, TASTING NEW THINGS, AND LEARNING.

YIELD: 4 SERVINGS

2 LARGE PINK GRAPEFRUITS, PEELED AND SLICED INTO SEGMENTS
2 RIPE AVOCADOS, HALVED, PITTED, AND SLICED
1 CUP DIAGONALLY SLICED FRESH MARINATED HEARTS OF PALM
½ CUP HERB VINAIGRETTE (PAGE 348), DIVIDED
8 CUPS MIXED BABY GREENS
¼ TEASPOON KOSHER SALT
¼ TEASPOON FRESHLY GROUND BLACK PEPPER

Combine the grapefruit segments, avocado slices, and hearts of palm in a medium bowl. Drizzle about half of the herb vinaigrette over the grapefruit mixture and toss gently to combine.

Arrange 3 to 5 grapefruit segments on each of four plates. Divide the avocado slices evenly among the plates. Place the mixed baby greens in the bowl with the hearts of palm and season lightly with salt and pepper, to taste. Drizzle the remaining herb vinaigrette over the lettuce and toss to combine. Divide the lettuce and hearts palm evenly among the plates. Serve immediately.

HEARTS OF ESCAROLE SALAD

In his culinary career Chris was introduced to escarole later than other varieties of lettuces. It is simply not something you see much of down south. Upon discovering its versatility and wonderful flavor, we have made it a staple of our winter cooking. Its dark green outer leaves are excellent cooked down with garlic and olive oil and its heart has a crisp, slightly bitter quality that lends depth and texture to many of our dishes, such as this unusual salad that blends the lettuce with Asian pears in a vinaigrette comprised of scuppernong juices.

YIELD: 4 SERVINGS

8 cups (10 ounces) torn escarole hearts
2 large (6-ounce) Asian pears, peeled, cored, and sliced into batons
¼ cup plus 1 tablespoon Scuppernong Vinaigrette (page 343)
¼ teaspoon kosher salt
¼ teaspoon freshly ground black pepper
4 ounces creamy blue cheese, cut into 8 (½-ounce) wedges

Combine the escarole, pears, and vinaigrette in a large mixing bowl and toss until well combined. Season the salad with the salt and pepper. Divide the salad mixture evenly among four salad plates. Arrange two blue cheese wedges on each plate and serve immediately.

BILL GOODRICH – LOCAL CHESTNUTS

Bill and his wife, Fran, have been great customers and friends for years. One year Bill invited us to a dove shoot and tour of his farm. It was at that time that we discovered Bill's chestnut trees. Typically, the chestnuts we were finding were dry, rather old and not very nutty or sweet, so we did not do much with them. Once we got Bill's chestnuts to the restaurant, we roasted them in the wood oven and ate them, warm, right out of the shell. That was when we realized what we had been missing—sweet, nutty richness that knocks your socks off. That was six or eight years ago and we still covet Bill's chestnuts, knowing that each year his trees might yield anywhere from just a few to a bumper crop as is typical with all nut-bearing trees. We would like to thank Bill and Fran for their commitment to us and to the annual chestnut harvest. It is these kinds of products and relationships that make our restaurant an interesting and exciting place to eat.

HEIRLOOM CAULIFLOWER GRATIN
with Roasted Chestnuts and Parmesan Cream

LOOK FOR HEADS OF CAULIFLOWER IN AN ARRAY OF COLORS—GOLD, PURPLE, WHITE, AND GREEN. WHILE SIMILAR IN FLAVOR AND TEXTURE, THE VIVID COLORS ADD VISUAL INTEREST TO A TRADITIONALLY PALE GRATIN.

YIELD: 8 SERVINGS

1 POUND WHITE HEIRLOOM CAULIFLOWER FLORETS,
   CUT INTO SMALL, BITE-SIZE PIECES
¾ POUND PURPLE HEIRLOOM CAULIFLOWER FLORETS,
   CUT INTO SMALL, BITE-SIZE PIECES
12 FRESH CHESTNUTS, ROASTED, PEELED, AND DICED
4 CUPS HEAVY CREAM
¾ CUP FRESHLY GRATED PARMESAN CHEESE
½ TEASPOON CHOPPED FRESH THYME
1½ TEASPOONS KOSHER SALT
½ TEASPOON FRESHLY GROUND BLACK PEPPER
1 TO 2 TEASPOONS BLACK TRUFFLE OIL (OPTIONAL)
1½ CUPS HERB BREADCRUMBS (PAGE 356)

Preheat the oven to 400°F.

Combine the cauliflower, chestnuts, and heavy cream in a medium stockpot or Dutch oven. Bring to a boil, reduce the heat to medium low, and simmer for 10 to 12 minutes or until the cauliflower is tender. Using a slotted spoon, remove the cauliflower and chestnuts from the cream and set aside to cool.

Add the Parmesan and thyme to the cream and return to a boil; reduce the heat to medium low, and simmer until the cream mixture is reduced by half and slightly thickened, about 20 minutes.

Return the cauliflower to the cream mixture and season with the salt and pepper. Drizzle the truffle oil, if using, into the cauliflower and cream mixture and stir to combine. Spoon the cauliflower mixture evenly into eight 8-ounce ramekins. Top each portion with 3 tablespoons of the herbed breadcrumbs.

Place the ramekins in the oven and bake for 4 to 5 minutes or until the topping is golden and the sides are bubbling. Serve warm.

HANGTOWN FRY

with Local Spinach and Pancetta

THE HANGTOWN FRY IS A WEST COAST DISH OF INTERESTING ORIGIN. LIKE AN OMELET MADE WITH EGGS, OYSTERS, AND BACON, IT WAS SERVED TO A HUNGRY GOLD PROSPECTOR AT THE EL DORADO HOTEL IN PLACERVILLE, CALIFORNIA, BACK IN THE DAY WHEN THE TOWN WAS KNOWN AS "HANGTOWN" FOR THE HANGING OF THREE DESPERADOES THERE. THE PROSPECTOR, WHO HAD JUST STRUCK IT RICH, DEMANDED THE MOST EXPENSIVE MEAL IN THE HOUSE. THE COOK TOLD HIM THAT EGGS WERE PRICEY BECAUSE THEY HAD TO BE CAREFULLY PACKED FOR SHIPMENT, THAT THE BACON CAME FROM BACK EAST, AND THAT FRESH OYSTERS ARRIVED ON ICE EACH DAY FROM THE BAY, MAKING ALL THREE DELICACIES. THE PROSPECTOR TOLD THE COOK TO JUST SCRAMBLE THEM ALL UP TOGETHER AND WITH THAT THE HANGTOWN FRY WAS BORN.

YIELD: 6 SERVINGS

1 QUART PEANUT OIL, FOR FRYING
30 FRESHLY SHUCKED APALACHICOLA OYSTERS,
  WELL DRAINED
3 TABLESPOONS BUTTERMILK
3 CUPS FRY MIX (PAGE 353)
12 LARGE FARM EGGS, LIGHTLY BEATEN
2 TABLESPOONS HEAVY CREAM
3 TABLESPOONS CHOPPED FRESH CHIVES
1½ TEASPOONS KOSHER SALT
1½ TEASPOONS FRESHLY GROUND BLACK PEPPER
2 TABLESPOONS UNSALTED BUTTER, DIVIDED
8 CUPS FRESH SPINACH, STEMS REMOVED
¼ CUP BACON VINAIGRETTE (PAGE 348), SLIGHTLY
  WARM OR AT ROOM TEMPERATURE
1 TABLESPOON CHIVE AÏOLI (PAGE 342), DIVIDED

Pour the oil into a deep-sided skillet to a depth of 2 inches. (Alternately, a deep fryer can be filled with peanut oil.) Preheat the oil to 360°F.

While the oil is heating, toss the oysters in the buttermilk to coat. Dredge the oysters in a shallow bowl filled with the fry mix, tossing to coat. Fry the oysters, in batches, until crispy and lightly golden, 1 to 1½ minutes, turning halfway through. Place the fried oysters on a paper towel–lined baking sheet and keep warm until ready to serve.

Combine the farm eggs, heavy cream, and chives in a medium mixing bowl, whisking well to blend. Season with the salt and pepper. Heat 1 teaspoon of the butter in an 8-inch nonstick skillet over medium heat. Add ½ cup of the egg mixture and cook, stirring gently with a heat-resistant spatula, for 2 to 3 minutes. The eggs should be gently scrambled but still hold together like an omelet. Carefully transfer the omelet onto a salad plate so that the eggs hold together in a circle. Repeat the process with the remaining butter and egg mixture, preparing a total of six omelets.

Combine the spinach and bacon vinaigrette in a large mixing bowl, tossing gently to coat. Season the salad with salt and pepper to taste. Divide the spinach salad evenly among each omelet. Arrange five oysters on each plate around each omelet. Drizzle ½ teaspoon of the chive aioli over each oyster and serve immediately.

BAKED 13-MILE OYSTERS

with Jalapeño, Lime, and Cilantro Butter

OYSTERS FROM BUDDY WARD'S 13-MILE SEAFOOD COMPANY IN APALACHICOLA, FLORIDA, ARE THE BEST OYSTERS WE HAVE EATEN ANYWHERE. THEY ARE PLUMP AND BRINY AND HAVE A RICH FLAVOR THAT IS NOT OVERPOWERING. THE CONFLUENCE OF WATERS FROM THE FRESH WATERS OF THE APALACHICOLA RIVER INTO THE SALTY APALACHICOLA BAY CREATES A PRISTINE ENVIRONMENT THAT IS PERFECT FOR GROWING OYSTERS. IF YOU LIVE ANYWHERE IN THE SOUTHEAST REGION OF THE UNITED STATES, ASK FOR 13-MILE OYSTERS BY NAME WHEN VISITING YOUR FISHMONGER.

YIELD: 6 SERVINGS

3 TABLESPOONS PEANUT OIL

4 SMALL JALAPEÑOS

2 TABLESPOONS GRATED LIME ZEST (FROM **4** LIMES)

3 TABLESPOONS GRATED FRESH LIME JUICE (FROM **2** LIMES)

½ CUP CHOPPED FRESH CILANTRO LEAVES

1 CUP (**2** STICKS) UNSALTED BUTTER, AT ROOM TEMPERATURE

1 TEASPOON KOSHER SALT PLUS MORE FOR BAKING THE OYSTERS

¼ TEASPOON FRESHLY GROUND BLACK PEPPER

36 SMALL TO MEDIUM APALACHICOLA OYSTERS IN THE SHELL

Heat the peanut oil in a small skillet over high heat. Add the jalapeños and cook until the skins are golden brown and blistered, about 1 minute. Carefully turn the jalapeños and cook an additional 1 to 1½ minutes or until the entire jalapeños are blistered. Transfer the jalapeños to a small bowl and cover with plastic wrap. Allow the jalapeños to sit for 5 minutes. Peel and discard the blistered skins and remove the stems and seeds. Finely chop the jalapeños and place in a mixing bowl. Add the lime zest, juice, cilantro, and butter to the jalapeños and stir, using a rubber spatula, until well combined. Season the butter mixture with the salt and pepper. Set aside at room temperature.

Preheat the oven to 450°F.

Sprinkle a jelly roll pan with an even layer of kosher salt, about ¼ inch thick. (This will keep the oyster shells from rolling around on the pan.) Shuck the oysters and place in an even layer on the prepared pan. Spoon a rounded ½ teaspoonful of the butter mixture into the center of each shucked oyster. The remaining butter will keep, refrigerated for up to one week or frozen for up to three months. Place the pan in the oven and bake for 6½ to 7 minutes or until the edges of the oysters begin to curl. Remove from the oven and set aside until the shells are cool enough to touch, about 5 minutes. Serve immediately.

BUDDY WARD & SON'S
13-MILE SEAFOOD COMPANY

Buddy Ward, with his wife, Martha Pearl, raised their family along a remote stretch of bay in Port St. Joe, Florida, named "13-Mile" after Buddy secured the oyster leases on the thirteen miles of the bay west of the town of Apalachicola along coastal Highway 30. Decades later, after Buddy's passing, his son Tommy took over the day-to-day operations of the family business. Tommy understands the trials and tribulations of life and business on the bay as only a native can. As a boy, he had explored the water's edge, finding old Indian artifacts like arrowheads near a spot called Picaleen Hole. He had helped the oystermen tong for oysters using large, wooden-handled metal tongs reminiscent of two large garden rakes that clamp together using scissor action. The oystermen would take the boats out and claw the sandy bottom, bringing up their weighty prize and dumping it on the flat-bottomed boat. Back at 13-Mile's seafood house, the oysters would be sorted and shucked or boxed for shipment. Tommy saw firsthand how the business was run and how it intertwined with the ecology of the bay and its tributaries. Tommy left Port St. Joe to attend college, but returned home to gain hands-on experience working at rival seafood houses.

Today, Tommy maintains the oyster leases and oversees all of the packing and distribution of an array of seafood. Independent fishermen bring their oysters, shrimp, crabs, fish, and clams to 13-Mile's headquarters to be weighed, washed, separated by size, and packed for sale. The Wards have developed enduring relationships with a lengthy list of clients eager to buy the day's haul. Tommy's trucking business rushes orders to clients, further ensuring quality from bay to kitchen door.

Tommy is a gregarious champion of the region and deeply passionate about preserving Apalachicola Bay and the way of life there. Hurricane Dennis practically destroyed company headquarters in 2005, but the community and family came together to rebuild so that life as they have known it on the bay endures as it has for so many generations.

An articulate man, Tommy is as comfortable talking to the local oystermen who tong out a living on the bay as he is with a powerful senator from Georgia while discussing their dispute over water rights. With his education and good-old-boy twinkle in his eye, Tommy could have done just about anything, but he was drawn back to the family business started by his dad and admits he wouldn't want to be or do anything else.

Tommy seeds his leases with clean scallop shells in the few short weeks before the oysters spawn. Once they spawn, the spat or baby oysters must have something to attach to in order to grow. Scallop shells have proven the ideal foundation for oysters to mature. The seeding and harvesting take place year-round. And while we like Bluepoints, Wellfleets, Hog Islands, and the entire world of oysters, we sell Tommy's oysters exclusively at Hot and Hot, simply because they are the best there is in terms of freshness and flavor and they are representative of our region. The oysters from 13-Mile are simply unparalleled.

An oyster's flavor is dictated as much by its genetic makeup as the quality of the water in which it matures and the mineral composition of the sediment and sand. It is very much like a wine grape's *terroir*—the effect the terroir or soil has on the flavor of the grapes. As it relates to the oyster industry, the salinity or freshness of the water affects the flavor of the oysters. All oysters require a balance of fresh water loaded with nutrients from swamps, riverbeds, and tributaries. They cannot survive in pure seawater. If the water is too saline, the oyster dies. This ideal balance of freshwater and sea is found in the bay of Apalachicola producing a plump, "stuffed" oyster, loaded with briny, clean flavor that is beyond compare.

Because so many factors come into play in producing this great product—water quality, environmental issues, weather, economics, management and people skills, it takes a truly dedicated person to eke out a living in this manner while championing all the causes necessary to keep oystering a viable enterprise. Tommy is as dedicated a gentleman as any you'll find.

SEARED DAY BOAT SCALLOPS

with Celery Root Slaw and Tamarind Sauce

PURCHASE "DAY BOAT" SCALLOPS FOR THIS RECIPE, WHICH MEANS THEY WERE HARVESTED FROM BOATS THAT ARE OUT ON THE WATER TO FISH ONE DAY AT A TIME. THIS IS THE BEST WAY TO ENSURE YOU ARE NOT GETTING SCALLOPS THAT HAVE BEEN DIPPED IN CHEMICALS USED IN THE SEAFOOD INDUSTRY TO INCREASE THE ABSORPTION RATE OF WATER THUS INCREASING THE WEIGHT OF THE SEAFOOD. THIS PRAC- TICE IS NOT A GOOD THING FOR THE FLAVOR OR TEXTURE OF THE SCALLOP. ALWAYS ASK IF THE SCALLOPS HAVE BEEN "DIPPED" AND, IF SO, DO NOT PURCHASE THEM. IF FOR SOME REASON YOU DO GET TREATED SCALLOPS, YOU WILL NOTICE A CHEMICALLY BITTER AFTER- TASTE THAT ROBS THE SCALLOP OF ITS NATURAL SWEETNESS—A CRIME!

YIELD: 6 SERVINGS

6 LARGE FRESH SCALLOPS (ABOUT **1** POUND), TRIMMED
¾ TEASPOON KOSHER SALT
¼ TEASPOON FRESHLY GROUND BLACK PEPPER
1 TABLESPOON OLIVE OIL
1 TABLESPOON UNSALTED BUTTER
3 CUPS CELERY ROOT SLAW (PAGE **370**)
2 TABLESPOONS TAMARIND SAUCE (PAGE **338**)

Pat the scallops dry and arrange in an even layer on a clean work surface. Season both sides with the salt and pepper.

Heat the olive oil in a heavy cast-iron skillet over medium-high heat. Just before the oil begins to smoke, add the scallops and cook for 2 minutes on the first side or until golden brown. Turn the scallops, add the butter, and reduce the heat to medium low. Continue cooking the scallops until well browned on both sides and cooked through, 2 to 2½ more minutes. Remove the scallops from the skillet.

Arrange ½ cup of the slaw on each of six appetizer plates. Place one scallop on each mound of slaw and drizzle each with ½ teaspoon of the tamarind sauce. Serve immediately.

PAN-SEARED FLOUNDER
with Shaved Fennel Salad, Olives, and Valencia Oranges

WHEN POSSIBLE, BUY "GIGGED" FLOUNDER. FLOUNDER GIGGERS CATCH BOTTOM-HUGGING FLOUNDER BY STABBING THEM WITH A PRONGED FORK, TYPICALLY AT NIGHT AND WITH THE AID OF ILLUMINATION FROM THE BOAT. SINCE THE BOATS ARE OUT ON THE WATER FOR ONLY A FEW HOURS EACH NIGHT, THE FLOUNDER ARE UNLOADED AT THE FISH HOUSE AND DELIVERED TO RESTAURANTS WITHIN HOURS OF BEING GIGGED. A WAY TO CHECK FOR FRESHNESS, PARTICULARLY WITH FLOUNDER, IS TO HOLD THE FLOUNDER BY ITS HEAD STRAIGHT OUT IN FRONT OF YOU. IT SHOULD NOT DROOP, BUT REMAIN STRAIGHT, FIRM, AND FLAT. IF IT GOES LIMP, IT HAS BEEN OUT OF THE WATER TOO LONG.

YIELD: 6 SERVINGS

4 VALENCIA ORANGES, PEELED AND SEGMENTED
6 CUPS CORED AND THINLY SLICED FENNEL BULB (ABOUT 2 LARGE)
⅔ CUP PITTED GREEN OR BLACK OLIVES, SUCH AS PICHOLINE, KALAMATA, OR NIÇOISE
¾ CUP VALENCIA ORANGE VINAIGRETTE (PAGE 345), DIVIDED
¼ CUP PEANUT OIL, DIVIDED
6 (8-OUNCE) SKIN-ON FLOUNDER FILLETS
1½ TEASPOONS KOSHER SALT
½ TEASPOON FRESHLY GROUND BLACK PEPPER

Combine the orange segments, fennel, and olives in a large mixing bowl. Add ½ cup of the vinaigrette and toss to combine. Set salad aside to marinate while the flounder is prepared.

Heat 1 tablespoon of the oil in a large, heavy skillet over high heat. Season the fillets on both sides with the salt and pepper. Add half of the fillets, skin side down, to the skillet and cook for about 3 minutes or until the skin is crispy. Turn the fillets, add 1 more tablespoon of peanut oil to the skillet, reduce the heat to medium, and continue cooking the fillets for 4 to 4½ minutes or until the fish is cooked through and flakes easily when tested with a fork. Transfer to a platter to keep warm until ready to serve. Wipe the skillet clean and repeat with the remaining oil and flounder fillets.

Spoon about 1 cup of the fennel salad onto each of six dinner plates. Arrange one fillet on top of each salad. Drizzle 2 teaspoons of the remaining vinaigrette over each fillet and serve immediately.

SWEET POTATO TORTELLONI

with Toasted Pine Nuts, Brown Butter, and Fried Sage

THE KEY TO GOOD TORTELLONI IS MAKING SURE THE DOUGH IS AS THIN AS POSSIBLE. THE SMALLEST SETTING ON YOUR PASTA MACHINE ROLLED THROUGH TWICE IS BEST. BE SURE TO COOK THE PASTA IN PLENTY OF BOILING SALTED WATER UNTIL THEY FLOAT, OTHERWISE THEY MAY OVERCOOK. THE AMOUNT OF BOILING WATER IS IMPORTANT SO THAT THE WATER NEVER LOSES ITS BOIL WHEN THE COOL PASTA IS ADDED. PASTA GETS MUSHY IF POACHED INSTEAD OF BEING BOILED. IN A PINCH, SUBSTITUTE STORE-BOUGHT CHEESE-FILLED TORTELLONI FOR THE SWEET POTATOES ONES IN THIS RECIPE.

YIELD: 6 SERVINGS

TORTELLONI:

4½ POUNDS SWEET POTATOES, ABOUT 10 SMALL POTATOES

2 TABLESPOONS OLIVE OIL

½ CUP (1 STICK) UNSALTED BUTTER, DICED

1½ TEASPOONS KOSHER SALT

¼ TEASPOON FRESHLY GROUND BLACK PEPPER

12 OUNCES SAFFRON PASTA DOUGH (PAGE 357)

ALL-PURPOSE FLOUR, FOR ROLLING PASTA DOUGH

SAUCE:

1 CUP (2 STICKS) UNSALTED BUTTER, AT ROOM TEMPERATURE

2 TEASPOONS BALSAMIC VINEGAR

24 FRESH SAGE LEAVES

¼ CUP PINE NUTS

2 TABLESPOONS MINCED FRESH CHIVES

½ TEASPOON KOSHER SALT

½ TEASPOON FRESHLY GROUND BLACK PEPPER

1 TABLESPOON AGED BALSAMIC VINEGAR (OPTIONAL)

TO PREPARE THE TORTELLONI:

Preheat the oven to 350°F.

Pierce the potatoes in several places with a sharp knife. Rub the outside of the potatoes with the oil and arrange on a baking sheet pan in an even layer. Bake the potatoes for 1 hour or until tender. Set the potatoes aside until cool enough to handle, about 15 minutes.

Peel the potatoes and place the flesh in the top of a food mill set over a bowl. (Alternately, a potato masher can be used.) Run the potatoes through the food mill, using a rubber spatula to press the potato through the mill, if needed. Add the butter, salt, and pepper to the potato mixture and stir gently until the butter is melted. Set the potato purée aside to cool to room temperature, about 30 minutes.

Divide the pasta dough into two equal portions. Lightly flour one portion and wrap the other portion in plastic wrap until ready to use (so it doesn't dry out). Roll the floured dough through a pasta machine, starting at the widest setting, repeating until you have reached the thinnest setting and the pasta dough is smooth and thin. (You should have an approximately 6 x 36-inch rectangle of dough.) Cut the dough into six 6-inch squares. Set the squares on a lightly floured surface and repeat the entire process with the reserved portion of dough.

Arrange six pasta squares in a single layer on a lightly floured rimmed baking sheet. Place 2 tablespoons of the cooled potato purée in the center of each square. Brush the edges of each pasta square with water. Fold opposite corners of each square together and press firmly to seal and form a triangle. Bring the opposite points of the triangle together to form a ring and press firmly to meld the ends together, using additional water, if needed. Continue with the remaining pasta and filling. (The tortelloni can be wrapped tightly in plastic wrap and refrigerated for up to two days.)

Bring a large pot of salted water to a boil. Add the tortelloni, a few at a time, to the water and cook for 2 to 3 minutes or until fork tender (al dente). Carefully remove the tortelloni from the water with a slotted spoon. Keep warm until ready to serve.

TO PREPARE THE SAUCE:

Melt the butter in a medium skillet over medium heat. Continue to cook the melted butter until it is golden brown and has a slightly nutty aroma, 4 to 5 minutes. (Be careful not to let the butter burn.) Add the vinegar, sage, pine nuts, and chives and remove the skillet from the heat. Season the butter mixture with the salt and pepper.

Toss the butter mixture with the cooked tortelloni until well coated. Evenly divide the tortelloni and butter mixture among six pasta bowls. Drizzle each serving with ½ teaspoon of the aged balsamic vinegar, if using. Serve immediately.

BOBWHITE QUAIL, SAUSAGE, AND WHITE BEAN CASSOULET

CASSOULET IS A CLASSIC SLOW-COOKED BEAN STEW ORIGINATING IN SOUTHWEST FRANCE THAT TYPICALLY COMBINES SAUSAGE WITH CONFIT OF DUCK. WE LIKE TO USE QUAIL, BUT FRESH BONE-IN CHICKEN PIECES WORK WELL TOO. THIS DISH IS A GREAT CATCHALL FOR MANY CUTS OF MEAT, INCLUDING PORK, GAME, AND SAUSAGE. TO MAKE THE PREPARATION IN THIS RECIPE LESS DAUNTING, YOU CAN BRAISE THE WHITE BEANS AND MAKE THE HAM HOCK BROTH A DAY OR TWO IN ADVANCE.

YIELD: 6 TO 8 SERVINGS

5 TABLESPOONS OLIVE OIL, DIVIDED
1 TABLESPOON UNSALTED BUTTER
4 CUPS ROUGHLY CHOPPED YELLOW ONIONS
3 CUPS HALVED AND ROUGHLY CHOPPED LEEKS (WHITE PART ONLY)
2 TEASPOONS CHOPPED FRESH THYME LEAVES, DIVIDED
2 CUPS PEELED AND ROUGHLY CHOPPED CARROTS
1¼ CUPS CHOPPED CELERY
2½ TEASPOONS KOSHER SALT, DIVIDED
1½ TEASPOONS FRESHLY GROUND BLACK PEPPER, DIVIDED
4 (6-OUNCE) SEMI-BONELESS QUAIL, HALVED
8 CUPS BRAISED WHITE BEANS (PAGE 369)
1 TABLESPOON CHOPPED FRESH SAGE
¼ CUP CHOPPED FRESH PARSLEY
¾ POUND SMOKED SAUSAGE, CUT INTO 8 (2-INCH) PIECES
1½ CUPS COOKED AND PICKED HAM HOCK MEAT (FROM SPICY HAM HOCK BROTH, PAGE 336)
6 DUCK CONFIT (PAGE 243) DRUMSTICKS OR THIGHS
4 CUPS HERBED BREADCRUMBS (PAGE 356)

Preheat the oven to 350°F.

Heat 2 tablespoons of the olive oil in a large skillet over medium heat. Add the butter, onions, and leeks and sauté for 5 minutes. Add 1 teaspoon of the thyme, the carrots, and celery and sauté for 5 more minutes. Season the vegetables with 1 teaspoon of the salt and ½ teaspoon of the pepper. Remove the vegetables from the heat and cool slightly.

Add the remaining 3 tablespoons olive oil to a large skillet and heat over medium high. Season both sides of the quail with 1 teaspoon of the salt and ½ teaspoon of the pepper. Add the quail to the hot oil and brown on each side for about 2 minutes. Remove from the heat and cool slightly.

Combine the braised white beans and the sautéed vegetables in a large bowl. Add the remaining teaspoon of the chopped thyme, the sage, parsley and the remaining ½ teaspoon each of salt and pepper and mix well.

Arrange ½ of the bean mixture in the bottom of a large 12-inch cast-iron skillet. Divide the browned quail meat, sausage, ham hock meat, and duck confit into six equal portions. Arrange the portions evenly over the braised beans in the skillet. Top with the remaining bean mixture. Sprinkle the herbed breadcrumbs evenly over the bean mixture.

Bake the cassoulet at 350°F for 45 to 50 minutes or until the breadcrumbs are browned and the cassoulet is heated through and bubbly.

SLOW ROASTED PORK SHOULDER

with Fall Vegetable Gratin and Mustard Greens

TO PROPERLY PREPARE THIS RECIPE, SOURCE A GOOD-QUALITY SEASON-
ING SALT AND PORK RUB (PAGE 381). ROASTING THE PORK ON TOP
OF THICK-CUT ONIONS KEEPS THE MEAT FROM GETTING TOO DARK ON
THE BOTTOM. AS THE JUICES FROM THE PORK RUN INTO THE BOTTOM
OF THE PAN AND BRAISE THE ONIONS, A FLAVORFUL JUS IS CREATED.
DON'T FORGET TO SERVE THIS PORK WITH PLENTY OF JUS FROM THE
BOTTOM OF THE ROASTING PAN.

YIELD: 6 SERVINGS

1 LARGE GARLIC CLOVE, SMASHED AND PEELED
1 (4 TO 4½-POUND) BONELESS PORK SHOULDER,
   TRIMMED OF EXCESS FAT
2 TABLESPOONS OLIVE OIL
2 TABLESPOONS HASTINGS CREATIONS PORK RUB
   (PAGE 381) OR ANY SALT-FREE PORK RUB
2 TABLESPOONS HASTINGS CREATIONS ANCHO PORK
   SALT (PAGE 381) OR KOSHER SALT
1 TABLESPOON FRESHLY GROUND BLACK PEPPER
2 LARGE SWEET ONIONS, PEELED AND SLICED INTO
   1-INCH-THICK RINGS
FALL VEGETABLE GRATIN (PAGE 372)
3 CUPS BRAISED MUSTARD GREENS (PAGE 170)

Preheat the oven to 300°F.

Rub the crushed garlic over the entire pork shoulder until fragrant. Discard the garlic clove. Brush the olive oil over the pork until well coated. Combine the rub, salt, and pepper in a small dish and sprinkle evenly over the pork shoulder. Using your hands, gently rub the seasonings into the meat.

Arrange the onion slices in an even layer in the bottom of a large baking dish or roasting pan. Place the seasoned pork on top of the onions, fat side up. Roast the pork at 300°F for 2 hours or until tender. Remove the pan from the oven and allow the pork to rest for 15 minutes.

Slice the gratin into six equal squares. Arrange one piece on each of six dinner plates. Spoon ½ cup of the braised greens around each gratin. Slice the pork shoulder into ½-inch-thick slices and arrange 2 to 3 slices over each serving. Serve immediately.

IDIE'S DAD AND GRILLED NEW YORK STRIP WITH POACHED EGG

Few people knew that Idie's dad, Jim, had trouble digesting food due to Crohn's disease, an inflammatory disease of the gastrointestinal system. After all, Jim always looked forward to his next meal and delighted in the joys of eating while keeping his Crohn's disease in check. At home, he devoted an enormous amount of attention to reviewing his food intake. Since he was taking so many medications, he maintained as healthy a diet as possible with well-rounded meals containing a protein, starch, and green vegetable. He most often stayed away from sweets, except for the occasional pound cake, which became his favorite dessert as he grew older. Jim was diagnosed when Idie was just five years old, so she had a firsthand view of its progression and the effect certain foods had on him. He simply could not tolerate corn, which became a problem when he moved to the South to live with Idie late in his life. He found the temptation of Alabama sweet corn irresistible. At least once or, bravely twice, each summer he indulged in his corn "fix." Mostly, Idie remembers him eating small portions, many times a day, which consisted of the three round meals and smaller snacks in between.

Breakfast was a favorite of Jim's. He never missed it. There was always an egg, poached or scrambled, a piece of sausage or bacon, a side of fresh fruit and a cup of hot coffee. Jim often scolded Idie for her skipped morning meal—she was not a breakfast person.

It was fitting, upon his passing, that Idie wanted to celebrate his life with family and food. Idie and Chris hosted a family-style dinner after his service. Originally, the room was set up with several tables of four, but Chris took charge and rearranged the dining room so that there was one long harvest table set to accommodate all thirty family members. Idie wanted it to be served family style with platters arriving at the table for everyone to share—the way meals were served when she was growing up. Course after course appeared at the table while wine was poured and guests shared stories of Jim and his wonderful life. When the Grilled New York Strip with Poached Egg and Rapini appeared at the table, Idie smiled as her eyes welled up with tears. There was that egg! Jim would have loved the dish—for breakfast!

Idie was surprised with a slideshow of old black-and-white photos of family get-togethers from her childhood. It was a time to laugh and reminisce. Zeb and Vincent, though young at the time, were present to witness and participate in this important rite of passage—of a life celebrated with food and family at a communal table. As the evening came to a close, Idie sat back quietly to observe the gathering and soak in the moment, knowing she could not have gotten through that day without her family's love and support. Since that day, in honor of Jim, the New York Strip with Poached Egg has been a mainstay on the Hot and Hot menu.

GRILLED NY STRIP

with Poached Farm Egg, Parmigiano-Reggiano, and Truffle Oil

MOST MEAT EATERS PREFER CERTAIN CUTS FOR DINNER. THE ADDITION OF A POACHED FARM EGG ALLOWS THIS ENTRÉE TO SPAN THE REALM OF BREAKFAST FARE TO LATE NIGHT DINNER. THE SHARPNESS OF THE PARMIGIANO-REGGIANO AND SCENT OF TRUFFLE OIL ELEVATES THIS DISH, BUT FEEL FREE TO ADJUST THE ACCOMPANIMENTS TO SUIT YOUR PALATE.

YIELD: 6 SERVINGS

24 FINGERLING POTATOES
2 (8-OUNCE) BUNCHES FRESH RAPINI OR BROCCOLI RABE
¼ CUP PLUS 2 TABLESPOONS EXTRA-VIRGIN OLIVE OIL
2 LARGE GARLIC CLOVES, PEELED
1 TEASPOON CRUSHED RED PEPPER FLAKES
6 (16-OUNCE) NEW YORK STRIP STEAKS
2 TABLESPOONS HASTINGS CREATIONS ALL-PURPOSE HERB SALT (PAGE 381) OR KOSHER SALT
2 TABLESPOONS PLUS ¼ TEASPOON FRESHLY GROUND BLACK PEPPER, DIVIDED
1 TEASPOON KOSHER SALT
6 LARGE POACHED EGGS (PAGE 374)
1½ CUPS FRESHLY GRATED PARMIGIANO-REGGIANO CHEESE
2 TABLESPOONS BLACK TRUFFLE OIL

LOCAL FARM EGGS – MCEWEN & SONS

We use fresh farm eggs gathered by Luke and Frank McEwen, Jr. who raise free-ranging hens without hormones or antibiotics on their family's Wilsonville, Alabama, property and save the proceeds of their sales for college. The eggs range from beige to brown to blue-gray and the yolks are plump and golden. Do not underestimate the flavor and quality of a great egg. It makes all the difference in this dish. If you do not have access to freshly gathered farm eggs, buy the freshest organic eggs from your grocery store.

Preheat the grill to medium-high heat (350°F to 400°F).

Place the potatoes in a medium saucepan with a small handful of salt. Add enough cold water to cover the potatoes and bring to a boil over high heat. Reduce the heat to medium low and simmer for 8 to 10 minutes or just until tender. Drain and set aside to cool completely, about 30 minutes. Cut the potatoes in half lengthwise.

Bring a medium saucepan of salted water to a boil over medium-high heat. Add the rapini and cook until bright green and tender, about 2 minutes. Drain the rapini and rinse under cold running water. Set aside.

Heat the olive oil in a small skillet over medium heat. Add the garlic and crushed red pepper and cook until the garlic begins to brown, 1 to 2 minutes. Remove from the heat and set aside to cool slightly.

Preheat the oven to 400°F.

Season the steaks evenly on both sides with the herb salt and 2 tablespoons of the pepper, using about 1 teaspoon of the salt and 1 teaspoon of the pepper on each steak. Grill the steaks over medium-high heat for 5 to 6 minutes on the first side, turn and continue cooking for 3 to 4 minutes (for medium) or until desired degree of doneness. Transfer steaks to a warm platter and loosely cover with aluminum foil for at least 5 minutes before serving.

Combine the olive oil mixture, potatoes, rapini, 1 teaspoon of the salt and ¼ teaspoon of the pepper in a large bowl and toss until well coated. Pour the vegetable mixture into a large baking dish and bake for 10 minutes or until heated through.

Divide the rapini and potato mixture evenly among six dinner plates. Arrange 1 steak on each serving of vegetables and top with a poached egg. Sprinkle ¼ cup of the cheese over each serving and drizzle with 1 teaspoon each of truffle oil. Serve immediately.

BRAISED VEAL CHEEKS

with Potato Gnocchi and Chanterelles

VEAL CHEEKS ARE NOT EASY TO FIND BUT ARE AVAILABLE BY SPECIAL ORDER FROM YOUR BUTCHER. SUBSTITUTE SHORT RIBS, PORK SHANKS, OR LAMB SHANKS IN A PINCH. VEAL CHEEKS ARE PHENOMENAL AND PARTICULARLY TENDER AND RICH IN FLAVOR, CONSIDERING THAT THEY ARE NOT AS FATTY AS MANY OF THE MEATS WE TYPICALLY LOOK TO FOR BRAISES.

YIELD: 6 SERVINGS

1¼ POUNDS (ABOUT 18) TRIMMED VEAL CHEEKS

2 TEASPOONS HASTINGS CREATIONS ALL-PURPOSE HERB SALT
    (PAGE 381) OR KOSHER SALT

1 TEASPOON FRESHLY GROUND BLACK PEPPER

3 TABLESPOONS PEANUT OIL

½ CUP ROUGHLY CHOPPED ONION

½ CUP ROUGHLY CHOPPED LEEKS (WHITE PART ONLY)

¼ CUP PEELED AND ROUGHLY CHOPPED CARROTS

¼ CUP ROUGHLY CHOPPED CELERY

2 CUPS VEAL STOCK (PAGE 335) OR LOW-SODIUM BEEF BROTH

12 TORPEDO ONIONS OR LARGE SPRING ONIONS, ROOTS AND
    GREEN TOPS TRIMMED AND RESERVED FOR ANOTHER USE

¼ CUP PLUS 1 TABLESPOON UNSALTED BUTTER, DIVIDED

2 TABLESPOONS MINCED SHALLOTS

1 TEASPOON CHOPPED FRESH THYME

½ POUND FRESH CHANTERELLE MUSHROOMS

48 TO 50 POTATO GNOCCHI (PAGE 359), COOKED UNTIL
    FORK TENDER (AL DENTE)

1 TEASPOON FRESH LEMON JUICE

2 TABLESPOONS CHOPPED FRESH PARSLEY

2 TABLESPOONS CHOPPED FRESH CHIVES

2 TEASPOONS BLACK TRUFFLE OIL (OPTIONAL)

Preheat the oven to 350°F.

Season the veal cheeks on both sides with the herb salt and pepper. Heat the peanut oil in a large, wide saucepan over medium-high heat. Add the cheeks, in batches and cook until well browned on both sides, 15 to 18 minutes total. Transfer the browned veal cheeks to a deep baking dish and set aside. Drain off and discard any excess oil left in the saucepan, reserving 1 tablespoon in the pan. Return the pan to medium heat and add the onion, leeks, carrots, and celery. Cook, stirring frequently, until the vegetables are softened and lightly caramelized, about 5 minutes. Add the veal stock and bring to a boil. Remove the saucepan from the heat and pour the veal stock and vegetable mixture over the browned cheeks. Cover the baking dish tightly with aluminum foil and bake for 2 hours or until tender.

While the veal cheeks are braising, add the onions, 2 tablespoons of the butter, and a pinch each of salt and pepper to a small baking dish. Cover the dish tightly with aluminum foil and bake at 350°F, shaking the pan halfway through, for 30 to 35 minutes or until the onions are tender. Set the onions aside until ready to serve.

Remove the cheeks from the braising liquid and transfer to a platter to keep warm. Strain the braising liquid through a fine-meshed sieve into a medium saucepan; discard the solids. Bring the braising liquid to a boil and cook until the liquid is reduced to 1 cup, 10 to 15 minutes.

Heat 1 tablespoon of the butter in a large sauté pan over medium-high heat. Add the shallots and thyme and cook, stirring constantly, for 1 minute. Add the chanterelle mushrooms, reduce the heat to medium low, and cook, stirring frequently, until the mushrooms are wilted and golden brown, about 5 minutes. Add the veal cheeks, 1 cup of the reduced braising liquid, and the roasted onions, and cook, stirring, until the liquid begins to simmer. Add the cooked gnocchi, lemon juice, parsley, and chives, and cook until heated through, about 1 minute. Remove from the heat and swirl in the remaining 2 tablespoons of butter and the truffle oil, if using.

Spoon the veal cheeks and gnocchi mixture equally into six wide shallow bowls (about three veal cheeks, two onions, and eight gnocchi per person). Serve immediately.

WHOLE-ROASTED, FREE-RANGE CHICKEN
with Winter Vegetables

EVERY HOUSEHOLD NEEDS A TRULY GREAT WHOLE ROASTED CHICKEN RECIPE FOR ITS REPERTOIRE. THIS IS A SIMPLE RECIPE THAT WE HAVE BEEN PREPARING AT LEAST ONCE A WEEK FOR THE LAST TWENTY YEARS. THE RESULTS ARE GREATLY IMPROVED BY PURCHASING A FREE-RANGE, ORGANIC CHICKEN, WHEN AVAILABLE. INCORPORATING EXOTIC, FLAVORFUL INGREDIENTS SUCH AS PORCINI OR MOREL MUSHROOMS, BABY ARTICHOKES, OR FINGERLING POTATOES ALSO ACHIEVES A SUPERIOR RESULT. OUR BOYS LOVE WHEN WE TAKE THE TIME TO CUT THE THIGHS AND LEGS AWAY FROM THE ROASTED CHICKEN TO PRODUCE EXTRA PAN DRIPPINGS. BE SURE TO SERVE THIS DISH WITH PLENTY OF CRUSTY BREAD FOR DIPPING.

YIELD: 6 SERVINGS

1 (4 TO 4½-POUND) WHOLE FREE-RANGE, ORGANIC CHICKEN

2½ TEASPOONS KOSHER SALT, DIVIDED

2 TEASPOONS FRESHLY GROUND BLACK PEPPER, DIVIDED

6 FRESH ROSEMARY SPRIGS, TORN IN HALF, DIVIDED

1 BUNCH (ABOUT 20) FRESH THYME SPRIGS, TORN IN HALF, DIVIDED

¼ CUP OLIVE OIL

¼ CUP (½ STICK) UNSALTED BUTTER

1 LARGE PARSNIP, PEELED AND COARSELY CHOPPED INTO 1-INCH PIECES

2 LARGE CARROTS, PEELED AND COARSELY CHOPPED INTO 1-INCH PIECES

1 MEDIUM TURNIP, PEELED AND CUT INTO 1-INCH WEDGES

¼ LARGE RUTABAGA, PEELED AND CUT INTO 1-INCH WEDGES

1 LARGE YELLOW ONION, PEELED, HALVED, AND SLICED INTO ½-INCH-WIDE SLICES

6 FINGERLING POTATOES, QUARTERED

¼ POUND ASSORTED WILD MUSHROOMS OR CREMINI MUSHROOMS

8 LARGE GARLIC CLOVES, PEELED

1½ TEASPOONS HASTINGS CREATIONS POULTRY SALT (PAGE 381) OR KOSHER SALT

CRUSTY FRENCH BAGUETTE, FOR SERVING

Rinse the chicken under cold running water, drain, and pat dry. Season the cavity with 1 teaspoon of the kosher salt and ½ teaspoon of the pepper. Stuff the cavity with half of the rosemary and half of the thyme. Tuck the wings behind the chicken and tie the legs together with butcher's twine. Allow the chicken to rest at room temperature for 30 minutes while the vegetables are being prepared.

Preheat the oven to 400°F.

Heat the olive oil and butter in a large cast-iron skillet over medium heat until the butter is melted. Add the next eight ingredients (parsnip through garlic) and the remaining rosemary and thyme sprigs, tossing until well coated. Season the vegetables with the remaining 1½ teaspoons kosher salt and 1 teaspoon of the black pepper. Cook the vegetables over medium heat, stirring occasionally, for 5 minutes. Transfer the vegetables to a large baking dish or roasting pan.

Season the outside of the chicken with the poultry salt and remaining ½ teaspoon of pepper. Arrange the chicken on top of the vegetables and roast at 400°F for 30 minutes. Reduce the oven temperature to 350°F and continue cooking for 40 to 45 minutes, basting occasionally with the pan juices, or until the chicken is golden brown and cooked through and the vegetables are tender. Remove from the oven and allow the chicken to rest for 10 minutes. Cut the legs and thighs away from the cavity of the chicken, allowing the juices to drain into the vegetables. Allow the chicken to rest an additional 5 to 10 minutes. Carve the chicken into eight pieces (two wings, two drumsticks, two thighs, and two breast halves.) Divide the vegetables and chicken evenly among six dinner plates and spoon the pan juices over each serving. Serve immediately with crusty bread slices.

POMEGRANATE SORBET
with Shortbread Cookies

Fresh pomegranates are a must for this recipe and are available from October through January. Look for dark red, unfaded fruit that is heavy in the hand. When you split the fruit, the seeds should be a deep, ruby red and plump with juice. An easy way to seed them is to halve them crosswise and hold the cut side down in the palm of your hand over a bowl. Beat the top of the fruit until the seeds fall out. The white pith is quite bitter, so be careful to remove it before placing the seeds in a strainer and pressing the juice from their pods. Pomegranates are rich in potassium and vitamin C. Serve this sorbet as a palate cleanser between courses or, as here, with cookies.

YIELD: ABOUT 4 CUPS SORBET AND 12 COOKIES

POMEGRANATE SORBET:

3 CUPS FRESH POMEGRANATE JUICE

1 CUP WATER

¾ CUP GRANULATED SUGAR

SHORTBREAD COOKIES:

3 CUPS ALL-PURPOSE FLOUR

½ TEASPOON SALT

1½ CUPS (**3** STICKS) PLUS **1** TABLESPOON UNSALTED
    BUTTER, AT ROOM TEMPERATURE, DIVIDED

1 CUP SIFTED CONFECTIONERS' SUGAR

¾ TEASPOON GRATED FRESH LEMON ZEST

½ TEASPOON PURE VANILLA EXTRACT

TO PREPARE THE SORBET:

Combine the juice, water, and sugar in a medium saucepan and bring to a boil over medium-high heat, stirring occasionally. Once the mixture begins to boil and the sugar is completely dissolved, remove from the heat and set aside to cool. Refrigerate the juice mixture until well chilled.

Freeze the chilled mixture in an ice cream machine according to the manufacturer's directions. Transfer the sorbet to a freezer-safe container and freeze until firm, at least 2 hours.

TO PREPARE THE COOKIES:

Preheat the oven to 300°F.

Sift together the flour and salt; set aside. Using 1 tablespoon of the softened butter, grease the bottom and sides of a 10-inch springform pan and set aside.

Combine the remaining 1½ cups of butter and the sugar in the bowl of a standing mixer fitted with the paddle attachment. With the machine on low, mix until well combined and pale yellow, stopping to scrape down the sides of the bowl as needed. Add the lemon zest and vanilla and mix just until incorporated.

With the mixer on low, add the sifted flour mixture a little at a time, until all of the flour has been added. Transfer the dough to the prepared springform pan and press gently into an even layer in the bottom of the pan. (The dough should be about ¾ inch thick.) Using the tip of a sharp knife, score the dough into 12 equal triangles, then pierce all over with a fork. Bake the shortbread at 300°F for 45 minutes or until cooked through and pale golden.

Using the tip of a sharp knife, cut the warm shortbread into triangles along the scored lines. Run a knife around the edges of the shortbread, to loosen. Allow the shortbread to cool in the pan for at least 30 minutes. Release the springform pan sides. Using a spatula, carefully remove the shortbread triangles.

Spoon ⅓ cup of the sorbet into twelve ice cream dishes and serve each immediately with a slice of warm shortbread.

APPLE AND ROSEMARY CROUSTADE
with *Caramel Sauce*

SOMETIMES YOU JUST NEED A CHANGE FROM OLD-FASHIONED APPLE PIE. A CROUSTADE IS A FREE-FORM PASTRY FILLED WITH ANY NUMBER OF THINGS. ROSEMARY, APPLES, AND FLAKY PASTRY ARE A MATCH MADE IN HEAVEN. CRISP, TART-SWEET APPLES LIKE WINESAP, YATES, MCINTOSH, OR ARKANSAS BLACK ARE PERFECT VARIETIES FOR THIS AUTUMN DESSERT. SIMMERING THE APPLES WITH ROSEMARY AND BUTTER INFUSES THE KITCHEN WITH A MAGICAL AROMA.

YIELD: 6 SERVINGS

2 POUNDS SWEET PASTRY DOUGH (PAGE 358)
1 LARGE EGG
1 TABLESPOON HEAVY CREAM
1 CUP (2 STICKS) UNSALTED BUTTER
⅓ CUP GRANULATED SUGAR
1 TABLESPOON FRESH ROSEMARY LEAVES
1 TEASPOON FRESHLY GRATED LEMON ZEST
⅛ TEASPOON FRESHLY GROUND BLACK PEPPER
PINCH OF SALT
2½ POUNDS (ABOUT 6 MEDIUM) BAKING APPLES, SUCH AS MCINTOSH, PEELED, CORED, AND SLICED INTO ¼-INCH-THICK SLICES
1 TABLESPOON TURBINADO SUGAR OTHER OR COARSE RAW SUGAR
1½ CUPS VANILLA ICE CREAM (PAGE 366)
¾ CUP CARAMEL SAUCE (PAGE 363)

Roll out the dough to ⅛-inch thickness on a lightly floured surface. Cut the dough into six 6-inch circles. Make 9 evenly spaced 1-inch slits around the edge of each pastry round, perpendicular to the edge.

Whisk together the egg and heavy cream in a small bowl. Brush the edges of the pastry rounds with the egg wash.

Melt the butter in a large skillet over medium heat. Add the granulated sugar, rosemary, lemon zest, pepper, and salt and cook, stirring until the sugar is melted, about 2 minutes. Reduce the heat to medium low, add the apples, and cook, stirring frequently, until tender, about 20 minutes. Remove from the heat and set aside to cool to room temperature, about 30 minutes. Pile an equal amount (about ½ cup) of the apple and butter mixture in the center of each pastry round, using about one whole apple, sliced, per pastry round. Fold the pastry around the apples, overlapping the pastry at the slits, and pressing to seal. There should be a 1-inch opening in the center of each tart. Brush the outside of the tarts with the remaining egg wash and sprinkle each with ½ teaspoon of the turbinado sugar.

Preheat the oven to 375°F.

Transfer the tarts to a parchment-lined jelly roll pan and refrigerate for 30 minutes. Bake the chilled tarts at 375°F for 30 minutes or until golden brown. Remove from the oven and allow the croustades to cool for 5 minutes. Transfer one tart onto each of six dessert plates. Top each with ¼ cup of vanilla ice cream and drizzle each with 2 tablespoons of the caramel sauce. Serve immediately.

PECAN TART

with Molasses Ice Cream

This recipe produces, quite possibly, the best pecan tart on the planet! It is simple, gooey, and not overtly sweet. Arrange the pecans on top after filling the prebaked tart shell to create a beautiful pattern. Store nuts in your freezer to keep their delicate oils from turning rancid. The molasses ice cream makes this Southern dessert extra special. We use unsulphured, dark molasses, which has a more delicate and clean sugarcane flavor.

YIELD: 1 (11-INCH) TART OR 6 SERVINGS

FOR THE CRUST:
12 ounces Sweet Pastry Dough, about 1 recipe (page 358)

FOR THE TART:
1¼ cups pecan pieces
2 large eggs
½ cup firmly packed dark brown sugar
¼ teaspoon salt
¼ cup melted unsalted butter
¾ cup dark corn syrup
1 teaspoon pure vanilla extract
1¼ cups whole pecan halves
1½ cups Molasses Ice Cream (page 366)

To Prepare the Crust:

Preheat the oven to 300°F

Place the chilled dough on a lightly floured surface. Roll the dough out into a 12-inch circle, a little less than ¼ inch thick. Transfer the circle to an 11-inch fluted tart pan and press the dough into the sides and bottom of the pan. Trim off and discard the excess pastry. Line the tart shell with a piece of parchment paper and fill with pie weights or dry beans.

Place the tart shell on a baking sheet pan and bake for 25 to 30 minutes or until lightly golden. Allow the tart shell to cool completely before removing the pie weights or beans.

To Prepare the Tart:

Preheat the oven to 325°F

Arrange the pecan pieces evenly in the bottom of the tart shell. Whisk together the eggs, brown sugar, salt, melted butter, corn syrup, and vanilla. Pour the egg mixture evenly over the pecan pieces. Arrange pecan halves on top of the filling in a decorative pattern.

Place the tart on a baking sheet pan and bake for 20 to 25 minutes or until the filling is set around the edges. (The center of the tart may still jiggle slightly.) Cool completely before slicing. Serve each slice with a small scoop (about ¼ cup) of molasses ice cream in the center of each piece.

PETALS FROM THE PAST

Petals from the Past is a nursery, educational facility, and display garden in Jemison, Alabama, south of Birmingham, owned and operated by horticulturists Jason and Shelley Powell. Over the years, Jason and Shelley have propagated plants from private gardens and old home sites in an effort to expand their unique offerings and provide the public with an opportunity to see mature plants in a natural setting rather than just nursery-pot miniature. Jason likes to brag that Shelley can identify rare plants from a car window zooming past at fifty-five miles per hour. Luckily, visitors to Petals from the Past can enjoy Shelley and Jason's finds at a more leisurely pace as they wander through the display gardens to determine the best selections to make for their own property. In addition to landscape plants, Jason and Shelley have an extensive selection of edibles. From brambles of blueberries and blackberries, rows of muscadine vines, an array of figs, citrus, persimmons, pomegranates, apples, and pears to an amazing variety of garden vegetables and herbs, their selection is abundant and quality beyond compare.

Our chef-purveyor relationship with Petals from the Past is quite new. We are interested in whatever they bring us because so much of what they grow is of a rare, heirloom sort. They find cultivars that have stood the test of time by surviving in the wild when other varieties were chosen, hybridized, and cultivated for commercial markets. These old plants often are found next to a decaying farmhouse, thriving amid the disrepair. These are plants that have endured with neglect yet surprise us with the overlooked quality of their fruits and vegetables.

This is the sort of farm-to-table relationship chefs dream about. Jason and Shelley have engaged us in conversation about what varieties and heirlooms we have liked so that they can take their cultivation of them to the next level. We get to serve products grown less than forty miles from our restaurant, often picked on the very day they are delivered to us. Jason appreciates being invited into our kitchen to hear how we will prepare his harvest instead of just dropping things off and heading out the door. Because we share his passion for these harvests, we think it is important to take time to bounce ideas off one another.

Petals from the Past is truly a family enterprise. Jason's dad, Dr. Arlie Powell, is a horticulturist and fruit tree expert and his mother does all the plant propagation for the nursery enterprise. Like us, the Powells are exceedingly passionate about what they do. Their mission is to preserve, propagate, and share heirlooms and old-fashioned varieties, using methods as natural as possible. In turn their offerings have become an important part of our seasonal dishes and another way they have found to expose the public to these unique varietals. Jason remembers bringing his mom and dad to Hot and Hot for dinner one evening and how it made his dad's year to see "Petals from the Past Fig Tart" on the menu. In no time, customers came into the nursery wanting a particular variety of something they had tasted at our restaurant. That is a compliment to both the grower and the chef.

Recently Jason came to us with a new apple variety called the "Cumberland Spur Apple" which they had discovered growing in southern Alabama. If the variety is picked early, it is reminiscent of a Granny Smith with a dry texture and a sweet-tart profile, but if picked at its peak of maturity, it is crisp with a sweet perfume and flavor. This is not the sort of ingredient we can simply order from some distributor. Our relationship with Petals from the Past has given us access to ingredients found nowhere else.

Thanks to the Powells, we have begun to tinker with Indian peaches in our kitchen. These rare stone fruits predate formal cultivation. They are rosy and firm and often used young for pickling or they can be fully ripened until sweet. Today they are growing this old variety at Petals from the Past. Like the Cumberland Spur Apple, such uncommon ingredients are a new artistic medium for us to use in the kitchen. Such wonders inspire us and bring the nuances of our craft back into focus and force us to look at cooking anew. The limited supply of these harvests is another one of the beauties of it. The harvest may be so small and fleeting that we are only able to showcase a particular ingredient for a single night. We want to highlight such rarity as best we can. It forces us to hone our skills while we expand our thinking. We are thrilled about the relationship we have developed with the Powells because their work inspires our cooking and leaves us in anticipation of what they might bring us next.

ITALIAN CHRISTMAS WITH THE MORANOS

CHRISTMAS PREPARATIONS AT OUR HOUSE SIGNAL MANY THINGS—THE HOMECOMING OF OUR BOYS ON HOLIDAY FROM BOARDING SCHOOL, THE COMPLETION OF ONE OF THE MOST PRODUCTIVE MONTHS OF OUR RESTAURANT LIFE, AND RENEWAL, AS WE RELAX TOGETHER AS A FAMILY. OUR HOUSE IS DECORATED BY THE FIRST OF THE MONTH WITH THE TREE GOING UP NO LATER THAN THREE WEEKS BEFORE CHRISTMAS. WE SPEND THE NEXT FEW WEEKS CROSSING OFF OUR LIST OF PRESENTS AS WE GET THEM PURCHASED, WRAPPED, AND UNDER THE DECORATED TREE. MENU PLANNING TAKES UP AMPLE TIME AS WELL.

IN OUR HOME, CHRISTMAS EVE DINNER IS THE MOST IMPORTANT MEAL OF THE HOLIDAY SEASON. THE ANTICIPATION AND MEANING OF THE EVENING FOR A CATHOLIC FAMILY IS SIGNIFICANT. AS WE DRESS FOR EVENING MASS, OUR TABLE IS ALREADY SET WITH FAMILY CHINA, THE CENTERPIECES ARRANGED, COURSES PLANNED OUT, AND THE WINE AND CHAMPAGNE CHILLED. AFTER CELEBRATING MASS, OUR FAMILY COMES TOGETHER FOR AN EVENING OF FELLOWSHIP AT THE TABLE.

OVER THE YEARS, THE MENU HAS COMBINED IDIE'S FAMILY TRADITIONS WITH SOME NEW TRADITIONS. OUR BOYS LOVE TO START WITH SHUCKED OYSTERS ON THE HALF SHELL, WITH ZEB USUALLY SHUCKING THE OYSTERS AND SERVING THEM TO US WITH LEMONS AND FRESHLY GRATED HORSERADISH. A CHEESE AND CHARCUTERIE PLATTER (SALAMI, MORTADELLA, PROSCUITTO, OLIVES, AND FENNEL) SITS ON THE TABLE ALONG WITH A BUCKET OF COLD CHAMPAGNE. AFTER CONVERSATION, MUCH LAUGHTER, AND CHRISTMAS SONGS PLAYING IN THE BACKGROUND, WE SIT DOWN TO OUR DINING ROOM TABLE. SOUP IS SERVED FIRST IN SMALL RAMEKINS JUST TO WHET OUR APPETITES AND THEN COURSES OF FISH, PASTA WITH HOMEMADE MEATBALLS, SAUSAGES, VEGETABLES, AND A SALAD ARRIVE IN RELAXED STAGES. DISCUSSIONS ABOUT LIFE, FAMILY, FRIENDS, AND POLITICS FILL THE EVENING AS WE SHARE IN THIS FEAST. THE MEAL ENDS WITH AN ASSORTMENT OF COOKIES, COFFEE, OR AN AFTER-DINNER DRINK. YEAR AFTER YEAR THIS FAMILY TRADITION HOLDS THE SAME MAGIC.

IDIE'S HOMEMADE SPAGHETTI AND MEATBALLS

———

COUSIN JOE'S CHEESE PIZZA

———

OVEN-ROASTED ITALIAN SAUSAGES

———

SAUTÉED RAPINI

———

FRIED CAULIFLOWER

———

TUNA MARINARA WITH RIGATONI

———

BREADED FRIED SHRIMP WITH COCKTAIL SAUCE

———

BASKET OF FRIED GREENS (CELERY FRITTERS)

———

CRANBERRY AND PISTACHIO TORRONE

———

SWEET ITALIAN COOKIES WITH LEMON GLAZE

- WINE PAIRINGS -

FOR THIS FESTIVE ITALIAN HOLIDAY FEAST WE CHOSE TWO ITALIAN WINE OPTIONS. THE BASTIANICH VESPA BIANCO IS A FLAGSHIP WHITE WINE FROM THE ITALIAN ESTATE OWNED BY RESTAURATEURS LIDIA BASTIANICH, JOE BASTIANICH, AND MARIO BATALI. IT IS A FULL-BODIED WINE MADE FROM A BLEND OF CHARDONNAY, SAUVIGNON BLANC AND PICOLIT GRAPES. THIS WINE HAS A WONDERFUL ACIDITY FROM THE SAUVIGNON BLANC GRAPES THAT IS BALANCED NICELY BY THE DEPTH OF THE CHARDONNAY GRAPES. IT HAS BEEN AWARDED THREE GLASSES FROM GAMBERO ROSSO FOR THE PAST TWO YEARS IN A ROW. AS WELL AS BEING A GOOD DRINKING WINE, IT PAIRS NICELY WITH FRIED FOODS SUCH AS THE FRIED CAULIFLOWER OR CELERY FRITTERS.

NO ITALIAN FEAST IS COMPLETE WITHOUT A RED WINE. THE LA MOZZA I PERAZZI MORELLINO DE SCANSANO IS ANOTHER WONDERFUL OFFERING FROM THE SAME BASTIANICH ESTATE. MADE PRIMARILY FROM SANGIOVESE GRAPES, IT EXHIBITS A GREAT ACIDITY WITH A NICE LONG FINISH, MAKING IT A GOOD WINE TO DRINK WITH FOOD. IT IS POWERFUL AND COMPLEX BUT NOT OVERLY HEAVY WITH FLAVORS OF CHERRY AND STRAWBERRY. IT STANDS UP WELL TO IDIE'S HOMEMADE SPAGHETTI AND MEATBALLS OR THE TUNA MARINARA WITH RIGATONI. WE ARE FOND OF BOTH SELECTIONS AND OFTEN SERVE THEM WITH PRIDE AT OUR CHRISTMAS TABLE.

Idie's Homemade Spaghetti and Meatballs

THIS IS A RECIPE PASSED DOWN TO IDIE FROM HER DAD AND IT HAS BECOME A HASTINGS FAMILY FAVORITE. THE DISH APPEARS EVERY CHRISTMAS EVE AND AT VARIOUS TIMES THROUGHOUT THE COOLER MONTHS OF THE YEAR. IT BECOMES A HEARTY MEAL WHEN PAIRED WITH A CRUSTY LOAF OF BREAD AND A GREEN SALAD. THE SECRET IS TO SPEND AN ENTIRE AFTERNOON SIMMERING AND SKIMMING THE SAUCE. BUON APPETITO!

YIELD: 8 TO 10 SERVINGS

½ CUP OLIVE OIL

8 BONE-IN PORK SPARERIBS, ABOUT 2 POUNDS

1 TEASPOON KOSHER SALT

2 TEASPOONS FRESHLY GROUND BLACK PEPPER, DIVIDED

8 FRESH MILD SWEET ITALIAN SAUSAGE LINKS, ABOUT 2¼ POUNDS

30 LARGE 1-INCH HOMEMADE MEATBALLS (PAGE 375)

1 (6-OUNCE) CAN TOMATO PASTE

6 (15-OUNCE) CAN TOMATO SAUCE, PREFERABLY AN IMPORTED ITALIAN BRAND

1 BAY LEAF

1 TABLESPOON DRIED OREGANO

1½ POUNDS SPAGHETTI OR RIGATONI, COOKED UNTIL FORK TENDER (AL DENTE)

1 CUP GRATED PECORINO ROMANO CHEESE, FOR SERVING

Heat the olive oil in a large Dutch oven over medium-high heat. Season the ribs on all sides with the salt and 1 teaspoon of the pepper. Cook the ribs, in batches, in the hot oil until well browned on all sides, 8 to 10 minutes. Remove the ribs from the pan as they brown and set aside on a rimmed baking sheet. Add the sausages, in batches, to the pan and cook until well browned on all sides, about 10 minutes per batch. Transfer the sausage to the rimmed baking sheet. Add the meatballs to the pan and cook until well browned on all sides, about 10 minutes.

Leave the browned meatballs in the pan and drain off the excess oil, leaving about ¼ cup of the oil in the pan. Add the tomato paste and cook, stirring constantly, for 2 to 3 minutes. Add the tomato sauce, bay leaf, oregano, and remaining teaspoon of pepper. Return the browned ribs and sausages to the pan and bring the mixture to a boil. Reduce the heat to medium low and simmer for at least 2½ hours or until the ribs are tender and the sauce has cooked down. While the sauce is simmering, skim off and discard any fat that rises to the top of the sauce.

Remove the sausages, meatballs, and ribs from the sauce with a slotted spoon or tongs. Remove and discard the bay leaf. Add the cooked pasta to the tomato sauce and toss until well coated. Spoon the pasta and tomato sauce into eight wide pasta bowls. Arrange one sausage link, one rib, and three to four meatballs onto each serving of pasta. Grate 2 tablespoons of the cheese over each portion and serve immediately.

Cousin Joe's Cheese Pizza

Idie's Aunt Mary made this pizza every Christmas. Today, her cousin Joe has taken over the job and has incorporated the use of his outdoor Italian brick pizza oven. Feel free to adapt this recipe to include a variety of topping variations such as fresh basil, goat cheese, mushrooms, sun-dried tomatoes, or your favorite pizza topping.

YIELD: 2 (12-INCH) ROUND PIZZAS

DOUGH:

2¼ teaspoons dry yeast

1¼ cups plus 2 tablespoons warm water (100°F to 110°F)

1 tablespoon honey

2 cups high-gluten flour

1¾ cups all-purpose flour plus more for flouring the work surface

¼ cup finely ground yellow cornmeal

1 teaspoon finely ground sea salt

2 tablespoons extra-virgin olive oil

SAUCE:

½ cup extra-virgin olive oil

2 tablespoons unsalted butter

1 cup finely chopped onion

½ teaspoon granulated sugar

1 (28-ounce) can whole peeled tomatoes

1 (10-ounce) can tomato purée

1 (10-ounce) can tomato sauce

½ teaspoon kosher salt

½ teaspoon freshly ground black pepper

PIZZA TOPPINGS:

4 ounces fontina cheese, freshly grated

4 ounces mozzarella cheese, freshly grated

4 ounces Pecorino-Romano cheese, freshly grated

To Prepare the Dough:

Dissolve the yeast in the warm water in a large bowl. Add the honey and let stand for 5 to 10 minutes or until the mixture begins to foam. Meanwhile, stir together the high-gluten flour, all-purpose flour, cornmeal, and salt to the yeast mixture. Add the yeast mixture and stir until a soft dough forms. Turn the dough out onto a lightly floured surface and knead for 5 minutes, adding additional flour, as needed, to prevent the dough from sticking to your hands.

Place the dough in a large bowl coated with the olive oil, turning to coat the dough. Cover and allow the dough to rise in a warm place (85°F), free from drafts, for 1½ hours or until doubled in size.

To Prepare the Sauce:

Heat the olive oil and butter in a heavy saucepan over medium heat. Add the onion and sugar and cook, stirring occasionally, until well caramelized, about 15 minutes. Add the whole tomatoes and their juices, crushing the tomatoes by hand as they are added to the onion mixture. Stir in the tomato purée, tomato sauce, salt and pepper and bring the mixture to a boil; reduce the heat to medium-low and simmer, stirring occasionally, for 1½ to 2 hours.

To Prepare the Pizza:

Preheat the oven to 425°F. If using a pizza stone, place in the oven while preheating.

Punch down the risen dough and divide into two equal portions. Arrange one portion on a lightly floured surface and roll or press gently into a 12-inch circle. Place the dough onto a perforated pizza pan or a large round baking sheet. Spread half of the sauce (about 1¼ cups) over the surface of the dough, leaving a ½-inch edge. Sprinkle half of each type of cheese over the sauce. Place the pizza in the oven and bake for 12 to 15 minutes or until lightly browned. Remove from the oven and cool for 5 minutes before slicing. Repeat with remaining dough, sauce, and cheese. Slice pizza into wedges and serve hot.

Oven-Roasted Italian Sausages

IF YOU DON'T HAVE TIME TO MAKE YOUR OWN ITALIAN SAUSAGE, WE RECOMMEND FINDING A GREAT BUTCHER OR ITALIAN MARKET TO PURCHASE ONES ALREADY PREPARED. ITALIAN SAUSAGE IS HEAVILY SPICED WITH FENNEL SEED AND GARLIC AND CAN BE PURCHASED EITHER SWEET OR HOT. WE TYPICALLY SERVE THE SWEET VARIETY GRILLED ON WARM ITALIAN ROLLS IN THE SUMMER AND USE IT IN SAUCES OR BRAISES IN THE WINTER MONTHS. WHILE THESE SAUSAGES CAN BE PREPARED IN A VARIETY OF WAYS, THE OVEN METHOD IS GREAT FOR WINTER MONTHS WHEN IT MAY BE TOO CHILLY TO GRILL OUTDOORS.

YIELD: 8 TO 10 SERVINGS
3 TABLESPOONS OLIVE OIL
2½ POUNDS MILD OR HOT ITALIAN SAUSAGES IN THE CASINGS, ABOUT 10 LINKS

Preheat the oven to 375°F.

Heat the olive oil in a large ovenproof skillet over medium heat just until smoking. Add the sausage links and cook about 4 minutes or until brown. Turn the sausages and place the skillet in the oven. Bake the sausages at 375°F for 10 to 12 minutes or until well browned on both sides and cooked through. Remove the sausages from the oven and set aside to cool for about 10 minutes. Serve warm.

Sautéed Rapini

RAPINI, ALSO CALLED BROCCOLI RABE, HAS TINY BROCCOLILIKE BUDS NESTLED IN BETWEEN LARGER, SLIGHTLY BITTER LEAVES. WHILE THIS VEGETABLE CAN BE PUNGENT, SAUTÉING IT IN RICH OLIVE OIL WITH CRUSHED RED PEPPER FLAKES IS A GREAT BALANCE TO THE BITTERNESS. ITALIANS USE RAPINI OFTEN, AND IDIE'S FAMILY IS FOND OF SERVING IT SAUTÉED, GRILLED, FRIED, OR BRAISED.

YIELD: 6 SERVINGS
3 (10-OUNCE) BUNCHES FRESH RAPINI, ENDS TRIMMED
½ CUP EXTRA-VIRGIN OLIVE OIL
¼ CUP PLUS 1 TABLESPOON PEELED AND THINLY SLICED FRESH GARLIC
¾ TEASPOON CRUSHED RED PEPPER FLAKES
½ TEASPOON KOSHER SALT

Bring a large pot of salted water to a boil over high heat. Prepare a cold water bath by filling a large bowl halfway with ice and water.

Add the rapini to the boiling water and cook for 1 minute or until bright green and tender. Remove the rapini with a slotted spoon and immediately plunge into the water bath. Stir gently until the rapini is cool to the touch, then drain and pat dry.

Heat the olive oil, garlic, and red pepper flakes in a large skillet over low heat until the garlic begins to turn a golden brown, 3 to 4 minutes. Add the rapini and salt and cook, stirring frequently, until tender, 3 to 4 minutes. Remove from the heat, season with additional salt, if needed, and serve immediately.

Fried Cauliflower (Cavolfiore Fritto)

This is a great alternative to steamed cauliflower and a wonderful vegetarian offering, seasoned with oregano, parsley, and Parmesan.

YIELD: ABOUT 24 PIECES OR 8 TO 10 SERVINGS

1 (2-pound) cauliflower head, trimmed and cut into
    1½ to 2-inch florets
2 quarts peanut oil, for frying
½ cup all-purpose flour
1¼ teaspoons kosher salt, divided
2 large eggs
1 large egg white
¾ cup dry plain breadcrumbs
2 tablespoons chopped fresh parsley
½ teaspoon dried oregano
¼ teaspoon freshly ground black pepper
½ cup finely grated Parmesan cheese

Fill a medium saucepan with water and kosher salt to taste and bring to a boil. Add the cauliflower and cook 5 to 7 minutes or until barely tender. Drain the cauliflower and cool completely. Pat the cauliflower dry, if needed.

Pour the oil into a deep-sided skillet to a depth of 3 inches. (Alternately, a deep fryer can be filled with peanut oil.) Preheat the oil to 350°F.

Combine the flour and ½ teaspoon of the salt in a small bowl. Whisk together the eggs and egg white in a separate small bowl. Combine the breadcrumbs, parsley, oregano, pepper, and the remaining ¾ teaspoon of salt in a medium mixing bowl. Dredge the cauliflower into the flour mixture, then dip in the egg mixture, and dredge in the breadcrumb mixture until well coated.

Fry the breaded cauliflower, in batches, in the hot oil for 1½ minutes or until golden brown. Transfer the cauliflower to a paper towel–lined plate to drain. Sprinkle the cheese immediately over the hot cauliflower and season with additional salt, if needed. Serve hot.

Tuna Marinara with Rigatoni

Use fresh or oil-packed canned tuna for this dish. We have made it both ways at the restaurant with great results, but fresh tuna is the ideal. Crushed red pepper flakes give the marinara just enough heat. If you like fish and pasta, give this entrée a try. It is quick and easy to make.

YIELD: 4 TO 6 SERVINGS

¼ cup plus 2 tablespoons extra-virgin olive oil, divided
2 (6-ounce) center-cut tuna loin steaks
1½ teaspoons kosher salt, divided
¾ teaspoon freshly ground black pepper, divided
¾ cup julienned onions
¼ cup peeled and thinly sliced fresh garlic, about 5 large cloves
¼ teaspoon crushed red pepper flakes
1 (28-ounce) can crushed tomatoes (such as San Marzano brand)
¼ teaspoon dried oregano
¼ cup drained capers, roughly chopped
¼ cup chopped fresh parsley
1 pound cooked rigatoni or spaghetti pasta

Heat ¼ cup of the extra-virgin olive oil in a medium saucepan over medium-high heat. Season the tuna steaks on all sides with 1¼ teaspoons of the salt and ½ teaspoon of the pepper. Add the tuna to the hot oil and sear on all sides until cooked through, 10 to 12 minutes. Remove the tuna from the saucepan and set aside.

Reduce the heat to medium and add the onions to the oil. Cook, stirring occasionally, for 5 minutes or until softened. Add the garlic and red pepper flakes and cook 4 minutes, stirring frequently, but being careful not to let the garlic burn. Return the seared tuna to the pan and break into large chunks with the back of a wooden spoon. Stir until the tuna flakes are well coated with the oil mixture, about 2 minutes. Add the crushed tomatoes, oregano, capers, and remaining ¼ teaspoon of salt and ¼ teaspoon of pepper and bring to a boil. Reduce the heat to medium low and simmer for 15 to 20 minutes, stirring occasionally. Remove the sauce from the heat and stir in the parsley. Toss the sauce with the cooked rigatoni and serve immediately.

Breaded Fried Shrimp with Cocktail Sauce

The secret to this recipe is the Pecorino Romano cheese, a hard grating cheese made from sheep's milk. Pecorino has a hard, yellowish rind and pale interior with a somewhat sharper flavor than Parmesan. You can substitute Pecorino for Parmesan in most recipes. The cheese gives the breading for the shrimp just the bite it needs. When testing this recipe, we could not make enough for the cooks in the kitchen. These shrimp make a great hors d'oeuvre.

YIELD: ABOUT 20 PIECES OR 4 SERVINGS

COCKTAIL SAUCE:

1 cup ketchup

1 tablespoon extra-hot prepared horseradish

1 teaspoon grated lemon zest

SHRIMP:

1 quart peanut oil, for frying

¾ cup plain dry breadcrumbs

2 tablespoons chopped fresh parsley

2 tablespoons ground Pecorino Romano cheese

1 teaspoon chopped fresh thyme

¾ teaspoon kosher salt

½ teaspoon freshly ground black pepper

2 large eggs

1 pound large (21 to 30 count) tail-on, deveined shrimp

To Prepare the Cocktail Sauce:

Whisk together the ketchup, horseradish, and lemon zest in a small glass or stainless steel bowl. Refrigerate until well chilled, about 30 minutes.

To Prepare the Shrimp:

Pour the peanut oil into a deep-sided skillet to a depth of 2 inches. (Alternately, a deep fryer can be filled with peanut oil.) Preheat the oil to 350°F.

Combine the breadcrumbs, parsley, cheese, thyme, salt, and pepper in a medium bowl. Place the eggs in a separate bowl and whisk until well beaten. Dip the shrimp into the beaten eggs and dredge in the breadcrumbs. Fry the shrimp in batches in the hot oil for 1½ minutes or until golden brown and cooked through. Transfer the shrimp to a paper towel–lined plate to drain. Serve hot with chilled cocktail sauce for dipping.

Basket of Fried Greens
(Celery Fritters)

TYPICALLY, COOKS WILL DISCARD THE TENDER GREEN LEAVES OF CELERY STALKS. THIS RECIPE USES ALL THE LEAVES, ROUGHLY CHOPPED. IT IS A GREAT WAY TO GET YOUR "GREENS" AND UTILIZE CELERY IN A NEW WAY. THIS IS A GREAT VEGETARIAN DISH FOR SNACKING.

YIELD: ABOUT 14 CAKES OR 8 TO 10 SERVINGS

3½ CUPS WASHED AND DRIED CELERY LEAVES, ROUGHLY CHOPPED, ABOUT 4 BUNCHES
2 (10-OUNCE) BOXES FROZEN CHOPPED SPINACH, THAWED AND WELL DRAINED
1½ TEASPOONS MINCED FRESH GARLIC
1 CUP ALL-PURPOSE FLOUR
¾ CUP GROUND PECORINO ROMANO CHEESE
¾ TEASPOON KOSHER SALT
¾ TEASPOON FRESHLY GROUND BLACK PEPPER
1 TEASPOON DRIED OREGANO
2 LARGE EGGS, LIGHTLY BEATEN
¼ CUP WATER
1 CUP PEANUT OIL, FOR FRYING

Stir together the first eight ingredients (celery leaves through oregano) in a medium bowl. Add the eggs and water and stir until a batter forms, about the consistency of pancake batter.

Heat the peanut oil in a 10-inch cast-iron skillet over medium-high heat. When the oil is hot (360°F to 375°F), spoon the batter, in batches, into the hot oil, using 2 rounded tablespoonfuls per cake. Cook the cakes for 1½ to 2 minutes on each side or until golden brown and cooked through. Transfer the cakes to a paper towel–lined plate to drain. Serve hot.

Cranberry and Pistachio Torrone (Nougat)

This candy transports Idie back to her childhood and excursions to Zanoni's grocery store in Cleveland where she looked forward to this sweet treat. The crunchy and chewy texture of this nougat of dried fruit and nuts flavored with lemon and vanilla will have you reaching for another. This candy is traditionally served during the holidays in Italy, but can be found year-round in most Italian food shops.

YIELD: ABOUT 16 TO 20 SQUARES

Confectionary rice paper, an edible paper found in
    specialty bakery stores
1 egg white
¼ teaspoon grated lemon zest
¼ teaspoon pure vanilla extract
2 cups confectioners' sugar
1 teaspoon liquid glucose, found in specialty bakery
    or cake decorating stores
2 tablespoons honey
2 tablespoons water
½ cup toasted shelled pistachios
½ cup dried cranberries

Line the sides and base of a 6 x 6 x 2-inch baking pan with parchment paper. Cut 2 pieces of rice paper that will fit inside the base of the baking pan. Arrange one of the pieces of rice paper in the bottom of the baking pan, on top of the parchment paper. Whisk the egg white in a heat-proof bowl until stiff. Whisk in the lemon zest and vanilla. Set aside.

Combine the confectioners' sugar, glucose, honey, and water in a small saucepan. Stir over very low heat until the mixture reaches the soft-crack stage, or 275°F on a candy thermometer. Remove from the heat. While whisking the egg white mixture constantly, slowly drizzle the hot syrup into the egg white mixture. Stir in the pistachios and cranberries and continue whisking until the mixture begins to turn glossy and stiffen.

Spread the mixture over the rice paper in the prepared pan, pressing it down well. Cover with another layer of rice paper, and place a weight, such as one or two bags of dried beans, lightly and evenly on the top. Set aside to cool completely. When cool, cut into squares and place the candy on a parchment-lined baking sheet. Wrap tightly in plastic wrap or store in an airtight container.

Sweet Italian Cookies with Lemon Glaze

IDIE'S GRANDMA MORANO AND NOW HER COUSIN PATTY MAKE THESE COOKIES EVERY YEAR FOR THE HOLIDAYS. AT THE RESTAURANT WE SERVE THEM AS AN ACCOMPANIMENT TO A CUP OF COFFEE IN THE COOL WINTER MONTHS. THE SMALL ROUND SIZE OF THIS COOKIE IS THE PERFECT FINISH TO A HEAVY MEAL IF YOU ARE YEARNING FOR SOMETHING SWEET TO ENJOY WITH YOUR COFFEE.

YIELD: ABOUT 3 DOZEN

COOKIES:

3 CUPS ALL-PURPOSE FLOUR, DIVIDED
½ CUP GRANULATED SUGAR
1 TABLESPOON BAKING POWDER
1 TABLESPOON FRESHLY GRATED ORANGE ZEST, ABOUT 1 ORANGE
3 LARGE EGGS
½ CUP VEGETABLE OIL
1 TABLESPOON PURE VANILLA EXTRACT

GLAZE:

¾ CUP CONFECTIONERS' SUGAR
1 TO 2 TABLESPOONS FRESH LEMON JUICE

TO PREPARE THE COOKIES:

Sift together 2 cups of the flour, the sugar, and baking powder into a large bowl. Stir in the orange zest. In a separate bowl, whisk together the eggs, vegetable oil, and vanilla. Make a well in the center of the flour mixture and gradually add the egg mixture to the flour mixture, until it is fully incorporated.

Sprinkle ½ cup of the flour on a clean work surface. Place the dough on the work surface and gently fold and knead the dough until all of the flour has been incorporated. Use the remaining ½ cup of flour on the work surface as needed to keep the dough from sticking. This recipe yields a soft, pliable dough that should hold its shape when rolled.

Preheat the oven to 375°F.

Divide the dough into six equal portions. Roll each portion into 22-inch-long logs. Cut the logs into 3-inch segments. Gently roll each segment into an even log, about ¼ inch thick. Close and pinch the edges to form small circle shapes.

Place the cookies on an ungreased baking sheet and bake until lightly golden and the bottoms are brown, 10 to 12 minutes. Transfer the cookies to a cooling rack and cool to room temperature.

TO PREPARE THE GLAZE:

Whisk together the confectioners' sugar and lemon juice in a small bowl. Drizzle the glaze over cooled cookies. The cookies can be served immediately or stored in an airtight container for up to 5 days.

CHAPTER 5

JANUARY
&
FEBRUARY

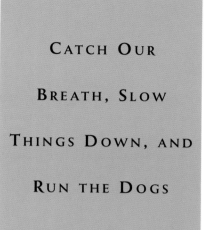

THE LONG HOLIDAY SEASON IS BEHIND US AND WE MOVE IN SLOW MOTION. LUCKILY, THE FRENZY OF THE HOLIDAYS IS FOLLOWED BY A SUBTLE LULL AT THE RESTAURANT AND AT HOME. IT SEEMS TO BE THAT WAY FOR OUR CHILDREN, TOO. THERE IS A COLLECTIVE SHIFT FROM HIGH GEAR INTO LOW. WE FIND OURSELVES COOKING DIFFERENTLY, THINKING DIFFERENTLY, AND SLOWING DOWN AT EVERY OPPORTUNITY AS A WAY TO SIMPLIFY OUR LIVES. THIS SHIFT IS REFLECTED IN THE CUISINE AT HOT AND HOT AND IN OUR HOME KITCHEN. COMFORT IS SOUGHT IN THE EASE OF ONE-POT DISHES LIKE A CHICKEN NOODLE OR OXTAIL SOUP, A BRAISED LAMB SHANK WITH ORECCHIETTE PASTA, OR CREAMED BOBWHITE QUAIL OVER RICE SERVED "OLD SCHOOL." BOBWHITE QUAIL WAS A TRADITIONAL SOUTHERN DISH SERVED IN HOMES BACK WHEN A MAN COULD WALK ANY FENCE AROUND A SMALL FARM AND SHOOT ENOUGH QUAIL OVER HIS OWN DOG FOR A RESPECTABLE DINNER. WE FIND SOLACE IN THESE HEARTY SOUPS, STEWS, AND BRAISES.

This time of year allows us to escape to the outdoors with our kids, friends, and bird dogs (English setters). Whether we're quail hunting on horseback on big tracts of land in northern Alabama or duck hunting in flooded timber or rice paddies with John Vawter and his boys, John Edward and Patrick, in Mississippi, we reconnect and wind down. And, of course, we end up at the table. The act of sitting down with friends over a great meal while bragging about our dogs, taking stock of our good fortune, and passing along to our children the value of our traditions, land, resources, and importance of conservation is what we call "memory cuisine."

What is memory cuisine? Most of us have family traditions —any number of events with family and friends and food—that prove profound. We both had many of these formative events as children. Chris' experiences made him the man, chef, and father he is. Idie's rich Italian heritage and large family gatherings left an indelible mark on her. Our respective childhoods were so rich with these experiences that we believe they formed us—our characters—in many ways. Unfortunately, for many families, such events

are rare in these busy times. Yet we strongly believe that occasions culminating in food set our compasses and solidified who we are and where we came from. These experiences fed the soul.

Another tradition this time of year is to bring together the staff of Hot and Hot Fish Club for a huge crawfish boil and Super Bowl party to show appreciation for all of their hard work. Each staffer brings a potluck dish for what, you might imagine, turns out to be a most amazing buffet. This "coming-together" of our restaurant family is both a time to reflect upon the year gone by and an occasion to regroup, and set our sights on the months to come.

In no time, those "months to come" are upon us. We gauge their arrival less by the calendar and more by the kitchen door. A purveyor such as Margaret Evans appears with a first harvest of the fleeting crop of wild watercress from local limestone springs sometime during the final weeks of February. When it appears (for perhaps two short months at best), we celebrate it by weaving it into the dishes on the menu such as Grilled Quail on Local Cress Salad with Blood Oranges. It is a first hint that spring is near.

GINGER
MARTINI

When Chris Bennett of Hollow Spring Farm brought us aromatic, wild ginger from his farm we knew we had to create something special. We experimented with a variety of dishes and came up with this refreshing cocktail. The wild ginger delivers enough spiciness to warm your bones on a chilly night, yet the drink is light enough to serve at an outdoor spring gathering.

YIELD: 1 SERVING

¼ cup Tanqueray Rangpur or other lime-infused gin
2 tablespoons Cointreau or other orange-flavored liqueur
1½ tablespoons Ginger Simple Syrup (page 362)
1 piece candied ginger, for garnish

Chill a martini glass for at least 20 minutes before serving. Combine gin, Cointreau, and simple syrup in a martini shaker filled halfway with ice. Shake until well chilled. Strain into a martini glass and drop the candied ginger into the bottom of the glass. Serve immediately.

HONEY TANGERINE
MOJITO

Honey tangerines are a type of tangerine named for their high sugar content. If you have never tasted a honey tangerine, find one. They are available in most large supermarkets between January and April. After sampling the fruit *au naturel*, try this recipe.

YIELD: 1 SERVING

8 fresh mint leaves
¼ cup light rum
2 tablespoons Mint Simple Syrup (page 362)
6 tablespoons freshly squeezed honey tangerine juice, chilled, about 2 small tangerines
2 tablespoons fresh lime juice
1 lime wedge, for garnish
1 fresh mint sprig, for garnish

Fill a martini shaker one-third full with ice. Tear mint leaves and add them to the shaker; muddle until mint is bruised and fragrant, about 1 minute. Add rum, simple syrup, honey tangerine juice, and lime juice. Shake until mixture is well chilled.

Strain mixture into 1 (12-ounce) Collins glass filled with ice. Garnish with a lime wedge and fresh mint sprig and serve immediately.

IDA MAE'S HOMEMADE CHICKEN NOODLE SOUP

IDIE (OFFICIALLY IDA MAE), CLAIMS THAT THE KEYS TO THIS FLAVOR-FUL SOUP ARE LOVE AND ATTENTION. SHE DOESN'T LIKE TO COVER HER SOUPS; INSTEAD, SHE SETS THEM ON A LOW SIMMER AND SKIMS THE TOP EVERY FIFTEEN TO TWENTY MINUTES. TENDING TO THIS SOUP IS ONE OF HER FAVORITE WAYS TO SPEND A CHILLY SUNDAY AFTERNOON. FOR A COMPLETE MEAL, ADD A SIMPLE GREEN SALAD AND A CRUSTY BAGUETTE. THIS SOUP ALSO FREEZES WELL; JUST FREEZE THE BROTH, VEGETABLES, AND CHICKEN WITHOUT ADDING THE PASTA.

YIELD: 5 QUARTS OR ABOUT 10 SERVINGS

- **5 TO 6 LARGE CELERY STALKS, INCLUDING LEAVES, SLICED DIAGONALLY INTO 1-INCH-THICK PIECES (ABOUT 3 CUPS)**
- **3 LARGE CARROTS, PEELED AND SLICED DIAGONALLY INTO 1-INCH-THICK PIECES (ABOUT 2 CUPS)**
- **1 LARGE ONION, PEELED AND COARSELY CHOPPED (ABOUT 2½ CUPS)**
- **1 (4½ TO 5-POUND) WHOLE ORGANIC CHICKEN, RINSED WITH COLD WATER AND PATTED DRY**
- **5 TO 6 FRESH THYME SPRIGS**
- **2 (8-INCH) FRESH ROSEMARY SPRIGS**
- **1 (32-OUNCE) CONTAINER LOW-SODIUM, ORGANIC CHICKEN BROTH OR CHICKEN STOCK (PAGE 335)**
- **1 (28-OUNCE) CAN WHOLE, PEELED TOMATOES, ROUGHLY CHOPPED**
- **KOSHER SALT, TO TASTE**
- **FRESHLY GROUND BLACK PEPPER, TO TASTE**
- **1 POUND DITALINI OR ORZO PASTA, COOKED _AL DENTE_**

Combine half of the celery, carrots, and onion in a two-gallon stockpot. Add the chicken to the pot and top with the remaining half of celery, carrots, and onions. (The vegetables should be surrounding the chicken.) Add the thyme, rosemary, chicken broth, and tomatoes. Add enough cold water to completely cover the chicken, about 10 cups. Season the broth with ¼ teaspoon each of the salt and pepper.

Bring the soup to a boil over high heat, reduce the heat to low, and simmer slowly for 2 hours, skimming foam off the top every 15 to 20 minutes. After 1 hour, taste the soup, adding more salt and pepper, as needed. After 2 hours, the chicken should be tender and the meat should easily pull away from the bones. Remove the chicken from the soup and set aside to cool slightly for handling, about 15 minutes. Remove the thyme and rosemary sprigs from the broth and discard. Season the broth with salt and pepper, as needed, and cover to keep warm.

Remove and discard the skin from the chicken. Pull the meat off of the bones in large chunks and discard the bones. Place about ½ cup of the chicken in each soup bowl. Add about ½ cup of cooked pasta to each serving. Add 1 to 1½ cups of reserved broth and vegetables to each bowl and serve immediately.

AMERINO JAMES MORANO—
"A WHOLE LOTTA LOVE"

For the last six years of his life, Idie's dad, "Jim" Morano, was a fixture in our lives both at home and at the restaurant. He packed up his worldly possessions while in failing health, leaving behind his brothers and sisters and all he knew in his hometown of Cleveland to move to Birmingham to be near us. Jim was a first-generation Italian-American of Calabrian roots; his parents came from Italy and settled in Clymer, Pennsylvania. His dad worked the coal mines while his mother raised eight children. Jim's father died young, most likely of black lung, and soon afterward his mother—hoping to spare her sons from a similar future and fate—moved the family to an Italian neighborhood in Cleveland. Jim's family lived a simple life, struggling through the Great Depression, yet finding strength in family, the Italian community, and the Catholic Church—St. Rocco's—that served as the cornerstone of the close-knit neighborhood where, eventually, Idie would grow up.

Once in Birmingham, Jim derived similar strength from our family, and from life at the restaurant. In his late seventies, standing proved difficult, but that didn't slow him down. The cooks always had "Prep for Jim" ready in the kitchen.

From ten o'clock every morning until three o'clock in the afternoon, he sat quietly at table number seven in the dining room, completing whatever task he was given—chopping, peeling, or dicing. He might visit with the cooks or lose himself in thought while Idie attended to business in the office. At noon, he joined the cooks for a staff lunch, and then returned to his task.

In the afternoon, Jim and Idie would head home to be there when our boys returned from school. Though busy helping with homework and getting our kids settled, Jim always found time to nurture some magical concoction on the stovetop. He never used a recipe, but loved to dote over chicken noodle or oxtail soup or another old-fashioned one-pot meal. His spaghetti and meatballs were famous. When anyone asked him his secret, he smiled and always responded that his trick was nothing but "a whole lotta love." He truly believed that if you loved on a dish all day long—simmering, skimming, stirring, and giving it lots of attention—it would be good. It always was. Standing side by side at the stove, Jim taught Idie how to dote on the ingredients in the pot. Our family continues to enjoy his bowlfuls of love today.

JIM'S OXTAIL SOUP

IDIE'S FATHER, JIM, MADE THIS SOUP EACH WINTER. ITS AROMA FILLED THE HOUSE BY THE TIME OUR BOYS CAME HOME FROM SCHOOL. THE RECIPE IS A VERY RUSTIC, HOME-STYLE ONE THAT CAN EASILY BE ADAPTED TO FIT YOUR PERSONAL TASTES. WE OCCASIONALLY SUBSTITUTE BEEF SHORT RIBS FOR OXTAIL, AND IDIE LIKES TO ADD FRESH GREEN BEANS ONE HOUR BEFORE THE END OF THE COOK TIME. THIS HAS BEEN A GREAT WAY TO GET OUR KIDS TO EAT GREEN VEGGIES. AT THE RESTAURANT WE SERVE A MORE REFINED VERSION WITH BLANCHED ROOT VEGETABLES AND COOKED BARLEY. AS LONG AS YOU TAKE THE TIME TO SIMMER, SKIM, AND "LOVE" THIS SOUP, WE KNOW YOU WILL BE HAPPY WITH THE RESULTS.

YIELD: ABOUT 10 CUPS OR 6 SERVINGS

5 TO 6 CELERY STALKS, INCLUDING LEAVES, SLICED DIAGONALLY INTO 1-INCH-THICK PIECES (ABOUT 3 CUPS)

3 LARGE CARROTS, PEELED AND SLICED DIAGONALLY INTO 1-INCH-THICK PIECES (ABOUT 2 CUPS)

1 LARGE ONION, PEELED AND ROUGHLY CHOPPED (ABOUT 2½ CUPS)

3 POUNDS BEEF OXTAIL, CUT INTO 3-INCH CROSS SECTIONS

5 TO 6 FRESH THYME SPRIGS

2 (8-INCH) FRESH ROSEMARY SPRIGS

1 (32-OUNCE) CONTAINER LOW-SODIUM, ORGANIC BEEF BROTH OR VEAL STOCK (PAGE 335)

1 (28-OUNCE) CAN PEELED WHOLE TOMATOES, ROUGHLY CHOPPED

KOSHER SALT, TO TASTE

FRESHLY GROUND BLACK PEPPER, TO TASTE

Combine half of the celery, carrots, and onion in a two-gallon stockpot. Add the oxtails to the pot and cover with the remaining celery, carrots, and onion. Add the thyme, rosemary, beef broth, and tomatoes. Add enough cold water to completely cover the mixture, about 1 quart. Season the soup with ¼ teaspoon each of salt and pepper.

Bring the soup to a boil over high heat, reduce the heat to low, and simmer slowly for 3 to 3½ hours, skimming foam off the top every 15 to 20 minutes. After 1 hour, taste the soup, adding more salt and pepper as needed. After 3 to 3½ hours, the meat should be tender and pull easily away from the bones.

Remove the meat from the soup and set aside to cool slightly, about 15 minutes. Remove the thyme and rosemary sprigs and discard . Season the broth with salt and pepper, as needed, and cover.

Pull the meat off of the bones and shred into thin pieces. Place about ¼ cup of meat in each soup bowl. Add 1 to 1½ cups of broth and vegetables to each bowl and serve immediately.

FROMAGERIE BELLE CHÈVRE, ELKMONT, ALABAMA

In north Alabama, in a little town called Elkmont, an award-winning farmstead produces goat cheese that rivals the best French chèvre. Two decades ago real estate executive Liz Parnell could not find the French-style chèvre she loved anywhere in the South. She set out to produce it herself by creating a full-scale factory that could utilize milk from nearby dairies, and thus Fromagerie Belle Chèvre was born. The resulting goat cheese, with its distinctive tang and milkiness, received critical acclaim from the very beginning.

Tasia Malakasis, to whom Liz recently passed the torch of business operations, shares this passion for cheese. Tasia brings years of high-tech marketing experience and culinary training to the company, though she states that nothing needed to change about the original recipe. One could tinker with it, but no two batches are ever exactly the same anyway. It is a perfect example of a product influenced by the seasons. Goats' milk in winter differs from summer's milk, and what a herd eats from one season to the next plays a large role in the flavor profile of the final product.

When using an ingredient as perfect and delicious as this one, the worst thing you can do as a cook is detract from it by mishandling it in your cooking. We might serve the Montrachet-style chèvre "as is" on a salad or mix it with a few fresh herbs and a dollop of crème fraîche to serve warm on a crouton for a soup or salad garnish. On our Hot and Hot cheese plate we pair it with spiced chutney for a contrast.

WINTER DENSITY AND RED STAR BIBB SALAD

with Warm Belle Chèvre Herb Toast

WINTER DENSITY AND RED STAR BIBB ARE VARIETIES OF MORE COMMON GREENS. THE WINTER DENSITY IS A SMALLER, LESS WATERY, SLIGHTLY DARK, AND MORE INTENSELY FLAVORED TYPE OF ROMAINE LETTUCE. THE RED BIBB IS A STURDIER-LEAVED BOSTON BIBB LETTUCE WITH A COMPACT HEAD AND MORE COMPLEX, CRISP FLAVOR THAN ITS STORE-BOUGHT COUSIN. TAKING THE EXTRA TIME TO SOURCE THESE UNCOMMON GREENS MAKES THIS SALAD EXCEPTIONAL, BUT IF THESE SPECIFIC VARIETIES ARE UNAVAILABLE, YOU CAN SUBSTITUTE BABY ROMAINE AND GREEN BIBB LETTUCE WITH DELICIOUS RESULTS.

YIELD: 4 SERVINGS

- 8 (¼-INCH-THICK) SLICES DAY-OLD CIABATTA OR FRENCH BREAD
- 2 TABLESPOONS OLIVE OIL
- 4 OUNCES FRESH BELLE CHÈVRE OR OTHER PLAIN GOAT CHEESE, AT ROOM TEMPERATURE
- ¼ CUP (2 OUNCES) HOMEMADE CRÈME FRAÎCHE (PAGE 352)
- ½ TEASPOON CHOPPED FRESH PARSLEY
- ½ TEASPOON CHOPPED FRESH CHIVES
- ½ TEASPOON CHOPPED FRESH CHERVIL
- ½ TEASPOON CHOPPED FRESH TARRAGON
- ½ TEASPOON FRESHLY GROUND BLACK PEPPER
- 6 OUNCES WINTER DENSITY LETTUCE OR OTHER TYPE OF HEARTY ROMAINE
- 8 OUNCES RED STAR BIBB LETTUCE OR OTHER TYPE OF BIBB LETTUCE
- ¼ TEASPOON KOSHER SALT
- ⅓ CUP GRENACHE VINAIGRETTE (PAGE 344)

Preheat the oven to 350°F.

Arrange ciabatta slices on a baking sheet and brush the tops with the olive oil. Bake for 8 to 10 minutes or until lightly toasted. Set aside.

Stir together the cheese, crème fraîche, parsley, chives, chervil, tarragon, and pepper in a bowl. Spread 1½ tablespoons of the goat cheese mixture on the toasted side of each ciabatta slice. Place the croutons, goat cheese side up, on the baking sheet and bake until the cheese is melted, about 2 minutes.

Combine the lettuces in a large bowl and season with the ¼ teaspoon salt and a pinch of freshly ground black pepper. Drizzle the vinaigrette over the lettuces and toss until well combined. Evenly divide the salad among four plates. Top each serving with two warm goat cheese croutons and serve immediately.

NANTUCKET BAY SCALLOP SEVICHE

SEVICHE IS ONE OF OUR FAVORITE APPETIZERS, BUT NOT NECESSARILY SOMETHING ONE THINKS OF AS KID-PLEAS-ING. CHRIS LEARNED TO LOVE IT WHILE HE WAS A YOUNG BOY. ONE EVENING AT SUNSET, HE CAUGHT A THREE-POUND REDFISH OFF A DOCK ON PAWLEYS ISLAND. BACK AT THE HOUSE, HIS UNCLE JOHN, HAD COME TO VISIT THE FAMILY WITH ALL SORTS OF EXOTIC INGREDIENTS IN TOW, SUCH AS GINGER, WASABI, AND CILANTRO. WHEN CHRIS ARRIVED WITH THE REDFISH, HIS UNCLE JOHN SUGGESTED THEY FILLET IT, SINCE IT WAS SO YOUNG AND BEAUTIFUL, AND THEN MAKE SEVERAL DIFFERENT COLD PREPARATIONS USING THE INGREDIENTS HE'D BROUGHT. THAT NIGHT THE FAMILY TRIED SEVICHE AND SASHIMI FOR THE FIRST TIME. IN THIS QUICK AND SIMPLE RECIPE, WE OCCASIONALLY SWITCH OUT THE BAY SCALLOPS FOR REDFISH OR SNAPPER AND SIMPLY SHORTEN THE MARINATING TIME.

YIELD: 6 SERVINGS

12 OUNCES NANTUCKET BAY SCALLOPS, CLEANED
4 TEASPOONS GRATED LEMON ZEST (FROM **2** LARGE LEMONS)
1 TABLESPOON FRESHLY SQUEEZE LEMON JUICE
1 TABLESPOON GRATED ORANGE ZEST (FROM **1** ORANGE)
3 TABLESPOONS FRESHLY SQUEEZED ORANGE JUICE
½ CUP FRESH CILANTRO LEAVES, FINELY CHOPPED
1 (**1**-OUNCE) JALAPEÑO PEPPER, SEEDED AND DICED
2 TABLESPOONS FINELY DICED RED ONION
½ TEASPOON KOSHER SALT
PINCH OF FRESHLY GROUND BLACK PEPPER

Chill six martini glasses for at least 30 minutes prior to use.

Place the scallops in a medium, stainless steel mixing bowl. Add the remaining ingredients, and stir to combine. Refrigerate the scallop mixture, covered, for 1 hour and 20 minutes, stirring occasionally.

Adjust the seasonings with additional salt, to taste, if necessary. Divide the seviche mixture evenly among the six chilled martini glasses and serve immediately.

OSPREY SEAFOOD

As sous chef at Bradley Ogden's Lark Creek Inn in Larkspur, California, Chris was responsible for purchasing seafood. As a Southerner unfamiliar with the West Coast's offerings, he had to get up to speed quickly. Supplier Michael Weinberg-Lynn at Osprey Seafood helped him get a handle on the area's seafood and its seasonal fluctuations. Through daily conversations the two got to know one another quite well and became friends.

On our days off, we would wander down to the wharf, which wasn't far from our apartment, to visit Michael. Once there, we would pick up fish, talk about fish, and learn as much as possible about the fish and shellfish available in that part of the world. Over the years, we have become quite close to many of our purveyors because what they do is so connected to what we do—it's what keeps our restaurant going.

These days, you'll see items like Nantucket Bay scallops on our menu because Michael also owns Osprey Seafood on the East Coast. That has been great for us, because it gives us access to a much broader array of outstanding seafood. His dedication to both locations is reflected in the quality of the seafood we get from both coasts.

The process by which Michael gets his products to us is pretty amazing. He typically arrives at his office at two or three in the morning and gets on the two-way radio with his boats out on the water to see what they've reeled in. As soon as they catch the fish on their lines, the fishermen lower their core temperature to 35°F at the spine without freezing their flesh. They then keep it at this precise temperature in the hold of the boats. The quick-cooling method keeps the fish pristine, with none of the bruising that a live fish thrashing and flopping around on the deck of the boat would produce. By around six in the morning, our time, Michael will call us to say his boats will dock in four or five hours with salmon, sardines, anchovies, and possibly halibut. We make our picks, and he notes our order.

Once at the dock, our order is packed on ice for transport to the airport. While we are just getting to work in Birmingham, our order is in flight. Arriving that afternoon to a box of Osprey's beautiful fish and shellfish, just plucked from the water that morning, ready to cook and serve to our guests that very night is awesome.

Because of purveyor relationships like those with Michael at Osprey, we succeed. Such relationships are truly the backbone of our business, and our suppliers become a part of our extended family and lives. What they provide us is critical to our restaurant and our way of cooking and eating. Michael is a mentor and friend whose relationship we count on to fill our menu with unparalleled seasonal seafood delicacies.

SALT-CURED ANCHOVIES

OSPREY SEAFOOD SENDS US FRESH WEST COAST ANCHOVIES THAT ARE MILDER THAN THEIR MEDITERRANEAN COUNTERPARTS. FOR THOSE OF YOU WILLING TO SOURCE FRESH ANCHOVIES AND REAP THE BENEFITS, I APPLAUD YOU. EVERY GREAT COOK WHO FILLS HIS OR HER PANTRY WITH GEMS SUCH AS THESE ELEVATES COOKING IN SO MANY WAYS.

YIELD: 1½ POUNDS

1½ POUNDS FRESH ANCHOVIES
5 CUPS COARSE SEA SALT
EXTRA-VIRGIN OLIVE OIL, FOR STORING

Remove the scales from the anchovies by scraping the outside of the anchovies with the back of a pairing knife. Use a paring knife to slice open their bellies and scrape away internal organs. Flatten the open cavity, belly side up. Cut off the head, leaving as much of the flesh as possible. Using the back of the paring knife, scrape from tail to head to dislodge the backbone. Remove and discard the thin backbone (or vertebrae) and bones. (The bones will easily pull up and away from the fillet in one piece.) Rinse the fillets with cold water and pat dry. Repeat with remaining fillets.

Evenly cover the bottom of a 13 x 9-inch glass or stainless steel baking dish with ¼ inch of the salt, about 1 cup. Arrange the anchovy fillets in an even layer on top of the salt. Add another ¼ inch of salt on top of the anchovies. Repeat with remaining anchovies and salt, ending with a layer of salt. Cover the baking dish tightly with plastic wrap and refrigerate for 2 to 4 weeks, tasting the anchovies occasionally, until the perfect amount of saltiness is reached.

When fully cured, wipe the salt off of the anchovy fillets with a clean towel. Place the fillets in a clean stainless steel or glass container and cover completely with a good-quality extra-virgin olive oil. Cover tightly and store in the refrigerator for up to six months. Salt-Cured Anchovies can be used in any recipe that calls for anchovies such as the Rouille (page 340) or the Green Goddess Dressing (page 347).

CRAWFISH RISOTTO
with *Preserved Meyer Lemons*

THIS RECIPE EXEMPLIFIES THE EQUAL IMPORTANCE OF USING GREAT INGREDIENTS AND RESTRAINT TO REACH A PERFECTLY BALANCED DISH. SIMPLE. INTENSE. SATISFYING.

YIELD: 4 SERVINGS

4 CUPS BASIC RISOTTO (PAGE 355)
¼ CUP FINELY DICED LEEKS (WHITE PART ONLY)
1 TO 1½ CUPS SHRIMP STOCK (PAGE 334)
1 TEASPOON KOSHER SALT
¼ TEASPOON FRESHLY GROUND BLACK PEPPER
8 OUNCES (¾ TO 1 CUP) COOKED CRAWFISH TAIL MEAT
2 TABLESPOONS DICED PRESERVED MEYER LEMON RIND (PAGE 351)
1 TABLESPOON PLUS 1 TEASPOON CHOPPED FRESH CHIVES
1 TABLESPOON PLUS 1 TEASPOON CHOPPED FRESH TARRAGON
1 TABLESPOON PLUS 1 TEASPOON CHOPPED FRESH CHERVIL
2 TABLESPOONS UNSALTED BUTTER
½ CUP LOOSELY PACKED MICROGREENS

Place the risotto and leeks in a large saucepan over medium heat and stir with a wooden spoon until warmed through. Slowly add the shrimp stock, ½ cup at a time, stirring until all of the liquid is absorbed. Repeat this process, adding ½ cup after each addition is absorbed, until the rice is creamy and al dente. (You may not need all 1½ cups of stock.)

Season the risotto with the salt and pepper, fold in the crawfish tail meat, and cook for 1 minute or just until heated through. Remove from the heat and stir in the preserved lemon, chives, tarragon, chervil, and butter. Spoon about 1¼ cups of the risotto into 4 shallow bowls and top each with 2 tablespoons of microgreens. Serve immediately.

MICROGREENS

By definition, microgreens are the sprouts of any particular type of vegetable, lettuce, or herb. They have an intense flavor and can add a refreshing punch of flavor to almost any dish. Microgreens can be tossed in a small amount of vinaigrette and served on their own as a salad or sprinkled over the top of a finished dish as a garnish. You can purchase microgreens in the produce section of many specialty grocery stores or they can be ordered through companies like The Chef's Garden or your favorite local chef. Microgreens can also be grown at home in shallow trays and potting soil or other type of moisture retaining medium. Once planted and watered, they can be ready to harvest in seven to fourteen days, depending on the vegetable, temperature, and light.

GRILLED QUAIL

On Local Cress and Blood Orange Salad

On any given February day in Alabama, you can shoot a limit of quail over your own setters, drive a few miles, and harvest the first tangle of wild cress from the many limestone springs. By supper you will be eating like a king. This is a perfect day for outdoorsmen, dog lovers, and foragers alike. Store-bought watercress can be substituted for the wild variety and the quail can be pan roasted if you're not up to firing up the grill after a long day's hunt.

YIELD: 6 SERVINGS

6 (6-OUNCE) SEMI-BONELESS WHOLE QUAIL
¼ CUP OLIVE OIL
1 SMALL GARLIC CLOVE, SMASHED AND PEELED
1½ TEASPOONS CHOPPED FRESH THYME
1½ TEASPOONS CHOPPED FRESH SAGE
1½ TEASPOONS CHOPPED FRESH PARSLEY
1¾ TEASPOONS KOSHER SALT, DIVIDED
1¾ TEASPOONS FRESHLY GROUND BLACK PEPPER, DIVIDED
9 CUPS (6 OUNCES) WILD WATERCRESS, WASHED AND TRIMMED
¼ CUP PLUS 2 TABLESPOONS BLOOD ORANGE VINAIGRETTE (PAGE 344), DIVIDED
36 BLOOD ORANGE SEGMENTS (ABOUT 3 ORANGES)
½ CUP TOASTED AND LIGHTLY SALTED PISTACHIO KERNELS

Clip and discard the last two segments of both wing tips on the quail. Rinse the quail under cold running water and pat dry. Place the quail in a large glass bowl with the olive oil, garlic, thyme, sage, and parsley and toss to coat. Cover and refrigerate for at least two hours or up to overnight.

Preheat the grill to medium-high heat (350°F to 400° F).

Remove the quail from the refrigerator and marinate at room temperature for 20 minutes. Remove the quail from the marinade and season on both sides with 1½ teaspoons of the salt and 1½ teaspoons of the pepper. Place the quail on the grill and cook for 5 to 6 minutes on each side or until golden brown and cooked through. Remove the quail from the grill and set aside to keep warm until ready to serve.

Toss the watercress and ¼ cup of the vinaigrette in a large bowl and season lightly with ¼ teaspoon each of salt and pepper. Divide the watercress evenly among six plates (about 1½ cups per person). Place five to six blood orange segments and 2 tablespoons of the pistachio kernels around each salad. Top each salad with the reserved quail and drizzle with 1 to 2 teaspoons of the remaining vinaigrette. Serve immediately.

DUCK CONFIT AND WARM MUSHROOM SALAD

The "confit" process is an age-old method that predates refrigeration and was used as a form of preserving meat for the winter where it would be stored in root cellars. The method involves salting and curing the meat through a long, slow, thorough cooking in its own rendered fat and storing it in the fat too which keeps the meat from oxidizing. It was this recipe that first inspired us to develop the Hastings Creations All-Purpose Herb Salt that we use in our restaurant. If you don't have our seasoning salt on hand, substitute the same amount of kosher salt.

YIELD: 4 SERVINGS

DUCK CONFIT:

4 (8-ounce) duck leg quarters (thigh and drumstick attached)
¼ cup Hastings Creations All-Purpose Herb Salt (page 381) or kosher salt
2 large garlic cloves, smashed and unpeeled
6 fresh thyme sprigs
1 (5-inch) fresh rosemary sprig
4 cups rendered (melted) duck fat

SALAD:

8 ounces assorted fresh mushrooms, such as chanterelle, oyster, porcini, or black trumpet
2 tablespoons peanut oil
1 tablespoon unsalted butter
2 tablespoons minced shallots
1 teaspoon chopped fresh thyme
8 cups torn frisée lettuce
¼ cup Lemon Dijon Vinaigrette (page 346)
Pinch of kosher salt
¼ teaspoon freshly ground black pepper

To Prepare the Duck Confit:

Season the duck legs liberally on all sides with the salt. Place the duck legs in a container in an even layer, cover, and refrigerate for 1½ hours.

Preheat the oven to 250°F.

Rinse the seasoned duck legs under cold, running water, wiping off as much of the salt as possible. Pat the legs dry with paper towels. Arrange the duck legs, garlic, thyme, and rosemary in a 6-quart saucepan with a tight-fitting lid. Cover the mixture with the duck fat and bring to a simmer over medium heat. Once the fat begins to simmer, cover the saucepan and place in the oven. Braise the legs for 2 to 2 hours and 20 minutes, or until the meat is meltingly tender. At this point, the duck confit can be used immediately or cooled and stored as described below.

Carefully transfer the legs and the liquid fat to a clean container and cool in an ice water bath, stirring occasionally. Remove the garlic, thyme, and rosemary from the braising liquid and store the duck legs covered in the fat in the refrigerator for use as needed. Duck confit will keep refrigerated for up to two weeks (as long as it is stored covered in the braising fat).

To Prepare the Salad:

Increase the oven temperature to 400°F.

Clean the mushrooms and cut into equal sizes; set aside.

Heat the peanut oil in a large cast-iron skillet over medium heat. Just before the oil begins to smoke, add the 4 duck confit leg quarters, skin side down, to the skillet. Cook the duck for 3 to 4 minutes or until the skins are golden brown and crispy. Remove the duck from the skillet and set aside.

Add the butter to the skillet and increase the heat to medium high. Once the butter is melted, add the shallots and cook for 30 seconds to 1 minute. (Be careful not to let the shallots get too brown.) Add the thyme and cleaned mushrooms and cook, stirring occasionally, until the mushrooms are softened, 3 to 4 minutes. Place the crispy duck legs on top of the mushrooms, skin side up, and place the skillet in the oven. Roast the entire mixture for 4 minutes or until the duck is heated through and most of the moisture has evaporated from the mushrooms. Set the pan aside to cool slightly (3 to 4 minutes).

Toss the lettuce with the vinaigrette in a large mixing bowl. Season the salad with the salt and pepper to taste. Arrange 2 cups of the salad on each of four plates. Evenly divide the roasted mushrooms over and around each mound of greens. Place 1 leg of warmed duck confit, skin side up, on each salad and serve immediately.

SEARED NANTUCKET BAY SCALLOPS

with Parsnip Purée and Citrus Sauce

THE NANTUCKET BAY SCALLOPS WE USE ARE FROM OUR FRIEND, MICHAEL WEINBERG-LYNN, WHO OWNS OSPREY SEAFOOD IN THE SAN FRANCISCO BAY AREA AS WELL AS AN EAST COAST OPERATION. WE MET MICHAEL WHEN WE LIVED IN CALIFORNIA AND PUT GREAT TRUST IN HIS INSTINCTS FOR THE HIGHEST-QUALITY SEAFOOD. BUILDING A RELATIONSHIP WITH A GREAT FISHMONGER IN YOUR OWN NEIGHBORHOOD WILL HELP YOU UNDERSTAND THE SEASONAL AVAILABILITY OF FISH AND SHELLFISH FROM YOUR REGION AND BEYOND AND SURELY ENHANCE YOUR MEALS. THOUGH WE NOW LIVE THOUSANDS OF MILES FROM MICHAEL, WE CONTINUE TO COUNT ON HIM AND OSPREY SEAFOOD TO SEND US THE FINEST-QUALITY SEAFOOD AVAILABLE FROM BOTH COASTS.

YIELD: 4 SERVINGS

20 OUNCES NANTUCKET BAY SCALLOPS (BETWEEN 65 AND 80 SMALL SCALLOPS), CLEANED

1¾ TEASPOONS KOSHER SALT, DIVIDED

¾ TEASPOON FRESHLY GROUND BLACK PEPPER

2 TABLESPOONS PEANUT OIL, DIVIDED

5 TABLESPOONS UNSALTED BUTTER, DIVIDED

¼ CUP MINCED SHALLOTS

2 TEASPOONS FINELY CHOPPED FRESH THYME

½ CUP FRESH CITRUS JUICE (SATSUMAS, HONEY TANGERINES, OR CLEMENTINES ALL WORK WELL)

3 CUPS PARSNIP PURÉE (PAGE 369)

2 TEASPOONS CHOPPED FRESH PARSLEY

Pat the scallops dry and season evenly on all sides with 1½ teaspoons of the salt and ½ teaspoon of the pepper.

Heat the peanut oil in a large, heavy skillet over medium-high heat. Just when the oil begins to smoke, add the scallops in a single layer, and cook until golden brown, 1½ to 2 minutes per side. Remove the scallops from the skillet and cover to keep warm until ready to serve.

Return the skillet to medium-high heat. Melt 3 tablespoons of the butter in the skillet and add the shallots and thyme. Cook for 1 minute, being careful not to let the shallots brown. Add the citrus juice and bring the mixture to a boil. Cook the sauce until the citrus juice is reduced by half, 2 to 3 minutes. Remove the skillet from the heat and add the remaining 2 tablespoons of butter, stirring until incorporated. Season the sauce with the remaining ¼ teaspoon of salt and ¼ teaspoon of pepper and stir in the parsley.

Spoon ¾ cup of the parsnip purée on each of four plates. Evenly divide the scallops over each mound of purée. Spoon 1½ tablespoons of the sauce over each plate and serve immediately.

UNCLE JOHNNY'S FISH STEW

For as long as anyone can remember, Chris' Uncle Johnny has made a rendition of his father's fish stew. It was a horrible concoction of tomatoes, rice, fish, and shrimp that was downright putrid by most accounts. Except for the seafood, most every ingredient came from a can. Each year, the family knew when the time had come for Uncle Johnny's fish stew. They had to psych themselves up in order to tough it out. After all, southerners are taught to be polite and respectful to their elders . . . no matter how awful the food. So when asked, "would you like more stew?" the standard answer was always a "no sir, but thank you, it was very good."

That food memory is seared in Chris' mind, but he also knew that a stew of Low-Country seafood could be equally phenomenal if fresh, ripe Southern ingredients at their peak of perfection were combined with the best of the area's seafood. Any good cook or chef who has experienced a cioppino, bouillabaisse, or any of the classic fish stews from around the world understands the enormous possibility of such a humble dish. It is through our travels and culinary experiences that the Hot and Hot restaurant menu goes beyond the purely southern vernacular. We don't offer "Low-Country Fish Stew" on the menu, instead we say "Southern Bouillabaisse" because we've moved so far beyond Uncle Johnny's less-than-mediocre recipe by taking some of those very same ingredients and treating them with an entirely different technique, adopted from the French in this instance.

By applying a different technique to many of those same ingredients, we have created an entirely new dish. Ours is a bouillabaisse rich with traditional Southern ingredients, but by all accounts a classic bouillabaisse in method. To a fish stock we add saffron, garlic, tomato, and fennel. We then add clams, shrimp, hard-shell crab, and fish indigenous to our region. And, like the French, we incorporate a *rouille* (a reddish sauce such as a bouillabaise). A fried soft-shell crab is the exclamation point on the finished dish.

These tweaks yield a finished stew that is neither purely Southern nor classically French. The French would no more serve a fried anything on top of their bouillabaisse. But that fried soft-shell crab elevates our stew to something outstanding and unique. It is through the building and layering of flavors throughout the cooking process that we perfect a distinctive backdrop for the seafood. Nothing is added to the pot haphazardly. While our technique might be complex and involved, the finished stew tastes simple and clean. Chris has tinkered with his Uncle Johnny's barebones fish stew recipe over the years until it has morphed into one of the signature dishes at Hot and Hot.

SOUTHERN BOUILLABAISSE

Having grown up in the salt marsh, Chris understands that fresh seafood is key to a great stew. This Southern Bouillabaisse is Chris' response to that horrible seafood experience that had been passed down in his family. The good news is that the horrible fish stew died with Chris' generation since he has replaced it with this fish stew built upon a classic we all know and love. It is important to start with fresh, good-quality seafood when preparing this dish. If a certain type of seafood is unavailable or not as fresh as it should be, feel free to leave it out or substitute another ingredient. For example, soft-shell crabs and stone crab claws are not always in season at the same time of year. You can prepare this dish with either type of crab without compromising the quality of the finished dish.

YIELD: 12 SERVINGS

SEAFOOD BROTH:

12 head-on large hoppers (or large pink shrimp)

½ pound bay scallops

6 long, thin strips of orange peel, white pith removed

1 small leek, cut in half and sliced into ½-inch-thick pieces

2 small carrots, peeled and roughly chopped (about 1½ cups)

2 celery stalks, roughly chopped

4 Roma tomatoes, crushed

2 large garlic cloves, peeled

2 cups roughly chopped fennel fronds

4 fresh thyme sprigs

2 bay leaves

12 long basil stems, leaves removed

2 quarts Vegetable Stock (page 334)

2 teaspoons toasted and ground Spanish saffron

BOUILLABAISSE:

¼ cup (½ stick) unsalted butter, divided

½ cup extra-virgin olive oil, divided

½ cup minced shallots, about 3 shallots

3 tablespoon finely chopped garlic, about 4 large cloves

8 fresh thyme sprigs

2 cups cored and thinly sliced fennel bulbs, about 1 bulb

2 cups peeled and thinly sliced carrots, about 2 small carrots

2 cups trimmed and diced celery stalks, about ¼-inch thick slices

2 cups halved and sliced leeks, about ½-inch thick pieces

1½ teaspoons kosher salt, divided

½ teaspoon freshly ground black pepper, divided

2 bay leaves

6 long, thin strips orange peel, white pith removed

12 littleneck clams, scrubbed

6 Roma tomatoes, blanched, peeled, seeded and quartered

12 (1-ounce) pieces black grouper fillet

4 large stone crab claws, cracked (optional)

12 mussels, scrubbed

2 tablespoons minced fennel fronds

1 cup finely chopped basil leaves

1 cup finely chopped flat-leaf parsley

6 Fried Soft-Shell Crabs (page 376) (optional)

12 slices grilled sourdough

Rouille (page 340)

To Prepare the Seafood Broth:

Peel the shrimp, leaving the heads and last tail segment intact. Set the shrimp aside to use for the bouillabaisse and reserve the shells. Pick the feet (tough muscle where the scallop attached to the shell) off of the bay scallops, reserve, and set aside the scallops for the bouillabaisse.

Combine the shrimp shells, reserved scallop feet, 6 small strips of orange peel and the next 10 ingredients (leek through vegetable stock) in a large, stainless steel saucepan. Bring the broth to a boil over medium-high heat, reduce the heat to low and simmer the stock for 40 minutes. Strain the broth through a fine-mesh sieve, discarding the solids. Stir in the saffron and set the broth aside until ready to use.

To Prepare the Bouillabaisse:

Heat 2 tablespoons of the butter and 6 tablespoons of the extra-virgin olive oil in a large, heavy-bottomed stainless steel pan over medium heat. Add the shallots, garlic, and thyme and cook, stirring, for 2 minutes; do not allow the vegetables to brown. Stir in the sliced fennel, carrots, celery, and leeks. Season the vegetables with ½ teaspoon of the salt and ¼ teaspoon of the pepper. Add the bay leaves and orange peels and continue cooking for about 5 minutes or until the vegetables are tender.

Add the clams and tomato quarters, cover, and cook for 2 minutes. Stir in the reserved seafood broth, increase the heat to high, cover and cook for 3 more minutes. Stir in the shrimp, grouper pieces, stone crab claws (if using) and mussels, cover, and cook for 1 to 2 more minutes or until the mussels have opened up.

Remove the lid and add the remaining 2 tablespoons of butter, remaining 2 tablespoons of extra-virgin olive oil, fennel fronds, basil, and parsley. Season the liquid with the remaining teaspoon of salt and remaining ¼ teaspoon of pepper.

Arrange the seafood and vegetables attractively in twelve wide soup bowls and ladle about ½ cup of the broth in each bowl (enough to come three-fourths of the way up the sides of the bowls). Top each bowl with ½ fried soft-shell crab (if using) and 1 grilled sourdough crouton smeared with several tablespoons of rouille. Serve immediately.

WADING FOR WATERCRESS

On a bracing early spring day about an hour's drive from Birmingham in Blount County, Margaret Evans parks her car on the side of a winding country road near Limestone Springs. With box in hand, she ducks her way through the tall pines, skirting the brush and low branches of blooming dogwood, budding oak leaf hydrangeas, and young maples. Hers is a pilgrimage for watercress, which is abundant in February and March and, if it's been cool and mild, perhaps through the first part of April. She has repeated this ritual annually since before we opened the restaurant.

We met Margaret when Chris was private chef for the Elton Stephens family, where Margaret continues to work today. In the Stephens' kitchen one day, she told him of a secret spot where wild watercress grew, and then brought in a basket to prove her story. She hasn't stopped since. Racing the calendar, weather, and a fleeting crop, she returns again and again to her favorite foraging spots where icy water bubbles up from the limestone spring, creating shallow pools of crystal-clear, mineral-rich water accented by barnacle-covered rocks and scurrying crawfish . . . and hopefully a mass of vibrant green, dime-size leaves of cress. She pulls it up by hand, long white roots trailing, until her box is full and for as long as these magical springs offer it up.

Varieties of cress, a member of the mustard family, are numerous, but it is watercress that is so prolific here. The goal is to get it young and tender before it bolts into leggy bloom and becomes too peppery for most palates. But when the timing is right and Margaret's huge boxes of watercress arrive at the Hot and Hot door, we celebrate it in every imaginable fashion on our menu until that particular season within the season has passed and our creative process moves on, dictated by the appearance of the next unique ingredient that only a lifetime of searching provides us.

GRILLED BLACK GROUPER ON WINTER VEGETABLE QUINOA

Quinoa (pronounced keen-wa) is an ancient, beadlike grain that is prepared like rice but cooks in half the time. It has a light texture and doesn't become gummy or sticky when cooked, making it an ideal starch to use in salads. We often prepare this meal in the summertime, using fresh produce instead of root vegetables, and serve it with fish or poultry. See page 378 for instructions on roasting vegetables.

YIELD: 6 SERVINGS

6 (6-ounce) black grouper fillets, each about ¾ inch thick
1½ teaspoons peanut oil
1½ teaspoons kosher salt
1½ teaspoons freshly ground black pepper
6 cups cooked quinoa
1 cup peeled and quartered roasted baby beets
1 cup peeled and quartered roasted baby turnips
1 cup peeled and quartered roasted cipollini onions
9 (4-inch-long) baby carrots, roasted, peeled, and halved
½ to ¾ cup Meyer Lemon Vinaigrette (page 346)
2 cups wild watercress

Preheat the grill to high heat (400°F to 450°F).

Brush both sides of the grouper fillets with the peanut oil and season evenly with the salt and pepper. Place the fillets on a hot grill and cook, for 6 to 7 minutes or until the fillet begins to pull away and loosen from the grill rack. Turn and cook an additional 4 to 5 minutes, or until the fillets are golden brown and cooked through. Remove from the heat and keep warm until ready to serve.

Combine the quinoa, beets, turnips, onions, and carrots in a large bowl. Drizzle ⅓ cup to ½ cup of the vinaigrette into the quinoa mixture and toss until lightly moistened. Fold in the watercress and divide evenly among six plates. Place a grouper fillet on each plate and drizzle the remaining vinaigrette over each serving.

MEYER LEMONS

The Meyer lemon season is usually at its peak in January. A hybrid citrus variety from China, Meyer lemons are a cross between a regular lemon and a mandarin orange. They have a sweet, slightly floral flavor that is less acidic than a regular lemon. The complex flavor and higher sugar content of a Meyer lemon makes it ideal to use in desserts, such as the Meyer Lemon Meringue Tarts (page 255), but we also like their flavor in vinaigrettes. To make the most of these slightly expensive lemons, we save the rinds after juicing and make Preserved Meyer Lemons (page 351) that will last long after their season has ended.

OVEN-ROASTED PHEASANT BREAST ON HUNTER-STYLE RISOTTO

THIS RICH, FLAVORFUL RISOTTO IS A COMFORTING DISH AT OUR TABLE AND IS A FORAGER'S DELIGHT. AN ASSORTMENT OF MUSHROOMS ALONG WITH THE SAUTÉED LIVERS AND ROASTED SWEET ONIONS MAKE THIS RISOTTO HEARTY ENOUGH TO STAND ON ITS OWN. IF PHEASANT IS UNAVAILABLE, YOU CAN SERVE THIS WITH CRISPY LEGS OF DUCK CONFIT (PAGE 243) OR ROASTED CHICKEN BREASTS.

YIELD: 6 SERVINGS

PHEASANT:

6 (6-OUNCE) BONELESS PHEASANT BREASTS
2 TEASPOONS KOSHER SALT
1 TEASPOON FRESHLY GROUND BLACK PEPPER
2 TABLESPOONS OLIVE OIL
1½ TABLESPOONS UNSALTED BUTTER

RISOTTO:

3 TABLESPOONS PEANUT OIL
¼ CUP FINELY DICED (¼-INCH) APPLEWOOD SMOKED BACON
2 TABLESPOONS FINELY CHOPPED DUCK OR CHICKEN LIVERS
2 TABLESPOONS FINELY CHOPPED DUCK OR CHICKEN GIBLETS
¼ CUP EQUAL PARTS FINELY DICED CARROTS, CELERY, AND ONIONS (MIREPOIX)
2 TABLESPOONS MINCED SHALLOTS
1/2 TEASPOON CHOPPED FRESH THYME
1 TABLESPOON MINCED GARLIC
2 CUPS ASSORTED WILD MUSHROOMS, SUCH AS SHIITAKE, OYSTER, CHANTERELLE, CREMINI, OR BLACK TRUMPET, CLEANED, STEMS REMOVED, AND ROUGHLY CHOPPED
1 CUP ROASTED, PEELED, AND QUARTERED CIPOLLINI ONIONS (PAGE 378)
3 CUPS BASIC RISOTTO (PAGE 355)
1½ CUPS CHICKEN STOCK (PAGE 335), SIMMERING
1 TABLESPOON SWEET PAPRIKA
2 TEASPOONS SPICY PAPRIKA
2¼ TEASPOONS KOSHER SALT
½ TEASPOON FRESHLY GROUND BLACK PEPPER
¼ CUP (½ STICK) UNSALTED BUTTER, DICED
1 TABLESPOON FRESH LEMON JUICE
BLACK TRUFFLE OIL (OPTIONAL)
6 TO 12 FRIED SAGE LEAVES (PAGE 376)

TO PREPARE THE PHEASANT:

Preheat the oven to 400°F.

Season the pheasant breasts on both sides with the salt and pepper. Heat the olive oil in a large skillet over medium-high heat. Add the pheasant to the hot skillet and sear until lightly browned, about 3 minutes. Turn the pheasants, add the butter, and place the skillet in the oven. Roast until the pheasant breasts are golden brown and cooked through, 7 to 10 minutes. Remove from the oven and cover to keep warm until ready to serve.

TO PREPARE THE RISOTTO:

Heat the oil in a 4-quart saucepan over medium heat. Add the bacon and cook until browned and crispy, about 8 minutes. Increase heat to medium high, add the livers and giblets and cook, stirring, until well browned, about 2 minutes. Add the mirepoix, shallots, and thyme and cook for 1 minute.

Add the garlic, wild mushrooms, and onion quarters and cook, stirring occasionally, until mushrooms are wilted, about 8 minutes. Reduce heat to medium and add the risotto. Stir in the chicken stock, ½ cup at a time, and stir until most of the liquid has been absorbed and the rice is al dente. (You may not need all of the stock.) Season the risotto with both types of paprika, salt, and pepper.

Remove the risotto from the heat and stir in the butter and lemon juice. Spoon about 1¼ cups of the risotto onto six dinner plates. Place 1 pheasant breast on each plate and drizzle each with black truffle oil, if desired. Garnish each plate with 1 or 2 pieces of fried sage and serve immediately.

CREAMED BOBWHITE QUAIL "OLD SCHOOL"
over Carolina Gold Rice

THIS RUSTIC MEAL IS AN ABSOLUTE CROWD PLEASER. IT IS SIMPLE TO PREPARE AND IS OUR FAVORITE WAY TO CLEAN OUT A FREEZER FULL OF QUAIL AFTER A SUCCESSFUL SEASON OF SHOOTING. FEEL FREE TO SUBSTITUTE ANY OF YOUR FAVORITE WILD MUSHROOMS IN PLACE OF THE CREMINI MUSHROOMS.

YIELD: 6 SERVINGS

12 (6-OUNCE) SEMI-BONELESS QUAIL
1 TABLESPOON PLUS 1 TEASPOON KOSHER SALT
2 TEASPOONS FRESHLY GROUND BLACK PEPPER
1 TABLESPOON CHOPPED FRESH THYME
¼ CUP VEGETABLE OIL
½ CUP (1 STICK) UNSALTED BUTTER
1 LARGE LEEK, HALVED AND THINLY SLICED CROSSWISE (ABOUT 2 CUPS)
1 POUND FRESH CREMINI MUSHROOMS, SLICED
2 CUPS CHICKEN STOCK (PAGE 335)
1½ CUPS HEAVY CREAM
2 TABLESPOONS CHOPPED FRESH PARSLEY
6 CUPS COOKED CAROLINA GOLD RICE (PAGE 353)

Rinse the quail under cold, running water and pat dry. Split the quail in half lengthwise and remove the backbones. Season the quail on both sides with the salt, pepper, and half of the thyme.

Heat the oil in a large, deep, cast-iron skillet or Dutch oven over medium-high heat. Add the quail, in batches, to the hot oil and cook until well browned on both sides, 3 to 4 minutes per side. Transfer the browned quail to a platter and set aside. Discard the oil from the skillet. Add the butter to the same skillet and melt over medium-high heat. Add the remaining ½ tablespoon of thyme and the leek to the butter and cook until softened, about 3 minutes. Add the mushrooms and cook an additional 5 minutes, stirring frequently. Add the stock, bring to a simmer, and cook for 3 minutes. Stir in the heavy cream and return the browned quail to the skillet. Bring the mixture to a simmer, reduce the heat, cover, and cook for 25 minutes. Uncover the quail and cook an additional 5 minutes or until the sauce is slightly thickened.

Remove the creamed quail from the heat and stir in the chopped parsley. Place 1 cup of the hot, cooked rice on each of six dinner plates. Spoon four quail halves and some of the sauce over each portion of rice and serve immediately.

BRAISED LAMB SHANKS
with Orecchiette Pasta and Gremolata

BRAISING TAKES TIME AND REQUIRES THAT ATTENTION IS PAID TO EACH STEP OF THE COOKING PROCESS. FOR THIS DISH WE BRAISE THE LAMB SHANKS, COVERED IN A LOW OVEN, SO THAT TIME AND CARE CAN BE APPLIED TO THE REMAINING INGREDIENTS IN THIS DISH. IF YOU TAKE THE TIME TO LEARN HOW TO PROPERLY BRAISE AND BECOME COMFORTABLE WITH THIS TECHNIQUE, WE PROMISE THAT YOU WILL BE REWARDED WITH GREAT RESULTS.

YIELD: 6 TO 8 SERVINGS

4 (16-OUNCE) LAMB SHANKS, TRIMMED
1½ TABLESPOONS KOSHER SALT
1 TABLESPOON FRESHLY GROUND BLACK PEPPER
2 TABLESPOONS PEANUT OIL
¼ CUP PLUS 2 TABLESPOONS UNSALTED BUTTER
4 CUPS COARSELY CHOPPED ONIONS, ABOUT 2 MEDIUM
1 CUP COARSELY CHOPPED LEEK (WHITE PART ONLY), ABOUT 1 SMALL
1½ CUPS COARSELY CHOPPED CARROTS, ABOUT 3 MEDIUM
1½ CUPS COARSELY CHOPPED CELERY, ABOUT 3 STALKS
1 BAY LEAF
1 FRESH ROSEMARY SPRIG
3 LARGE GARLIC CLOVES, SMASHED AND PEELED
3 CUPS SEEDED AND CHOPPED TOMATOES (ONE 32-OUNCE CAN CHOPPED, UNDRAINED TOMATOES CAN BE SUBSTITUTED FOR FRESH TOMATOES)
6 CUPS VEAL STOCK (PAGE 335) OR REDUCED-SODIUM BEEF BROTH
8 CUPS COOKED ORECCHIETTE PASTA, ABOUT 1¼ POUNDS DRIED PASTA
1½ TEASPOONS GRATED ORANGE ZEST, ABOUT 1 ORANGE
½ TEASPOON GRATED LEMON ZEST, ABOUT 1 LEMON
6 TABLESPOONS CHOPPED FRESH PARSLEY
1 TEASPOON CHOPPED FRESH GARLIC

Season the lamb shanks on all sides with the salt and pepper. Heat the peanut oil in a large, heavy Dutch oven over medium-high heat. Add the shanks and cook until well browned on all sides, 10 to 12 minutes. Transfer the shanks to a deep-sided baking dish or roasting pan. Discard oil from the skillet, reduce the heat to medium, and add the butter. Once the butter is melted, add the onions, leeks, carrots, celery, bay leaf, garlic cloves, rosemary, and thyme. Preheat the oven to 300°F.

Cook, stirring often until the vegetables are well caramelized, 8 to 10 minutes. Add the tomatoes and cook 2 to 3 minutes, stirring frequently. Add the stock and bring the mixture to a simmer. Pour the vegetable and stock mixture over the lamb shanks and cover the baking dish tightly with aluminum foil. Braise the shanks for 3 to 3½ hours or until the meat is tender and pulls away easily from the bones.

Transfer the braised lamb shanks to a platter and cover to keep warm. Strain the braising liquid through a fine-meshed strainer or chinois and discard the solids. Pour the strained liquid into a small saucepan and bring to a boil; reduce the heat to medium and allow the sauce to simmer until reduced by half, about 1 hour. Skim off any fat that rises to the top of the braising liquid, as needed.

While the broth is reducing, pick the meat off the braised lamb shanks, discarding the fat and bones. Add the picked meat to the reduced lamb jus and cook just until heated through, about 5 minutes. Add the cooked pasta and stir until warm, 1 to 2 minutes. Remove from the heat and stir in the orange and lemon zest, the parsley and garlic. Serve immediately.

ROASTED PORK LOIN

with Farro, Artichokes and Parmesan

AT THE RESTAURANT AND AT HOME WE ARE ALWAYS LOOKING FOR UNUSUAL INGREDIENTS AND METHODS TO KEEP OUR DISHES INTERESTING AND FLAVORFUL. FARRO IS ANCIENT GRAIN OF WHICH WE HAVE BECOME FANS. SIMILAR IN SIZE TO THE ARBORIO RICE USED IN RISOTTO, FARRO IS TRADITIONALLY COOKED IN A DIFFERENT MANNER. BY COOKING IT LIKE A RISOTTO, WE HAVE FOUND THAT IT BECOMES A WONDERFUL FOIL FOR OTHER INGREDIENTS, LIKE ARTICHOKE, YET WITH A NUTTIER FLAVOR AND MORE DISTINCTIVE TEXTURE THAN CLASSIC RISOTTO. TRY IT . . . WE LOVE IT.

YIELD: 6 SERVINGS

PORK:

3 TABLESPOONS OLIVE OIL

1 (3-POUND) BONELESS PORK LOIN

2 TABLESPOONS HASTINGS CREATIONS ALL-PURPOSE HERB SALT (PAGE **385**) OR KOSHER SALT

1 TABLESPOON FRESHLY GROUND BLACK PEPPER

¼ CUP VEGETABLE OIL

FARRO WITH ARTICHOKES:

2 TABLESPOONS OLIVE OIL

½ CUP MINCED ONION

½ TEASPOON FINELY CHOPPED FRESH THYME

2 CUPS FARRO, PICKED THROUGH

6 CUPS HOT CHICKEN STOCK (PAGE **335**)

1 CUP FINELY DICED (ABOUT **4**) BRAISED ARTICHOKES (PAGE **373**)

1 TEASPOON GRATED LEMON ZEST

1 TEASPOON KOSHER SALT

½ TEASPOON FRESHLY GROUND BLACK PEPPER

1 TABLESPOON UNSALTED BUTTER

½ CUP GRATED PARMESAN CHEESE

1 TABLESPOON CHOPPED FRESH PARSLEY

1 TABLESPOON CHOPPED FRESH CHIVES

TO PREPARE THE PORK:

Preheat the oven to 400°F.

Rub the olive oil over the pork loin and season evenly with the herb salt and black pepper. In a heavy cast-iron skillet, heat the vegetable oil until hot and almost smoking. Add the pork loin and sear on all sides until well browned, about 4 minutes per side. Place the loin on a cooking rack set inside a roasting pan and roast for 20 minutes. Reduce the oven temperature to 325°F and cook for an additional 20 to 30 minutes or until a thermometer inserted into the center of the pork loin registers 160°F. Remove from the oven and let the loin rest for 15 minutes in a warm spot.

TO PREPARE THE FARRO:

Heat the oil in a rondeau or wide saucepan with deep sides over medium heat. Add the onion and thyme and sauté until transparent, without browning, 3 to 4 minutes. Add the farro and stir with a wooden spoon until the grains are coated with oil and slightly toasted, about 2 minutes. Add ½ cup of hot chicken stock to the farro and stir constantly with a wooden spoon until all of the liquid is absorbed. Repeat this process, adding ½ cup of chicken stock each time, until all of the stock has been added and the farro is cooked through, 20 to 25 minutes.

Stir in the diced artichokes, lemon zest, salt, and pepper and cook until heated through, about 1 minute. Remove the farro from the heat and fold in the butter, cheese, parsley, and chives, stirring until the butter is melted.

To serve, slice the pork loin into about 18 slices, each about ½ inch thick. Spoon about ¾ cup of the farro mixture onto each of six dinner plates. Arrange three slices of the pork over each plate and serve immediately.

MEYER LEMON MERINGUE TART

PREPARING A HOMEMADE LEMON CURD LIKE THE ONE USED IN THIS FILLING IS A WONDERFUL WAY TO UTILIZE MEYER LEMONS. FOR THE RESTAURANT WE MAKE THESE INDIVIDUAL TARTS TOPPED WITH A STAR-SHAPED MERINGUE FOR AN IMPRESSIVE DESSERT. IF YOU DON'T HAVE INDIVIDUAL TART PANS, TRY THIS TART IN AN EIGHT-INCH TART OR PIE PAN AND INCREASE THE BAKING TIME FOR THE FILLING BY SEVEN TO TEN MINUTES OR UNTIL IT'S SET.

YIELD: 8 (4-INCH) TARTS OR 8 SERVINGS

CRUST:

3 CUPS STORE-BOUGHT GRAHAM CRACKER CRUMBS
¼ CUP PLUS 2 TABLESPOONS GRANULATED SUGAR
¾ CUP (1½ STICKS) UNSALTED BUTTER, MELTED

FILLING:

3 LARGE EGGS
5 LARGE EGG YOLKS
⅓ CUP PLUS 2 TABLESPOONS GRANULATED SUGAR
¼ TEASPOON SALT
3 TABLESPOONS GRATED MEYER LEMON ZEST
¾ CUP FRESHLY SQUEEZED MEYER LEMON JUICE
¼ CUP PLUS 3 TABLESPOONS UNSALTED BUTTER,
   CUT INTO SMALL PIECES

MERINGUE:

3 LARGE EGG WHITES
⅛ TEASPOON CREAM OF TARTAR
¾ CUP GRANULATED SUGAR

TO PREPARE THE CRUST:

Preheat the oven to 350°F.

Combine the graham cracker crumbs and sugar in a large mixing bowl. Add the melted butter and toss thoroughly until the butter is evenly incorporated. Divide the mixture evenly into 8 (4-inch) fluted tart pans, using about ½ cup of the crumbs per pan. Press the mixture firmly into the sides and bottom of the tart pans.

Arrange the tart pans on a baking sheet and bake for 12 to 15 minutes or until the crusts are lightly browned. Remove from the oven and cool completely.

TO PREPARE THE FILLING:

Combine the eggs, egg yolks, sugar, and salt in a small, non-reactive, heavy saucepan and whisk until well combined, about 1 minute. Stir in the lemon zest, lemon juice, and butter. Cook the mixture over medium heat until it is thick enough to coat a spoon, about 5 to 7 minutes. (Be careful not to allow the mixture to boil or the eggs will curdle.) Transfer the filling into a clean, stainless steel bowl and cover the surface with plastic wrap. Refrigerate the filling until completely cool.

Divide the cooled filling evenly among the eight tart shells, smoothing the tops with a rubber spatula.

TO PREPARE THE MERINGUE:

Increase the oven temperature to 375°F. Fill a medium saucepan one-third of the way with water and bring the water to a boil.

Add the egg whites to the bowl of a standing mixer and whisk on low speed until slightly frothy, 1 to 2 minutes. Add the cream of tartar and continue mixing on low speed, adding the sugar one tablespoon at a time until all of the sugar has been added. Remove the bowl from the mixer and place over the hot water, whisking continually until the sugar has melted and the meringue is warm, 4 to 5 minutes. Return the bowl to the standing mixer and whisk on medium speed until stiff peaks form, 2 to 3 minutes.

Transfer the meringue to a pastry bag fitted with a large star tip. Pipe the meringue into star shapes in a circular pattern on the top of each tart until the tops are entirely covered. Return the tarts to the oven and bake for 10 to 12 minutes or until the tops of the meringue stars are lightly browned and slightly firm to the touch. Serve immediately.

HOT AND HOT DOUGHNUTS

Espresso Cream and Brittle, Banana Bavarian Cream Filled and Chocolate Orange Glazed

WHEN WE FIRST OPENED HOT AND HOT FISH CLUB, WE KNEW WE WANTED TO PREPARE DOUGHNUTS FOR THE DESSERT MENU. WE HAVE ALWAYS ENJOYED DOUGHNUTS AT BRUNCH AND THOUGHT IT WOULD BE A FUN TWIST FOR DESSERT. WHILE THE GARNISHES AND SAUCES MAY BE TIME CONSUMING, THEY PRODUCE A DRAMATIC RESULT. TO SIMPLIFY, PREPARE THE DOUGHNUTS AND FILL THEM WITH THE SAUCE OF YOUR CHOICE OR A HIGH-QUALITY JELLY. THIS IS ONE OF THE FEW DESSERT ITEMS THAT HAVE REMAINED ON OUR RESTAURANT'S DESSERT MENU SINCE WE FIRST OPENED.

YIELD: 16 DOUGHNUTS OR 4 SERVINGS

SPONGE:
¾ OUNCES DRY YEAST
¾ CUP WARM MILK (105°F TO 115°F)
1 CUP BREAD FLOUR

DOUGH:
¾ TEASPOON GRATED LEMON ZEST
¼ CUP GRANULATED SUGAR
1 LARGE EGG
2 LARGE EGG YOLKS
3 TABLESPOONS MELTED BUTTER
1½ CUPS BREAD FLOUR
1 TEASPOON SALT

DOUGHNUT ASSEMBLY:
PEANUT OIL, FOR FRYING
¼ CUP CINNAMON SUGAR (PAGE 367)
¼ CUP VANILLA SUGAR (PAGE 367)
¼ CUP BANANA BAVARIAN CREAM (PAGE 364)
½ CUP ESPRESSO CREAM (PAGE 363)
4 (2-INCH) PIECES ESPRESSO BRITTLE (PAGE 364)
4 (1-INCH) PIECES SUGARED VANILLA BEAN (PAGE 367)
¾ CUP CHOCOLATE ORANGE SAUCE (PAGE 362)
4 DRIED ORANGE SLICES (PAGE 367)

TO PREPARE THE SPONGE:

Stir the yeast into the warm milk and let stand for 10 minutes. Place the flour in a large mixing bowl, add the yeast mixture and stir until the mixture is incorporated. Cover the bowl and place in a warm spot for about 20 minutes. The sponge will double in size.

TO PREPARE THE DOUGH:

Bring a small pot of water to a simmer. Combine the lemon zest, sugar, egg, and egg yolks in a heat-proof bowl, whisking until blended. Place the bowl with the lemon zest mixture over the pot of simmering water and heat, whisking constantly, until the mixture reaches about 110°F. Transfer the egg mixture to the bowl of a standing mixer and whisk until the mixture is slightly thickened, pale yellow, and doubled in size.

Attach a paddle attachment to the standing mixer and add the melted butter, bread flour, salt, and the sponge to the egg mixture. Mix on low until a dough forms; increase the mixer speed to medium and mix for 3 minutes. Transfer the dough to a lightly greased large mixing bowl, cover, and place in a warm place, free from drafts. Allow the dough to rise for 1 hour and 20 minutes. The dough will double in size.

TO PREPARE THE DOUGHNUTS:

Preheat the peanut oil in a deep fryer or in a heavy-bottomed stockpot to 350°F.

Punch down the risen dough and place on a lightly floured surface. Divide the dough into 16 equal pieces. Roll each piece into a ball and place on a lightly greased baking sheet, about 2 inches apart. Cover the baking sheet loosely and place it in a warm place, free from drafts. Allow the dough to rise for 1 hour or until the rolls have doubled in size.

Gently remove the dough from the baking sheet, being careful not to deflate the doughnuts. Place 2 or 3 portions of dough, into the oil, round side down first. Fry for about 45 seconds, gently turn the doughnuts with a slotted spoon, and fry an additional 45 seconds to 1 minute, or until golden brown. Remove the doughnuts with a slotted spoon and drain in a paper towel–lined bowl.

Roll eight of the hot doughnuts in the cinnamon sugar and the remaining four doughnuts in the vanilla sugar. Spoon the banana cream into a squeeze bottle or a pastry bag fitted with a small, round tip. Poke a small hole into the side of the four vanilla sugared doughnuts with the tip of the squeeze bottle or pastry tip until the doughnuts are filled.

Spread 2 tablespoons of the espresso cream in a small circle on each of four large plates. Place 1 of the cinnamon sugared doughnuts on each circle of espresso cream and top with a piece of espresso brittle. Place one Bavarian cream filled doughnut on each plate next to the espresso doughnuts and top each with a small piece of sugared vanilla bean. Place a third doughnut on each plate and cover with 2 to 3 tablespoons of the chocolate orange sauce. Top with a slice of dried orange and serve immediately.

CHOCOLATE DEVIL'S FOOD CAKE

with Vanilla Ice Cream

Pssst . . . The secret is the beets. Trust us; this cake is rich, moist, and sure to please. We adapted the beet technique from Chef Bradley Ogden's chocolate cake recipe at the Lark Creek Inn. It has become our son Vincent's favorite cake for birthdays and special occasions. We like to see if our friends and guests can guess the secret ingredient. There have been no first-time guesses in thirteen years.

YIELD: 1 (9-INCH) ROUND CAKE OR 6 TO 8 SERVINGS

CAKE:

2 cups all-purpose flour

¾ cup unsweetened cocoa powder

1¾ cups granulated sugar

1½ teaspoons baking soda

¾ teaspoon salt

½ teaspoon baking powder

¼ teaspoon freshly ground cardamom seeds

1½ cups buttermilk

3 large eggs

½ teaspoon pure vanilla extract

½ cup Homemade Crème Fraîche (page 352)

½ cup peeled and finely grated raw red beets (about 3 ounces)

¾ cup (1½ sticks) unsalted butter, melted and cooled slightly

FROSTING:

2 cups (4 sticks) unsalted butter, at room temperature

⅔ cup unsweetened cocoa powder

2 (16-ounce) boxes confectioners' sugar

½ cup whole milk

1 teaspoon pure vanilla extract

FOR SERVING:

2 cups large milk chocolate curls (optional)

2⅔ cups Vanilla Ice Cream (page 366)

To Prepare the Cake:

Preheat the oven to 325°F.

Lightly spray the bottom of two 9-inch round cake pans with vegetable oil cooking spray and line with parchment paper. Grease the parchment paper and sides of the pans with softened butter and dust with flour to coat. Tap out any excess flour and then set the pans aside.

Sift together the flour, cocoa powder, sugar, baking soda, salt, baking powder, and cardamom into a large mixing bowl. In a separate bowl, whisk together the buttermilk, eggs, and vanilla. Stir the buttermilk mixture into the flour mixture. Fold in the crème fraîche and grated beets. Add the melted butter and stir just until combined.

Divide the batter evenly between the prepared cake pans. Place the pans in the center of the oven and bake for 35 to 37 minutes or until the sides begin to pull away from the pan and the center is set but soft. Allow the cakes to cool in the pans for 10 minutes. Invert the cakes onto a wire cooling rack and cool completely.

To Prepare the Frosting:

Combine the butter and cocoa powder in the bowl of a standing mixer fitted with a paddle attachment. Whip the butter on low until combined, then increase the speed to medium. Continue mixing until the mixture is smooth and well combined.

With the machine on low, gradually add the confectioners' sugar and milk, alternating until all has been added. You will need to stop the machine occasionally to scrape down the sides while mixing. Add the vanilla and stir just until combined.

To Serve:

Spread 1 tablespoon of the frosting on the bottom of the cake plate and place one of the cake layers, top side down, on the plate. (The frosting will help keep the cake from sliding.) Spread 1 cup of the frosting on top of the cake and top with the second cake layer, top side down. Ice the sides and top of the cake with the remaining frosting. Garnish the top of the cake with chocolate curls, if desired, and serve each piece with a scoop of vanilla ice cream (about ⅓ cup per serving).

CRAWFISH BOIL AND PIG ROAST

After working nonstop from October straight through December at the restaurant, there comes a noticeable downshift in January. Both the restaurant and catering sides of our business have been in high gear all holiday season, so we relish the slower pace. It's the ideal time to bring the staff together and the Super Bowl is the event around which we gather. In addition to our entire staff and their families, our boys invite their friends over to join in the festivities and watch the game.

At this time of year, the crawfish have begun to appear and are really fantastic, so a crawfish boil makes perfect sense. Roasting a whole pig is another tradition we've maintained each year because it is a delicious way to feed a crowd and in many ways a nod to those celebratory feasts you find in so many cultures—whether a lamb at Easter, a goat for a wedding, or a turkey for Thanksgiving. For us, this annual party is an important day to thank everyone for their amazingly hard work all year. Hosting the party outside the restaurant and in our home is really important to us too. We are opening our doors to our extended family.

Like any great feast, the preparations begin days earlier. We set up a makeshift kitchen out in the backyard. Even though they're our guests, our cooks have to get in there and get involved. They simply can't stay away. Typically the cooks will be outside tending to the pig and cooking up the crawfish while kids from the neighborhood run all over the place and adults mingle inside. We all watch the game, eat, and simply hang out. The mood is festive and light. We really look forward to the time we take each year to relax with our staff and connect outside of the frenzy of our workplace. January and the Crawfish Boil and Pig Roast have become that welcome punctuation mark at the end of a busy season.

CRAWFISH, FOOTBALL, BEER, AND BOUDIN WITH THE STAFF AND FRIENDS

CRAWFISH BOIL

———

CAJUN-STYLE BOUDIN SAUSAGE
ROASTED PIG

———

ENDIVE SALAD WITH KUMQUATS
AND PECORINO

———

CHICKEN AND CONECUH COUNTY
SAUSAGE GUMBO

———

GERMAN POTATO SALAD

- BEER PAIRINGS -

ALTHOUGH WE USUALLY PAIR OUR MENUS WITH WINE, WE FEEL THAT THIS MEAL GOES BEST WITH A COLD BEER. A WHEAT-BASED BEER SOFTENS THE SPICINESS OF THE CRAWFISH BOIL, WHILE A PALE ALE IS BEST SERVED WITH OUR GUMBO. ABITA WHEAT BEER (ONLY AVAILABLE FROM JUNE THROUGH SEPTEMBER) MADE BY THE ABITA BREWING COMPANY IS ONE OF OUR FAVORITE, LOCAL WHEAT BEERS. FOR A PALE ALE, TRY ATLANTA BREWING COMPANY'S PEACHTREE PALE ALE WHICH IS STURDIER THAN SOME PALE ALES AND HAS A SLIGHT BITTERNESS WITH NOTES OF CITRUS, OR LOOK FOR A GOOD PALE ALE IN YOUR AREA. WHATEVER YOU CHOOSE, RELAX AND ENJOY YOURSELVES SURROUNDED BY FESTIVE FOOD AND FRIENDS.

Crawfish Boil

The boiling liquid we prepare is super-seasoned so that the intense flavors penetrate into crawfish quickly without overcooking the meat. That's why the soaking time for the crawfish is so short. We always start with live, Louisiana crawfish. If unavailable from your local fish market, try ordering from an online source such as the Louisiana Crawfish Company or the Cajun Grocer (see Sources, page 380).

YIELD: 4 SERVINGS

8 pounds live crawfish
3 lemons, halved
1 orange, halved
2 garlic heads, halved
2 large onions, quartered
5 bay leaves
6 to 8 fresh thyme sprigs
1½ cups plus 2 tablespoons cayenne pepper (about 6 ounces)
2 cups kosher salt (about 19 ounces)
3 (12-ounce) bottles light beer
3 gallons fresh cold water

Fill a large container (an ice chest works well) with fresh cold water and add the crawfish. Allow the crawfish to soak in the water for 30 minutes. Drain the water off the crawfish and refill the container with fresh, cold water. Repeat this process 3 more times to purge any excess mud from the crawfish.

Combine the next 10 ingredients (lemons through water) in a large, 5 or 6 gallon stockpot. Bring the liquid to a boil and allow the mixture to boil hard for 5 minutes.

Add the crawfish to the water and return the water to a boil. Cover and allow the crawfish to boil for 5 minutes, turn off the heat, and steep for 15 minutes. Remove and taste one of the crawfish tails to check the seasonings. If the crawfish are not spicy or salty enough, steep for an additional 5 to 10 minutes. Using a large slotted scoop or basket, remove the crawfish from the liquid and serve immediately.

SIDE DISHES FROM OUR STAFF PARTY

As you can imagine, when a group of restaurant folks get together for a party, the food is going to be amazing. Each year when we host our annual party, our staff signs up to bring side dishes to accompany the crawfish boil and pig roast. It's not only a chance for them to relax and enjoy the game but they also have an opportunity to express their creativity through food. We've enjoyed everything from salads and dips to heartier side dishes such as braised beluga lentils and potato salad, and decadent cakes and pies. Occasionally, we are so excited by a dish that it ends up on our restaurant dinner menu a few weeks later. The German Potato Salad (page 272) is one example of a side dish that is now one of our staple menu items.

Cajun-Style Boudin Sausage

What goes better with a traditional crawfish boil than home-made Cajun-style boudin sausage? The hot sausages can be served as a side dish, but also make a great meal on their own. At the restaurant, we often serve homemade boudin atop braised winter greens with a side of coarse-grain mustard. If you don't have the Hastings Creations Pork Rub, you can still make this dish by substituting any type of salt-free, store-bought pork rub, although the flavors won't be as intense.

YIELD: 10 TO 12 LINKS

1 tablespoon peanut oil
1¼ pounds pork shoulder, cut into 2-inch cubes
½ pound fresh pork liver, rinsed in cold water, pat-
    ted dry and cut into 2-inch cubes
½ cup diced yellow onion
¼ cup seeded and diced poblano pepper
¼ cup diced celery
1 bay leaf
½ teaspoon finely chopped fresh garlic
3½ cups Spicy Ham Hock Broth (page 336)
1½ cups cooked medium-grain white rice
1 tablespoon Hastings Creations Ancho Pork Salt
    (page 381) or kosher salt
1 teaspoon freshly ground black pepper
¾ teaspoon Hastings Creations Pork Rub (page 381)
    or store-bought, salt-free pork rub
½ cup finely chopped fresh parsley
¾ cup thinly sliced green onions
1 (½-inch diameter) hog casings, about 2 feet in length
¼ cup (½ stick) unsalted butter

Heat the peanut oil in a large rondeau or wide saucepan over medium-high heat. Add the pork shoulder and liver and sauté until well browned, 8 to 10 minutes. Add the onion, poblano, celery, and bay leaf and cook, stirring occasionally, until the vegetables are softened, 4 to 5 minutes. Stir in the garlic and cook for 30 seconds. Add the ham hock broth and stir to scrape up any browned bits from the bottom of the pan. Bring the mixture to a boil, reduce the heat, and simmer until the meat is tender, about 1½ hours.

Remove the bay leaf and stir in the cooked rice during the last 5 minutes of simmering. Cover the pan, remove it from the heat and allow the mixture to steep for 30 minutes or until the rice has soaked up most of the liquid from the meat mixture.

Season the meat mixture with the Ancho pork salt, pepper, and pork rub. Stir in the parsley and green onions. While the mixture is still slightly warm, push it through a meat grinder fitted with a ⅛-inch die. Either using a feeding tube or a funnel, stuff the sausage into the casings, making 3-inch long links. Sausages can be cooked immediately or chilled until ready to cook.

Before serving, preheat the oven to 375°F.

If the sausages have been chilled, allow them to sit at room temperature for 20 minutes before cooking. Add the butter and sausages to a large, cast-iron skillet. Place in the oven and roast until the boudin is golden brown and heated through, 17 to 20 minutes, turning the sausages over halfway through. Serve hot.

ROASTED PIG: HOW TO

We select pigs between 50 and 60 pounds dressed weight (gutted and scalded with the head on). Give the pig a rinse, pat it dry, and cover it with a basic brine made from salt, water, fresh garlic, and bay leaves and refrigerate it for at least 48 hours. Remove the pig from the brine and pat it dry thoroughly before rubbing it all over with a little vegetable oil. Give it a liberal seasoning with our Hastings Creations Pork Rub (page 381) or your favorite salt-free pork rub and refrigerate the seasoned pig again for at least 24 hours.

The day of the cooking, pull the pig out of the refrigerator and allow it to come to room temperature. (This is a crucial step as it enables it to cook more evenly and retain moisture as it cooks.) Before you start cooking, season the entire pig generously with our Hastings Creations Ancho Pork Salt (page 381).

As for the cooking, there are many, many methods of this art form, so find one you are comfortable with. If this is a first time event, a great way to roast a pig that doesn't require a shovel or pit is to use a La Caja China (page 382). It looks like a box-shaped wheelbarrow with a metal tray on top. The pig cooks in slow, steady heat generated by the coals that sit on top of the metal tray. This product is easy to use and can be used for other types of large cuts such as ribs, pork shoulders, and whole turkeys or chickens. During our staff Super Bowl party, small groups seem to form around La Caja China to warm their hands over the hot coals and anticipate the coming meal. Once the pig reaches an internal temperature of 187°F the metal tray is lifted higher so the pig skin can become crispy and brown. When tender, the meat under the skin will pull easily.

Endive Salad with Kumquats and Pecorino

THIS IS A GREAT SEASONAL SALAD FOR THE WINTERTIME. WE LOVE TO USE THE PLUMP, TANGY KUMQUATS FROM A NEARBY NURSERY CALLED PETALS FROM THE PAST (PAGE 215), BUT ANY TYPE OF FRESH CITRUS SEGMENTS WORK WELL. THE TWO DIFFERENT WAYS THE ENDIVE LEAVES ARE SLICED GIVE IT GREAT TEXTURE AND HELP THE VINAIGRETTE COAT THE SALAD EVENLY. IF YOU ARE PREPARING THIS FOR A PARTY, MAKE SURE THE ENDIVE LEAVES ARE CUT JUST BEFORE SERVING OR THE EDGES MAY TURN BROWN.

YIELD: 4 SERVINGS

3 CUPS CHOPPED ENDIVE LEAVES, CUT CROSSWISE INTO ½-INCH-WIDE SLICES

2 CUPS THINLY JULIENNED ENDIVE LEAVES

2 CUPS CHOPPED RADICCHIO LETTUCE, CUT INTO ½-INCH-WIDE STRIPS

10 TO 12 KUMQUATS, SLICED LENGTHWISE INTO 4 WEDGES AND SEEDS REMOVED

24 ORANGE SEGMENTS, SUCH AS MANDARINS, SATSUMAS, HONEY TANGERINES, OR BLOOD ORANGES

6 TABLESPOONS CITRUS VINAIGRETTE (PAGE 344)

½ CUP TOASTED WALNUTS

¼ TEASPOON KOSHER SALT

¼ TEASPOON FRESHLY GROUND BLACK PEPPER

32 (2-INCH-LONG) STRIPS SHAVED PECORINO CHEESE

Combine the chopped and julienned endive, radicchio, kumquats, and orange segments in a large bowl. Drizzle with the vinaigrette and toss to combine. Add the walnuts, salt, and pepper and toss again.

Evenly divide the salad among four salad plates. Place about 8 strips of pecorino cheese over each salad and serve immediately.

German Potato Salad

RATHER THAN COOK RED-SKINNED POTATOES IN THE CRAWFISH BOIL, WE SERVE THIS SALAD ON THE SIDE. SINCE THIS POTATO SALAD CAN BE SERVED WARM OR AT ROOM TEMPERATURE, IT'S THE PERFECT SIDE DISH FOR OUR STAFF PARTY OR ANY LARGE BUFFET.

YIELD: ABOUT 7 CUPS OR 6 SERVINGS

2 OUNCES SMOKED SLAB BACON, CUT INTO ¼-INCH CUBES (ABOUT ⅓ CUP)

2½ POUNDS SMALL, RED-SKINNED POTATOES

2 TABLESPOONS PLUS ½ TEASPOON KOSHER SALT, DIVIDED

3 TABLESPOONS SHERRY VINEGAR

1 TABLESPOON WHOLE-GRAIN DIJON MUSTARD

¼ CUP THINLY SLICED GREEN ONIONS

½ TEASPOON CHOPPED FRESH THYME

¼ CUP OLIVE OIL

¼ TEASPOON FRESHLY GROUND BLACK PEPPER

Place the bacon in a large skillet over medium-low heat and cook until golden brown and crispy, 6 to 8 minutes. Remove the bacon with a slotted spoon and drain on paper towels; set aside. Reserve 2 tablespoons of the rendered bacon grease.

Cut the potatoes into 1-inch cubes, leaving the skins intact. Place the potatoes in a large stockpot and add enough cold water to cover the potatoes by 2 inches. Place small 2 tablespoons of the salt into the water and bring to a boil. Simmer the potatoes for about 10 minutes or until fork-tender. (Be careful not to overcook the potatoes or the salad will be mushy.)

Whisk together the vinegar, mustard, green onions, and thyme. Slowly add the olive oil into the vinegar mixture while whisking constantly. Season the vinaigrette with the remaining ½ teaspoon of salt and the pepper. Store the vinaigrette at room temperature until the potatoes are tender.

Drain the cooked potatoes and toss with the reserved bacon grease and the vinaigrette. Taste and adjust the seasonings with additional salt and pepper, if needed. Serve the potato salad warm or at room temperature.

Chicken and Conecuh County Sausage Gumbo

CONECUH IS A COUNTY IN SOUTH ALABAMA. THE CONECUH SAUSAGE COMPANY IS A SMALL, FAMILY-OWNED OPERATION THAT HAS BEEN MAKING WELL-SEASONED SAUSAGES AND CURED MEATS SINCE 1947 IN THE SMALL TOWN OF EVERGREEN. THIS IS OUR TRIBUTE TO THEIR WONDERFUL PRODUCTS AND IT IS HAS BEEN THE PERFECT ACCOMPANIMENT TO OUR STAFF CRAWFISH BOIL EVERY JANUARY. THERE ARE MANY TYPES OF GUMBO, BUT WE PREFER THOSE THAT START WITH A MEDIUM-DARK ROUX. TO ACHIEVE THE PERFECT DEPTH OF FLAVOR, THE COLOR OF THE ROUX MUST MATCH THE RETRO RED-DISH-BROWN TILES ON THE FLOOR IN OUR KITCHEN. IF YOU LIKE YOUR GUMBO SPICY, TRY THE CAJUN-SMOKED OR SPICY AND HOT HICKORY-SMOKED STYLES OF CONECUH SAUSAGE.

YIELD: ABOUT 16 CUPS OR 10 TO 12 SERVINGS

1 CUP PEANUT OIL
1¼ CUPS ALL-PURPOSE FLOUR
3 CUPS DICED ONION, ABOUT 2 MEDIUM ONIONS
1 CUP DICED CELERY, ABOUT 2 STALKS
1 CUP SEEDED AND DICED RED BELL PEPPER, ABOUT 2
    MEDIUM PEPPERS
1 CUP SEEDED AND DICED POBLANO PEPPER, ABOUT 3
    MEDIUM PEPPERS
2 TABLESPOONS MINCED GARLIC
2 BAY LEAVES
2 TEASPOONS FRESH THYME LEAVES
1 (12-OUNCE) BOTTLE LIGHT BEER
7 CUPS CHICKEN STOCK (PAGE 335)
1 TABLESPOON PLUS 1 TEASPOON SALT
2 TEASPOONS FRESHLY GROUND BLACK PEPPER
1 TEASPOON CAYENNE PEPPER
1 POUND CONECUH BRAND SMOKED SAUSAGE OR OTHER
    SPICY SMOKED SAUSAGE, SUCH AS ANDOUILLE
1½ POUNDS OKRA (FRESH OR FROZEN AND THAWED), SLICED
2 CUPS SEEDED AND DICED TOMATOES
1½ POUNDS COOKED CHICKEN, PULLED INTO 2-INCH PIECES
1 CUP CHOPPED GREEN ONION TOPS
4 TO 5 CUPS COOKED RICE, FOR SERVING

Heat the oil in a large, heavy-bottomed skillet over medium heat. Whisk in the flour and cook, stirring constantly, until the mixture darkens to a rich, reddish-brown color, 30 to 35 minutes. (Be careful not to let the flour burn or the gumbo will taste burned.)

Once the roux reaches the desired color, add the onion, celery, and peppers and cook, stirring, for 2 to 3 minutes. Add the garlic, bay leaves, and thyme and cook an additional 1 to 2 minutes. Whisk in the beer, stirring to scrape any browned bits on the bottom of the skillet. Transfer the roux mixture to a large Dutch oven or stockpot, over medium-high heat. Add the chicken stock, salt, pepper, and cayenne and bring the mixture to a boil. Reduce the heat and simmer the gumbo for 20 minutes, stirring occasionally.

While the gumbo is simmering, slice the sausage length-wise and then crosswise into ½-inch-thick slices. Place the sausage in a large skillet over medium heat and cook, stirring occasionally, until the sausage is rendered and lightly browned, 8 to 10 minutes. Transfer the sausage to a paper towel–lined plate and pat dry.

Add the cooked sausage, okra, and tomatoes to the gumbo and simmer an additional 30 minutes, stirring occasionally. Stir in the chicken and cook an additional 10 minutes. Taste and adjust the seasonings, adding more salt or pepper, if needed. Just before serving, remove and discard the bay leaves and stir in the green onions. Ladle the gumbo into warm soup bowls and top with cooked rice. Serve hot.

CHAPTER 6

MARCH
&
APRIL

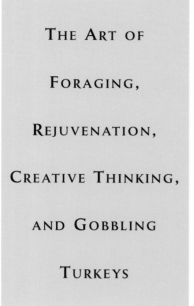

The Art of Foraging, Rejuvenation, Creative Thinking, and Gobbling Turkeys

With the arrival of March and April warmth begins radiating through our bones. The brief and nuanced slowdown of the first months of the year shifts to a quickened pace, fueled partly by the anticipation of spring and partly by our loyal patrons lining up for our latest seasonal interpretations. Vegetables are sprouting, honeysuckles are blooming, and there is general excitement at the restaurant about the products our purveyors have begun appearing with at the kitchen door. Our fishmongers tell us that coastal water temperatures will soon hit them magical number of 68°F, signaling that the pompano and cobia are about to embark on their annual spring run. First-of-the-season soft-shell crabs have also begun to appear. Anticipation of the spring run of shad along the Eastern seaboard gets our mouths watering for shad roe. The thought of grits, smoked bacon, and shad roe whether for breakfast, lunch, or dinner quite simply gets Southern folks fired up. All our die-hard shad roe-loving customers start calling with one question: "How long till shad roe?" When our response is "Right now. Come on!" a great deal of excitement ensues among the cooks and patrons this time of year.

In the cool air of the Appalachian Mountains, Chris' dad ventures out to harvest wild ramps, which he ships to us. Simultaneously, baby leeks, tender favas, and tiny peas are appearing while Vidalia onions, full of sweetness, are being plucked from the soil in nearby Georgia. Both foraged and cultivated gems find their way into appetizers like baby leeks vinaigrette topped with soft-boiled farm egg or a risotto dotted with earthy morels and English peas. Even pea tendrils, the tiny shoots of the climbing vine, garnish the freshest pompano. Before they've been allowed to mature to red ripeness, plump green tomatoes star in a robust chutney for our cheese plate. Ours is a life and style of cooking tied to the seasons within seasons—those brief moments where the flavors of specific ingredients are perfect.

Chris' pursuit of the eastern wild turkey is nothing short of an obsession. Being in the woods at the crack of dawn in the springtime is a truly magical experience. Day breaks and the woods wake up as the turkeys' gobbles thunder through the hardwoods. We are in awe of our surroundings—the wild, budding Easter lilies; the crisp, cool air; and springtime's great chess match played out through the hunt. Over the years we have had the opportunity to gather with some great legends of the sport to soak up their insightful stories of turkey hunting and life's lessons learned over a half century of participation. The stories of their experiences are priceless and deserving of a place in the Smithsonian's archives. Through our rich Southern tradition of storytelling, we make sure their wisdom endures. In the woods we reconnect with the land, old friends, each other, and our children and, in doing so, find rejuvenation. Such days always end at the table, breaking bread, telling tales, and passing along our shared histories.

Whether it is crabs, shrimp, flounder or oysters for family meals at Pawleys Island, or game from hunting and fishing trips around the country or here at home, foraging has been a part of our lives for many years. Foraging has both a literal and more contemporary context for us. It is one of the cornerstones of our success at the restaurant. It is in our DNA. The art of foraging is in the-knowing-where-to-look and whom to ask. Throughout this chapter and the rest of the book, we share with you the places and purveyors we turn to for the prized ingredients we use at Hot and Hot Fish Club so that you have access to the same outstanding products we use. They are certain to inspire your creativity and rejuvenate your cooking. We share the stories behind the ingredients while paying homage to the land and its bounty, those who work the soil . . . and, of course, the noble eastern gobbler.

PINEAPPLE-SAGE
LEMON CELEBRATION

As spring draws near we look forward to tiny boxes of fresh herbs from The Chef's Garden. When we tasted the crisp, herbal flavor of pineapple sage for the first time, we decided to create this cocktail to celebrate the arrival of spring.

YIELD: 1 SERVING

2 FRESH PINEAPPLE SAGE LEAVES
2 OUNCES (¼ CUP) ORANGE-FLAVORED VODKA
1½ TABLESPOONS SIMPLE SYRUP (PAGE 362)
1 TABLESPOON FRESH LEMON JUICE
1 TABLESPOON FRESH LIME JUICE
1 (2-INCH) LEMON PEEL, TWISTED, FOR GARNISH
1 FRESH PINEAPPLE SAGE SPRIG, FOR GARNISH

Fill a martini shaker one-third full with ice. Tear the pineapple sage leaves and add them to the ice; muddle until the leaves are bruised and fragrant, about 1 minute. Add the orange vodka, simple syrup, lemon juice, and lime juice. Shake until the mixture is well chilled.

Strain the muddled pineapple sage mixture into a 12-ounce Collins glass filled with ice. Garnish with a lemon twist and a pineapple sage sprig and serve immediately.

HOT AND HOT SPICY 'TINI

MAKING YOUR OWN PEPPER-INFUSED VODKA IS EASY AND VERSATILE. ONCE STRAINED, THE INFUSED VODKA WILL KEEP UNDER REFRIGERATION INDEFINITELY. WE USE IT TO SPICE UP OUR BLOND MARY (PAGE 76) AND IDIE'S HOMEMADE PASTA SAUCES. BLUE CHEESE-STUFFED OLIVES CAN BE PURCHASED, BUT THEY'RE EASY TO MAKE AND ALSO KEEP WELL REFRIGERATED. PURCHASE LARGE PIMIENTO-STUFFED GREEN QUEEN OLIVES AND REMOVE THE PIMIENTO WITH A TOOTHPICK. FILL A PASTRY BAG FITTED WITH A THIN, ROUND TIP WITH CREAMY GORGONZOLA THAT HAS BEEN SOFTENED AT ROOM TEMPERATURE. PIPE THE CHEESE INTO THE OLIVES AND YOU'RE DONE! THESE ARE A GREAT NIBBLE FOR ANY MARTINI AND THEIR SALTINESS REALLY BALANCES THE SPICINESS OF THIS COCKTAIL.

YIELD: 1 SERVING

5 FRESH RED CAYENNE CHILE PEPPERS (ABOUT **2** OUNCES)
½ SMALL (**8**-OUNCE) ONION, PEELED AND CUT INTO
   4 WEDGES
1 (**750**ML) BOTTLE VODKA
2½ TABLESPOONS OLIVE JUICE
1 BLUE CHEESE-STUFFED GREEN QUEEN OLIVE, FOR GARNISH

Bring a small pot of water to a boil. Remove the stems from the chiles and blanch in the boiling water for 30 seconds and drain. Place the chiles on a clean kitchen towel and pat dry. While they are still warm, cut two vertical slits through them with a paring knife. Combine the warm chiles and 2 of the onion wedges in a sterile 1-liter jar with a tight-fitting lid. Reserve the remaining onion wedges for another use. Pour the vodka over the vegetables and cover the jar. Allow the mixture to sit in a dark, cool place at room temperature for three to four days.

After three days, taste the vodka, to determine the spiciness. The mixture can continue to soak for 1 more day, if more spice is needed. When ready, strain the vodka through a fine-meshed sieve and discard the chiles and onions. The strained vodka can be poured back into its original vodka bottle (that has been cleaned) or into a sterile 1-liter jar. Refrigerate the vodka until ready to use.

Chill a martini glass for at least 20 minutes before serving. Fill a martini shaker halfway with ice. Add 2 ounces (¼ cup) of the pepper-infused vodka, and the olive juice and shake until well chilled. Strain the mixture into a chilled martini glass. Drop a blue cheese-stuffed olive into the bottom of the glass and serve immediately.

SHE-CRAB SOUP

This super seasonal soup is made often in the springtime with live female crabs laden with roe (called the tamale). Be sure to buy them from a reputable fish market known for quality and freshness and make certain the crabs are active before purchasing them. You can pinpoint female crabs by finding those with slightly orange tips on their blue claws.

YIELD: ABOUT 4 QUARTS OR 10 TO 12 SERVINGS

½ cup (1 stick) unsalted butter
2 large onions, peeled and roughly chopped (about 5 cups)
1 large leek, white part roughly chopped (about 1 cup)
2 celery stalks, roughly chopped (about 1 cup)
5 fresh thyme sprigs
3 fresh tarragon sprigs
1 bay leaf
4 cups (1 quart) Shrimp Stock (page 334)
12 live blue crabs
8 cups (2 quarts) heavy cream
3 cups cooked Carolina Gold Rice (page 353) or other cooked long-grain rice
1 teaspoon kosher salt
Pinch of freshly ground black pepper
½ pound (about 1 cup) lump crabmeat

Melt the butter in a large, heavy stockpot or Dutch oven over medium heat. Add the onions, leek, celery, thyme, tarragon, and bay leaf. Cook, stirring occasionally, until the vegetables are soft, about 10 minutes. Be careful not to allow the vegetables to brown. Increase the heat to high, add the shrimp stock, and bring the mixture to a boil. Once the liquid is at a rolling boil, add the live crabs, cover, and steam for 15 minutes, stirring occasionally. Once the crabs are cooked through and bright red, remove them from the stockpot and set aside to cool slightly. Reserve the broth.

Clean the crabs by removing the apron, the hard, top outer shell, and the legs. Add the hard, outer shell and the legs to the reserved broth mixture. Remove and reserve any bright orange roe from the crabs. Remove and discard the feathery, grayish colored lungs. Pick and through the crabmeat and reserve any meat from the inner chambers of the shell, being careful not to include any cartilage.

Add the cream to the shell and broth mixture and bring to a simmer. Reduce the heat and allow the mixture to simmer for 40 minutes or until the cream has thickened slightly. Add the reserved orange-colored roe to the soup and simmer an additional 5 minutes. Remove from the heat and remove and discard the thyme sprigs, tarragon sprigs, and bay leaf.

Strain the soup through a colander, pressing gently on the solids to extract as much liquid as possible. Combine the cooked rice and strained soup in a blender and process until smooth and well blended. Season the soup with the salt and pepper and add the picked crabmeat. Ladle the soup into soup bowls and top each serving with about 1 tablespoon of the lump crabmeat. Serve immediately.

CRAWFISH BISQUE

We save the peeled crawfish shells and tail meat from the Crawfish Boil (page 266) and utilize their spicy flavor to enhance this bisque. The picked shells and meat can be frozen separately, for up to two months. They can be added to the cream mixture in their frozen state, just allow a few extra minutes for the shell and meat to heat through.

YIELD: ABOUT 8½ CUPS OR 8 SERVINGS

¼ cup (½ stick) unsalted butter
3½ cups cored and diced fennel bulb, about
    1 large fennel bulb
3 cups halved and thinly sliced leeks, about
    2 large leeks, white part only
1 bay leaf
4 fresh thyme sprigs
2½ tablespoons roughly chopped fresh tarragon
1 cup seeded and diced Roma tomatoes, about
    4 large
1 teaspoon kosher salt
½ teaspoon freshly ground black pepper
¼ teaspoon cayenne pepper
½ cup brandy
2½ pounds cooked and peeled crawfish heads
    and tails (about 1 gallon)
2 quarts (8 cups) heavy cream
2 tablespoons finely chopped fresh tarragon
2 tablespoons finely chopped fresh fennel fronds
1 teaspoon grated lemon zest
1 cup cooked crawfish tails

Melt the butter in a large Dutch oven or stockpot over medium heat. Add the fennel, leeks, bay leaf, thyme sprigs, and the roughly chopped tarragon. Cook for 5 minutes, stirring occasionally. Add the tomatoes and continue cooking until the vegetables are tender and softened but not caramelized, about 5 more minutes. Season the vegetables with the salt, pepper, and cayenne. Deglaze the mixture with the brandy and cook for 30 seconds, stirring constantly. Add the crawfish shells, stirring until the shells are coated with the vegetable mixture, about 2 minutes. Pour the cream over the shells, making sure the shells are covered by at least ½ inch, and bring to a simmer. Allow the mixture to simmer over low heat for 45 to 50 minutes. Remove the soup mixture from the heat and cool slightly, about 10 minutes.

Remove and discard the bay leaf and thyme sprigs. Ladle the soup mixture (both the shells and broth) into a blender until it is half full. Blend the mixture, on high, until smooth and transfer the mixture to a clean container. Repeat with remaining broth and shells. Strain the blended soup through a fine-meshed sieve, pressing lightly on the solids to extract as much liquid as possible.

Ladle 1 cup of the strained soup into each of eight serving bowls and garnish each with ¼ teaspoon of the finely chopped tarragon, ¼ teaspoon of the fennel fronds, ⅛ teaspoon of the lemon zest, and 2 tablespoons of the crawfish tails. Serve immediately.

CRESCENT MOON ORGANIC FARM

On a small, independent farm in rural Sopchoppy, Florida, Jack Simmons and his girlfriend, Carmen, coax an amazing range of produce to ripe perfection each and every season and micro-season. We were introduced to Crescent Moon Organic Farm through our consulting relationship with the St. Joe Company, a property developer along the Florida Panhandle and another chef in the region who tipped us off to the great things happening over at Crescent Moon. Jack and Carmen grow everything organically on a simple, understated spit of land, yet produce some of the most impressive produce with which we've had the opportunity to work. Now we are beneficiaries of their farm's products as far north as Birmingham.

Jack and Carmen certainly weren't making deliveries the six hours to Birmingham from the start. But, as vacation season was ending, local Panhandle restaurants were transitioning to limited hours and required fewer ingredients. This put Jack and Carmen in a bit of a predicament with their growing season in full swing, fields planted, and an abundant harvest on the horizon. When Jack called us at Hot and Hot to say he had a crop ready to harvest and not enough customers to take it all, we knew we had to help him out.

Trucking goods from Crescent Moon to Birmingham might be seen as environmentally excessive, but Jack's pickup (and all his farm machines) runs on bio-diesel. From the restaurants that buy his produce he gets discarded vegetable oil. Using pumps, pipes, and a chemist's skill, he turns that food-grade oil into bio-diesel, making the long trip both environmentally and economically sound. It's a win-win situation. Crescent Moon Organic Farm continues to prosper and our patrons get to taste the magic of his fields.

A typical delivery might mean boxes of Red Star Bibb, Winter Density Romaine, and all manner of leaf lettuces, herbs, and arugula, as well as root vegetables, such as carrots, turnips, beets, and rutabagas. With spring we also get radishes and new potatoes. In a few more months, he'll bring okra, heirloom tomatoes, field peas, eggplants, blackberries, persimmons, peppers, and the list goes on and on and on. Crescent Moon's harvests are a great example of the micro-seasons within a season. We stay in touch with Jack and Carmen to learn about what crops are ready for harvest, then allow our menu to evolve accordingly.

Occasionally, Jack has more to offer than we can comfortably buy, so we call other chefs and grocers in our area so that he can deliver to them while he's here. This makes Jack's trip doubly beneficial while fostering great relationships between our community of close-knit chefs and storeowners who appreciate access to great ingredients and people like Jack and Carmen.

SPRING VEGETABLE SALAD

The key to this salad is finding a variety of spring vegetables. Using your "foraging skills," visit farmers' markets, green grocers, and roadside stands, or talk with local chefs and discover what is in season in your area. Almost any fresh, local vegetable can be added to this salad. After all, this recipe is only a guideline for those confident enough to embrace their own creative view. If you can't find Vidalia onions, pearl onions will work too.

YIELD: 6 SERVINGS

1 TABLESPOON OLIVE OIL

1 TEASPOON MINCED SHALLOTS

¼ TEASPOON CHOPPED FRESH THYME

6 OUNCES FRESH CHANTERELLE MUSHROOMS

½ TEASPOON SALT, DIVIDED

¼ TEASPOON FRESHLY GROUND BLACK PEPPER, DIVIDED

6 SMALL BEETS, ROASTED, PEELED, AND EACH CUT INTO 4 WEDGES (ABOUT 24 WEDGES) (PAGE 378)

9 JUMBO ASPARAGUS, PEELED, BLANCHED, AND CUT IN HALF LENGTHWISE (ABOUT 18 PIECES)

6 SMALL SPRING VIDALIA ONIONS, BRAISED (PAGE 377)

6 FRESHLY DUG FINGERLING POTATOES, COOKED UNTIL TENDER AND SLICED IN HALF

6 (4-INCH-LONG) BABY CARROTS, TRIMMED, PEELED, BLANCHED, AND CUT IN HALF LENGTHWISE

1 CUP FRESH ENGLISH PEAS, BLANCHED

1½ CUPS COOKED CRANBERRY BEANS OR OTHER FRESH FIELD PEA OR BEAN

½ CUP CHERVIL VINAIGRETTE (PAGE 346)

2 CUPS FRESH PEA TENDRILS OR WATERCRESS

Heat the olive oil in a large skillet over medium-high heat. Add the shallots and thyme and sauté for 30 seconds. Add the chanterelles and cook, stirring frequently, until golden brown, 5 to 8 minutes. Season the mushrooms with ¼ teaspoon of the salt and ⅛ teaspoon of the pepper. Remove the mushrooms from the heat and let cool to room temperature, about 15 minutes.

Combine the beets, asparagus, onions, potatoes, carrots, peas, and beans in a large mixing bowl. Add the cooled mushrooms and vinaigrette and season the vegetables with the remaining ¼ teaspoon of salt and ⅛ teaspoon of pepper; toss until the vegetables are well coated with the dressing.

Evenly divide the vegetables among six salad plates, arranging them in a nice pattern. Add the pea tendrils to the mixing bowl and toss with any remaining vinaigrette from the bottom of the bowl. Arrange 3 to 4 tendrils (about ⅓ cup) on top of each salad. Drizzle any remaining vinaigrette over each salad and serve immediately.

SOURCING LOCAL INGREDIENTS

Whenever possible, learn about and buy ingredients at your local farmers' market, a roadside stand, or a nearby organic farm. If you eat something spectacular at a restaurant, ask the chef or waiter about it and where you might find the ingredient for cooking at home; then seek it out. Perhaps you saw an heirloom fruit or vegetable on a television cooking show or on vacation that you haven't seen at your local grocer. Talk to your store manager about it and ask if the store can order it for you. You are the customer and they value your input. Better yet, ask an area farmer to grow it. If he is willing, put him in touch with your grocer. When a farmer knows he has a market for a product, he's much more apt to cultivate it. Creating a dialogue with those from whom you get your ingredients is imperative to the process of sourcing the very best. When all else fails, perhaps it is something you can grow in your backyard. Visit your local nursery or garden shop and ask questions, order seeds, and get your hands dirty. If you live in an urban area, start a potted garden on your balcony or roof. You'll reap uncommon rewards and eat better for it.

GRILLED JUMBO ASPARAGUS

with Head-On Florida Hoppers and Preserved Lemon Vinaigrette

FLORIDA HOPPERS ARE NOT FROGS! THEY ARE A VARIETY OF PINK SHRIMP WITH A DISTINCTIVE RED SPOT ON THEIR TAIL. BELOVED BY BOAT CAPTAINS AND LAND LOVERS ALIKE, THE HOPPER IS ONE OF OUR FAVORITES OF THE FIVE WILD, AMERICAN SHRIMP VARIETIES.

YIELD: 6 SERVINGS

12 LARGE, SHELL-ON FLORIDA HOPPERS OR OTHER LARGE, PINK SHRIMP
2 TEASPOONS GRATED LEMON ZEST, ABOUT ½ LEMON
1 TABLESPOON COARSELY CHOPPED FRESH FLAT-LEAF PARSLEY
4 FRESH THYME SPRIGS, PICKED AND COARSELY CHOPPED
1 TABLESPOON COARSELY CHOPPED FRESH BASIL
½ FRESH GARLIC CLOVE, PEELED AND COARSELY CHOPPED
¼ CUP OLIVE OIL
¼ TEASPOON SALT
⅛ TEASPOON FRESHLY GROUND BLACK PEPPER
18 JUMBO ASPARAGUS, TRIMMED, PEELED, AND BLANCHED
¾ CUP PRESERVED LEMON VINAIGRETTE (PAGE 345)
½ CUP LOOSELY PACKED MICROGREENS

Combine the shrimp, lemon zest, parsley, thyme, basil, garlic, and olive oil in a large bowl, tossing to coat well. Season the shrimp with the salt and pepper. Cover and refrigerate the shrimp for at least 2 hours.

Soak three (12-inch) wooden skewers in cold water for at least 20 minutes before grilling. Preheat the grill to medium-high (350°F to 400° F).

Remove the shrimp from the marinade and skewer four shrimp onto each wooden skewer. Grill the shrimp skewers over medium heat until shrimp are slightly charred and just cooked through, 4 to 5 minutes. Remove the shrimp from the skewers and set them aside to cool slightly. Peel the shrimp, leaving the last tail segment intact and cover to keep warm until ready to serve.

Just before serving, place the asparagus, grilled shrimp, and vinaigrette in a large bowl. Toss well and season lightly with salt and pepper, if needed. Arrange three asparagus spears on each of six plates. Place two shrimp on top of each serving of asparagus. Drizzle 1 tablespoon of the vinaigrette from the bowl around each plate. Garnish each plate with about 2 tablespoons of the microgreens and serve immediately.

MOREL AND ENGLISH PEA RISOTTO
with Lemon Oil

THE SWEETNESS OF THE FRESH PEAS AND THE EARTHINESS OF THE MOREL MUSHROOMS, ACCENTED BY THE LEMON OIL, MAKE THIS DISH PROFOUND IN ITS SIMPLICITY. WE OFTEN SPEAK WITH FOLKS WHO ARE INTIMIDATED BY PREPARING RISOTTO. THE KEY IS TO RELAX, FOLLOW A GOOD RECIPE, AND BEGIN TO FEEL THE PROCESS. THE REST TAKES CARE OF ITSELF.

YIELD: 4 SERVINGS

- 1 POUND (28 TO 32) FRESH MOREL MUSHROOMS, CLEANED
- 2 TABLESPOONS UNSALTED BUTTER
- 2½ TABLESPOONS MINCED SHALLOTS
- 1 TEASPOON CHOPPED FRESH THYME
- ½ TEASPOON KOSHER SALT, DIVIDED
- ¼ TEASPOON FRESHLY GROUND BLACK PEPPER, DIVIDED
- 4 CUPS BASIC RISOTTO (PAGE 355)
- 1 TO 1½ CUPS VEGETABLE STOCK (PAGE 334), SIMMERING
- 1⅓ CUPS FRESH ENGLISH PEAS, BLANCHED
- 1 TABLESPOON PLUS 1 TEASPOON CHOPPED FRESH PARSLEY
- 1 TABLESPOON PLUS 1 TEASPOON CHOPPED FRESH CHIVES
- 2 TEASPOONS LEMON OIL (PAGE 382)

Trim the ivory-colored stems to the base of the morels. Set the top portion aside. Thinly slice the stems and set aside. Melt the butter in a large 4-quart saucepan over medium-high heat. Add the morels, sliced stems, shallots, and thyme to the pan and cook until softened, 4 to 5 minutes. Season the mushrooms with ⅛ teaspoon each of the salt and pepper.

Stir the risotto into the mushroom mixture. Add ½ cup of the hot vegetable stock and stir constantly with a wooden spoon until all of the liquid is absorbed. Repeat this process, adding ½ cup of the stock each time, until the rice is creamy and al dente. (You may not need all 1½ cups of the stock.) Season the risotto with the remaining salt and pepper. Stir in the English peas and cook, stirring, for 1 minute or until the peas are heated though. Remove the risotto from the heat and stir in the parsley and chives. Spoon about 1¼ cups of the risotto into each of four shallow bowls and drizzle each serving with ½ teaspoon of the lemon oil. Serve immediately

PROSCIUTTO AND
SPRING VIDALIA ONION SALAD
with Parmesan Vinaigrette

SPRING VIDALIA ONIONS ARE ONE OF THOSE "MARKERS" OF SPRING FOR SOUTHERNERS. THEY ARRIVE IN EARLY SPRING, THE SIZE OF A LARGE GREEN ONION OR SCALLION, AND MORPH INTO FULL GROWN ONIONS BY SUMMER. ROASTING BRINGS OUT THEIR DELICATE, SWEET FLAVOR, WHICH IS COMPLIMENTED BY THE SALTINESS OF THE PROSCIUTTO AND PARMESAN.

YIELD: 6 SERVINGS

12 THIN SLICES (ABOUT 4½ OUNCES) PROSCIUTTO DI PARMA OR
    OTHER GOOD-QUALITY AGED HAM
6 SPRING VIDALIA ONIONS, ROASTED AND HALVED (PAGE **377**)
6 CUPS (4 OUNCES) FRESH WATERCRESS
3 TABLESPOONS PARMESAN VINAIGRETTE (PAGE **346**)
PINCH OF KOSHER SALT
⅛ TEASPOON FRESHLY GROUND BLACK PEPPER
12 (2-INCH-LONG) PARMESAN SHAVINGS

Arrange 2 slices of prosciutto in the center of six salad plates, slightly overlapping. Place 2 roasted onion halves in a circle around the prosciutto on each plate.

Combine the watercress and vinaigrette in a large mixing bowl and toss until combined. Season the salad with the salt and pepper. Arrange 1 cup of the watercress mixture in the center of each salad plate (on top of the onions and prosciutto). Place 2 slices of Parmesan over the top of each salad. Serve immediately.

WILD TURKEY SALAD

with First of the Season Morels and Watercress

Opening day of turkey hunting in Alabama is one of the most anticipated days on our calendar. We share this favorite recipe for wild turkey in the hope that doing so will bring us luck in harvesting a prized gobbler. If you don't have a good shot at a wild turkey this year, substitute fresh domestic turkey breast. Partially freezing the turkey breast makes for easier slicing. Happy hunting and eating!

YIELD: 4 SERVINGS

TURKEY:

¼ cup buttermilk

1 tablespoon Dijon mustard

1½ teaspoons kosher salt, divided

1 teaspoon freshly ground black pepper

12 (⅛-inch-thick) slices wild turkey breast, about 4 to 5 ounces

3 cups Fresh Breadcrumbs (page 353)

¼ cup peanut oil, for cooking

SALAD:

1 tablespoon olive oil

1 tablespoon minced shallots

¼ teaspoon chopped fresh thyme

3 ounces fresh morel mushrooms

Pinch of kosher salt

Pinch of freshly ground black pepper

12 cups (1½ bunches) loosely packed fresh watercress

¼ cup Lemon Dijon Vinaigrette (page 346)

2 ounces fresh chèvre, crumbled

2 tablespoons finely chopped fresh chives

To Prepare the Turkey:

Combine the buttermilk and mustard with ½ teaspoon of the salt and ½ teaspoon pepper in a shallow dish. Add the turkey slices, turning to coat. Cover and allow the turkey to marinate in the refrigerator for 1 hour.

Season the breadcrumbs with the remaining teaspoon of salt and ½ teaspoon of pepper. Dredge the turkey slices in the breadcrumbs, pressing to make sure the crumbs adhere to the turkey. Place the breaded turkey on a parchment paper–lined plate. (At this point the turkey can be covered and refrigerated up to 2 hours, if needed.) Just before serving, heat the peanut oil in a large cast-iron skillet over medium-high heat until hot. Add the turkey, in batches, and cook 1½ to 2 minutes on each side or until golden brown. Remove from the heat and drain on a paper towel–lined plate. Repeat with remaining turkey slices. Cover to keep warm.

To Prepare the Salad:

Heat the olive oil in a small skillet over medium-high heat. Add the shallots, thyme, and mushrooms and cook until softened, 4 to 5 minutes. Season the mushrooms with a pinch of salt and pepper and remove from the heat. Allow the mushrooms to cool for 10 minutes before tossing the salad.

Combine the watercress and the cooled mushrooms in a large bowl with the vinaigrette, tossing until well coated. Layer one-third of the watercress mixture on each of four serving plates. Top each salad with 1 slice of fried turkey. Repeat the layers two more times. Crumble about ½ ounce of the goat cheese and ½ tablespoon of the chives over each salad and serve immediately.

SWEET GRASS DAIRY

In southern Georgia, a dairy family took an economic gamble and gave up on conventional dairy practices in an effort to return their livestock to living and grazing outdoors the old-fashioned, natural way. The quality of the resulting milk proved theirs was a gamble well taken. Soon they added goat herds to the operation and before long a farmstead cheese making enterprise became a natural outgrowth of the business.

From Sweet Grass Dairy we get some of the best regional cheeses. At the restaurant and for guests at home, we showcase several of their varieties on a cheese plate with accompaniments of our Green Tomato Chutney, Sesame Brittle, a drizzle of Red Mountain Honey and a scattering of nuts. With offerings that include fresh, semiripened, and naturally aged cheeses, we are assured of an assortment that runs the gamut in texture, color, and flavor, whether made from goats' or cows' milk. This is what makes Sweet Grass Dairy a perfect choice for a well-rounded cheese plate from a single producer.

Cheese making is yet another culinary undertaking that is influenced by the seasons. As the goats and cows consume different vegetation seasonally, the flavor of their milk varies in turn. That variation affects the flavor profile of the cheese. Seasonal fluctuations force the cheese maker, much like a chef, to be flexible when determining when his product is ready for the offering. Like cooking, cheese making is an endeavor dictated by natural influences on maturity and flavor.

THE HOT AND HOT CHEESE PLATE

Hot and Hot Fish Club is one of the best places in Birmingham to nibble on a fantastic cheese plate. With a variety of seasonal fruits and homemade garnishes such as sesame brittle, banana-nut bread, and seasonal chutney, this is not your average cheese plate. We feature a variety of local and imported specialty, artisanal cheeses from numerous different dairies and fromageries. The cheeses on the menu are continually revolving which gives our customers a chance to try something new on each visit. We like to serve cheese platters at home to our friends and family as a simple appetizer or dessert. The Green Tomato Chutney (page 295) and the Sesame Brittle (page 296) are two of our favorite garnishes to serve on a cheese platter.

GREEN TOMATO CHUTNEY

Our favorite application for this chutney is alongside a plate of local cheeses. In the fall, as the harvest changes, we substitute local Kiefer pears, grown by our friend Dave Garfrerick, for the green tomatoes.

YIELD: ABOUT 1 QUART

1½ pounds (3 to 4 medium) firm green tomatoes, cored and finely diced (about 1¼ cups)

2 small garlic cloves, smashed and peeled

¾ cup white vinegar

3 tablespoons white wine

2½ tablespoons fresh lemon juice

¼ cup plus 2 tablespoons granulated sugar

½ teaspoon kosher salt

2 bay leaves, torn

6 fresh thyme sprigs

1½ teaspoons yellow mustard seeds

1½ teaspoons whole white peppercorns

1½ teaspoons whole coriander

½ teaspoon fennel seed

½ teaspoon celery seed

¼ teaspoon whole cumin seed

Prepare an ice water bath.

Combine the tomatoes, garlic cloves, vinegar, wine, lemon juice, sugar, and salt in a medium saucepan. Place the remaining ingredients (bay leaves through cumin seed) in a 5-inch square of cheesecloth, gather the edges together and tie the cheesecloth securely with butcher's twine.

Add the spice sachet to the saucepan and bring the entire mixture to a boil over medium-high heat. Reduce the heat to low and simmer the chutney for 5 minutes or until the tomatoes are well-spiced but still slightly firm. Discard the spice sachet and immediately transfer the chutney to a stainless steel bowl set inside a water bath. Stir the chutney occasionally until cooled. Refrigerate until the chutney is well chilled. This mixture will keep in an airtight container in the refrigerator for up to one month.

SESAME BRITTLE

For an easy summertime appetizer, we often choose a selection of fresh cheeses, drizzle them with local honey and toasted pecans and serve a batch of this homemade Sesame Brittle alongside. Pair with a crusty baguette and a side of Green Tomato Chutney (page 295) and you'll have the perfect beginning or ending to any meal.

YIELD: ABOUT 3 DOZEN (2 TO 3-INCH) PIECES

- ½ cup (about 3 ounces) whole unsalted almonds
- ¼ cup plus ½ teaspoon (about 1½ ounces) white sesame seeds
- ¼ cup plus 1 tablespoon (about 1½ ounces) black sesame seeds
- ½ cup (about 4 ounces) granulated sugar
- 1½ tablespoons bread flour
- ¼ teaspoon salt
- ½ cup (1 stick) unsalted butter, melted
- 3 tablespoons whole milk
- 1 tablespoon light corn syrup

Place the almonds in a food processor and process until finely ground (about the same size as the sesame seeds). Combine the ground almonds, white sesame seeds, black sesame seeds, sugar, bread flour, and salt in a large mixing bowl. Add the melted butter, milk, and corn syrup and stir until well combined. Chill the mixture until firm, at least 4 hours. (The mixture will keep, refrigerated, for up to 2 weeks.)

Preheat the oven to 300°F and allow the mixture to sit at room temperature for about 15 minutes.

Meanwhile, cut 4 pieces of parchment paper large enough to fit inside a large jelly roll pan (about 16 x 12 inches). Place 2 of the parchment pieces on a clean work surface and evenly divide the mixture between the sheets (about ¾ cup each). Place 1 piece of the remaining parchment paper over each portion of the mixture and roll out until the mixture is about the same size as the parchment paper. Transfer the parch-

ment paper and mixture to 2 jelly roll pans and carefully remove and discard the top piece of parchment paper. (If some of the mixture peels off with the parchment, use a rubber spatula to scrape it back onto the jelly roll pan.)

Bake the brittle at 300°F, one pan at a time, for 13 to 15 minutes, rotating the pan halfway through the baking time. When ready, the brittle will be golden brown with bubbling edges. Remove from the oven and allow the brittle to cool completely on the pans before removing. Break the brittle into 2 to 3-inch jagged pieces and serve. The brittle will keep in an airtight container in the freezer for up to one month.

ALLIGATOR POINT CLAMS

In a little bay surrounding the Alligator Point peninsula on the Florida panhandle, some of the best clams you've ever tasted are being nurtured. This particular bay has a salinity and sediment profile that's absolutely ideal for raising clams. The state has designated Alligator Harbor a pristine area suitable for farm raising clams. Local fishermen are able to buy leases to raise and harvest clams in the bay. Tiny seed clams are placed in mesh bags, dated, and then buried in the sandy bottom with the exact location of each bag marked on a grid. The ebb and flow of the tidal currents covers the clams with sand and seawater comprised of the perfect recipe of nutrients to make the clams grow plump and juicy. Varying sizes of clams are harvested based on the number of days buried. The smallest clams have spent the least number of days on the floor of the bay; medium clams take a little longer and so forth. Variations in size are desirable at market.

A. D. Folks and Tanglefoot (that's his Indian name) are clammers we've come to know at Alligator Point. In waders, knee or chest high in the bay, depending on the tide, they work their clam lease, pulling up specific bags by hand based on a designated maturity date and using the mapped locations. Once harvested, the clams are cleaned and graded by size for sale. We've eaten clams all over the world and agree that there is none better than an Alligator Point clam.

The "wow" quality of these clams is beginning to get noticed as the product slowly makes its way into restaurants. It is exciting to watch the reactions of those tasting an Alligator Point clam for the first time. To understand the clams' uniqueness, it helps to look them as you would a fine wine because it's really all about the *terroir*—only in this case it's just happens to be underwater. An Alligator Point seed clam buried in a different bay would have an altogether different flavor and texture due to the different minerals in the sand and salinity level of the water. There is something truly special about the forces at work in the bay at Alligator Point that incubates such a knockout clam. One favorite way we eat them is steamed with a little bit of butter right out of the shell, but they are ridiculously good any way you try them—tender, fat, sweet and salty, meaty, and unlike any other clam you've tasted.

GRILLED COBIA

with Alligator Point Clam Vinaigrette

COBIA IS A FIRM, WHITE-FLESHED FISH THAT STANDS UP WELL TO GRILLING. USING MESQUITE OR HICKORY WOOD IN YOUR GRILL GIVES THE COBIA A NUTTY SMOKINESS THAT COMPLIMENTS ITS NATURAL FLAVORS. WHEN DRIZZLED WITH THE CLAM VINAIGRETTE, IT'S A MATCH MADE IN HEAVEN.

YIELD: 4 SERVINGS

⅓ CUP PLUS 2 TABLESPOONS OLIVE OIL, DIVIDED

3 LARGE SHALLOTS, PEELED AND SLICED, ABOUT ½ CUP

6 FRESH THYME SPRIGS

1 DRIED ARBOL CHILE PEPPER

1 BAY LEAF

1 CUP VERJUS (OR DRY WHITE WINE)

3 DOZEN (ABOUT 2 POUNDS) SMALL ALLIGATOR POINT CLAMS, SCRUBBED (MAY SUBSTITUTE LOCAL SMALL LITTLENECK CLAMS)

3 TABLESPOONS FRESH LEMON JUICE

2 TEASPOONS MINCED SHALLOTS

1 TEASPOON CHOPPED FRESH THYME

1 TEASPOON CHOPPED FRESH PARSLEY

1 TEASPOON CHOPPED FRESH CHIVES

⅓ CUP EXTRA-VIRGIN OLIVE OIL

1 TABLESPOON KOSHER SALT, DIVIDED

1½ TEASPOONS FRESHLY GROUND BLACK PEPPER, DIVIDED

12 JUMBO ASPARAGUS STALKS, BOTTOM ENDS TRIMMED, PEELED, AND BLANCHED

2 TABLESPOONS PEANUT OIL, DIVIDED

4 (6 TO 7-OUNCE) COBIA FILLETS

Heat 2 tablespoons of the olive oil in a large, ovenproof rondeau or saucepan over medium-high heat. Add the shallots, thyme sprigs, chile pepper, and bay leaf and cook for 2 minutes. Increase the heat to high, add the verjus, and bring the mixture to a boil. Once boiling, add the clams, cover, and cook for 10 minutes. (Check the pan every 2 to 3 minutes, pulling the clams out of the saucepan and reserving them, as they open.)

Once all of the clams have opened, remove the saucepan from the heat and pull the remaining clams out of the broth. Return the broth to a simmer over medium-high heat and cook until reduced to ⅓ cup, about 7 to 10 minutes. Allow the mixture to cool slightly. While the broth is cooling remove the clams from their shells, discarding the shells. Strain the cooled broth through a fine-meshed sieve into a clean mixing bowl. Add the shelled clams to the broth, along with the lemon juice, shallots, chopped thyme, parsley, and chives. Whisk in the remaining ⅓ cup olive oil and the extra-virgin olive oil. Season the vinaigrette with ½ teaspoon of the salt and ¼ teaspoon of the pepper. Set vinaigrette aside, at room temperature, for up to 30 minutes until ready to serve.

Preheat the grill to high (400°F to 450°F).

Toss the asparagus spears with 1 tablespoon of the peanut oil and season with ½ teaspoon of the salt and ¼ teaspoon of the pepper; set aside. Brush the cobia fillets with the remaining tablespoon of peanut oil and season on both sides with the remaining 2 teaspoons of salt and the remaining 1 teaspoon of pepper.

Place the asparagus on the hot grill and cook, turning occasionally, 3 to 4 minutes or until tender. Remove the asparagus from the grill and cover to keep warm. Place the cobia on the hot grill and cook 4 to 5 minutes on each side, or until the fish is cooked through and flakes easily when tested with a fork. Arrange three asparagus spears and one cobia fillet on each of four dinner plates. Spoon ¼ cup of the vinaigrette over each fillet and serve immediately.

WHOLE-ROASTED MINGO SNAPPER ON PIPÉRADE

with Herb Croutons

Mingo, also known as vermilion snapper, is a smaller, shallow water fish. The true American red snapper is much larger and is a deep-water fish. While they share a similar flavor, the mingo snapper is lighter and flakier.

YIELD: 6 SERVINGS

6 (12 to 16-ounce) whole Mingo snappers, fins trimmed, gills removed, cleaned, and scaled

1 tablespoon plus ¾ teaspoon kosher salt, divided

1¾ teaspoons freshly ground black pepper, divided

2 lemons, thinly sliced

36 fresh thyme sprigs

1 cup plus 2 tablespoons roughly chopped fresh basil

½ cup (1 stick) plus 1 tablespoon unsalted butter, divided

2 tablespoons extra-virgin olive oil, divided

4 garlic cloves, peeled and sliced

2 large yellow onions, cut into 1-inch squares (about 6½ cups)

2 large red bell peppers, seeded and cut into 1-inch squares (about 2 cups)

2 large yellow bell peppers, seeded and cut into 1-inch squares (about 2 cups)

2 poblano peppers, seeded and cut into 1-inch squares (about 1½ cups)

2 cups seeded and diced Roma tomatoes

1 cup assorted heirloom cherry tomatoes, such as red, sungold, and purple cherry, halved

1 cup verjus or dry white wine

2 fresh basil sprigs

3 tablespoons Lemon Oil (page 382)

2 tablespoons finely chopped fresh basil

1 tablespoon finely chopped fresh parsley

1 tablespoon finely chopped fresh chives

1½ cups Herb Croutons (page 356)

Rinse the snappers under cold, running water, and pat both the inside and out with paper towels until dry. Season the inside cavity of each fish with ½ teaspoon of the salt and ¼ teaspoon of the pepper. Stuff each cavity with 3 to 4 lemon slices, 6 sprigs of thyme and 3 tablespoons roughly chopped basil. Refrigerate stuffed snappers until ready to cook.

Preheat the oven to 400°F.

Melt ½ cup of the butter and 1 tablespoon of the extra-virgin olive oil in a large rondeau or Dutch oven over medium heat. Add the garlic and cook, stirring, for 1 minute, being careful not to let the garlic get too brown. Add the onions and cook until softened, about 5 minutes, stirring frequently. Stir in the peppers and cook until slightly softened, 8 to 10 minutes. Add the Roma and cherry tomatoes, verjus, and basil sprigs, increase the heat to medium-high and simmer for 3 minutes. Season the vegetables with the remaining ¾ teaspoon of the salt and remaining ¼ teaspoon of pepper and remove from the heat.

Divide the pepper mixture evenly between two (13 x 9-inch) baking dishes. Arrange 3 stuffed snappers in each baking dish on top of the pepper mixture. Bake the fish for 20 to 25 minutes or until cooked through. Remove the snappers from the baking dish. Stir together the lemon oil, remaining tablespoon of butter, parsley, basil, and chives and add to the cooked pepper and tomato mixture. Spoon 1 cup of the pipérade onto each of six plates. Place one fish on each mound of pipérade and sprinkle each with ¼ cup of the herb croutons. Serve immediately.

PAN-SEARED POMPANO

with Spring Vegetable Risotto and Pea Tendrils

RAMPS ARE A MEMBER OF THE LILY FAMILY AND ARE FOUND WILD THROUGHOUT THE APPALACHIAN MOUNTAIN RANGE. THEY GROW WELL IN ANY MOUNTAINOUS REGION ABOVE THREE THOUSAND FEET. THEIR DISTINCT, PUNGENT FLAVOR IS A CROSS BETWEEN AN ONION AND SPICY, WILD GARLIC, WITH A HINT OF SWEETNESS. YOU CAN SUBSTITUTE LEEKS IF YOU CAN'T FIND ANY RAMPS.

YIELD: 4 SERVINGS

POMPANO:

4 (6-OUNCE) SKIN-ON POMPANO FILLETS
2 TEASPOONS KOSHER SALT
1 TEASPOON FRESHLY GROUND BLACK PEPPER
2 TABLESPOONS PEANUT OIL

RISOTTO:

3 TABLESPOONS UNSALTED BUTTER, DIVIDED
1 TABLESPOON MINCED SHALLOTS
1 TEASPOON CHOPPED FRESH THYME
2½ CUPS BASIC RISOTTO (PAGE 355)
1 TO 1½ CUPS VEGETABLE STOCK (PAGE 334), SIMMERING
½ TEASPOON KOSHER SALT
¼ TEASPOON FRESHLY GROUND BLACK PEPPER
½ CUP CHOPPED FRESH RAMPS (1-INCH PIECES), ABOUT 4 WHOLE RAMPS
½ CUP DICED BRAISED FENNEL (PAGE 377)
¾ CUP PEELED, BLANCHED, AND DICED BABY CARROTS
¾ CUP BLANCHED AND PEELED FRESH FAVA BEANS
½ CUP PEELED, BLANCHED, AND DICED ASPARAGUS (1-INCH PIECES)
¼ CUP BLANCHED SWEET ENGLISH PEAS
8 FRESH PEA TENDRILS, FOR GARNISH

TO PREPARE THE POMPANO:

Season the pompano fillet on both sides with the salt and pepper. Heat the peanut oil in a large skillet over medium-high heat. Add the fillets, skin side down, to the pan and cook about 3 minutes or until the skin is golden brown. Turn the fillets and cook an additional 2 minutes or until the fillets are cooked through and flake easily when tested with a fork. Transfer pompano to a platter and cover to keep warm.

TO PREPARE THE RISOTTO:

Melt half of the butter in a 4-quart saucepan over medium-high heat. Add the shallots and thyme and cook until softened, about 1 minute. Add the risotto and cook, stirring, until heated through, about 1 minute. Add ½ cup of the hot vegetable stock and stir constantly with a wooden spoon until all of the liquid is absorbed. Repeat this process, adding ½ cup of the stock each time, until the rice is creamy and al dente. (You may not need all 1½ cups of the stock.) Season the risotto with the salt and pepper and stir in the fresh ramps. Cook the ramps for 30 seconds and add the fennel, carrots, fava beans, asparagus, and English peas. Cook the risotto, stirring, for 1 minute or until the vegetables are heated through but still retain their bright color. Remove the risotto from the heat and stir in the remaining 1½ tablespoons of butter until melted.

Spoon 1½ cups of the spring vegetable risotto on each of four dinner plates. Arrange one pompano fillet over each portion, skin side up. Place two pea tendrils over each serving and serve immediately.

SHAD ROE

Each spring when he was a child, as the weather warmed, Chris' maternal grandmother and mother would have animated discussions about shad roe, look for shad roe, buy shad roe, and prepare shad roe for as long as it was available to them. His first experience of this regional delicacy was of the salted variety, quite possibly from a can, and he detested it. Eating the egg sack of a shad is certainly a stretch for any kid, and even for most adults it is an acquired taste. The roe has a strong, distinctive flavor that is difficult to forget, yet for those who grew up near the rivers that feed the Atlantic, it is truly memory cuisine.

Growing up in Charlottesville, Virginia, Chris' mother lived near a great system of rivers navigated by throngs of spawning shad each spring. They would swim up from the ocean laden with roe to be snagged by commercial fisherman. The roe has always been prized over the meat of the shad simply because the body of the fish, while delicious, has such an intricate and complex bone structure it is very impractical to fillet for sale. A properly cleaned and boned shad fillet looks almost mangled so not all that visually appealing for market.

Chris' mom and grandmother would also get fresh shad roe at the beach in early June. There they would cook the egg sack in the grease left from frying bacon and serve it with grits, eggs, and a side of bacon. His first taste of fresh, unsalted shad roe made a positive impression. Sure, it was a bit funky, but a little funk can be endured when paired with bacon, plus he loved grits and eggs. It seemed shad roe served Southern style was the perfect introduction. Shad roe was growing on him.

For a lot of Southerners of middle age on up, shad roe is a very sought after delicacy that heralds springtime. It is a marker of time. When shad roe appears, you know spring is truly here. Gathering at certain times of year and chasing after one ingredient, or seeking out another, yields these uncommon food experiences that, perhaps solely out of nostalgia, become part of our adult lives—our memory cuisine.

We maintain many of the food traditions of our childhoods as much out of wistful longing as an extension of our roles at the restaurant. It's these food memories that become the fodder for our creativity, the genesis of dishes we refine, tweak, and reinterpret until they land on the menu anew. Many patrons who come to Hot and Hot for shad roe when it's "that time" do so because of fond memories of it, yet we can promise they leave with a renewed appreciation of it served in a fresh and contemporary way.

BACON-WRAPPED SHAD ROE

with Anson Mills Grits and Caper Brown Butter Sauce

THE TRICK HERE IS TO SLICE THE BACON VERY THIN. IF YOU DON'T HAVE ACCESS TO A MEAT SLICER, PURCHASE A SLAB OF BACON AND HAVE A BUTCHER SLICE IT INTO VERY THIN STRIPS. WHEN THE BACON IS SLICED THIN ENOUGH, IT WILL BE EASY TO WRAP AROUND THE SHAD AND ADHERES LIKE SKIN TO THE ROE SACK DURING COOKING.

YIELD: 4 SERVINGS

2 PAIRS (5 OUNCES EACH) SHAD ROE, MEMBRANES INTACT
8 TO 10 THIN SLICES (4 OUNCES) BACON
1 TABLESPOON PEANUT OIL
¼ CUP (½ STICK) UNSALTED BUTTER
4 TEASPOONS MINCED SHALLOTS
2 TABLESPOONS DRAINED CAPERS
2 TABLESPOONS FRESH LEMON JUICE
PINCH OF KOSHER SALT
2 TEASPOONS CHOPPED FRESH PARSLEY
1⅓ CUPS COOKED ANSON MILLS ANTEBELLUM
    COARSE WHITE GRITS (PAGE 380)

Gently rinse the roe in cold water. Using scissors, separate the two halves of each pair, being careful not to puncture the roe sac. Gently pat each roe half dry.

Wrap each roe half with 2 to 3 slices of bacon, slightly overlapping the bacon with each wrap. (The roe should be completely covered by the bacon.)

Heat the peanut oil in a large cast-iron skillet over medium-low heat. Add the roe and cook until the bacon is rendered and crispy on each side, 10 to 12 minutes. Remove the shad roe from the pan, set aside, and keep warm.

Increase the heat to medium and melt the butter in the skillet. Continue to cook the butter until it turns a light, golden brown color and smells slightly nutty. Add the shallots to the butter and cook for 30 seconds. Add the capers and cook, just until the foam subsides, about 30 seconds. Add the lemon juice and a pinch of salt and remove the skillet from the heat. Stir in the parsley.

Spoon ⅓ cup of the cooked grits on each of four appetizer plates. Arrange one piece of cooked shad roe over each mound of grits. Drizzle 1½ to 2 tablespoons of the sauce over each shad roe and serve immediately.

ALLIGATOR POINT CLAM PAELLA

We love the idea of pairing clams and saffron in this classic dish. If you don't have access to Alligator Point Clams, you can substitute small littleneck clams. Feel free to add additional seafood such as mussels, shrimp, or crawfish, as you see fit.

YIELD: 6 SERVINGS

2 tablespoons unsalted butter

2 tablespoons extra-virgin olive oil

4 garlic cloves, peeled and sliced

2 dried Arbol chile peppers, broken in half

1 tablespoon saffron threads

1 pound smoked chorizo sausage, sliced into 1-inch slices

1 large onion, peeled and diced (about 2½ cups)

1 large red bell pepper, seeded and cut into 1-inch squares (about 1¼ cups)

1 large yellow bell pepper, seeded and cut into 1-inch squares (about 1¼ cups)

1 large poblano pepper, seeded and cut into 1-inch squares (about 1 cup)

4 fresh thyme sprigs

1 bay leaf

3 dozen (about 2 pounds) small Alligator Point clams, scrubbed

2 cups uncooked long-grain rice

4 cups Chicken Stock (page 335)

1 tablespoon kosher salt

1 teaspoon freshly ground black pepper

Preheat the oven 400°F.

Heat the butter and olive oil in a large paella pan or rondeau over medium heat. Add the garlic, broken chile peppers, and saffron and cook for 3 minutes, stirring frequently. Stir in the sausage and cook until lightly browned, about 3 minutes. Add the onion, peppers, thyme sprigs, and bay leaf and cook until the vegetables are softened, 6 to 7 minutes, stirring often. Add the clams and cook, stirring, for 2 minutes. Stir in the rice and cook, stirring frequently, for 1 minute. Add the chicken stock, salt, and pepper and bring the mixture to a boil. Once the liquid begins to boil, cover and place the pan in the oven. Roast for 20 to 25 minutes or until the rice is cooked through and the clams are open.

Remove the bay leaf and thyme sprigs from the paella. Spoon about 2 cups of the rice and sausage mixture onto each of six dinner plates, arranging the clams over and around the rice. Serve hot.

GRILLED WILD TURKEY BREAST
with Grilled Vegetables and Sauce Gribiche

WHEN PREPARING WILD TURKEY, WE LIKE TO "SALT" OR "KOSHER" THE MEAT BY TOSSING IT IN OUR HOUSE-MADE POULTRY SALT AND MARINATING IT FOR ABOUT AN HOUR. ALTHOUGH IT MAY SEEM LIKE MORE SALT THAN YOU WOULD NORMALLY ADD, THE END RESULT IS VERY FLAVORFUL. THIS PROCESS IS NOT COMPLICATED AND SOFTENS THE SLIGHTLY GAMEY FLAVOR OF THE WILD TURKEY MEAT.

YIELD: 6 SERVINGS

12 (3-OUNCE) WILD TURKEY BREAST STEAKS
1 TABLESPOON HASTINGS CREATIONS POULTRY SALT (PAGE 381) OR KOSHER SALT
½ TEASPOON FRESHLY GROUND BLACK PEPPER
1 GARLIC CLOVE, CRUSHED AND PEELED
¼ CUP EXTRA-VIRGIN OLIVE OIL
2 (8-OUNCE) HEADS RADICCHIO LETTUCE, CUT LENGTHWISE INTO 6 WEDGES EACH
2 LARGE (1-POUND) FENNEL BULBS, CORES TRIMMED AND CUT INTO 6 WEDGES EACH
6 SPRING VIDALIA ONIONS, CUT IN HALF LENGTHWISE
12 JUMBO ASPARAGUS STALKS, BOTTOM PART TRIMMED, PEELED, AND BLANCHED (PAGE 377)
3 TO 4 TABLESPOONS LEMON OIL (PAGE 382)
1 TABLESPOON KOSHER SALT
1½ TEASPOONS FRESHLY GROUND BLACK PEPPER
1½ CUPS SAUCE GRIBICHE (PAGE 337)

Toss the turkey steaks with the poultry salt, pepper, garlic clove, and extra-virgin olive oil in a large bowl until well seasoned. Cover the steaks and chill for 1 hour.

Preheat the grill to medium high (350°F to 400°F).

Remove the turkey steaks from the refrigerator and allow them to continue to marinate at room temperature for 20 minutes before grilling.

Combine the radicchio wedges, fennel wedges, onions, and asparagus stalks in a large bowl. Drizzle with the lemon oil, salt, and pepper and toss to combine.

Grill the vegetables on all sides, until lightly charred and tender: 1 to 2 minutes for the radicchio, 5 to 7 minutes for the fennel, 3 to 4 minutes for the onions, and 3 to 4 minutes for the asparagus. Set the vegetables aside and cover to keep warm.

Remove the turkey steaks from the marinade and discard the garlic clove and any excess oil. Grill the steaks for 3 to 4 minutes on each side, or until cooked through.

To serve, arrange two pieces of the turkey steaks on each dinner plate. Place two wedges of radicchio, two wedges of fennel, one onion half, and two asparagus stalks on each plate. Spoon ¼ cup of the sauce gribiche over and around each plate and serve immediately.

BRAISED RABBIT
with Vegetable Ragout

Any manner of fresh vegetables can be used to prepare this dish. Spring Vidalia onions make a good substitute for the torpedo onions, which are similar in size and have a purple-colored outer layer. Farm-raised rabbit can be found in most specialty markets and can be cut into five pieces (two rear legs, two front legs, and the loin) by the butcher if you're unsure how to portion the rabbit for this dish. For a more refined presentation, purchase three whole rabbits and use only the hind leg quarters for the braise. A flavorful stock can be made from the remaining halves of the rabbits.

YIELD: 6 SERVINGS

2 (2¼-pound) whole rabbits, each cut into 5 pieces

1 tablespoon plus ½ teaspoon kosher salt, divided

2½ teaspoons freshly ground black pepper, divided

3 tablespoons olive oil

1 large onion, peeled and roughly chopped (about 2 cups)

3 small carrots, peeled and roughly chopped (about 1 cup)

4 fresh thyme sprigs

½ cup (about ¾ ounce) dried porcini mushrooms

1 bay leaf

6 cups Chicken Stock (page 335)

3 tablespoons unsalted butter, divided

1 tablespoon minced shallots

¼ teaspoon chopped fresh thyme

½ pound (about 18) fresh morel mushrooms

5 small spring torpedo onions, braised and halved (page 377)

4 small carrots, peeled and cut into 1-inch oblique cut (or diagonally cut), and blanched (about 2 cups)

1 cup fresh peeled and blanched fava beans

1 teaspoon chopped fresh parsley

1 teaspoon chopped fresh chives

Preheat the oven to 400°F.

Season the rabbit pieces on all sides with 1 tablespoon of the salt and 2 teaspoons of the pepper. Heat the olive oil in an 6 to 8-quart ovenproof stockpot over medium-high heat. Add the rabbit pieces in batches and sear until golden brown on all sides, 4 to 5 minutes per side. Transfer the browned rabbit to a platter and set aside. Repeat with remaining rabbit pieces.

Add the onion, carrots, and thyme sprigs and cook for 5 minutes, stirring to scrape up any browned bits from the bottom of the stockpot. Add the porcini mushrooms and cook an additional 2 minutes, stirring occasionally. Add the bay leaf, chicken stock, and browned rabbit pieces to the stockpot. Bring the mixture to a boil, cover, and place the stockpot in the oven. Allow the rabbit mixture to braise for 45 to 50 minutes, or until the rabbit is fork tender.

Remove the rabbit pieces from the braising liquid and let them cool at room temperature for 20 minutes. Meanwhile, strain the braising liquid through a fine-meshed sieve into a medium saucepan. Bring the strained liquid to a boil and cook over medium-high heat until the stock is reduced by half, about 30 to 35 minutes. Reserve 1 cup of this braising liquid for the ragout. Save the remaining 2 cups of liquid for another use, such as braising liquid in the Cajun-Style Boudin Sausage (page 269).

Melt 2 tablespoons of the butter in a large sauté pan over medium heat. Add the shallots and chopped thyme and cook for 1 minute, stirring frequently. Add the morels and cook for 5 to 6 minutes, stirring frequently. Add the braised onions, carrots, and fava beans and stir until heated through, 1 to 2 minutes. Place the braised rabbit pieces on top of the vegetable mixture and add the reserved liquid, the remaining ½ teaspoon of salt and ½ teaspoon of pepper. Bring the mixture to a simmer and place in the oven. Bake the ragout at 400°F for 10 minutes or until everything is heated through.

Transfer the rabbit pieces and the vegetables to a large serving platter with a slotted spoon. Return the skillet and its liquid to medium heat and bring to a simmer. Remove the sauce from the heat and whisk in the remaining tablespoon of butter, the parsley, and the chives. Pour the sauce over the rabbit and vegetable ragout and serve immediately.

WHOLE-ROASTED BABY CHICKEN
with Crawfish and Tasso Jambalaya

IT IS ESSENTIAL TO ALLOW THE CHICKENS TO SIT AT ROOM TEMPERATURE FOR ABOUT ONE AND ONE-HALF HOURS BEFORE BEGINNING THE COOKING PROCESS. IF COLD BIRDS ARE PLACED DIRECTLY IN A HOT OVEN, THE MEAT WILL NOT COOK EVENLY AROUND THE BONES AND MAY NOT BE AS MOIST. IF USING CHICKENS THAT WERE FROZEN, MAKE SURE THEY ARE PROPERLY THAWED BEFORE ROASTING.

YIELD: 6 SERVINGS

CHICKENS:

6 (1 TO 1¼-POUND) BABY CHICKENS, POUSSINS, OR CORNISH GAME HENS, RINSED AND PATTED DRY

1 TABLESPOON KOSHER SALT, DIVIDED

2 TEASPOONS FRESHLY GROUND BLACK PEPPER, DIVIDED

24 FRESH THYME SPRIGS (ABOUT 4 OUNCES)

2 TABLESPOONS OLIVE OIL, DIVIDED

JAMBALAYA:

½ CUP (1 STICK) UNSALTED BUTTER

2 CUPS DICED SWEET ONION, ABOUT 1 LARGE

½ CUP DICED CELERY, ABOUT 2 SMALL RIBS

1 TABLESPOON MINCED FRESH GARLIC

1 BAY LEAF

1 CUP SEEDED AND DICED RED BELL PEPPER, ABOUT 1 LARGE

¾ CUP SEEDED AND DICED POBLANO PEPPER, ABOUT 1 LARGE

½ CUP SEEDED AND DICED YELLOW BELL PEPPER, ABOUT ½ LARGE

1½ CUPS FINELY DICED TASSO HAM (ABOUT ½ POUND)

2 CUPS UNCOOKED LONG-GRAIN RICE

1 TABLESPOON KOSHER SALT

½ TEASPOON FRESHLY GROUND BLACK PEPPER

½ TEASPOON SMOKED PAPRIKA

½ TEASPOON ANCHO CHILI POWDER

4½ CUPS SPICY HAM HOCK BROTH (PAGE 336) OR CHICKEN STOCK (PAGE 335)

¼ TEASPOON CAYENNE PEPPER

2 CUPS COOKED AND PEELED CRAWFISH TAIL MEAT (PAGE 266)

1 CUP FINELY CHOPPED GREEN ONION TOPS (ABOUT 1 BUNCH)

½ CUP FINELY CHOPPED FRESH PARSLEY

3 TABLESPOONS CHOPPED FRESH CHIVES

TO PREPARE THE CHICKENS:

Preheat the oven to 400°F.

Season the inside cavity of each chicken with ¼ teaspoon each of salt and pepper. Stuff 4 fresh thyme sprigs into each cavity. Tie the legs of each chicken securely with butcher's twine and tuck the wing tips behind each chicken. Lightly grease a jelly roll pan with 1 tablespoon of the olive oil. Arrange the chickens on the pan, tail to tail. Rub the remaining tablespoon of olive oil over the chickens and season the outsides evenly with the remaining 1½ teaspoons of salt and ½ teaspoon of pepper. Roast the chickens in the oven for 45 to 50 minutes, or until golden brown and cooked through. Allow chickens to rest for 5 minutes before serving.

TO PREPARE THE JAMBALAYA:

While the chickens are roasting, melt the butter in a large rondeau or Dutch oven over medium-high heat. Add the onion, celery, garlic, and bay leaf and sauté for 5 to 7 minutes, or until the vegetables are softened. Add the peppers and continue to cook, stirring occasionally, for about 3 minutes. Add the tasso ham and cook for 2 minutes. Stir in the rice, salt, pepper, paprika, and ancho chili powder and cook, stirring constantly, for 1 to 2 minutes. (The rice should be well coated with the fat from the pan.) Slowly add the broth and bring the mixture to a boil. Once boiling, cover the pan, reduce the heat to low, and simmer for 20 to 22 minutes or until the rice is cooked through and most of the liquid is absorbed.

Uncover and stir in the crawfish tail meat and green onions and cook for 1 minute or until heated through. Remove from the heat and stir in the parsley.

Spoon about 1½ cups of the jambalaya mixture onto each of six dinner plates. Arrange one chicken on each plate and sprinkle each with ½ tablespoon of the chives. Serve immediately.

FORAGERS AND FOOD LOVERS

Chris Bennett, a former employee and chef by trade, has a family farm nearby. Walking his land like all landowners do, but also as a culinarian, he discovers things like wild persimmons, sassafras, wild ginger, wild strawberries, and mulberries to forage and bring to us. We have other relationships like this too. The other day, some of our cooks found a mulberry tree in a park and harvested them for use here. While regulations don't allow us to serve fish we catch or game we hunt, we have the luxury of offering wild foraged fruits and vegetables.

For years, restaurants have relied on foragers to bring in wild mushrooms like morels. Yet we've expanded our reach beyond procurement of just the more expected wild items thanks to an assortment of passionate folks who seek out wild ingredients that your grandmother might have used but you just don't see in markets. Chris Bennett has become one of the key people who bring us these amazing foraged finds. Because he knows his land, he is always there when these uncommon gems are in season. By bringing them to our door, he enables us to add an incredibly unique layer to our cuisine that is absolutely of the moment. It is a taste of right now. If it is wild strawberries that he brings, we celebrate them for just the nanosecond of time nature provides.

Our patrons delight in these uncommon ingredients and the mind-blowing flavor that they bring to dishes. When we make our honeysuckle simple syrup with fresh blossoms in spring and drizzle it over wild strawberries and plump mulberries for a 100 percent "wild" dessert, we always watch the reaction of diners. It is quite fulfilling to witness someone taste the perfume of honeysuckle and the absolutely explosive flavor of these tiny wild strawberries and mulberries. Again, food is magic, like a time warp, the flavors transport our guests back to childhood and those days of standing by the honeysuckle bush, tasting the nectar of honeysuckles, one by one. It's a heady experience that we are honored to provide, which truly embodies our philosophy of cooking and eating.

LEMON BUTTERMILK TARTS

with Wild Strawberries and Mulberries

ZEB, OUR OLDEST SON, HAS ALWAYS LOVED THE FLAVOR OF LEMON. WHEN WE HAVE THESE TARTS IN OUR REFRIGERATOR, HE WILL EAT THE MAJORITY OF THEM—SOMETIMES EVEN FOR BREAKFAST! HE LOVES THE ZING OF THE LEMON FLAVOR COMBINED WITH THE SWEET WILD BERRIES. IF WILD BERRIES ARE UNAVAILABLE, YOU CAN SUBSTITUTE LOCAL, RIPE STRAWBERRIES, WHICH HAVE A RICH, RED COLOR THROUGHOUT AND AN INTENSE BERRY FLAVOR.

YIELD: 8 SERVINGS

1½ POUNDS SWEET PASTRY DOUGH (PAGE **358**),
    A DOUBLE RECIPE
4 LARGE EGGS, LIGHTLY BEATEN
1⅓ CUPS GRANULATED SUGAR
¼ CUP BUTTERMILK
2 TABLESPOONS FINELY GROUND YELLOW CORNMEAL
½ CUP (**1** STICK) UNSALTED BUTTER, MELTED AND
    SLIGHTLY COOLED
¼ CUP FRESH LEMON JUICE
1 TABLESPOON GRATED LEMON ZEST
¼ TEASPOON FRESHLY GRATED NUTMEG
1 POUND (ABOUT **2** CUPS) SMALL WILD STRAWBERRIES
    AND MULBERRIES, STEMS PICKED AND HULLED
1 CUP WHIPPED CREAM (PAGE **367**)

Preheat the oven to 375°F.

Place the pastry dough on a lightly floured surface and roll out to ⅛-inch thickness. Cut the dough into 8 (6-inch) circles. Fit the dough circles into 8 (4-inch) fluted tart pans, pressing the dough into the bottom and sides of the pans. Trim off any excess dough around the edges of the tart pans. Cut 8 squares of parchment paper to fit inside each tart pan. Once the tart shells are lined with the parchment squares, fill each shell with pie weights or baking beans and place the tart pans on a baking sheet.

Bake the tarts at 375°F for 15 minutes. Remove the tarts from the oven and remove the parchment and pie weights from each tart. Return the tart shells to oven and continue baking for 5 to 7 minutes, or until lightly golden and slightly crispy to the touch. Allow the tart shells to cool completely at room temperature.

Reduce the oven temperature to 325°F.

Whisk together the eggs and sugar in a large mixing bowl until the mixture is pale yellow and slightly thickened. Stir in the buttermilk, cornmeal, and melted butter, mixing just until smooth. Add the lemon juice and zest. Divide the custard evenly between the prebaked shells and grate 1 to 2 scrapes of fresh nutmeg over each tart.

Bake the tarts at 325°F for 20 to 22 minutes or until the edges are set and the tops are golden brown. (The center of the tarts may still jiggle slightly when ready.) Allow the tarts to cool to room temperature before serving.

To serve, arrange the whole strawberries and mulberries, cut side down, in a circular pattern on top of each tart until the entire top is covered with berries. Spoon 2 tablespoons of the whipped cream onto each tart. Serve immediately.

LEMON BUTTERMILK TART

Before opening Hot and Hot Fish Club, Chris worked as a private chef for the Stephens family in Birmingham and Idie often prepared bread and desserts at home for Chris to serve at the Stephens' home. One family member, Donald Comer, was a self-taught cook with a passion for the perfect piecrust. He had been working on perfecting a tart shell to meet his high standards. Meanwhile, Idie was doing the same thing, not realizing that she and Donald shared this same interest in "pastry arts." One day, Donald requested that Chris serve a lemon tart, and, now knowing how particular Donald was about tart shells, Idie experimented until she developed a recipe that consistently worked well and pleased Mr. Comer. She concentrated, too, on the lemon filling. It had to have pure lemon flavor that stood out from first bite to last. After several attempts, she mastered this lemon buttermilk tart, which we still serve today. The tanginess of the buttermilk is a wonderful counterpoint to the tartness of the lemon. Idie began making this tart regularly, first for the Stephens family and, eventually, for the restaurant.

After having been served this tart at a function in Seaside, Florida, a gentleman approached Idie and asked where she had purchased the lemons, mentioning he had never tasted such intense lemon flavor in a tart. He loved how the tartness of the lemons "popped" in his mouth only to be followed by the perfect balance of vanilla and whipped cream. That moment was a great lesson in letting the pure essence of ingredients shine. Tinkering combined with an ample dose of restraint allows something as simple as a lemon tart to be spectacular. We have served this tart at the restaurant from day one onward.

LAVENDER POUND CAKE
with *Meyer Lemon Glaze*

IDIE'S FATHER ALWAYS LOVED POUND CAKE. FOR A MAN WHO DIDN'T HAVE MUCH OF A SWEET TOOTH, HE WAS CERTAINLY PASSIONATE ABOUT FINDING A RICH, MOIST POUND CAKE WHEREVER WE WENT. DURING THE FIRST FEW YEARS AFTER OPENING HOT AND HOT FISH CLUB, IDIE SERVED A BASIC POUND CAKE GARNISHED WITH LOCAL BERRIES AND FRESH WHIPPED CREAM. WHEN A CUSTOMER CALLED AND REQUESTED A LAVENDER POUND CAKE FOR A SPECIAL CELEBRATION, IDIE CREATED THIS RECIPE AND PAIRED IT WITH A MEYER LEMON GLAZE. POUND CAKE IS NOW ONE OF HER FAVORITE WAYS TO COOK WITH LAVENDER.

YIELD: 1 (10-INCH) CAKE OR 10 TO 12 SERVINGS

CAKE:
1½ CUPS (3 STICKS) PLUS 2 TEASPOONS UNSALTED BUTTER, AT ROOM TEMPERATURE, DIVIDED

1 (8-OUNCE) PACKAGE CREAM CHEESE, AT ROOM TEMPERATURE

3 CUPS GRANULATED SUGAR

1 TABLESPOON PURE VANILLA EXTRACT

1 TO 2 TEASPOONS DRIED LAVENDER BLOSSOMS

6 LARGE EGGS, AT ROOM TEMPERATURE

3 CUPS CAKE FLOUR, SIFTED

MEYER LEMON GLAZE:
1¼ CUPS CONFECTIONERS' SUGAR, SIFTED

2 TABLESPOONS FRESHLY SQUEEZED MEYER LEMON JUICE, ABOUT 1 SMALL LEMON

¼ TEASPOON PURE VANILLA EXTRACT

TO PREPARE THE CAKE:

Preheat the oven to 325°F. Lightly grease a 10-inch tube pan with 2 teaspoons of the butter.

Combine the remaining 1½ cups of butter and the cream cheese in the bowl of a standing mixer fitted with a paddle attachment. Whip the butter mixture until well combined. With the machine on low, add the sugar in a slow, steady stream. Add the vanilla and lavender blossoms and continue mixing until the mixture is light and fluffy, stopping to scrape down the sides of the bowl as needed.

With the machine on low, add the eggs, one at a time, stopping to scrape the sides of the bowl between each addition. Add the flour, one cup at a time, stopping to scrape the bowl occasionally. Once the flour is well incorporated, pour the batter into the prepared pan and place a rack in the center of the oven.

Bake for about 1 hour and 15 minutes or until a cake tester or skewer inserted into the center of the cake comes out clean. Cool the cake in the pan for 10 to 15 minutes before unmolding. Allow cake to cool completely before glazing. You can dust with extra confectioners' sugar for added presentation.

TO PREPARE THE GLAZE:

Whisk together the confectioners' sugar, Meyer lemon juice, and vanilla. Drizzle the glaze over the top of the cooled cake. Allow the glaze to set and drip slightly down the sides of the cake for 5 minutes before serving.

THE HOT AND HOT FISH CLUB
CHOCOLATE SAMPLER

At the restaurant, we serve a dessert platter with miniature portions of our favorite chocolate desserts. This dessert was created in honor of Idie's addiction to chocolate. As a child, Idie's father used to bring her a piece of chocolate everyday after school. Not surprisingly, this habit was the beginning of her love for all things chocolate. Different types of chocolate have been used throughout the years at the restaurant, including El Rey, Valrhona, and currently Callebaut. Although Idie's personal preference is milk chocolate, we prep all of these desserts using a dark, Belgian-style chocolate that is made with over 50 percent cocoa solids. Idie's philosophy behind the chocolate sampler platter is to feature chocolate in different applications, showcasing different textures, consistencies, and flavors. For example, the Chocolate Caramel Mousse is light and airy while the Chocolate-Black Pepper Cookie with Cardamom is crispy and slightly spicy. You don't have to make all of these desserts at once like we do. Each chocolate item is decadent enough to stand on its own.

CHOCOLATE CARAMEL MOUSSE

YIELD: ABOUT 3½ CUPS OR 10 SERVINGS

3¾ OUNCES (ABOUT ½ CUP) DARK CHOCOLATE MORSELS
1 CUP GRANULATED SUGAR
3 TABLESPOONS WATER
1½ CUPS HEAVY CREAM, DIVIDED
3 TABLESPOONS UNSALTED BUTTER
⅛ TEASPOON SALT
PINCH OF FRESHLY GROUND BLACK PEPPER
½ CUP PLUS 2 TABLESPOONS CANDIED PEANUTS (PAGE 363)

Place the chocolate in the top of a double boiler or stainless steel bowl set over a pot of simmering water. Allow the chocolate to melt, stirring occasionally, until smooth. Remove from the heat and set aside in a warm place.

Combine the sugar and water in a small saucepan over medium-high heat. Stir just until the mixture begins to boil and the sugar is dissolved. Continue cooking, without stirring, until the mixture reaches 360°F (dark caramel stage) on a candy thermometer and turns a dark amber color. Immediately remove the caramel from the heat and whisk in ¾ cup of the cream, the butter, salt and pepper. Set the caramel aside until it reaches room temperature, about 10 minutes.

Stir the melted chocolate into the cooled caramel and set aside at room temperature.

Whip the remaining ¾ cup of heavy cream until medium peaks form. Fold the whipped cream, in thirds, into the chocolate caramel mixture. Refrigerate the mousse until well chilled, about 2 hours. Spoon ⅓ cup of the mousse into ten dessert cups or ramekins. Sprinkle each serving with 1 tablespoon of the candied peanuts and serve immediately.

CHOCOLATE TRUFFLES

YIELD: ABOUT 16 SERVINGS

½ CUP PLUS 2 TABLESPOONS HEAVY CREAM
2 TEASPOONS GRATED ORANGE ZEST, ABOUT 1 ORANGE
12 OUNCES (ABOUT ¾ CUP PLUS 1½ TABLESPOONS) DARK CHOCOLATE MORSELS, FINELY CHOPPED
PINCH OF SALT
½ CUP (1 STICK) UNSALTED BUTTER, AT ROOM TEMPERATURE
2 CUPS UNSWEETENED COCOA POWDER, FOR COATING TRUFFLES

Combine the heavy cream and orange zest in a small saucepan over medium heat. Allow the mixture to come to a boil, cover, and remove from the heat. Steep the cream for 30 minutes.

Place the chopped chocolate in a medium mixing bowl and set aside. Line the bottom of a 6 x 6 x 2-inch baking pan with parchment paper and set aside.

Return the steeped cream mixture to a simmer over medium heat. Once the mixture begins to boil, remove and strain through a fine-meshed strainer set over the bowl of dark chocolate. Allow the cream and chocolate mixture to sit at room temperature for 1 minute without stirring.

Add the salt and butter to the chocolate mixture and whisk just until smooth. Be careful not to overmix. Pour the chocolate mixture into the prepared baking pan and chill over night until firm.

Invert the chilled chocolate mixture onto clean surface and remove the parchment paper. Cut the chocolate into sixteen equal squares and place in a small bowl of cocoa. Toss the squares until well coated and serve immediately or chill until ready to serve.

CHOCOLATE POT DE CRÈME

YIELD: 4 SERVINGS

8 OUNCES (ABOUT **1** CUP AND **2** TABLESPOONS) BITTERSWEET
    CHOCOLATE MORSELS
1 CUP HEAVY CREAM
¾ CUP WHOLE MILK
6 LARGE EGG YOLKS
2 TEASPOONS KAHLÚA OR OTHER COFFEE-FLAVORED LIQUEUR
½ CUP WHIPPED CREAM (PAGE **367**), FOR GARNISH

Place the chocolate in a stainless steel bowl or in the top of a double boiler set over a pot of gently simmering water. Stir the chocolate occasionally, just until melted. Remove the bowl from the heat and set aside.

While the chocolate is melting, combine the cream and milk in a medium saucepan over medium heat. Allow the mixture to scald (but not boil) and remove from the heat. Whisk the melted chocolate into the cream mixture. Return the saucepan to the stove over medium heat and whisk just until the mixture begins to simmer.

Remove the chocolate from the heat and slowly add the hot mixture to the egg yolks in a thin stream, while whisking constantly. Return the chocolate mixture to the saucepan. Prepare a water bath by filling a 13 x 9-inch baking dish halfway with ice and a small amount of water. Find a clean (preferably stainless steel), shallow container that will fit inside the water bath and set aside. (An 8 x 8-inch baking dish will work well.)

Return the chocolate mixture to the stove and cook over medium heat until the mixture reaches 160°F, stirring constantly. Immediately pour the mixture into the 8 x 8-inch baking dish and set it inside the ice bath. Stir until the mixture cools to about 90°F.

Stir the Kahlúa into the custard mixture and strain through a fine-meshed strainer. Spoon the custard evenly into four (½-cup) serving bowls or custard cups and chill for at least 2 hours before serving. Spoon several tablespoons of the whipped cream over each custard, just before serving. The pot de crème custards will keep in the refrigerator for up to three days.

CHOCOLATE–BLACK PEPPER COOKIE

with Cardamom

YIELD: ABOUT 3½ DOZEN

3 CUPS ALL-PURPOSE FLOUR

1½ CUPS UNSWEETENED COCOA POWDER

½ TEASPOON SALT

¾ TEASPOON FRESHLY GROUND BLACK PEPPER, DIVIDED

1 TEASPOON GROUND CINNAMON

1 TEASPOON FRESHLY GROUND CARDAMOM

1½ CUPS (**3** STICKS) UNSALTED BUTTER, AT ROOM TEMPERATURE

2 CUPS GRANULATED SUGAR

2 LARGE EGGS

1 TEASPOON PURE VANILLA EXTRACT

2 TABLESPOONS WHITE SANDING SUGAR OR COARSE RAW SUGAR,
   FOR GARNISH

Sift together the flour, cocoa powder, salt, ½ teaspoon of the pepper, the cinnamon, and cardamom into a clean, dry mixing bowl; set aside.

Add the butter and sugar to the bowl of a standing mixer with a paddle attachment. Cream the butter mixture on medium speed until light and fluffy. Scrape down the butter mixture from the side of the bowl and continue to mix on medium speed for 1 more minute.

Reduce the speed to low and add the egg, mixing just until incorporated. Add the vanilla, stirring just until it is incorporated. With the mixer on the lowest speed, begin adding the sifted flour mixture, a little at a time, until all of the ingredients have been added. Remove the dough from the mixing bowl and divide evenly between 2 sheets of parchment paper. Using the parchment paper, form each portion of the dough into a long log, about 2 inches in diameter, with the parchment paper surrounding the dough. Wrap each log securely in plastic wrap and chill the dough until firm, at least 4 hours. (At this point, the dough will keep in the freezer for up to 2 months.)

Preheat the oven to 325°F and line several rimmed baking sheets with parchment paper.

Stir together the sanding sugar and remaining ¼ teaspoon of black pepper in a small bowl. Unwrap the cookie dough and slice the logs into ¼-inch-thick slices. Arrange the slices on the prepared baking sheets about 1 inch apart. Sprinkle the tops of the cookies with the sanding sugar mixture, using about ⅛ teaspoon per cookie.

Bake the cookies for 12 to 15 minutes or until the cookies are mostly set in the middle. Allow the cookies to cool on the baking sheets for 5 minutes before transferring them to a cooling rack. Cool completely before serving.

MOLTEN CHOCOLATE LAVA CAKES

We often chill the lava cake batter before baking at the restaurant. This works well at home, especially if you're trying to prepare items ahead of time. The batter is good when chilled, covered, for up to one week. You can also pour the batter into the prepared ramekins and chill for up to two hours. If the cakes are chilled in the ramekins, be sure to add one to two minutes to the baking time. When properly cooked, these lava cakes will still have a liquid center.

YIELD: 10 SERVINGS

6 ounces (about 1 cup) good-quality bittersweet
    chocolate morsels
¾ cup (1½ sticks) plus 1 tablespoon unsalted butter,
    softened, divided
½ cup granulated sugar, divided
3 large eggs
3 large egg yolks
¼ cup sifted confectioners' sugar, for garnish
¾ cup Whipped Cream (page 367), for garnish

Fill a saucepan or base of a double boiler one-third of the way full with water and bring to a simmer.

Combine the chocolate and ¾ cup of the butter in a stainless steel bowl or in the top of a double boiler and place over the gently simmering water. Stir the chocolate occasionally, just until melted. Remove the bowl from the heat and set aside to cool slightly, about 5 minutes.

Place ¼ cup plus 2 tablespoons of the sugar, the eggs, and egg yolks in a large bowl and whisk until the mixture is pale yellow, slightly thickened, and almost doubled in volume. Stir the egg mixture into the melted chocolate, stirring until well incorporated.

Preheat the oven to 400°F.

Using a clean pastry brush, coat the inside of ten (⅓-cup) ramekins or baking dishes with the remaining tablespoon of softened butter. Spoon the remaining 2 tablespoons of granulated sugar into the buttered ramekins and roll the sugar in each ramekin until the sides are lightly coated. Shake any excess sugar out of the ramekins.

Spoon 3 tablespoons of the lava cake batter into the prepared ramekins. Bake the cakes for about 12 minutes, or until the edges of the cakes have risen and are slightly firm. (The center of the cakes may still be slightly sunken in, when ready.) Immediately invert the ramekins and place the cakes on dessert plates. Serve immediately with a light dusting of confectioners' sugar and a small dollop of whipped cream.

FAMILY TRIP TO ROME

Archbishop Joseph Marino, a Birmingham native, now archbishop nuncio to Bangladesh, worked for the Vatican in Rome for a number of years and returns to Alabama from time to time to visit his father. Since we are Catholic, and many of our friends know Archbishop Marino well, it was suggested we contact him when planning a family trip to Italy. The archbishop was living in London at that time, but graciously offered us the use of his flat in Rome, a driver, and arranged tours for us to places we might not otherwise have had access.

Experiencing Rome had been a lifelong dream of Idie's ever since childhood where she attended Catholic school and mass at her largely Italian-American neighborhood cathedral, St Rocco's Church, in Cleveland. She had long dreamed of visiting the great cathedrals of Rome, visiting St. Peter's Basilica, and attending Mass at Vatican Square. It wasn't just about seeing the sites; it was about connecting to the place and its people—her people. Of course we also saw the ruins and museums and immersed ourselves in the city's art, history, and religion, but we didn't do it from the ivory tower of a fancy hotel, we experienced Rome as the locals do.

The archbishop's flat faces a courtyard constantly abuzz with activity—kids playing, old couples sitting and talking on benches, and people making their way to the bustling open-air market around the corner. It is a quintessential Italian setting—beautiful old buildings flanking a square dotted with trees centered on a fountain or aquifer where one can stop to fill a jug with water just as they did centuries ago. Occupants gaze out of the upper windows of the buildings to watch the activity below while laundry flaps in the breeze and the echo of conversations bounce off the old stone walls. The flat provided us a glimpse of daily Roman life. We did our laundry at the Laundromat, bought bread at the corner bakery, selected a bouquet for the table from a nearby flower stand, purchased a paper from the newsstand, shopped daily in the markets, and cooked at home more than we ate out.

The market down the street from our flat was a beautiful place to behold and we made daily stops there. Arranged in a lovely fashion were sausages of every variety, fresh fish, langoustines, and a rainbow of produce. One day we bought some tiny sausages and plump cherry tomatoes and cooked them with lots of garlic and basil and served them over pasta. This, with oven-roasted langoustines and a simple salad, was like the Italian version of that simple, but pivotal meal Idie and I shared so many years ago in San Francisco—only this time the experience, shared with our children, was made even better. Every meal we prepared there is etched in our memory because each was so simple yet amazing because the ingredients used were so utterly perfect.

Our very first night, suffering from jet lag, we all felt a bit rough around the edges, so we stayed in and cooked our first meal on Italian soil. After a quick trip to the market, we braised greens, stewed some tomatoes and zucchini, and roasted a chicken and served it with fresh bread. It revived us. The next day, we headed back to the market and selected a handful of fresh porcini. We went about our day exploring the city and returned to the flat to prepare another simple meal. With the bones from the previous night's chicken, the trimmings of the porcini, and some fresh herbs, we created the most incredible, rich, deep broth that we used to moisten pasta topped with the earthy porcini, garlic, and herbs. It was that kind of simple cooking with standout ingredients that often awes. Those meals we shared are no exception and are as imprinted in our collective memories as are the city's cathedrals, museums, and ancient ruins.

WHEN IN ROME

CHEESE PLATE WITH LOCAL FRUIT AND WINE

SALT-ROASTED SEA BREAM OR "ORATE"

PORCINI MUSHROOM PASTA

ARUGULA SYLVETTA SALAD WITH GARLIC BRUSCHETTA

- WINE PAIRINGS -

THE ELEGANT, ENGAGING FLAVORS OF A GAVI ARE A PERFECT MATCH TO THE SALT-ROASTED SEA BREAM. ONE OF OUR FAVORITE PRODUCERS IS BROGLIA WHICH PRODUCES THE GAVI DI GAVI LA MEIRANA. ITS DELICATE AROMA HAS HINTS OF ANISE AND FLOWERS. IT IS CRISP AND DRY WITH A GREAT FINISH.

CHEESE PLATE WITH LOCAL FRUIT AND WINE

Every day in Rome we stopped by the market around the corner from our borrowed flat and picked up cheese, olives, fruit, and bread. We would sit down together to enjoy a cheese plate as a snack, a light lunch, or to hold us until dinner was ready. To replicate that experience at home, we venture out to roadside stands and specialty shops seeking those perfectly fresh and unique items that make a cheese plate special. Learn what options you have locally. Farmstead cheese-makers like Belle Chèvre or Sweet Grass Dairy in our area provide us access to cheeses that enable us to showcase some of the wonders of our region. Along with a variety of local cheeses, our restaurant cheese plate is filled with homemade garnishes, fruit, and nuts. These are the little accents that elevate our cheese platter from simple to spectacular.

To create your own, start with a basket of good, crusty bread, including one type of homemade sweet bread, such as persimmon, plum, dried fig, or banana bread. Add another sweet element such as local honey on the comb drizzled over and around the cheeses. Honey adds a sweet note that balances some of the more acidic cheeses. Include a relish or chutney as a tart component to cut through the richness of certain cheeses. The type of chutney we serve is dictated by the seasons: green tomato chutney in the spring and summer and pear chutney in the fall. Toasted nuts or sesame brittle lend crunch and texture to a cheese plate. Seasonal fruit is a last essential element to all of our cheese platters. We incorporate a variety of berries, wild apples, pears, local peaches, strawberries, or pomegranates, based on the season.

Salt-Roasted Sea Bream or "Orate"

This is a great dish to enjoy with your family or friends. Cracking the salt crust at the table to produce a perfectly steamed whole fish is a show stopper! For added flavor, we often prepare the crust mixture using our house blend Hastings Creations Seafood Salt, which is full of citrus and herbs that create a lovely aroma while roasting.

YIELD: 6 SERVINGS

1 (4½ to 5-pound) fresh whole sea bream or other white-fleshed fish, such as snapper
1 tablespoon kosher salt
1 teaspoon freshly ground black pepper
2 large lemons, thinly sliced
6 fresh basil sprigs
15 to 20 fresh thyme sprigs
20 cups Hastings Creations Seafood Salt (page 381) or kosher salt
20 large egg whites

Preheat the oven to 400°F.

Remove the gills and clean the cavity of the fish well, then trim the fins. Rinse the cavity with cold, running water, and pat dry. Season both sides of the internal cavity with 1 tablespoon of kosher salt and the pepper. Stuff both sides of the cavity with the lemon slices, basil, and thyme and set aside.

Line a large baking dish or jelly roll pan (about 12 x 18 inches) with parchment paper. Combine the seafood salt and egg whites in a large bowl, mixing thoroughly until it forms a wet, cementlike consistency. Pack 4 to 5 cups of the salt mixture in an even layer in the baking dish, about ½ inch thick. Place the bream on top of the salt layer and pack the remaining salt mixture over the fish, creating an even layer of salt in a dome shape, at least ½ inch thick. The salt mixture should be thick enough to create a good seal over the fish.

Bake the fish at 400°F for 45 minutes. Remove from the oven and allow the salt-crushed bream to cool for 15 minutes on the baking sheet. With the back of a large, metal spoon, crack open the dome and carefully remove the salt layer. (The salt will crack and come apart in two or three large pieces.) With a clean kitchen towel, brush any excess salt off of the fish. Transfer the entire fish to a serving tray and serve immediately.

Porcini Mushroom Pasta

Unless you are in Italy, fresh porcini mushrooms can be difficult to source and expensive. Dried porcinis are a good
alternative for infusing the mushroom stock and any type of
fresh, seasonal mushroom can be exchanged for the fresh
porcini mushrooms used in this recipe. Add one ounce of
dried porcini mushrooms to the chicken stock instead of the
mushroom trimmings.

YIELD: 4 SERVINGS

1 pound fresh porcini mushrooms
2 cups Chicken Stock (page 335)
2 fresh thyme sprigs
3 cups uncooked hand-shaped pasta
3 tablespoons olive oil
1 cup sliced cipollini onions, about 3 large
¾ teaspoon coarse sea salt, divided
¼ teaspoon freshly ground black pepper
1 ounce freshly grated Parmesan cheese
2 tablespoons chopped fresh parsley, for garnish

Trim approximately ¼ inch off the bottom of the porcini mushrooms. Peel the outer skin of the mushroom stems up to the cap of the mushrooms. Trim away any blemishes off the bottom, sides, and tops of the mushroom caps, reserving the porcinis and all of the trimmings.

Combine the mushroom trimmings, chicken stock, and thyme in a small saucepan and bring to a boil over medium-high heat. Reduce the heat and allow the broth to simmer for 7 to 10 minutes or until a richly infused, aromatic broth has formed. Strain the broth (you will need about ¼ cup) and set aside.

Bring a large pot of salted water to a boil and cook the pasta according to the package directions, reserving about 1 cup of the pasta water. Meanwhile, heat the olive oil in a large sauté pan over medium-high heat. Add the sliced cipollini onions and cook, stirring occasionally, until lightly caramelized, about 10 minutes. Add the reserved porcinis and cook, stirring occasionally, until lightly browned, about 8 minutes. Season the mushroom mixture with ¼ teaspoon of the salt and add the reserved mushroom broth and bring to a simmer. Allow the mixture to simmer for about 2 minutes. Add the cooked pasta, the remaining ¼ teaspoon of salt, and the pepper; toss until well combined and heated through, about 1 minute.

Spoon about 1½ cups of the pasta into each of four pasta bowls. Grate about ¼ ounce of the Parmesan cheese over each portion and garnish each with ½ tablespoon of the parsley. Serve immediately.

Arugula Sylvetta Salad
with Garlic Bruschetta

FOR MOST OF OUR VINAIGRETTES WE USE A BLEND OF REGULAR 100 PERCENT OLIVE OIL AND EXTRA-VIRGIN OLIVE OIL. BUT BECAUSE ARUGULA SYLVETTA HAS SUCH A STRONG, PEPPERY FLAVOR, WE LIKE TO MAKE A VINAIGRETTE WITH A RICH, FULL-FLAVORED EXTRA-VIRGIN OLIVE OIL TO BALANCE THE SPICINESS OF THE GREENS. WITH FEW INGREDIENTS, THIS IS A SIMPLE SALAD TO PUT TOGETHER AT HOME.

YIELD: 6 SERVINGS
¼ CUP (½ STICK) UNSALTED BUTTER
2 LARGE GARLIC CLOVES, CRUSHED AND PEELED
PINCH OF KOSHER SALT
12 (¼-INCH-THICK) BAGUETTE SLICES
12 CUPS LIGHTLY PACKED ARUGULA SYLVETTA OR WILD ARUGULA
½ CUP EXTRA-VIRGIN OLIVE OIL VINAIGRETTE (PAGE 344)

Preheat an oven to 375°F.

Combine the butter, garlic, and salt in a small saucepan over medium heat. Once the butter has melted, cover and remove from the heat. Allow the butter to steep for 5 minutes.

Arrange the baguette slices on a baking sheet. Brush the top side of each slice with the garlic butter, reserving the garlic cloves for a later use. Bake the baguette slices at 375°F for 7 to 10 minutes or until lightly browned and crispy. While the bread is still hot, rub each slice with the reserved garlic cloves until fragrant. Set aside and keep warm.

Combine the arugula and vinaigrette in a large mixing bowl and toss until well combined. Arrange about 2 cups of the greens on each of six salad plates. Place two warm bruschetta on each plate and serve immediately.

BASIC RECIPES
&
TECHNIQUES

EVERY KITCHEN NEEDS BASIC RECIPES FOR EVERYDAY COOKING. STAPLE RECIPES SUCH AS A BASIC VINAIGRETTE OR SALAD DRESSING, A HOMEMADE MAYONNAISE RECIPE, OR CHICKEN STOCK ARE ESSENTIAL FOR ANY HOME COOK. THIS SECTION PROVIDES EVERY-DAY RESOURCES TO ENHANCE EVEN THE MOST BASIC COOKING. WE FEEL STRONGLY THAT GREAT COOKING BEGINS HERE AND WE WANT TO PROVIDE A FOUNDATION OF BASIC RECIPES THAT HELP YOU ELEVATE YOUR COOKING.

SAUCES AND STOCKS

VEGETABLE STOCK

YIELD: ABOUT 7 CUPS

8 CUPS VEGETABLE TRIMMINGS, SUCH AS ONION CORES
   OR PEELS, CELERY ENDS OR TOPS, CARROT PEELS,
   LEEK TOPS, OR BELL PEPPER TRIMMINGS
1 GARLIC CLOVE, SMASHED AND PEELED
6 FRESH PARSLEY SPRIGS
3 FRESH THYME SPRIGS
½ TEASPOON KOSHER SALT
2 QUARTS COLD WATER

Combine all of the ingredients in a medium stockpot and bring to a boil over high heat. Reduce the heat to medium low and simmer for about 30 minutes, skimming away any foam that rises to the top. Strain the broth through a fine-meshed strainer or sieve. The vegetable stock can be used immediately or chilled and stored in an airtight container in the refrigerator for up to four days or frozen for up to one month.

FISH STOCK

YIELD: ABOUT 1 QUART

3 CUPS SHRIMP SHELLS
1 CUP FISH BONES OR SCRAPS FROM ANY WHITE-
   FLESHED FISH, OMITTING ANY INNARDS OR GILLS
2 FRESH THYME SPRIGS
1 BAY LEAF
½ LARGE CARROT, ROUGHLY CHOPPED
1 CELERY STALK, ROUGHLY CHOPPED
½ LARGE ONION, PEELED AND QUARTERED
1 TEASPOON KOSHER SALT
6 CUPS COLD WATER

Combine all of the ingredients in a large stockpot and bring to a boil over high heat. Reduce the heat to medium low and simmer for 30 minutes. Strain the stock through a fine-meshed strainer or sieve. The stock can be used immediately or chilled and refrigerated for up to three days.

....

VARIATION: TO MAKE **SHRIMP STOCK**, INCREASE THE AMOUNT OF SHRIMP SHELLS TO **4** CUPS AND OMIT THE FISH BONES OR SCRAPS. PROCEED WITH THE RECIPE AS DIRECTED.

CHICKEN STOCK

We like to prepare the stocks we make at home using the whole chicken method. It gives the stock a richer flavor and yields tender cooked chicken for use in other dishes. At the restaurant, we generally use the chicken bone method.

YIELD: ABOUT 5 QUARTS

1 (5-POUND) WHOLE CHICKEN OR 3 TO 4 POUNDS CHICKEN BONES

3 MEDIUM ONIONS, PEELED AND ROUGHLY CHOPPED (ABOUT 8 CUPS)

4 LARGE CARROTS, PEELED AND ROUGHLY CHOPPED (ABOUT 2 CUPS)

4 CELERY STALKS, ROUGHLY CHOPPED (ABOUT 2 CUPS)

2 LARGE GARLIC CLOVES, SMASHED AND PEELED

6 FRESH THYME SPRIGS

1 BAY LEAF

1 TABLESPOON KOSHER SALT

5 QUARTS COLD WATER

FOR THE WHOLE CHICKEN METHOD:

Rinse the chicken under cold running water and pat dry. Place the chicken in a large stockpot or Dutch oven and add the remaining ingredients. Bring the mixture to a boil, reduce the heat to low, and simmer for 45 to 50 minutes, skimming off any foam that rises to the top. Remove the whole chicken from the broth mixture and set aside to cool slightly. Continue to simmer the broth mixture for an additional 30 minutes, skimming occasionally. Strain the broth through fine-meshed sieve or strainer and discard the solids. The stock can be used immediately or chilled and kept refrigerated for up to three days or frozen for up to one month. The meat can be pulled off of the chicken and reserved for another use.

FOR THE CHICKEN BONE METHOD:

Rinse the bones under cold running water and drain. Place the bones in a large stockpot or Dutch oven and add the remaining ingredients. Bring the mixture to a boil, reduce the heat to low, and simmer for 1 hour, skimming off any foam that rises to the top. Strain the broth through a fine-meshed sieve or strainer and discard the bones and vegetables. The stock can be used immediately or chilled and kept refrigerated for up to three days or frozen for up to one month.

VEAL STOCK

If oxtail or rib bones are unavailable, you can use any type of veal or beef bones for this stock. For a richer, more gelatinous stock, the liquid can be reduced to the desired consistency once the bones and vegetables are removed.

YIELD: ABOUT 4 QUARTS (1 GALLON)

2 POUNDS VEAL BONES

2 POUNDS OXTAILS

2 POUNDS BEEF OR VEAL RIB BONES

3 MEDIUM ONIONS, PEELED AND ROUGHLY CHOPPED (ABOUT 8 CUPS)

4 LARGE CARROTS, PEELED AND ROUGHLY CHOPPED (ABOUT 2 CUPS)

4 CELERY STALKS, ROUGHLY CHOPPED (ABOUT 2 CUPS)

2 LARGE GARLIC CLOVES, SMASHED AND PEELED

6 FRESH THYME SPRIGS

1 BAY LEAF

6 ROMA TOMATOES, ROUGHLY CHOPPED

1 TABLESPOON KOSHER SALT

6 QUARTS COLD WATER

Preheat the oven to 400°F.

Rinse the bones under cold running water and pat dry. Arrange the bones in an even layer in a large roasting pan. Roast the bones at 400°F for 50 to 60 minutes or until golden brown. Place the roasting pan on the stovetop over medium-high heat. Add the onions, carrots, celery, garlic, thyme, and bay leaf to the bone mixture and cook over medium-high heat, stirring frequently, until the vegetables are well browned, 5 to 8 minutes. Add the tomatoes and continue to cook, stirring frequently, for 10 to 15 minutes or until slightly caramelized. Transfer the bone and vegetable mixture to a large stockpot or Dutch oven and add the salt and water. Bring the mixture to a boil over high heat, reduce the heat to low, and simmer for 6 hours, skimming off any foam that rises to the top. Strain the broth through a fine-meshed sieve or strainer and discard the bones and vegetables. The stock can be used immediately or chilled and kept refrigerated for up to five days or frozen for up to two months.

SPICY HAM HOCK BROTH

At the restaurant we cut and cure our own ham hocks which give this broth an excellent meaty flavor. If you are using store-bought ham hocks, the broth may need to be reduced slightly for extra flavor and there won't be as much meat to pull off the bones as on fresh smoked ham hocks. Since our ham hock cure tends to lend less salt to the broth, you may need to taste and adjust the seasonings in this recipe when using store-bought ham hocks.

When preparing this broth, don't throw away the braised ham hocks. They are useful in a variety of ways such as Braised White Beans (page 371).

YIELD: ABOUT 6 CUPS

2 tablespoons peanut oil
3 smoked ham hocks (about 3¼ pounds)
2 medium yellow onions, peeled and quartered
2 small celery stalks, chopped (about ¾ cup)
1 large carrot, peeled and chopped (about ¾ cup)
4 Roma tomatoes, quartered and chopped (about 3 cups)
4 garlic cloves, smashed and peeled
6 black peppercorns
2 fresh thyme sprigs
1 bay leaf
1 dried Arbol chile pepper, broken in half
3 quarts water

Place the oil in a large Dutch oven or stockpot over medium heat. Add the ham hocks and cook until lightly browned, 3 to 4 minutes on each side. Add the remaining ingredients and bring the mixture to a boil. Reduce the heat to low and allow the hocks to boil gently until the liquid has reduced by half, about 2 hours. Skim off any fat that rises to the top off of the broth while simmering.

Once the mixture has reduced, remove the ham hocks and set aside to cool. Pick the meat off the ham hock bones and reserve the meat for another use. (The picked ham hock meat can be refrigerated for up to three days.) Strain the broth through a fine-meshed sieve or strainer and use immediately or chill until ready to use. The broth will keep refrigerated for up to three days or frozen for up to two months.

BBQ SAUCE

YIELD: ABOUT 6 CUPS

1 quart bottled chili sauce
1 orange, roughly diced (peel and segments)
1 lemon, roughly diced (peel and segments)
1 cup molasses
½ cup firmly packed light brown sugar
1 cup balsamic vinegar
4 serrano peppers, roughly chopped (including the seeds)
2 cups Veal Stock (page 335) or reduced-sodium beef broth
4 garlic cloves, smashed and peeled
8 fresh thyme sprigs
2 bay leaves
3 cups chopped onions (about 1½ medium onions)
¼ cup Dijon mustard
2 tablespoons Ancho chili powder

Combine all of the ingredients in a heavy-bottomed saucepan and bring to a boil over high heat. Reduce the heat to medium low and simmer for 30 minutes. Remove the sauce from the heat and strain through a fine-meshed strainer or sieve, pressing on the inside of the strainer with a rubber spatula to release as much liquid as possible. The sauce can be used immediately or chilled and refrigerated in an airtight container for up to one week.

WHITE BARBECUE SAUCE

YIELD: ABOUT ¾ CUP

½ CUP HOMEMADE CRÈME FRAÎCHE (PAGE 352)
1 TABLESPOON BASIC AÏOLI (PAGE 342)
1 TABLESPOON CHAMPAGNE VINEGAR
1½ TEASPOONS GRANULATED SUGAR
¼ TEASPOON KOSHER SALT
1 TO 2 TEASPOONS COARSELY GROUND BLACK PEPPER

Whisk together the crème fraîche, aïoli, vinegar, and sugar in a medium mixing bowl. Season the sauce with the salt and pepper. Allow the sauce to chill for at least 20 minutes before serving. The barbecue sauce will keep in an airtight container in the refrigerator for up to three days.

SAUCE GRIBICHE

YIELD: ABOUT 2¼ CUPS

1 TABLESPOON DIJON MUSTARD
¼ CUP CHAMPAGNE VINEGAR
¾ CUP OLIVE OIL
1 TABLESPOON CHOPPED FRESH TARRAGON
2 TEASPOONS CHOPPED FRESH PARSLEY
1½ TEASPOONS CHOPPED FRESH CHIVES
1½ TEASPOONS CHOPPED FRESH CHERVIL
¾ TEASPOON KOSHER SALT
¼ TEASPOON FRESHLY GROUND BLACK PEPPER
4 LARGE HARD-BOILED EGGS, PEELED AND GRATED
2 TABLESPOONS DRAINED CAPERS

Whisk together the mustard and vinegar in a medium mixing bowl. While whisking constantly, slowly drizzle the oil into the mustard mixture until well combined. Stir in the tarragon, parsley, chives, and chervil and season with the salt and pepper. Fold in the grated eggs and capers and refrigerate for 30 minutes before serving. Make sure to stir the sauce again before serving.

ANCHO CHILI SAUCE

YIELD: ABOUT 1⅓ CUPS

2 ANCHO CHILE PEPPERS
1 LARGE RED BELL PEPPER, ROASTED, PEELED, AND CHOPPED
¼ CUP FRESH LIME JUICE
1 SMALL GARLIC CLOVE, PEELED
½ CUP OLIVE OIL
½ TEASPOON KOSHER SALT
PINCH OF FRESHLY GROUND BLACK PEPPER

Bring 2 cups of water to a boil in a medium saucepan. Add the ancho peppers to the boiling water, cover, and remove the pan from the heat. Steep the peppers for 1 hour. Drain off the water and pat the peppers dry. Slice the peppers in half and remove the stems and seeds. Using the back of a knife blade, scrape the chile flesh away from the peels; discard the peels.

Place the chile flesh, red bell pepper, lime juice, and garlic clove in a blender. Process on high until the mixture is puréed. With the machine running, drizzle the olive oil into the chile mixture in a slow, steady stream until all of the oil has been added and the sauce is slightly thickened. Season the sauce with the salt and pepper, stirring until incorporated.

This sauce can be used right away or refrigerated until ready to serve. Ancho chile sauce will keep in an airtight container in the refrigerator for up to two days.

TAMARIND SAUCE

THE TAMARIND SAUCE HERE CAN HAVE A NUMBER OF SUBSTITUTES SUCH AS WORCESTERSHIRE SAUCE OR YOUR FAVORITE STEAK SAUCE; HOWEVER, TAMARIND PODS AND BRICKS OF PASTE ARE AVAILABLE AT SPECIALTY MARKETS AS WELL AS ASIAN AND LATIN MARKETS. THE POD COMES FROM A TREE NATIVE TO TROPICAL AFRICA. ITS GROUND PULP LENDS THAT DISTINCTIVE SWEETNESS TO WORCESTERSHIRE AND PICKAPEPPA SAUCES. WE URGE YOU TO TRY THE RICH, TANGY FLAVOR AND PERFECT CONSISTENCY OF OUR HOMEMADE TAMARIND SAUCE.

YIELD: ABOUT 3 CUPS

¼ CUP PEANUT OIL

5 CUPS ROUGHLY CHOPPED YELLOW ONION, ABOUT 2 MEDIUM ONIONS

2 CUPS PEELED AND ROUGHLY CHOPPED CARROT, ABOUT 2 MEDIUM CARROTS

4 LARGE GARLIC CLOVES, SMASHED AND PEELED

8 ROMA TOMATOES, QUARTERED

4 WHOLE SALT-CURED ANCHOVY FILLETS (PAGE 239)

2 ANCHO CHILE PEPPERS, EACH CUT INTO 3 PIECES

2 DRIED ARBOL CHILE PEPPERS

24 DRIED TAMARIND PODS, PEELED, VEINS REMOVED, AND CUT INTO 1-INCH PIECES

4 WHOLE CLOVES

1 TEASPOON WHOLE ALLSPICE

1 TEASPOON WHOLE PEPPERCORNS

2 WHOLE STAR ANISE PODS

2 TEASPOONS MUSTARD SEEDS

12 FRESH THYME SPRIGS, TORN IN HALF

4 BAY LEAVES, TORN IN HALF

1½ CUPS MOLASSES

2 CUPS BALSAMIC VINEGAR

2 CUPS RED WINE

1 QUART VEAL STOCK (PAGE 335) OR REDUCED-SODIUM BEEF BROTH

Heat the oil in a stainless steel stockpot over medium heat. Add the onions and the next 14 ingredients (carrots through bay leaves) and cook, stirring occasionally, for 10 minutes. Be careful not to allow the vegetables to caramelize or color too much.

Add the molasses, balsamic vinegar, red wine, and veal stock. Bring the mixture to a boil, reduce the heat to medium low, and simmer for 1½ to 2 hours or until the sauce is thick and slightly sticky. Remove the mixture from the heat and strain through a fine-meshed strainer or sieve. Serve warm or chill and keep refrigerated in an airtight container for up to two weeks.

COCONUT CURRY DIPPING SAUCE

YIELD: ABOUT 3 CUPS

1 TABLESPOON PEANUT OIL

1 TABLESPOON GRANULATED SUGAR

½ CUP ROUGHLY CHOPPED SWEET ONION, ABOUT ¼ LARGE ONION

½ CUP ROUGHLY CHOPPED CELERY STALK, ABOUT 1 STALK

¾ CUP PEELED AND ROUGHLY CHOPPED CARROT, ABOUT 1 MEDIUM CARROT

¾ CUP SEEDED AND ROUGHLY CHOPPED RED BELL PEPPER, ABOUT ½ LARGE

¾ CUP SEEDED AND ROUGHLY CHOPPED YELLOW BELL PEPPER, ABOUT ½ LARGE

¾ CUP DICED RED TOMATO, ABOUT ½ LARGE TOMATO

¾ TEASPOON PEELED AND MINCED FRESH GINGER

2 TEASPOONS RED CURRY PASTE

2 FRESH CILANTRO SPRIGS

2 FRESH BASIL SPRIGS

1 FRESH MINT SPRIG

1 KAFFIR LIME LEAF

1 LEMONGRASS STALK, CUT INTO 3-INCH-LONG PIECES

1½ TEASPOONS FISH SAUCE

1½ TEASPOONS RICE WINE VINEGAR

2 (13½-OUNCE) CANS COCONUT MILK

2 TEASPOONS FRESH LIME JUICE

Heat the peanut oil in a large saucepan over medium heat. Add the sugar and stir constantly until dissolved, about 1 minute. Add the onion, celery, carrot, and peppers and cook, stirring occasionally, until the vegetables are softened, 5 to 8 minutes. (Make sure that the vegetables do not brown.) Add the tomato, ginger, and curry paste and continue cooking, stirring frequently, for 3 to 5 minutes. Add the next 8 ingredients (cilantro through coconut milk) and bring the mixture to a boil; reduce the heat to medium low and simmer for 25 to 30 minutes. Remove the sauce from the heat and stir in the lime juice.

Strain the sauce through a fine-meshed sieve or strainer into a clean container. Allow the sauce to cool to room temperature, about 20 minutes. Serve the sauce at room temperature with the Seafood Spring Rolls (page 139). This sauce will keep in an airtight container in the refrigerator for up to four days.

SPICY RÉMOULADE SAUCE

YIELD: ABOUT 2 CUPS

1½ CUPS BASIC AÏOLI (PAGE 342) OR STORE-BOUGHT
    MAYONNAISE
1 TABLESPOON DIJON MUSTARD
2 TABLESPOONS FRESH LEMON JUICE
1 TABLESPOON TARRAGON VINEGAR
1 RED BELL PEPPER, ROASTED, PEELED, SEEDED, AND
    FINELY CHOPPED
1 JALAPEÑO PEPPER, ROASTED, PEELED, SEEDED, AND
    FINELY CHOPPED
1 LARGE HARD-BOILED EGG, PEELED AND GRATED
2 TABLESPOONS COOKED, PEELED, AND GRATED
    POTATO
1 TABLESPOON DRAINED AND ROUGHLY CHOPPED
    CAPERS
1½ TEASPOONS DRAINED AND CHOPPED CORNICHONS
¼ CUP SLICED GREEN ONIONS
1 TABLESPOON CHOPPED FRESH TARRAGON
1 TABLESPOON CHOPPED FRESH PARSLEY
⅛ TEASPOON CAYENNE PEPPER
¼ TEASPOON KOSHER SALT
⅛ TEASPOON FRESHLY GROUND BLACK PEPPER

Whisk together the aïoli, Dijon, lemon juice, and vinegar in a large bowl until smooth. Stir in the remaining ingredients. Refrigerate for at least 20 minutes before serving. The rémoulade sauce will keep refrigerated in an airtight container for up to three days.

SUMMER TOMATO SAUCE

WE PREFER TO COOK SUMMER TOMATO SAUCES WITH ONLY FRESH TOMATOES. THIS TYPE OF SAUCE COOKS FOR A SHORTER PERIOD OF TIME THAN A WINTER TOMATO SAUCE MADE WITH CANNED TOMATOES. THE RESULT IS A LIGHT, FRESH SAUCE THAT CAN ACCOMPANY A VARIETY OF ITEMS SUCH AS PASTA, SEAFOOD, OR CHICKEN.

YIELD: ABOUT 9 CUPS

¼ CUP EXTRA-VIRGIN OLIVE OIL
2 LARGE ONIONS, HALVED AND THINLY SLICED (ABOUT
    5 CUPS)
3 GARLIC CLOVES, SMASHED AND PEELED
6 POUNDS (ABOUT 10 MEDIUM) RIPE RED TOMATOES,
    CORED AND COARSELY CHOPPED
1½ OUNCES (ABOUT 3 LARGE) FRESH BASIL SPRIGS
2 TABLESPOONS KOSHER SALT
½ TEASPOON FRESHLY GROUND BLACK PEPPER

Heat the olive oil in a large saucepan or rondeau over medium heat. Add the onions and garlic and cook, stirring frequently, until lightly caramelized, about 15 minutes. Add the tomatoes, basil, and salt and bring to a simmer. Allow the sauce to simmer for 30 minutes, stirring occasionally. Remove the sauce from the heat and set aside to cool slightly, about 20 minutes.

Place a food mill over a large bowl or saucepan and ladle a small amount of the cooled tomato sauce into the mill. Turn the mill until all of the liquid is extracted. Repeat with the remaining tomato sauce, discarding the skins and solids, as needed. Season the strained sauce with the pepper. The sauce can be used immediately or chilled and kept in an airtight container in the refrigerator for up to one week.

ROUILLE

Anchovies are very pungent and also range in flavor. The anchovies we use for the Salt-Cured Anchovies (page 239) are from the Pacific Coast and are milder than their Atlantic or Mediterranean cousins. Pacific anchovies are also larger than the Atlantic or Mediterranean ones. Although canned anchovies can be substituted for the home-made salt-cured version, be aware of this difference in flavor and add them to this dish carefully. The anchovies in this sauce can easily dominate a dish if too many are added.

YIELD: ABOUT 1½ CUPS

1 LARGE (7 OUNCES) RED BELL PEPPER, WELL CHARRED

½ TO 1 SALT-CURED ANCHOVY FILLET (PAGE 239)

1 CUP ROUGHLY CHOPPED ONION (ABOUT ½ ONION

1 CUP ROUGHLY CHOPPED ROMA TOMATOES, ABOUT 2 LARGE TOMATOES

2 GARLIC CLOVES, CRUSHED AND PEELED

1 DRIED ARBOL CHILE PEPPER, BROKEN IN HALF

¼ CUP RED WINE

¼ CUP BALSAMIC VINEGAR

½ CUP CHICKEN STOCK (PAGE 335)

1 CUP BASIC AÏOLI (PAGE 342) OR STORE-BOUGHT MAYONNAISE

GRILLED SOURDOUGH CROUTONS, FOR SERVING

Remove the stem and most of the seeds from the red bell pepper and roughly chop the remaining pepper, leaving the charred skin attached to the flesh.

Combine the chopped pepper and the next 8 ingredients (anchovy through chicken stock) in a medium saucepan. Bring the mixture to a simmer, reduce the heat, and cook at a slow simmer, stirring occasionally, for 40 to 45 minutes, or until all of the liquid has evaporated from the saucepan. (Make sure to stir the mixture more often towards the end of cooking to keep the mixture from sticking to the saucepan.) The mixture should look slightly dry when ready.

Purée the vegetable mixture in a blender until a smooth paste is formed. Strain the paste through a fine-meshed sieve or strainer, pressing the mixture with a rubber spatula to extract as much liquid as possible. Refrigerate the strained paste until well chilled, about 30 minutes.

Whisk together the chilled rouille paste and the aïoli until smooth. Spread 1 to 2 tablespoons of the rouille on warm grilled sourdough croutons and serve immediately. The rouille will keep refrigerated in an airtight container for up to two days before using.

BROWN BUTTER VINAIGRETTE

YIELD: ABOUT 1 CUP

1 CUP (2 STICKS) UNSALTED BUTTER, DIVIDED
1 TABLESPOON MINCED SHALLOTS
1 TEASPOON CHOPPED FRESH THYME
¼ CUP BALSAMIC VINEGAR
½ TEASPOON KOSHER SALT
¼ TEASPOON FRESHLY GROUND BLACK PEPPER

Dice half of the butter (1 stick) into ½-inch pieces and chill for at least 20 minutes.

Melt the remaining stick of butter in a medium skillet over medium heat. Continue cooking until the melted butter is golden brown and has a slightly nutty aroma, 4 to 5 minutes. Add the shallots and thyme and cook, stirring constantly, for 20 to 30 seconds. Add the vinegar, salt, and pepper and cook, stirring constantly, for 30 seconds. Reduce the heat to low and slowly whisk in the chilled butter, several pieces at a time, swirling the pan constantly, until all of the butter has been added. (Be careful not to add the butter into the sauce too quickly or to allow the sauce to become too hot or the sauce may separate.) Serve immediately.

LEMON BUTTER SAUCE

YIELD: ABOUT ¾ CUP

1 CUP WHITE WINE
¼ CUP WHITE WINE VINEGAR
2 TABLESPOONS MINCED SHALLOTS
1 FRESH THYME SPRIG
2 TABLESPOONS HEAVY CREAM
¾ CUP (1½ STICKS) UNSALTED BUTTER, DICED AND CHILLED
2 TEASPOONS FRESH LEMON JUICE
1 TABLESPOON CHOPPED FRESH PARSLEY
2 TABLESPOONS DRAINED CAPERS
¼ TEASPOON KOSHER SALT
PINCH OF FRESHLY GROUND BLACK PEPPER

Combine the white wine, vinegar, shallots, and thyme in a small saucepan. Bring the mixture to a boil, reduce the heat to medium-low and simmer until the mixture is reduced to 2 tablespoons of liquid. Remove and discard the thyme sprig. Add the cream and cook until the mixture thickens slightly and can coat the back of a spoon, about 1 minute.

Whisk the diced butter into the wine mixture, a few pieces at a time, until all of the butter has been incorporated. (Be careful not to add the butter into the sauce too quickly or to allow the sauce to become too hot or the sauce may separate.) Remove the sauce from the heat and stir in the lemon juice, parsley, and capers. Season the sauce with the salt and pepper and serve immediately.

BASIC AÏOLI

Because of the slight risk of salmonella, raw eggs should not be served to the very young, the ill or elderly, or to pregnant women. If you are concerned about this, try adding ½ teaspoon finely chopped fresh garlic to 1½ cups of a good-quality, store-bought mayonnaise.

YIELD: ABOUT 1½ CUPS

2 LARGE EGG YOLKS
1½ CUPS OLIVE OIL, DIVIDED
½ SMALL GARLIC CLOVE, PEELED
1 TABLESPOON FRESH LEMON JUICE
1 TABLESPOON WATER, IF NEEDED
¼ TEASPOON KOSHER SALT
⅛ TEASPOON FRESHLY GROUND BLACK PEPPER

Place the egg yolks in a food processor and process on high for 2 minutes. With the machine running, slowly drizzle ½ cup of the olive oil into the egg yolks, until slightly thickened. Add the garlic and lemon juice and process until combined.

Add the remaining olive oil in a slow, steady stream into the egg mixture while the machine is running. Thin the mixture with 1 tablespoon of water, if needed. (When all of the oil has been added, the mixture should be creamy and thickened.) Season the aïoli with the salt and pepper. Refrigerate the aïoli for at least 30 minutes before using. The aïoli will keep refrigerated for up to three days.

VARIATIONS:

To make **CHIVE AÏOLI**, whisk ¼ cup finely chopped fresh chives, ¼ teaspoon kosher salt, and ¼ teaspoon freshly ground black pepper into the prepared aïoli and proceed as directed.

To make **WASABI AÏOLI**, whisk 1 tablespoon prepared wasabi paste into ½ cup of prepared aïoli and refrigerate as directed. The heat can be adjusted by adding additional wasabi paste, to taste, if needed.

To make **BASIL AÏOLI**, measure 1 ounce (about 1½ cups loosely packed) fresh basil leaves. Place one-third of the basil into the bowl of a mortar and pestle. Add a pinch of salt and grind until the basil is a smooth consistency. Transfer the basil purée to a mixing bowl and repeat with the remaining basil. Fold 1½ cups of prepared aïoli into the basil mixture. Season the aïoli with additional salt and pepper, if needed and proceed as directed.

SCUPPERNONG VINAIGRETTE

YIELD: ABOUT 1 CUP

2 CUPS (ABOUT 12 OUNCES) FRESH SCUPPERNONG GRAPES

½ CUP PLUS **2** TABLESPOONS BLONDE VERJUS, DIVIDED

2 TABLESPOONS MINCED SHALLOTS

2 TABLESPOONS CHOPPED FRESH PARSLEY

2 TABLESPOONS CHOPPED FRESH CHIVES

1½ TEASPOONS CHOPPED FRESH THYME

2 TABLESPOONS CHAMPAGNE VINEGAR

½ CUP OLIVE OIL

½ TEASPOON KOSHER SALT

¼ TEASPOON FRESHLY GROUND BLACK PEPPER

Combine the scuppernongs and ½ cup of the verjus in a small saucepan over medium-high heat. Bring the mixture to a boil, reduce the heat to medium low, and simmer for 5 minutes or until the grape skins begin to pop and almost all of the liquid has evaporated. Remove from the heat and pour the grapes and any liquid through a fine-meshed sieve or strainer into a clean mixing bowl, pressing on the solids to extract as much juice as possible. Discard the solids and set the juice aside to cool.

Add the shallots, parsley, chives, thyme, vinegar, and the remaining 2 tablespoons of verjus to the scuppernong juice. Slowly add the olive oil to the juice mixture, in a steady stream while whisking constantly. Season the vinaigrette with the salt and pepper. The vinaigrette can be used immediately or stored in an airtight container in the refrigerator for up to two days.

POMEGRANATE VINAIGRETTE

YIELD: ABOUT 1½ CUPS

2 LARGE POMEGRANATES OR ⅓ CUP **100%** PURE POMEGRANATE JUICE

2 TEASPOONS MINCED SHALLOTS

3 TABLESPOONS CHAMPAGNE VINEGAR

¼ CUP PLUS **3** TABLESPOONS EXTRA-VIRGIN OLIVE OIL

¼ TEASPOON CHOPPED FRESH THYME

2 TEASPOONS CHOPPED FRESH PARSLEY

1 TEASPOON CHOPPED FRESH CHIVES

¼ TEASPOON KOSHER SALT

PINCH OF FRESHLY GROUND BLACK PEPPER

Cut the pomegranates in half and place in a large bowl. Using the back of a large spoon, hit the outside of the pomegranate halves to remove the seeds. Reserve the seeds and discard tough outer rind. Pick out and discard the pith that separates the seed clumps.

Set a fine-meshed sieve or strainer over a medium bowl. Place half of the pomegranate seeds into the strainer and press the seeds with a rubber spatula to remove any juice. Discard the solids. (You should have about ⅓ cup of pomegranate juice.) Add the remaining pomegranate seeds to the juice and stir in the shallots and vinegar. Slowly drizzle the olive oil into the juice mixture while whisking constantly until all of the oil is incorporated. Stir in the thyme, parsley, and chives and season the vinaigrette with the salt and pepper. The vinaigrette can be used immediately or refrigerated in an airtight container for up to two days.

EXTRA-VIRGIN OLIVE OIL VINAIGRETTE

SPENDING A LITTLE EXTRA MONEY ON A GOOD-QUALITY EXTRA-VIR-GIN OLIVE OIL IS THE KEY TO ANY VINAIGRETTE. FRESH, RIPE LEMONS AND A FULL-FLAVORED EXTRA-VIRGIN OLIVE OIL WILL MAKE THIS SIM-PLE VINAIGRETTE STAND OUT.

YIELD: ABOUT ¾ CUP

½ CUP FULL-FLAVORED, FIRST COLD PRESS, EXTRA-VIRGIN OLIVE OIL
¼ CUP FRESH LEMON JUICE
¼ TEASPOON KOSHER SALT
¼ TEASPOON FRESHLY GROUND BLACK PEPPER
¼ TEASPOON FINELY CHOPPED FRESH THYME

Whisk together all of the ingredients until well combined. Use immediately or chill for up to two days.

GRENACHE VINAIGRETTE

YIELD: ABOUT ½ CUP

¼ CUP GRENACHE VINEGAR
1 TEASPOON MINCED SHALLOTS
½ TEASPOON MINCED FRESH THYME
⅓ CUP EXTRA-VIRGIN OLIVE OIL
2 TABLESPOONS OLIVE OIL
¼ TEASPOON KOSHER SALT
¼ TEASPOON FRESHLY GROUND BLACK PEPPER

Whisk together the vinegar, shallots and thyme. Slowly driz-zle the oils into the vinegar mixture while whisking con-stantly. Season the vinaigrette with the salt and pepper. Use immediately or refrigerate the vinaigrette for up to two days.

CITRUS VINAIGRETTE

THIS IS A WONDERFUL, BASIC CITRUS VINAIGRETTE. WE PREPARE A NUMBER OF VARIATIONS FROM THIS RECIPE SUCH AS THE BLOOD ORANGE VINAIGRETTE, LISTED BELOW. FRESH GRAPEFRUIT JUICE, HONEY TANGERINE JUICE OR SATSUMA JUICE CAN ALL BE SUBSTITUTED FOR THE ORANGE JUICE IN THIS RECIPE. FOR BEST RESULTS, STAY AWAY FROM STORE-BOUGHT CITRUS JUICES AS THEY LEND A SLIGHTLY METAL-LIC FLAVOR TO THE VINAIGRETTE.

YIELD: ABOUT ½ CUP

1 CUP FRESH ORANGE JUICE
1 TABLESPOON GRATED ORANGE ZEST
2 TEASPOONS FRESH LEMON JUICE
1 TEASPOON FRESH LIME JUICE
1 TABLESPOON MINCED SHALLOTS
1 TEASPOON FINELY CHOPPED FRESH THYME
1 TABLESPOON FINELY CHOPPED FRESH PARSLEY
¼ TEASPOON KOSHER SALT
PINCH OF FRESHLY GROUND BLACK PEPPER
2 TABLESPOONS OLIVE OIL
2 TABLESPOONS EXTRA-VIRGIN OLIVE OIL

Place the orange juice in a small saucepan and bring to a boil over high heat. Reduce the heat to medium low and simmer until the orange juice has reduced to about ¼ cup. Add the orange zest to the reduced juice and continue simmering until the mixture has reduced to about 3 tablespoons. Remove the pan from the heat and allow the juice mixture to cool completely.

Whisk together the cooled orange mixture, lemon juice, lime juice, shallots, thyme, and parsley. Season the juice mix-ture with the salt and pepper. Slowly pour the oils into the juice mixture in a slow, steady stream while whisking constantly. Continue whisking until the vinaigrette is slightly thickened. Use the vinaigrette immediately or refrigerate until ready to serve. The vinaigrette will keep refrigerated for up to two days.

VARIATION: TO MAKE BLOOD ORANGE VINAIGRETTE, SUBSTITUTE 1 CUP FRESHLY SQUEEZED BLOOD ORANGE JUICE AND 1 TABLESPOON GRATED BLOOD ORANGE ZEST FOR THE ORANGE JUICE AND ZEST IN THE CITRUS VINAIGRETTE RECIPE. PROCEED WITH THE RECIPE AS DIRECTED.

VALENCIA ORANGE VINAIGRETTE

YIELD: ¾ CUP

2 TABLESPOONS FRESH LEMON JUICE,
    ABOUT 1 SMALL LEMON
¼ CUP FRESH VALENCIA ORANGE JUICE,
    ABOUT 1 ORANGE
1 TABLESPOON CHOPPED FRESH PARSLEY
1 TABLESPOON CHOPPED FRESH CHIVES
1 TABLESPOON CHOPPED FRESH FENNEL FRONDS
½ TEASPOON KOSHER SALT
¼ TEASPOON FRESHLY GROUND BLACK PEPPER
¼ CUP EXTRA-VIRGIN OLIVE OIL
¼ CUP OLIVE OIL

Whisk together the lemon juice, orange juice, parsley, chives, and fennel fronds. Season the juice mixture with the salt and pepper. Slowly pour the oils into the juice mixture in a slow, steady stream while whisking constantly. Continue whisking until the vinaigrette is slightly thickened. The vinaigrette can be used immediately or stored in an airtight container in the refrigerator for up to two days. Before serving bring the chilled vinaigrette to room temperature and whisk well.

SESAME VINAIGRETTE

YIELD: ABOUT 1½ CUPS

¾ CUP PURE SESAME OIL
¼ CUP FRESH LIME JUICE
¼ CUP SOY SAUCE
¾ CUP THINLY SLICED GREEN ONIONS,
    ABOUT 3 GREEN ONIONS

Whisk together all of the ingredients together in a medium bowl. Adjust the seasoning with additional soy sauce, if needed. The vinaigrette can be used immediately or refrigerated in an airtight container for up to three days.

PRESERVED LEMON VINAIGRETTE

YIELD: ABOUT 3½ CUPS

2 PRESERVED MEYER LEMONS (PAGE 351
1 CUP FRESH LEMON JUICE
1 CUP EXTRA-VIRGIN OLIVE OIL
1½ TEASPOONS CHOPPED FRESH PARSLEY
1½ TEASPOONS CHOPPED FRESH CHIVES
1½ TEASPOONS CHOPPED FRESH THYME
1½ TEASPOONS MINCED SHALLOTS

Peel the preserved lemons and discard the inside pulp. Remove the white pith from the lemon peel and discard. Finely chop the lemon rind and place in a large mixing bowl. Add the remaining ingredients to the bowl and whisk well to combine. Serve at room temperature. This vinaigrette will keep refrigerated in an airtight container for up to three days. Be sure to bring the vinaigrette to room temperature and whisk well before serving.

WALNUT VINAIGRETTE

YIELD: 1¼ CUPS

2 TEASPOONS MINCED SHALLOTS
½ TEASPOON CHOPPED FRESH THYME
½ CUP CHAMPAGNE VINEGAR
⅓ CUP WALNUT OIL
⅓ CUP OLIVE OIL
¼ TEASPOON KOSHER SALT
PINCH OF FRESHLY GROUND BLACK PEPPER

Whisk together the shallots, thyme, and vinegar in a small mixing bowl. Add the walnut and olive oils to the vinegar mixture, whisking constantly. Season the vinaigrette with the salt and pepper. The vinaigrette can be used immediately or refrigerated in an airtight container for up to three days.

LEMON DIJON VINAIGRETTE

THIS IS ONE OF OUR MOST WIDELY USED VINAIGRETTES. IT IS VERY VERSATILE AND THE VARIATIONS ARE ENDLESS. IF YOU ARE SAVING THE VINAIGRETTE FOR A LATER USE, FOR BEST RESULTS, BE SURE TO STRAIN AND DISCARD THE CHOPPED SHALLOTS AND HERBS. FRESH SHALLOTS AND HERBS CAN BE ADDED AGAIN, JUST BEFORE SERVING.

YIELD: ABOUT 2 CUPS

½ CUP PLUS 2 TABLESPOONS FRESH LEMON JUICE
¼ CUP DIJON MUSTARD
½ CUP OLIVE OIL
½ CUP EXTRA-VIRGIN OLIVE OIL
2 TABLESPOONS MINCED SHALLOTS
2 TABLESPOONS FINELY CHOPPED FRESH PARSLEY
½ TEASPOON FINELY CHOPPED FRESH THYME
½ TEASPOON KOSHER SALT
½ TEASPOON FRESHLY GROUND BLACK PEPPER

Whisk together the lemon juice, mustard, and olive oils. Stir in the shallots, parsley, and thyme. Season the vinaigrette with the salt and pepper. Use immediately or refrigerate for up to two days.

VARIATIONS:

TO MAKE **CHERVIL VINAIGRETTE**, WHISK IN ½ CUP OF FINELY CHOPPED FRESH CHERVIL TO THE PREPARED VINAIGRETTE AND PROCEED AS DIRECTED.

TO MAKE **MEYER LEMON VINAIGRETTE**, SUBSTITUTE ½ CUP PLUS 2 TABLESPOONS OF FRESHLY SQUEEZED MEYER LEMON JUICE FOR THE REGULAR LEMON JUICE AND ADD ½ TEASPOON OF GRATED MEYER LEMON ZEST AND PROCEED AS DIRECTED.

TO MAKE **PARMESAN VINAIGRETTE,** WHISK IN 2 CUPS OF FRESHLY GRATED, LOOSELY PACKED PARMESAN CHEESE TO THE PREPARED VINAIGRETTE AND PROCEED AS DIRECTED.

BALSAMIC VINAIGRETTE

YIELD: 2 CUPS

1 CUP BALSAMIC VINEGAR
1 CUP FINELY CHOPPED FRESH CHIVES
½ CUP CHOPPED GREEN ONIONS
½ CUP EXTRA-VIRGIN OLIVE OIL
½ CUP OLIVE OIL
¼ TEASPOON KOSHER SALT
⅛ TEASPOON FRESHLY GROUND BLACK PEPPER

Whisk together the vinegar, chives, and green onions in a medium bowl. Slowly whisk the oils into the vinegar mixture until well blended and slightly emulsified. Season the vinegar mixture with the salt and pepper. The vinaigrette can be used immediately or stored in an airtight container in the refrigerator for up to five days. Be sure to bring the chilled vinaigrette to room temperature and whisk well before serving.

CREAMY HERB DRESSING

YIELD: ABOUT 1¼ CUPS

1 CUP BASIC AÏOLI (PAGE **342**) OR STORE-BOUGHT MAYONNAISE
1 TABLESPOON PLUS 1 TEASPOON BLOND VERJUS
1 TABLESPOON PLUS 1 TEASPOON TARRAGON VINEGAR
2½ TEASPOONS DIJON MUSTARD
1 TABLESPOON CHOPPED FRESH TARRAGON
1 TABLESPOON CHOPPED FRESH CHIVES
1 TABLESPOON CHOPPED FRESH PARSLEY
1 TABLESPOON CHOPPED FRESH CHERVIL
¼ TEASPOON KOSHER SALT
⅛ TEASPOON FRESHLY GROUND BLACK PEPPER

Whisk together the aïoli, verjus, tarragon vinegar, and Dijon mustard until smooth. Stir in the herbs and season with the salt and pepper. The dressing can be used immediately or refrigerated in an airtight container for up to three days.

GREEN GODDESS DRESSING

YIELD: 2¼ CUPS

½ CUP CHOPPED FRESH PARSLEY LEAVES
2 TABLESPOONS CHOPPED FRESH CHIVES
2 TABLESPOONS CHOPPED FRESH BASIL LEAVES
2 TABLESPOONS CHOPPED FRESH TARRAGON
2 TO 3 RIPE HAAS AVOCADOS, HALVED AND PITTED
½ TEASPOON MINCED FRESH GARLIC
1½ TEASPOONS MINCED SHALLOTS
2 TABLESPOONS FRESH LIME JUICE
¼ CUP BASIC AÏOLI (PAGE 342) OR STORE-BOUGHT
   MAYONNAISE
½ TEASPOON ANCHOVY PASTE
2½ TABLESPOONS TARRAGON VINEGAR
1 TABLESPOON PLUS ½ TEASPOON KOSHER SALT
¾ TEASPOON FRESHLY GROUND BLACK PEPPER

Combine the first 8 ingredients (parsley through lime juice) in the bowl of a large food processor. Process until well blended and there are no large chunks of avocado remaining. Add the remaining ingredients to the food processor and process on high until the dressing is slightly thickened. The dressing can be used immediately or kept refrigerated in an airtight container for up to two days.

CHIVE DRESSING

BECAUSE OF THE SLIGHT RISK OF SALMONELLA, RAW EGGS SHOULD NOT BE SERVED TO THE VERY YOUNG, THE ILL OR ELDERLY, OR TO PREGNANT WOMEN. IF YOU ARE CONCERNED ABOUT THIS, TRY ADDING ½ TEASPOON FINELY CHOPPED FRESH GARLIC, ¼ CUP FINELY CHOPPED FRESH CHIVES, AND A PINCH OF SALT AND PEPPER TO 1 CUP OF A GOOD-QUALITY, STORE-BOUGHT MAYONNAISE.

YIELD: ABOUT 1¼ CUPS

1 SMALL GARLIC CLOVE, PEELED AND FINELY MINCED
6 TABLESPOONS FINELY CHOPPED FRESH CHIVES
1 LARGE EGG YOLK
2 TABLESPOONS FRESH LEMON JUICE
½ TEASPOON KOSHER SALT
¼ TEASPOON FRESHLY GROUND BLACK PEPPER
1 CUP OLIVE OIL
¼ CUP HOMEMADE CRÈME FRAÎCHE (PAGE 352)

Combine the garlic and chives in small bowl. Add the egg yolk, lemon juice, salt, and pepper and whisk to combine. Add the oil in a thin, steady stream while whisking vigorously to create an emulsion. Stir in the crème fraîche. You may need to add a drop or two of water if the dressing is too thick. Cover and chill the dressing for at least 20 minutes before serving. This dressing will keep refrigerated in an airtight container for up to two days.

HERB VINAIGRETTE

YIELD: ABOUT 1 CUP

1 TABLESPOON CHOPPED FRESH PARSLEY

1½ TEASPOONS CHOPPED FRESH CHIVES

1 TEASPOON CHOPPED FRESH CHERVIL

1 TEASPOON CHOPPED FRESH TARRAGON

¼ TEASPOON CHOPPED FRESH THYME

½ TEASPOON MINCED SHALLOTS

¼ CUP CHAMPAGNE VINEGAR

1 TABLESPOON TARRAGON VINEGAR

½ CUP PLUS 2 TABLESPOONS EXTRA-VIRGIN OLIVE OIL

½ CUP PLUS 2 TABLESPOONS OLIVE OIL

¼ TEASPOON SALT

⅛ TEASPOON FRESHLY GROUND BLACK PEPPER

Combine the first 8 ingredients (parsley through tarragon vinegar) in a large mixing bowl. Slowly whisk in the oils until well blended and slightly emulsified. Season the vinaigrette with the salt and pepper. Set aside until ready to use, making sure to stir well again before using. The vinaigrette will keep refrigerated for up to two days.

BACON VINAIGRETTE

YIELD: 1¾ CUPS

½ CUP PLUS 1 TABLESPOON OLIVE OIL, DIVIDED

2 CUPS FINELY CHOPPED BENTON'S BACON (ABOUT ¼-INCH PIECES) OR OTHER THICK-CUT SMOKED BACON

¼ CUP MINCED SHALLOTS

¼ CUP SHERRY VINEGAR

2 TEASPOONS CHOPPED FRESH THYME

¼ TEASPOON KOSHER SALT

⅛ TEASPOON FRESHLY GROUND BLACK PEPPER

Heat 1 tablespoon of the olive oil in a heavy skillet over medium heat. Add the bacon and cook, stirring occasionally, until rendered, about 20 minutes. Add the shallots, stir well, and remove from the heat. Transfer the bacon mixture (including the rendered fat) to a mixing bowl. Stir in the vinegar and remaining ½ cup of oil, whisking until well blended. Add the thyme and season with the salt and pepper. Use warm or at room temperature.

CONDIMENTS AND GARNISHES

TAPENADE

YIELD: ABOUT 2 CUPS

1 CUP PITTED AND FINELY CHOPPED KALAMATA OLIVES
1 CUP PITTED AND FINELY CHOPPED PICHOLINE OLIVES
2 TABLESPOONS DRAINED AND FINELY CHOPPED CAPERS
1 TABLESPOON FINELY CHOPPED FRESH PARSLEY
1 TABLESPOON FINELY CHOPPED FRESH THYME
1½ TEASPOONS DIJON MUSTARD
¼ TEASPOON MINCED SALT-CURED ANCHOVY FILLET (PAGE 239)
¼ TEASPOON FINELY GRATED LEMON ZEST
⅛ TEASPOON GRATED ORANGE ZEST
5 TABLESPOONS EXTRA-VIRGIN OLIVE OIL

Combine the olives, capers, parsley, thyme, mustard, anchovy, and zests in a medium bowl. Drizzle olive oil into the bowl and stir well to combine. Allow the mixture to sit at room temperature for 30 minutes before serving. The tapenade will keep in the refrigerator in an airtight container for up to one week.

CHOWCHOW

YIELD: ABOUT 3½ CUPS

1 CUP DISTILLED WHITE VINEGAR
½ CUP WATER
½ CUP GRANULATED SUGAR
4 FRESH THYME SPRIGS
1 BAY LEAF
2 CUPS FINELY CHOPPED YELLOW ONION
1 CUP SEEDED AND FINELY CHOPPED RED BELL PEPPER
1 CUP SEEDED AND FINELY CHOPPED YELLOW BELL PEPPER
¾ CUP SEEDED AND FINELY CHOPPED POBLANO PEPPER

Combine the vinegar, water, sugar, thyme, and bay leaf in a medium saucepan and bring to a boil over medium-high heat. Add the remaining ingredients and return the mixture to a boil. Reduce the heat to medium low and simmer for 25 to 30 minutes, or until the vegetables are tender. At this point the relish will still be liquidy, but do not drain off the excess liquid. Remove the saucepan from the heat and allow the relish to cool to room temperature. Discard the thyme sprigs and bay leaf. The relish can be used immediately or stored in the refrigerator in an airtight container for up to two weeks.

BASIL PESTO

YIELD: 1¼ CUPS

2 OUNCES (ABOUT 1¼ CUPS LIGHTLY PACKED) FRESH
    BASIL LEAVES
¾ OUNCE (ABOUT 1 CUP LIGHTLY PACKED) FRESH
    FLAT-LEAF PARSLEY LEAVES
1½ TABLESPOONS PINE NUTS, TOASTED AND COOLED
¼ CUP FRESHLY GRATED PARMESAN CHEESE
½ TEASPOON FRESH LEMON JUICE
¼ TEASPOON GRATED LEMON ZEST
¾ TO 1 CUP OLIVE OIL, CHILLED
¼ TEASPOON KOSHER SALT
PINCH OF FRESHLY GROUND BLACK PEPPER

Bring a medium pot of salted water to a boil over high heat.
Prepare an ice water bath by filling a large bowl halfway with
ice and a small amount of water.

Blanch the basil and parsley leaves in the boiling water
for several seconds or until the leaves turn bright green.
Remove the leaves from the boiling water and immediately
plunge in the ice water bath, stirring until well chilled. Drain
the leaves and wring dry. Roughly chop the blanched herbs.

Combine the blanched herbs, pine nuts, Parmesan, lemon
juice, and lemon zest in a blender or small food processor.
With the machine on low, process the mixture until everything
is roughly chopped, about 30 seconds. Increase the speed to
medium and pour the olive oil into the blender, processing
until the mixture is smooth and slightly thickened. Be careful
not to over process the pesto or the herbs may turn brown.

Season the pesto lightly with the salt and pepper. The
pesto can be used immediately or refrigerated until ready to
use. To store, place the pesto in an airtight container and lay
a piece of plastic wrap directly over the surface of the pesto.
The pesto will keep refrigerated for up to two days.

BLACK BEAN SALSA

ALTHOUGH YOU CAN SUBSTITUTE CANNED AND RINSED BLACK BEANS,
THE SALSA WILL NOT HAVE THE RICH, MEATY FLAVOR THAT THE
BRAISED BEANS GIVE. YOU MAY NEED TO ADJUST THE SALT AND PEP-
PER, WHEN USING CANNED BEANS. THIS SALSA WILL KEEP
REFRIGERATED IN AN AIRTIGHT CONTAINER FOR UP TO FIVE DAYS.

YIELD: 6½ CUPS

¾ CUP FINELY CHOPPED POBLANO PEPPER
¾ CUP FINELY CHOPPED YELLOW BELL PEPPER
¾ CUP FINELY CHOPPED RED BELL PEPPER
4 CUPS BRAISED BLACK BEANS (PAGE 371), DRAINED
½ CUP CHOPPED FRESH CILANTRO LEAVES
1 TEASPOON GRATED LIME ZEST
¼ CUP FRESH LIME JUICE
2 TABLESPOONS EXTRA-VIRGIN OLIVE OIL
2 TABLESPOONS FINELY CHOPPED FRESH CHIVES
¾ TEASPOON KOSHER SALT
¼ TEASPOON FRESHLY GROUND BLACK PEPPER

Combine the first 9 ingredients (poblano pepper through
chives) together in a large bowl. Season the bean mixture
with the salt and pepper and serve at room temperature. This
salsa will keep refrigerated in an airtight container for up to
five days.

PEACH MOJO

YIELD: 2½ CUPS

2 CUPS PITTED AND CHOPPED, FIRM-RIPE PEACHES
¼ CUP PLUS 2 TABLESPOONS OLIVE OIL
¼ CUP PLUS 2 TABLESPOONS FRESH LIME JUICE
½ CUP FINELY CHOPPED RED ONION
1 TABLESPOON SEEDED AND MINCED JALAPEÑO
2 TEASPOONS CHOPPED FRESH CILANTRO
½ TEASPOON KOSHER SALT
⅛ TEASPOON FRESHLY GROUND BLACK PEPPER

Combine all of the ingredients in a large bowl and stir well. Allow the mojo to macerate at room temperature for at least 30 minutes before serving. This mixture will keep refrigerated in an airtight container for up to three days.

PRESERVED MEYER LEMONS

THE THINGS THAT YOU CAN DO WITH THESE LEMONS, SUCH AS SAUCES, VINAIGRETTES, AND BRAISES, MAKE THIS RECIPE WORTH THE LONG WAIT AND EFFORT. IF MEYER LEMONS ARE UNAVAILABLE, YOU CAN SUBSTITUTE REGULAR LEMONS WITH SIMILAR RESULTS.

YIELD: ABOUT 1 QUART OR 12 LEMON HALVES

6 MEYER LEMONS, HALVED
2 CUPS KOSHER SALT
½ CUP COLD WATER

Juice the lemon halves, reserving 1 cup plus 2 tablespoons of the juice and the lemon rinds. Combine the lemon rinds, reserved lemon juice, salt, and cold water in a sterile, 1-quart glass container with a tight-fitting lid. Make sure to leave a small amount of air space before tightening the lid on the jar. Once the lid is in place, gently shake the jar until the ingredients are well mixed. Allow the lemons to sit in a cool, dark place for three to four weeks, gently shaking the jar each day.

Preserved Meyer lemons will keep in the jar for up to one year and do not need to be refrigerated. To use, rinse the lemon rinds under running water and remove and discard the pulp. Dice the lemon rinds and use according to the recipe instructions.

HOMEMADE CRÈME FRAÎCHE

YIELD: 2 CUPS

1¾ CUPS HEAVY CREAM
2 TABLESPOONS BUTTERMILK

Whisk together the cream and buttermilk just to combine. Pour into a sterilized 2-cup jar (a mayonnaise or pickle jar works well) and cover tightly. Allow the mixture to sit at room temperature for two days.

After 24 hours, the crème fraîche will have thickened. If the mixture is slightly separated, whisk until smooth. The crème fraîche can be used immediately or refrigerated until ready to use. Homemade crème fraîche will keep refrigerated for up to two weeks.

VARIATIONS:

To make **HONEYSUCKLE CRÈME FRAÎCHE,** whisk together 1¾ cups prepared crème fraîche, 2 tablespoons Honeysuckle Simple Syrup (page 362), and 1 tablespoon finely chopped honeysuckle blossoms (page 23) until the mixture begins to stiffen and medium-firm peaks form. Cover and chill for about 4 hours to allow the honeysuckle flavors to permeate the crème fraîche. The mixture will keep refrigerated in an airtight container for up to one week.

To make **GARLIC CRÈME FRAÎCHE,** preheat the oven to 350°F. Slice off the top third of 1 garlic head, horizontally. Arrange the larger portion on a small square of aluminum foil. Drizzle 1 teaspoon of olive oil over the cut garlic and sprinkle with ¼ teaspoon of kosher salt. Place the top third of the cut garlic on top of its base and wrap the entire piece of garlic with the foil. Bake for 45 minutes to 1 hour or until the pulp is tender and golden brown. Set the garlic aside to cool slightly. Squeeze the garlic cloves out of their papery husks and place in a fine-meshed sieve or strainer. Press the cloves through the strainer into a small bowl. Add 1 cup of prepared crème fraîche and ¾ teaspoon kosher salt to the roasted garlic and whisk until smooth. Cover and refrigerate the mixture for at least 30 minutes before serving. The mixture will keep refrigerated in an airtight container for up to one week.

To make **CILANTRO CRÈME FRAÎCHE,** whisk together 1¾ cups prepared crème fraîche, 2 tablespoons fresh lime juice, and ½ teaspoon grated lime zest until smooth. Add 3 tablespoons chopped fresh cilantro, ½ teaspoon kosher salt, and ¼ teaspoon freshly ground black pepper. Cover and refrigerate the mixture for at least 30 minutes before serving. The mixture will keep refrigerated in an airtight container for up to five days.

ANSON MILLS CAROLINA GOLD RICE

YIELD: ABOUT 3 CUPS

1 CUP (ABOUT 7 OUNCES) ANSON MILLS CAROLINA
   GOLD RICE (PAGE 380)
4 CUPS COLD WATER
2 TEASPOONS KOSHER SALT

Place the rice in a fine-meshed sieve or strainer and rinse with cold running water until the water runs clear. Drain well and pour the rice into a large bowl. Fill the bowl with enough water to cover the rice and set aside to soak at room temperature for 1 hour; drain well.

Fill a 2-quart saucepan with 4 cups cold water and the salt and bring to a boil over high heat. Add the soaked rice, stir, and allow the mixture to return to a boil. Reduce the heat to low and simmer, uncovered, for 15 minutes, stirring occasionally, until the rice is tender with no hard starch at the center of each grain. Drain the rice through a fine-meshed sieve or strainer and use immediately. The cooked rice will keep refrigerated in an airtight container for up to one week.

FRESH BREADCRUMBS

SEVERAL RECIPES CALL FOR FRESH BREADCRUMBS AS OPPOSED TO DRY BREADCRUMBS. TO ACHIEVE THE CORRECT RESULTS, START WITH A FRESH FRENCH BAGUETTE, TORN INTO 2-INCH PIECES. PLACE THE BREAD PIECES IN THE BOWL OF A FOOD PROCESSOR AND PULSE UNTIL THE BREAD FORMS A UNIFORM CRUMB CONSISTENCY. AT THIS POINT THE FRESH BREADCRUMBS CAN BE USED IMMEDIATELY OR STORED IN AN AIRTIGHT CONTAINER IN THE FREEZER FOR UP TO THREE MONTHS.

FRY MIX

YIELD: ABOUT 3 CUPS

1 CUP FINELY GROUND YELLOW CORNMEAL
1 CUP CORN FLOUR
1 CUP ALL-PURPOSE FLOUR
2 TABLESPOONS PLUS 1 TEASPOON KOSHER SALT
½ TEASPOON CAYENNE PEPPER
½ TEASPOON FRESHLY GROUND BLACK PEPPER

Combine all of the ingredients in a large bowl and mix well. Store the fry mix in a dry, airtight container at room temperature until ready to use.

ANSON MILLS WHITE ANTEBELLUM GRITS

If the grits are going to sit for a while before serving, place a piece of plastic wrap directly on the surface of the grits and cover. This will keep a skin from forming on the top of the grits as well as help to keep the grits warm.

YIELD: ABOUT 3 CUPS OR 6 SERVINGS

1 TABLESPOON UNSALTED BUTTER
½ TEASPOON MINCED GARLIC
1 TEASPOON CHOPPED FRESH THYME
3 CUPS CHICKEN STOCK (PAGE 335), DIVIDED
1½ CUPS HEAVY CREAM
1 CUP WHITE ANTEBELLUM COARSE GRITS FROM
    ANSON MILLS (PAGE 380)
1 TEASPOON KOSHER SALT
½ TEASPOON FRESHLY GROUND BLACK PEPPER

Melt the butter in a 4-quart saucepan over medium-high heat. Add the garlic and thyme and cook, stirring constantly for 30 seconds, being careful not to burn the garlic.

Add 2½ cups of the chicken stock and the heavy cream and bring the mixture to a boil. Upon boiling, add the grits in a slow, steady stream while whisking constantly. Once the mixture returns to a simmer, reduce the heat to low. Cook the grits at a simmer, stirring frequently, for 25 minutes. (The grits will begin to thicken after about 10 minutes.) Once the grits begin to look dry, stir in the remaining ½ cup chicken stock and continue cooking the grits for an additional 15 to 20 minutes or until the grits are tender. Season the grits with the salt and pepper and remove from the heat. Serve immediately.

MCEWEN AND SONS YELLOW STONE-GROUND GRITS

YIELD: ABOUT 3 CUPS OR 6 SERVINGS

1 TABLESPOON UNSALTED BUTTER
½ TEASPOON MINCED GARLIC
1 TEASPOON CHOPPED FRESH THYME
2½ CUPS CHICKEN STOCK (PAGE 335), DIVIDED
1½ CUPS HEAVY CREAM
1 CUP YELLOW STONE-GROUND COARSE GRITS FROM
    MCEWEN AND SONS (PAGE 381)
1 TEASPOON KOSHER SALT
½ TEASPOON FRESHLY GROUND BLACK PEPPER

Melt the butter in a 4-quart saucepan over medium-high heat. Add the garlic and thyme and cook, stirring constantly for 30 seconds, being careful not to burn the garlic.

Add 2 cups of the chicken stock and the heavy cream and bring the mixture to a boil. Upon boiling, add the grits in a slow, steady stream while whisking constantly. Once the mixture returns to a simmer, reduce the heat to low. Cook the grits at a simmer, stirring frequently for 15 minutes. (The grits will begin to thicken after about 10 minutes.) Once the grits begin to look dry, stir in the remaining ½ cup chicken stock and continue cooking the grits for an additional 15 to 20 minutes or until the grits are tender. Season the grits with the salt and pepper and remove from the heat. Serve immediately.

BASIC RISOTTO

This basic risotto recipe is a technique we use at the restaurant but is often helpful for home cooks as well. In this method we are essentially parcooking the risotto and finishing it just before serving. This way you can prepare the part of the risotto that takes the most time in advance, chill the rice, and finish it just before serving without the rice getting cold or clumpy. We prefer to make risotto with Vialone Nano, which is a medium-grain rice originally from the Mantova and Veneto regions of Italy. Vialone Nano is shorter and thicker than Arborio and holds twice its weight in liquid, creating a very hearty and creamy risotto. For information on ordering this product, see Earthly Delights in our Sources Guide (page 381). If Vialone Nano is unavailable, you can substitute Arborio rice with similar results.

YIELD: ABOUT 6½ CUPS

3 tablespoons peanut oil
1 cup finely chopped white onion
½ cup minced leeks (white part only)
2 cups Vialone Nano or Arborio rice
1 cup dry white wine
4 cups hot Chicken Stock (PAGE **335**)

Heat the oil in a rondeau or wide saucepan with deep sides over medium heat. Add the onion and leeks and sauté until transparent for about 3 to 4 minutes, being careful not to let the vegetables to brown. Add the rice and stir with a wooden spoon until the rice is coated with oil and slightly toasted, about 2 minutes. Add the wine and cook, stirring constantly, until all of the wine is absorbed.

Add ½ cup hot chicken stock and stir constantly with a wooden spoon until all of the liquid is absorbed. Repeat this process, adding ½ cup of chicken stock each time, until all of the stock has been added. Remove the pan from the heat and spread the risotto evenly onto a jelly roll pan to cool completely.

....

VARIATION: To serve the Basic Risotto immediately, do not remove the risotto from the heat and add 1 additional cup of hot Chicken Stock, stirring until the rice is creamy and al dente. Adjust the seasonings with kosher salt and freshly ground black pepper to taste. Remove the risotto from the heat and stir in 1 to 2 tablespoons of unsalted butter. Serve immediately.

HERB BREADCRUMBS

YIELD: ABOUT 6½ CUPS

1 (8-OUNCE) FRESH FRENCH BAGUETTE, TORN INTO 2-INCH PIECES

2 TABLESPOONS CHOPPED FRESH THYME LEAVES

¼ CUP CHOPPED FRESH PARSLEY LEAVES

3 TABLESPOONS CHOPPED FRESH CHIVES

1½ TEASPOONS GRATED LEMON ZEST

½ TEASPOON FINELY CHOPPED GARLIC

1½ TEASPOONS KOSHER SALT

¾ TEASPOON FRESHLY GROUND BLACK PEPPER

½ CUP (1 STICK) UNSALTED BUTTER, MELTED

Place the bread in the bowl of a food processor and pulse until a uniform crumb consistency is achieved. Transfer the crumbs to a large mixing bowl. Add the next 7 ingredients (thyme through pepper) and mix well. Drizzle the melted butter over the crumbs and toss to evenly coat. The herb breadcrumbs can be used immediately or stored in an airtight container in the refrigerator for up to one week.

HERB CROUTONS

YIELD: ABOUT 3 CUPS

¼ CUP (½ STICK) UNSALTED BUTTER

2 TABLESPOONS EXTRA-VIRGIN OLIVE OIL

1 GARLIC CLOVE, SMASHED AND PEELED

3 CUPS FINELY DICED (¼ INCH) DAY-OLD BREAD, SUCH AS CIABATTA OR OTHER PEASANT-STYLE BREAD

2 TEASPOONS GRATED LEMON ZEST, ABOUT 1 LEMON

2 TABLESPOONS CHOPPED FRESH PARSLEY

2 TABLESPOONS CHOPPED FRESH CHIVES

Preheat the oven to 400°F.

Melt the butter and olive oil in a small saucepan over medium heat. Add the garlic and cook for about 3 minutes, being careful not to allow the garlic to brown. Remove the butter mixture from the heat and discard the garlic. Combine the melted butter mixture in a large bowl with the diced bread and toss until well coated. Spread the bread in an even layer on a rimmed baking sheet.

Bake the bread at 400°F for 6 to 8 minutes or until golden brown and toasted. Remove from the oven and toss the croutons with the lemon zest, parsley and chives. Serve warm.

SAFFRON PASTA DOUGH

YIELD: 2 POUNDS

2 TABLESPOONS SAFFRON THREADS
1 CUP HOT WATER (ABOUT **200°F**)
4 CUPS PLUS **2** TABLESPOONS BREAD FLOUR
¾ TEASPOON KOSHER SALT
¼ TEASPOON FRESHLY GROUND BLACK PEPPER
2 LARGE FARM EGGS OR REGULAR FREE-RANGE EGGS

Combine the saffron threads and hot water in a nonreactive container. Cover and steep for 10 minutes. Strain the saffron mixture, discarding the saffron threads and reserving the liquid.

While the saffron is steeping, combine the flour, salt, and pepper in the bowl of a standing mixer with a dough hook attachment. With the machine running, add the eggs and mix until the eggs are combined. Drizzle in the steeping liquid, 1 tablespoon at a time until a soft dough is formed. Wrap the dough in plastic wrap and refrigerate for at least 2 hours or up to three days. The dough will keep frozen for up to one month.

....

VARIATION: TO MAKE SAFFRON PAPPARDELLE, DIVIDE THE PASTA DOUGH INTO THREE EQUAL PORTIONS. LIGHTLY FLOUR ONE PORTION AND WRAP THE OTHER PORTIONS IN PLASTIC WRAP UNTIL READY TO USE (SO THEY DO NOT DRY OUT). ROLL THE FLOURED DOUGH THROUGH A PASTA MACHINE, STARTING AT THE WIDEST SETTING, REPEATING UNTIL YOU HAVE REACHED THE THINNEST SETTING AND THE PASTA DOUGH IS SMOOTH AND THIN. THE PASTA DOUGH CAN THEN BE RUN THROUGH A PAPPARDELLE PASTA ATTACHMENT OR CUT INTO 1½-INCH-WIDE STRIPS. PLACE THE PAPPARDELLE NOODLES ON A LIGHTLY FLOURED SURFACE, AND REPEAT THE ENTIRE PROCESS WITH THE RESERVED PORTION OF DOUGH. THE NOODLES CAN BE COVERED WITH PLASTIC WRAP AND REFRIGERATED FOR UP TO ONE DAY BEFORE USING. TO COOK THE PAPPARDELLE, PLACE IN A LARGE POT OF BOILING SALTED WATER FOR 2 MINUTES, STIRRING OCCASIONALLY, OR UNTIL AL DENTE.

SAVORY PASTRY DOUGH

At the restaurant we melt and chill leaf fat (the fat that surrounds the kidneys) from the fresh hogs we receive from Fudge Family Farms. We then make pastry dough using equal parts butter and leaf fat for an extra flaky crust. You can also use a food processor to prepare this dough, but be careful not to overmix; just pulse the machine until the pastry begins to come together. The amount of water you add to the dough may vary each time, depending on the humidity. If you use a food processor to mix the dough, make sure you allow enough time (at least two hours) for the dough to rest before using.

YIELD: ABOUT ¾ POUND (12 OUNCES)

1¼ cups all-purpose flour
¼ teaspoon salt
½ cup (1 stick) unsalted butter, diced and well chilled
4 to 5 tablespoons (about ¼ cup) ice cold water

Sift together the flour and salt into a medium bowl. Using a pastry cutter or a fork, add the butter to the flour mixture until it resembles a coarse meal. Add the water, one tablespoon at a time, stirring just until the mixture begins to stick together and form a dough.

Turn out the dough onto a piece of plastic wrap and wrap tightly into a small disk. Chill the dough for at least 2 hours before using.

VARIATIONS:

To make **SWEET PASTRY DOUGH**, add 1 tablespoon of granulated sugar to the flour and salt mixture and proceed as directed.

To make **OYSTER CRACKERS**, (Yield: about 80 crackers) add ¼ teaspoon of freshly ground black pepper to the flour and salt mixture and proceed as directed. Preheat the oven to 375°F. Once the dough has rested, unwrap and place on a well-floured work surface. Roll out the dough until it is almost paper thin, sprinkling additional flour as needed to keep the dough from sticking. Use a 1½-inch round cutter to cut circles out of the dough and place on a parchment paper–lined baking sheet. Do not reroll the dough scrapes as it will make the crackers tough. Whisk together 1 large egg and 1 tablespoon of water. Using a pastry brush, lightly brush the egg wash over the tops of the crackers. Sprinkle kosher salt over the tops of the crackers and bake for 7 to 10 minutes or until slightly puffed and golden brown. Watch the crackers closely towards the end of the baking time as they will brown quickly. Allow the crackers to cool completely on the baking sheet before serving.

POTATO GNOCCHI

Since homemade gnocchi can be a time consuming process, we like to make a sizeable batch at one time and freeze the extra gnocchi for a later use. To do so, spread the gnocchi in an even layer on a rimmed baking sheet pan sprinkled lightly with flour. Allow the gnocchi to freeze completely on the baking sheet before transferring to an airtight, freezer-safe container. The gnocchi will keep frozen for up to one month and can be boiled directly from the frozen state in about the same time as fresh gnocchi.

YIELD: ABOUT 104 DUMPLINGS OR 12 SERVINGS

2 large (1½ pounds) Idaho baking potatoes, peeled and cut into 2-inch cubes

3 large egg yolks

⅛ teaspoon grated fresh nutmeg

½ cup (1 ounce) finely grated, loosely packed Parmesan cheese

1½ cups all-purpose flour, plus more for dusting

Place the potatoes in a stockpot and cover with cold water and several generous pinches of kosher salt. Bring to a boil over high heat and cook until tender, about 15 minutes. Drain and place the potatoes on a baking sheet and set aside until cool enough to handle.

Pass the potatoes through a potato ricer or food mill set over a large bowl. Add the egg yolks, nutmeg, and Parmesan cheese to the potato mixture and stir until well incorporated. Gradually add 1½ cups of the flour until a soft dough is formed. (You may not need all of the flour.)

On a lightly floured work surface, knead the potato mixture several times and cover lightly with plastic wrap or a tea towel to keep from drying out.

Lightly flour the work surface again with additional flour. Divide the dough into four equal portions. Working with one portion at a time, roll the dough into a long rope shape, about 1 inch thick. Cut the strand of dough into 1-inch-long pieces and place dumplings on a lightly floured baking sheet. Repeat with the remaining dough.

Bring a large pot of salted water to a simmer. Lightly press a fork into the tops of the dumplings, if desired. Drop the dumplings, in batches, into the gently simmering water and cook for 2 to 3 minutes, or until the dumplings begin to rise to the top of the water. Remove the dumplings with a slotted spoon and place on a large baking sheet. If the dumplings are not being used immediately, drizzle with several tablespoons of olive oil to keep the dumplings from sticking together.

AREPA CAKE

YIELD: 8 TO 9 CAKES

2 CUPS MASA HARINA (MEXICAN FLOUR)
½ **CUP ALL-PURPOSE FLOUR**
¾ **TEASPOON BAKING POWDER**
1½ **TEASPOONS KOSHER SALT**
½ **TEASPOON FRESHLY GROUND BLACK PEPPER**
¾ **CUP SLICED GREEN ONIONS**
1 CUP FRESHLY SHAVED CORN KERNELS
3 CUPS BUTTERMILK
1 LARGE EGG
½ **CUP PEANUT OIL, DIVIDED**

Stir together the masa harina, all-purpose flour, baking powder, salt, and pepper in a large bowl. Add the green onions and corn kernels and stir to combine.

Whisk together the buttermilk and egg in a small bowl until smooth. Stir the buttermilk mixture into the masa harina mixture until moistened.

Heat 2 tablespoons of the peanut oil in a 10-inch cast-iron skillet over medium heat. Pour ½ cup of the batter into the skillet and spread into a 5-inch circle. Cook for 2½ to 3 minutes. Turn the cake and cook an additional 2 minutes or until golden brown and cooked through. Remove the cake from the skillet and keep warm until ready to serve. Repeat with the remaining batter, adding more peanut oil to the skillet, as needed. Serve hot.

HUSHPUPPIES

USING FRESH, SWEET RIPE CORN WILL ADD A TOUCH OF SWEETNESS TO THE HUSHPUPPIES. IF FRESH CORN IS OUT OF SEASON, YOU CAN SUBSTITUTE THAWED FROZEN SWEET CORN KERNELS.

YIELD: ABOUT 3 DOZEN

3 CUPS PEANUT OIL, FOR FRYING
1½ **CUPS FINELY GROUND YELLOW CORNMEAL**
½ **CUP ALL-PURPOSE FLOUR**
1 TEASPOON BAKING POWDER
1½ **TEASPOONS SALT**
½ **TEASPOON FRESHLY GROUND BLACK PEPPER**
1 CUP SHAVED FRESH CORN KERNELS
¾ **CUP MINCED GREEN ONIONS**
1½ **CUPS BUTTERMILK**
1 LARGE EGG

Pour the peanut oil into a deep-sided skillet to a depth of 3 inches. (Alternately a deep fryer can be filled with peanut oil.) Preheat the oil to 375°F.

Combine the cornmeal, flour, baking powder, salt, and pepper in a large bowl. Stir in the corn and green onions. In a separate bowl, whisk together the buttermilk and egg. Add the buttermilk mixture to the cornmeal mixture and stir until the entire mixture is moistened.

Place rounded tablespoonfuls of the batter into the preheated oil and fry for 2 to 3 minutes, turning halfway through, or until golden brown and cooked through. Remove from the oil with a slotted spoon and drain on paper towel–lined plates. Allow hushpuppies to cool for 1 to 2 minutes and serve hot.

WILD PERSIMMON JAM

IF WILD PERSIMMONS ARE UNAVAILABLE, LOOK FOR REGULAR PERSIM-MONS THAT ARE RIPE AND SOFT TO THE TOUCH. THE SOFTER THE PERSIMMON SKINS ARE THE BETTER RESULTS YOU WILL HAVE WHEN PREPARING THIS JAM.

YIELD: ABOUT 1⅓ CUPS

6 MEDIUM-SIZED RIPE PERSIMMONS (ABOUT 1¾ POUNDS)
1 CUP GRANULATED SUGAR

Remove the peel from the persimmons and roughly chop the pulp. Use the back of a knife to scrape as much juice and pulp as possible from the peel. You should have about 2 cups of pulp.

Combine the persimmon pulp and sugar in a small saucepan and bring to a boil over medium-high heat. Reduce the heat to medium-low and allow the mixture to simmer for 30 minutes, stirring frequently, or until thickened. Set aside to cool to room temperature. The jam can be used immediately or stored in the refrigerator in an airtight container for up to two weeks.

VANILLA CRÈME ANGLAISE

YIELD: 1½ CUPS

1 CUP HALF-AND-HALF
¼ VANILLA BEAN, SPLIT IN HALF LENGTHWISE
3 LARGE EGG YOLKS
¼ CUP GRANULATED SUGAR
PINCH OF SALT

Pour the half-and-half into a small saucepan. Scrape the vanilla beans into the half-and-half and add the vanilla bean pods. Heat the half-and-half over medium heat just until scalded, about 5 minutes. Remove from the heat.

Whisk together the egg yolks, sugar, and salt until slightly thickened and pale yellow. Pour the hot half-and-half mixture into the egg mixture in a slow, steady stream while whisking constantly.

Prepare an ice water bath by filling a large bowl halfway with ice and a little water.

Pour the entire mixture back into the saucepan and cook, stirring constantly, for 3 to 5 minutes or until the custard coats the back of a spoon.

Strain the mixture through a fine-meshed strainer or sieve into a clean container set inside the prepared water bath. Stir occasionally until cool. The anglaise can be served warm or covered and chilled before serving. The anglaise will keep in an airtight container in the refrigerator for up to one week.

SIMPLE SYRUP

This syrup is very versatile. In addition to being used as a base for many of our desserts, it can be flavored with a variety of seasonings such as lemon peel, lavender, cinnamon, or our two favorites, fresh ginger and mint, listed below. These recipes can easily be doubled or tripled and when chilled, will keep fresh for up to one week.

YIELD: ABOUT 2¼ CUPS

2 CUPS GRANULATED SUGAR
1 CUPS WATER

Combine the sugar and water in a small saucepan and bring to a boil, stirring occasionally, until the sugar is dissolved. Boil for 30 seconds and remove the saucepan from the heat. Cool the syrup to room temperature. Refrigerate the syrup until well chilled.

VARIATIONS:

To make **GINGER SIMPLE SYRUP**, add one 2-ounce piece fresh ginger that has been peeled and julienned (about ½ cup) to the sugar and water mixture before bringing it to a boil. Once the mixture boils, cover, and remove the saucepan from the heat. Allow the syrup to steep for 30 minutes. Strain the syrup through a fine-meshed strainer and refrigerate the syrup until well chilled.

To make **MINT SIMPLE SYRUP**, add 4 to 5 fresh mint sprigs (about ¾ ounce) to the sugar and water before bringing it to a boil. Once the mixture boils, cover, and remove the saucepan from the heat. Allow the syrup to steep for 30 minutes. Strain the syrup through a fine-meshed sieve or strainer and refrigerate the syrup until well chilled.

To make **HONEYSUCKLE SIMPLE SYRUP**, pack 3 ounces of fresh golden-yellow honeysuckle blossoms into a 1-quart mason jar with a tight-fitting lid. Pour 2¼ cups of hot, prepared simple syrup over the fresh blossoms and allow the mixture to cool to room temperature. Once cool enough to touch, seal the jar and chill overnight. The honeysuckle syrup will keep refrigerated for up to two weeks. Both the syrup and the honeysuckle blossoms can be used in recipes.

CHOCOLATE ORANGE SAUCE

YIELD: ABOUT 2 CUPS

12 OUNCES BITTERSWEET CHOCOLATE, CUT INTO SMALL CHUNKS
1½ TABLESPOONS GRATED ORANGE ZEST, ABOUT 2 ORANGES
¼ CUP FRESH ORANGE JUICE, ABOUT 2 ORANGES
½ CUP HEAVY CREAM
2 TABLESPOONS UNSALTED BUTTER

Fill a medium saucepan or the bottom of a double boiler with water and place over medium heat. Bring the water to a simmer.

Combine all of the ingredients in a heat-proof bowl or the top of a double boiler and set over simmering water. Stir occasionally until melted. Remove the sauce from the heat and whisk until smooth. Use the sauce immediately or keep warm until ready to serve.

WHITE CHOCOLATE SAUCE

YIELD: ABOUT 3 CUPS

2 CUPS GOOD-QUALITY WHITE CHOCOLATE, ROUGHLY CHOPPED
¾ CUP HEAVY CREAM
1 TABLESPOON PLUS 1 TEASPOON LIGHT CORN SYRUP

Fill a medium saucepan or the bottom of a double boiler halfway with water and place over medium heat. Bring the water to a simmer.

Combine the chocolate and cream in a heat-proof bowl or the top of a double boiler and place on top of the saucepan. Whisk the chocolate-cream mixture until the chocolate is melted.

Remove the sauce from the heat and stir in the corn syrup. Set the sauce aside to cool to room temperature. Serve warm or at room temperature.

RASPBERRY COULIS

YIELD: ABOUT 2 CUPS

8 PINTS FRESH RASPBERRIES
2 CUPS GRANULATED SUGAR
2½ TABLESPOONS FRESH LEMON JUICE

Combine the raspberries, sugar, and lemon juice in a small saucepan over medium heat. Bring the mixture to a boil, stirring occasionally, to dissolve the sugar. When the mixture begins to boil, reduce the heat to medium low and cook, stirring occasionally, for 8 to 10 minutes, or until slightly thickened.

Place the raspberry mixture in a fine-meshed strainer or sieve set over a clean bowl. Using a rubber spatula, lightly press the raspberry mixture through the strainer, extracting as much of the liquid as possible. Discard the solids and chill the coulis completely before using. The coulis will keep refrigerated in an airtight container for up to one week.

CANDIED PEANUTS

YIELD: ABOUT 2 CUPS

1 LARGE EGG WHITE, AT ROOM TEMPERATURE
2½ CUPS LIGHTLY SALTED PEANUTS
3 TABLESPOONS LIGHT BROWN SUGAR

Preheat the oven to 225°F. Lightly coat a rimmed baking sheet with vegetable cooking spray.

Whisk the egg white by hand in a medium bowl, just until foamy. Fold in the peanuts, stirring to coat well. Sprinkle the brown sugar over the peanuts and stir to combine. Spread the peanuts in an even layer on the prepared baking sheet.

Bake for 1 hour at 225°F, stirring occasionally, or until the peanuts are golden brown and lightly toasted. Allow the peanuts to cool on the baking sheet before using. Use immediately or store in an airtight container for up to one week.

CARAMEL SAUCE

YIELD: 1½ CUPS

1 CUP GRANULATED SUGAR
¼ CUP WATER
1 CUP HEAVY CREAM
1 TABLESPOON UNSALTED BUTTER
PINCH OF FINELY GROUND SEA SALT
1 TO 2 DROPS PURE VANILLA EXTRACT

Combine the sugar and water in a heavy-bottomed medium saucepan. Stir over medium heat until the sugar dissolves. Increase the heat to medium-high and allow the mixture to boil without stirring until it reaches 350°F (dark caramel stage) on a candy thermometer and turns a deep amber color, about 10 minutes. Instead of stirring, brush down the sidse of the saucepan with a wet pastry brush and gently swirl the pan while the mixture is cooking. Once the desired color is achieved, remove from the heat and carefully add the cream. You may want to stand back as the cream is added as it will bubble vigorously. Whisk in the butter, sea salt, and vanilla and set aside to cool to room temperature. Serve warm or at room temperature.

ESPRESSO CREAM

YIELD: ABOUT 2 CUPS

1 (16-OUNCE) CONTAINER MASCARPONE
1½ CUPS CONFECTIONERS' SUGAR
3½ TABLESPOONS FRESHLY BREWED ESPRESSO, CHILLED

Whisk together the mascarpone and the confectioners' sugar in a small bowl until smooth. Drizzle the espresso into the mascarpone mixture and whisk until well combined. Chill for at least 30 minutes before serving or up to three days.

ESPRESSO BRITTLE

YIELD: ABOUT 20 PIECES

½ CUP WHOLE ESPRESSO BEANS
1¾ CUPS GRANULATED SUGAR
¼ CUP WATER
2 TABLESPOONS LIGHT CORN SYRUP

Line a rimmed baking sheet with a heat-proof, nonstick baking mat, such as a Silpat brand baking mat. Evenly spread the espresso beans over the baking mat and set aside.

Combine the sugar, water, and corn syrup in a heavy-bottomed medium saucepan. Stir over medium heat until the sugar dissolves. Increase the heat to medium-high and allow the mixture to boil without stirring until it reaches 340°F (light caramel stage) on a candy thermometer and turns a light amber color, 8 to 10 minutes. Instead of stirring while the mixture is cooking, brush down the sides of the saucepan with a wet pastry brush and gently swirl the pan. Once the mixture achieves the desired color, remove from the heat and pour evenly over the espresso beans into the prepared baking sheet. Allow the brittle to cool completely.

Crack the brittle into even-size pieces and use immediately or store in an airtight container in the freezer for up to one month.

CANDIED PECANS

YIELD: ABOUT 2 CUPS

2 TABLESPOONS UNSALTED BUTTER
2 TABLESPOONS FIRMLY PACKED LIGHT BROWN SUGAR
2 TABLESPOONS WATER
¼ TEASPOON CAYENNE PEPPER
¼ TEASPOON KOSHER SALT
2 CUPS PECAN HALVES

Preheat the oven to 300°F.

Combine the butter, brown sugar, water, cayenne, and salt in a large, ovenproof skillet over medium heat, stirring occasionally, until the butter is melted and the sugar is dissolved. Add the pecans and toss until well coated. Place the skillet in the oven and bake for 10 minutes, stirring halfway through, until the pecans are golden brown and toasted. Using a heat-proof rubber spatula, transfer the pecan mixture to a baking sheet and set aside to cool completely.

Separate the pecans, if needed, and use immediately or store in an airtight container at room temperature for up to four days.

BANANA BAVARIAN CREAM

YIELD: ABOUT 1½ CUPS

½ CUP PASTRY CREAM (PAGE 365)
3 RIPE BANANAS, PEELED AND CUT INTO CHUNKS
½ CUP WHIPPED CREAM (PAGE 367)

Place the pastry cream in the bowl of a standing mixer fitted with a paddle attachment and beat until smooth. Add the bananas and continue beating until the bananas are well mashed. Fold the whipped cream into the banana mixture until fully incorporated. Chill the cream for at least 30 minutes before serving. This mixture will keep refrigerated in an airtight container for up to two days.

PASTRY CREAM

YIELD: ABOUT 4½ CUPS

4 CUPS (1 QUART) HALF-AND-HALF
¼ VANILLA BEAN, SPLIT IN HALF LENGTHWISE
1 CUP PLUS 2 TABLESPOONS GRANULATED SUGAR
½ CUP CORNSTARCH
PINCH OF SALT
7 LARGE EGG YOLKS
¼ CUP (½ STICK) UNSALTED BUTTER, AT ROOM TEM-PERATURE

Pour the half-and-half into a medium saucepan and scrape the vanilla bean seeds into pan. Add the vanilla bean pods to the half-and-half mixture and bring to a boil. Immediately remove the half-and-half from the heat, cover, and allow the vanilla to steep for 30 minutes.

Whisk the sugar, cornstarch, and salt in a mixing bowl until smooth. Add the egg yolks and whisk until combined. Set aside.

Return the saucepan to the heat and bring to a simmer. Remove the half-and-half mixture from the heat and slowly pour the egg mixture into the hot half-and-half while whisking constantly until all of the egg mixture has been added. Return the mixture to the stove and cook over medium heat while whisking constantly until the mixture thickens to a puddinglike consistency. You may begin to see one large bubble appear on the surface of the custard when ready. Remove the custard from the heat and whisk in the softened butter. Strain the mixture through a fine-meshed strainer or sieve and chill completely before using. This mixture will keep refrigerated in an airtight container for up to one week.

MACADAMIA NUT BISCOTTI

THESE TRADITIONAL ITALIAN COOKIES ARE A FAVORITE OF IDIE'S. THEY ARE OFTEN SERVED ALONGSIDE DESSERTS AT THE RESTAURANT, BUT ARE ALSO A GREAT ADDITION TO A CUP OF COFFEE OR CAPPUCCINO. THIS RECIPE MAKES PLENTY, BUT THE COOKIES WILL KEEP WELL FOR UP TO THREE WEEKS IN AN AIRTIGHT TIN OR CONTAINER.

YIELD: ABOUT 6½ DOZEN

2¾ CUPS ALL-PURPOSE FLOUR
1⅔ CUPS GRANULATED SUGAR
1 TEASPOON BAKING POWDER
½ TEASPOON SALT
½ TEASPOON TOASTED AND FRESHLY GROUND ANISE SEEDS
1½ TABLESPOONS GRATED LEMON ZEST, ABOUT 1 LEMON
½ TEASPOON FRESHLY GRATED NUTMEG
3 LARGE EGGS
3 LARGE EGG YOLKS
1 TEASPOON PURE VANILLA EXTRACT
1 (6-OUNCE) JAR DRY-ROASTED, LIGHTLY SALTED MACADAMIA NUTS

Combine the flour, sugar, baking powder, salt, anise seeds, lemon zest, and nutmeg in the bowl of a standing mixer. Using the paddle attachment, stir the flour mixture on low until combined. In a separate bowl, lightly whisk together the eggs, egg yolks, and vanilla. With the mixer on low, add the egg mixture in a slow, steady stream. Continue mixing until the eggs are almost incorporated. Stir in the macadamia nuts and set the dough aside.

Preheat the oven to 325°F.

Line a rimmed baking sheet with parchment paper. Divide the dough in half and place on a generously floured surface. Roll each half of the dough into a log shape, about 14 inches long. Carefully transfer the logs to the prepared baking sheet and gently flatten the tops until each log is about 3 inches wide and ¾ inch thick. Bake for 30 to 35 minutes or until lightly browned. Remove from the oven and allow the biscotti to cool completely.

Decrease the oven temperature to 250°F.

Cut the cooled biscotti logs into ¼-inch-thick slices, about 35 to 40 slices per log. Arrange the slices, cut side down, on a baking sheet. Bake the biscotti at 250°F for 35 to 40 minutes or until golden brown and crispy. Serve warm or room temperature. To store, allow the biscotti to cool to room temperature before placing in an airtight container.

VANILLA ICE CREAM

At home we prefer to use a White Mountain brand hand-crank ice cream freezer to make slow-churned ice cream. When you're pressed for time, any electric tabletop ice cream freezer will work well.

YIELD: ABOUT 5 CUPS

4 CUPS HEAVY CREAM
½ VANILLA BEAN, SPLIT
8 LARGE EGG YOLKS
½ CUP GRANULATED SUGAR
PINCH OF SALT

Add the cream to a 2-quart saucepan and place over medium-high heat. Scrape the vanilla bean seeds into the cream and add the scraped bean pods to the cream. Bring the mixture to a simmer and remove from the heat.

Prepare a water bath by filling a large bowl halfway with ice and a small amount of water.

Whisk together the egg yolks and sugar in a large, stainless steel bowl until they are pale yellow and slightly thickened. Slowly drizzle the hot cream mixture into the egg mixture, while whisking continuously. Add a pinch of salt and pour the entire mixture back into the saucepan and cook over medium heat, stirring constantly, for 2 to 3 minutes or until the mixture coats the back of a spoon.

Remove from the heat and strain the mixture through a fine-meshed sieve or strainer into a stainless steel bowl. Set the bowl in the prepared ice water bath, stir until cool, and refrigerate overnight (about 8 hours). Pour the mixture into an ice cream machine and freeze according to the manufacturer's directions. Transfer the ice cream into a freezer-safe container and freeze for at least 2 hours or until firm. The ice cream will keep in an airtight container in the freezer for up to one month.

VARIATIONS:

To make **LEMON VERBENA ICE CREAM** (Yield: about 5 cups), add 2 (2 to 3-inch) fresh lemon verbena sprigs to the cream and vanilla mixture and bring to a simmer. Cover the saucepan and remove from the heat. Allow the cream mixture to steep for 30 minutes. Remove and reserve the lemon verbena sprigs. Continue with the vanilla ice cream recipe as directed. Return the reserved lemon verbena sprigs to the cooked custard while the mixture chills in an ice water bath. Strain before freezing according to the manufacturer's directions. Proceed with the recipe as directed.

To make **BUTTERMILK ICE CREAM** (Yield: about 6 cups), add 1½ cups whole-milk buttermilk to the cooled vanilla ice cream custard. Freeze the ice cream mixture according to the manufacturer's directions and proceed with the recipe as directed.

To make **CINNAMON ICE CREAM** (Yield: about 5 cups), break 3 cinnamon sticks in half and add them to the cream and vanilla mixture and bring to a simmer. Cover the saucepan and remove from the heat. Allow the cream mixture to steep for 1 hour; strain and discard the cinnamon sticks. Proceed with the recipe as directed.

To make **NUTMEG ICE CREAM** (Yield: about 5 cups), add 1 tablespoon freshly grated nutmeg to the cream and vanilla mixture and bring to a simmer. Cover the saucepan and remove from the heat. Allow the cream mixture to steep for 30 minutes. Proceed with the recipe as directed.

To make **MOLASSES ICE CREAM** (Yield: about 5½ cups), stir ½ cup unsulphured molasses into the cooked custard mixture and strain through a fine-meshed sieve or strainer. Proceed with the recipe as directed.

VANILLA SUGAR

YIELD: ABOUT 2 CUPS

2 CUPS GRANULATED SUGAR
2 VANILLA BEANS, SPLIT IN HALF LENGTHWISE

Combine the sugar and vanilla bean in a dry, airtight container at room temperature for at least one week or up to two months.

VARIATIONS:

TO MAKE **SUGARED VANILLA BEANS**, REMOVE THE VANILLA BEANS FROM THE VANILLA SUGAR AND CUT INTO 1-INCH-LONG PIECES. USE AS A GARNISH FOR DOUGHNUTS OR OTHER VANILLA-FLAVORED DESSERTS.

TO MAKE **CINNAMON SUGAR** SUBSTITUTE 1 TEASPOON FRESHLY GROUND CINNAMON FOR THE VANILLA BEANS AND PROCEED WITH THE RECIPE AS DIRECTED.

TO MAKE **LEMON SUGAR** COMBINE ½ CUP FRESHLY GRATED LEMON ZEST WITH THE SUGAR IN A LARGE MIXING BOWL. USING YOUR HANDS, RUB THE ZEST AND SUGAR MIXTURE TOGETHER, RELEASING THE OILS INTO THE SUGAR. SPREAD THE MIXTURE IN AN EVEN LAYER ON A RIMMED BAKING SHEET AND SET ASIDE TO DRY AT ROOM TEMPERATURE OVERNIGHT (ABOUT 8 HOURS). TRANSFER THE LEMON SUGAR MIXTURE TO A DRY, AIRTIGHT CONTAINER AND STORE FOR UP TO TWO MONTHS.

DRIED ORANGE SLICES

YIELD: 15 TO 18 SLICES

1 LARGE ORANGE, UNPEELED

Preheat the oven to 250°F.

Slice the orange on a mandoline into thin (¹⁄₁₆-inch) rounds. Arrange the orange slices in an even layer on an ovenproof, nonstick baking mat (such as Silpat brand) inside a rimmed baking sheet. Bake the orange slices at 250°F for 25 to 30 minutes. Remove from the oven and turn the orange slices. Return the oranges to the oven and bake for an additional 25 to 30 minutes or until the slices are dry, crisp, and lightly browned. Set the orange slices aside to cool to room temperature. The orange slices will keep in an airtight container at room temperature for up to one month.

WHIPPED CREAM

YIELD: ABOUT 1 CUP

½ CUP HEAVY CREAM, CHILLED
1 TEASPOON LEMON SUGAR (PAGE 367)

Place the cream in a large bowl (or standing mixer with whisk attachment) and whisk until firm peaks form and the mixture has doubled in size. Add the lemon sugar and continue whisking just until incorporated. The whipped cream should hold its shape and slightly topple over when the whisk is removed from the bowl. Use whipped cream immediately or chill for up to 1 hour.

PURPLE MASHED POTATOES

YIELD: 6 CUPS

**3 POUNDS PURPLE PERUVIAN POTATOES, WASHED,
PEELED, AND CUT INTO 2-INCH PIECES**
4 TEASPOONS KOSHER SALT, DIVIDED
½ CUP (1 STICK) UNSALTED BUTTER, DICED
1 CUP HEAVY CREAM
½ TEASPOON FRESHLY GROUND BLACK PEPPER

Place the potatoes in a medium saucepan; add enough water to cover the potatoes by 1 inch and add 2 teaspoons of the salt. Bring the potatoes to a boil over high heat, reduce the heat to medium, and simmer for 10 to 12 minutes or until tender. Drain the potatoes and place in a food mill or potato ricer set over the warm saucepan. Run the potatoes through the food mill or ricer. Add the butter and cream to the potatoes and stir gently until the butter is melted. Season the potatoes with the remaining 2 teaspoons of salt and the pepper. Serve warm.

FENNEL MASHED POTATOES

YIELD: 4 CUPS

**1¼ CUPS CORED AND ROUGHLY CHOPPED FENNEL,
ABOUT ½ LARGE BULB**
¾ CUP HEAVY CREAM
**1½ POUNDS IDAHO POTATOES, PEELED AND CUT INTO
2-INCH PIECES**
2¾ TEASPOONS KOSHER SALT, DIVIDED
3 TABLESPOONS UNSALTED BUTTER
¼ TEASPOON FRESHLY GROUND BLACK PEPPER

Combine the fennel and cream in a small saucepan over medium heat. Bring the mixture to a boil, reduce the heat to medium low, and simmer for 15 minutes or until the fennel is tender. Transfer the cream and fennel mixture to a blender and process on high until puréed. Set the fennel cream aside and keep warm until ready to use.

Place the potatoes in a medium saucepan; add enough water to cover the potatoes by 1 inch and add 2 teaspoons of the salt. Bring the potatoes to a boil over high heat, reduce the heat to medium, and simmer for 10 to 12 minutes or until tender. Drain the potatoes and place in a food mill or potato ricer set over the warm saucepan. Run the potatoes through the food mill or ricer. Add the reserved fennel cream and the butter and stir gently until the butter is melted. Season the potatoes with the remaining ¾ teaspoon of salt and the pepper. Serve warm.

CREAMY COLESLAW

YIELD: ABOUT 2 QUARTS OR 8 SERVINGS

3 TABLESPOONS GRANULATED SUGAR

¼ CUP PLUS ½ TABLESPOON CIDER VINEGAR

1 TEASPOON KOSHER SALT

¼ TEASPOON FRESHLY GROUND BLACK PEPPER

1½ CUPS BASIC AÏOLI (PAGE **342**) OR STORE-BOUGHT
    MAYONNAISE

2 SMALL (1-POUND) HEADS GREEN CABBAGE, HALVED,
    CORED AND THINLY SHAVED

1 LARGE CARROT, PEELED AND GRATED

Whisk together the sugar, vinegar, salt, and pepper until well combined. Add the aïoli and whisk until smooth. Toss the cabbage and carrot with the dressing. Adjust the seasonings with additional salt and pepper, if needed. The slaw can be served immediately or chilled until ready to serve.

PARSNIP PURÉE

YIELD: ABOUT 3 CUPS

1½ POUNDS PARSNIPS, PEELED AND SLICED ½ INCH
    THICK

2½ CUPS WHOLE MILK

¾ TEASPOON KOSHER SALT

¼ TEASPOON FRESHLY GROUND BLACK PEPPER

Bring the sliced parsnips and milk to a boil in a 6-quart saucepan. Once the mixture begins to boil, reduce the heat and simmer until the parsnips are tender, about 15 minutes. Allow the parsnips to cool in the milk for 10 minutes.

    Drain the parsnips, reserving ½ cup of the milk. Place the parsnips and the reserved ½ cup milk in a blender along with the salt and pepper. Process until the mixture is smooth, stopping occasionally to scrape down the sides as needed. Serve immediately.

BRAISED WHITE BEANS

YIELD: ABOUT 6 CUPS

1 CUP (ABOUT ½ POUND) DRIED GREAT NORTHERN
    BEANS OR OTHER WHITE BEANS

1 TABLESPOON PEANUT OIL

½ POUND BONELESS PORK SHOULDER, CUT INTO
    1-INCH CUBES

2 CUPS SPICY HAM HOCK BROTH (PAGE **336**)

1 SMOKED HAM HOCK

2 SLICES THICK-CUT APPLE-SMOKED BACON, ROUGHLY CHOPPED

1 BAY LEAF

3 LARGE GARLIC CLOVES, PEELED

6 FRESH THYME SPRIGS

1½ TEASPOONS KOSHER SALT

½ TEASPOON FRESHLY GROUND BLACK PEPPER

1 MEDIUM ONION, PEELED AND QUARTERED

Place the beans in a medium pot and add enough water to cover the top of the beans. Bring the mixture to a boil over high heat, cover, and turn off the heat. Allow the beans to steep for 10 minutes. Uncover, drain the beans, and rinse well under cold running water. Set the beans aside to cool slightly.

    Heat the peanut oil in a large Dutch oven or stockpot over medium heat. Add the pork shoulder cubes and cook until all of the sides are well browned, about 8 minutes. Add the blanched beans and the remaining ingredients to the Dutch oven and bring to a boil. Reduce the heat to medium low, cover, and simmer until the beans are tender, stirring occasionally, about 1½ hours. The beans will still have a significant amount of liquid when cooked.

    Remove the bean mixture from the heat. Remove the ham hock and set aside until cool enough to touch. Pull the meat off the ham hock and discard the bone. Return the ham hock meat to the beans. Shred the pork shoulder cubes in the beans. Remove and discard the bay leaf and thyme sprigs. The beans can be drained and served warm or cooled and stored covered in their broth in the refrigerator for up to four days.

CELERY ROOT SLAW

YIELD: 5 CUPS

¼ CUP APPLE CIDER VINEGAR

2 TABLESPOONS GRANULATED SUGAR

¾ CUP BASIC AÏOLI (PAGE 342) OR STORE-BOUGHT
    MAYONNAISE

¾ TEASPOON KOSHER SALT

¼ TEASPOON FRESHLY GROUND BLACK PEPPER

6 CUPS PEELED AND GRATED CELERY ROOT, ABOUT 2
    MEDIUM CELERY ROOTS

1 CUP PEELED AND GRATED CARROT, ABOUT 2 LARGE
    CARROTS

3 TABLESPOONS CHOPPED FRESH CHIVES

Combine the vinegar and sugar in a small saucepan and bring to a boil over high heat, stirring until the sugar is dissolved. Remove from the heat and refrigerate until well chilled.

Whisk together the vinegar mixture, aïoli, salt, and pepper until smooth. Add the celery root, carrot, and chives, tossing until well combined. The slaw can be served immediately or chilled for up to 1 hour before serving.

RATATOUILLE

YIELD: ABOUT 4 CUPS

¼ CUP PLUS 2 TABLESPOONS EXTRA-VIRGIN OLIVE OIL

1 CUP CHOPPED YELLOW ONION, ABOUT ½ INCH THICK

1¼ TEASPOONS CHOPPED FRESH THYME

1 CUP PEELED AND CHOPPED EGGPLANT, ABOUT ½
    INCH THICK

1 TEASPOON MINCED GARLIC

1 CUP SEEDED AND CHOPPED RED BELL PEPPER, ABOUT
    ½ INCH THICK

1 CUP SEEDED AND CHOPPED YELLOW BELL PEPPER,
    ABOUT ½ INCH THICK

1 CUP CHOPPED ZUCCHINI, ABOUT ½ INCH THICK

1 CUP CHOPPED YELLOW SQUASH, ABOUT ½ INCH
    THICK

1 CUP PEELED, SEEDED, AND CHOPPED RIPE TOMATOES

¾ TEASPOON KOSHER SALT

½ TEASPOON FRESHLY GROUND BLACK PEPPER

2 TABLESPOONS FINELY CHOPPED FRESH BASIL

1 TABLESPOON CHOPPED FRESH CHIVES

1 TABLESPOON CHOPPED FRESH PARSLEY

Heat the olive oil in a large saucepan or deep-sided skillet over medium-low heat. Add the onion and thyme and cook for 3 to 4 minutes, or until translucent. Add the eggplant and cook for 3 minutes. Stir in the garlic and cook, stirring constantly, for 1 minute. Add the bell peppers, zucchini, and squash and cook, stirring frequently, for 4 minutes. Add the tomatoes and cook, stirring occasionally, for 3 minutes. Season the vegetables with the salt and pepper. Stir in the basil, chives, and parsley and remove from the heat. Serve immediately.

BRAISED VEGETARIAN WHITE BEANS

YIELD: ABOUT 3 CUPS

2 CUPS (ABOUT 1 POUND) DRIED GREAT NORTHERN BEANS OR OTHER WHITE BEANS
6 CUPS VEGETABLE STOCK (PAGE 334) OR WATER
1 BAY LEAF
3 LARGE GARLIC CLOVES, PEELED
6 FRESH THYME SPRIGS
1½ TABLESPOONS KOSHER SALT
½ TEASPOON FRESHLY GROUND BLACK PEPPER
1 MEDIUM ONION, PEELED AND QUARTERED
2 LARGE CARROTS, PEELED AND ROUGHLY CHOPPED
2 CELERY STALKS, ROUGHLY CHOPPED

Place the beans in a medium pot and add enough water to cover the top of the beans. Bring the mixture to a boil over high heat, cover, and turn off the heat. Allow the beans to steep for 10 minutes. Uncover, drain the beans, and rinse well under cold running water. Set the beans aside to cool slightly.

Combine the blanched beans and the remaining ingredients in a large Dutch oven or stockpot over medium-high heat and bring to a boil. Reduce the heat to medium low, cover, and simmer until the beans are tender, stirring occasionally, about 1½ hours. The beans will still have a significant amount of liquid when cooked.

Remove the bean mixture from the heat and discard the bay leaf and thyme sprigs. The beans can be drained and served warm or cooled and stored covered in their broth in the refrigerator for up to four days.

BRAISED BLACK BEANS

YIELD: ABOUT 6 CUPS

2 CUPS DRIED BLACK BEANS
1 TABLESPOON PEANUT OIL
¼ CUP FINELY CHOPPED THICK-CUT APPLEWOOD SMOKED BACON
1 SMOKED HAM HOCK
1 ANCHO CHILE PEPPER, CUT INTO 3 PIECES
1 DRIED ARBOL CHILE PEPPER, BROKEN IN HALF
3 LARGE GARLIC CLOVES
1 LARGE ONION, PEELED AND QUARTERED
5 CUPS WATER
1 TABLESPOON KOSHER SALT

Place the beans in a medium stockpot and add enough cold water to cover. Bring the beans to a boil over high heat, cover, and turn off the heat. Allow the beans to steep for 10 minutes. Strain the beans and rinse well in cold water. Set aside to cool slightly.

Heat the peanut oil in a large Dutch oven or stockpot over medium heat. Add the bacon and cook until brown and crispy, about 8 minutes. Add the ham hock and cook, stirring frequently, for 2 minutes. Add the blanched beans and the remaining ingredients to the Dutch oven and bring to a boil. Reduce the heat to low, cover, and simmer until the beans are tender, stirring occasionally, about 1½ hours. The beans will still have a significant amount of liquid when fully cooked.

Remove the bean mixture from the heat and set aside to cool slightly. Strain off and discard the excess liquid from the beans. Remove ham hock and reserve for another use. Remove and discard the ancho and Arbol chile peppers and onion quarters. The beans can be used immediately or stored in an airtight container in the refrigerator for up to one week.

FIELD PEAS

YIELD: ABOUT 3 CUPS

1 TABLESPOON OLIVE OIL

2 SLICES THICK-CUT APPLEWOOD SMOKED BACON,
   FINELY CHOPPED

½ SWEET ONION, PEELED AND CHOPPED

1 BAY LEAF

2 FRESH THYME SPRIGS

3 CUPS FRESH FIELD PEAS, SUCH AS BLACK-EYED, PINK-
   EYED, OR CROWDER PEAS

4 CUPS COLD WATER

1 TEASPOON KOSHER SALT

½ TEASPOON FRESHLY GROUND BLACK PEPPER

Heat the olive oil in a medium saucepan over medium heat. Add the bacon and cook, stirring frequently, until crispy, about 3 minutes. Add the onion, bay leaf, and thyme sprigs and cook until the onion is softened and translucent, about 4 minutes. Stir in the peas. Add the water and bring the mixture to a boil. Reduce the heat to medium low and simmer for 12 to 15 minutes, or just until tender. Remove the peas from the heat and season with the salt and pepper to taste. Serve warm.

FIELD PEA LIQUOR – IF RESERVING THE PEAS FOR LATER USE, ALLOW THE PEAS TO COOL IN THEIR BRAISING LIQUID. THE PEAS CAN THEN BE STORED AND REHEATED IN THEIR BRAISING LIQUID. SEVERAL RECIPES CALL FOR FIELD PEA LIQUOR WHICH IS THE PEA BRAISING LIQUID THAT HAS BEEN STRAINED THROUGH A FINE-MESHED SIEVE OR STRAINER.

FALL VEGETABLE GRATIN

YIELD: 6 TO 8 SERVINGS

¼ CUP (½ STICK) UNSALTED BUTTER, DIVIDED

1 LARGE GARLIC CLOVE, PEELED AND SMASHED

1½ TEASPOONS HASTINGS CREATIONS ALL-PURPOSE
   HERB SALT (PAGE 381) OR KOSHER SALT, DIVIDED

½ POUND FINGERLING POTATOES, UNPEELED AND
   SLICED LENGTHWISE INTO ⅛-INCH SLICES

1 SMALL (½-POUND) RUTABAGA, PEELED AND SLICED
   INTO ⅛-INCH SLICES

2 LARGE PARSNIPS, PEELED AND SLICED LENGTHWISE
   INTO ⅛-INCH SLICES

1 LARGE (½-POUND) TURNIP, PEELED AND SLICED INTO
   ⅛-INCH SLICES

1 TABLESPOON CHOPPED FRESH THYME, DIVIDED

1½ CUPS HEAVY CREAM

Preheat the oven to 350°F.

Melt the butter in a small saucepan over low heat with the garlic. Pour 1 tablespoon of the melted butter into an 8 x 8-inch baking dish. Using the smashed garlic clove, spread the butter around the bottom and sides of the baking dish; discard the garlic. Sprinkle ¼ teaspoon of the herb salt over the bottom and sides of the buttered dish.

Arrange an even layer of sliced potatoes, rutabaga, parsnips, and turnip over the bottom of the baking dish, slightly overlapping the vegetables until the entire surface is covered. Drizzle 1 tablespoon or less of the melted butter over the vegetables and sprinkle with ½ teaspoon of the thyme and ½ teaspoon of the herb salt. Repeat the layers, arranging sliced vegetables, butter, thyme, and herb salt in the dish until the dish is almost full. End with a layer of large round turnip slices, creating a concentric pattern on the top of the gratin.

Pour the cream over the gratin, pressing the vegetables down gently to coat. Cover the baking dish with aluminum foil and bake for 30 minutes. Uncover the gratin and continue baking for 20 to 25 minutes or until the vegetables are tender and the gratin is golden brown on top. Allow the gratin to cool for 10 to 15 minutes before serving. Serve hot.

BRAISED ARTICHOKES

YIELD: 4 ARTICHOKE HEARTS

3 SMALL LEMONS, CUT IN HALF, DIVIDED
4 (12-OUNCE) ARTICHOKES
4 CUPS VEGETABLE STOCK (PAGE 334)
½ CUP WHITE WINE
½ CUP OLIVE OIL
¼ CUP FRESH LEMON JUICE
3 FRESH THYME SPRIGS
½ BAY LEAF
1 DRIED ARBOL CHILE PEPPER
2 TEASPOONS KOSHER SALT
1 TEASPOON FRESHLY GROUND BLACK PEPPER

Squeeze 2 of the lemon halves into a medium bowl and fill with enough cold water to cover the artichokes. Clean the artichokes one at a time by taking off the hard, outer leaves. Use a spoon to scrape out the pointy thistles and use a knife to trim away any remaining leaves or husk. Peel away the tough, outer layer of the stems. You should be left with just the heart and the peeled stem. Place the cleaned artichokes in the lemon water.

Combine the remaining 4 lemon halves, the vegetable stock, and the remaining ingredients in a medium saucepan. Remove the artichokes from the lemon water and add to the saucepan. Bring the artichoke mixture to a boil over high heat, reduce the heat, and simmer until the artichokes are tender, 12 to 15 minutes. Allow the artichokes to cool slightly, 10 minutes. Serve warm.

FRIED ONION RINGS

YIELD: 4 SERVINGS

3 MEDIUM YELLOW ONIONS, PEELED AND CUT INTO ½-INCH-THICK RINGS
1 TABLESPOON PLUS ½ TEASPOON KOSHER SALT, DIVIDED
2¼ TEASPOONS FRESHLY GROUND BLACK PEPPER, DIVIDED
½ CUP BUTTERMILK
3 CUPS PEANUT OIL, FOR FRYING
1 CUP ALL-PURPOSE FLOUR
1 CUP CORNMEAL
1 CUP CORN FLOUR

Season the onions with ½ teaspoon of the salt and ¼ teaspoon of the pepper and combine with the buttermilk in a small bowl; toss until well coated.

Combine the flour, cornmeal, and corn flour in a wide baking dish and season with the remaining tablespoon of the salt and 2 teaspoons of the pepper. Dredge the onion rings, one at a time in the cornmeal mixture, turning to coat well. Repeat with the remaining onion rings. Allow the onion rings to sit in the cornmeal mixture for 20 to 25 minutes to help absorb moisture and make them extra crispy when fried. Remove the onion rings from the cornmeal mixture, shaking off any excess flour.

Pour the oil into a deep-sided skillet to a depth of 2 inches. (Alternately, a deep fryer can be filled with peanut oil.) Preheat the oil to 375°F.

Place the onion rings, in batches, in the preheated oil and fry for 1½ to 2 minutes or until golden brown. Transfer the onion rings to a paper towel–lined baking sheet and season with additional salt and pepper, if needed. Serve immediately.

MISCELLANEOUS BASIC RECIPES

SAUSAGE STUFFING

YIELD: 1½ POUNDS (ABOUT 6 CUPS)

2 TABLESPOONS OLIVE OIL
2 POUNDS FRESH SAUSAGE, CASINGS REMOVED
½ CUP MINCED SHALLOTS
3 CUPS FRESH BREADCRUMBS
1 TABLESPOON CHOPPED FRESH PARSLEY
1 TABLESPOON CHOPPED FRESH THYME
1 TABLESPOON CHOPPED FRESH SAVORY
1 TEASPOON FRESHLY GROUND BLACK PEPPER
½ TEASPOON KOSHER SALT

Heat the olive oil in a large skillet over medium heat. Add the sausage and cook, stirring frequently, until the sausage is crumbled and well browned, 8 to 10 minutes. Add the shallots and cook an additional 3 minutes. Remove the sausage mixture from the heat and drain off the excess grease, reserving ¼ cup of the drippings.

Transfer the sausage mixture to a large mixing bowl and add the breadcrumbs and the remaining ingredients; toss until well combined. Stir in the reserved ¼ cup of sausage drippings and stir until well moistened. The stuffing can be used immediately or refrigerated in an airtight container for up to two days.

POACHED EGGS

YIELD: 6 SERVINGS

2 QUARTS WATER
¼ CUP DISTILLED VINEGAR
1 TEASPOON KOSHER SALT
6 LARGE EGGS, WELL CHILLED

Combine the water, vinegar, and salt in a shallow, wide saucepan with 2-inch sides. Bring to a boil over high heat, reduce the heat to low, and allow the mixture to simmer for 2 minutes. Crack the cold eggs one at a time into a small dish. Slowly pour the egg from the dish into the simmering water and cook for 3½ to 4 minutes (for soft poached eggs), carefully turning halfway through. Remove the eggs with a slotted spoon and drain on a paper towe–lined plate. Serve immediately.

BROWN SUGAR CURE

YIELD: ABOUT 4 CUPS

3 CUPS FIRMLY PACKED DARK BROWN SUGAR
1 CUP KOSHER SALT
2 DRIED ARBOL CHILI PEPPERS, BROKEN INTO
  SEVERAL PIECES
1 VANILLA BEAN, SPLIT IN HALF LENGTHWISE AND
  FINELY CHOPPED

Combine all of the ingredients in a food processor and pulse until well blended. Use immediately or store in an airtight container at room temperature for up to two weeks.

HOMEMADE MEATBALLS

YIELD: ABOUT 30 (1-INCH) LARGE MEATBALLS
OR 60 (½-INCH) SMALL MEATBALLS

½ POUND LEAN GROUND BEEF

½ POUND GROUND VEAL

½ POUND GROUND PORK

3 TABLESPOONS MINCED YELLOW ONION

1 TEASPOON MINCED GARLIC

3 TABLESPOONS CHOPPED FRESH PARSLEY

½ TEASPOON DRIED OREGANO

2 TABLESPOONS FRESHLY GRATED PECORINO ROMANO CHEESE

½ CUP BREADCRUMBS (MADE FROM STALE ITALIAN BREAD)

1 LARGE EGG

¾ TEASPOON KOSHER SALT

¼ TEASPOON FRESHLY GROUND BLACK PEPPER

1 TABLESPOON VEGETABLE OIL OR VEGETABLE COOK-
ING SPRAY

Combine the first 12 ingredients (ground beef through pepper) together in a large mixing bowl. Mix by hand until well combined.

For large meatballs, shape the meat mixture into 1-inch balls and set aside until ready to cook when preparing Idie's Homemade Spaghetti and Meatballs (page 219).

For small meatballs, preheat the oven to 375°F.

Use a flattened teaspoonful of the meat mixture and form into small ½-inch balls. Lightly coat a baking sheet with the vegetable oil or cooking spray and arrange the meatballs onto the baking sheet.

Bake the small meatballs for 5 to 7 minutes, or until lightly browned. Set aside for use in Aunt Emma's Italian Wedding Soup (page 179). Once cooked and cooled, the meatballs can be kept frozen in an airtight container for up to two months. Make sure to thaw the frozen meatballs completely in the refrigerator before adding them to the soup.

FRIED SOFT-SHELL CRABS

FOR TIPS ON HOW TO PROPERLY CLEAN A SOFT SHELL CRAB, SEE THE SIDEBAR (PAGE 28).

YIELD: 6 SERVINGS

1 CUP BUTTERMILK
½ TEASPOON CAYENNE PEPPER
¼ TEASPOON FRESHLY GROUND BLACK PEPPER
½ TEASPOON KOSHER SALT, DIVIDED
6 SOFT-SHELL CRABS, CLEANED
3 CUPS PEANUT OIL, FOR FRYING
2 CUPS FRY MIX (PAGE 353)

Combine the buttermilk, cayenne, black pepper, and ¼ teaspoon of the salt in a mixing bowl and whisk to combine. Add the crabs and toss well to coat. Transfer the bowl to the refrigerator and marinate for at least 30 minutes or up to 2 hours.

Pour the peanut oil into a deep-sided skillet to a depth of 3 inches. (Alternately a deep fryer can be filled with peanut oil.) Preheat the oil to 360°F.

Remove the crabs from the buttermilk and dredge in the fry mix, one at a time. Set aside on a baking sheet. Fry the crabs for 3 to 4 minutes, or until golden brown and cooked through. Season the hot crabs with the remaining ¼ teaspoon of salt, if needed. Serve immediately.

FRIED SAGE LEAVES

YIELD: 30 LEAVES

1 CUP PEANUT OIL, FOR FRYING
30 FRESH SAGE LEAVES
PINCH OF KOSHER SALT

Pour the peanut oil into a deep-sided skillet to a depth of ½ inch. (Alternately a deep fryer can be filled with peanut oil.) Preheat the oil to 300°F. Pick fresh sage leaves off of the stem. Fry the sage leaves in the preheated oil for 1 minute or until crispy and dark green. Carefully remove the leaves from the hot oil and drain on a paper towel–lined plate. Sprinkle the leaves with a pinch of kosher salt and use immediately. Fried sage leaves can be used as a garnish on a variety of dishes. Once fried, they will keep in an airtight container at room temperature for up to one day, but are best served immediately.

VARIATION: TO MAKE **FRIED CAPERS,** DRAIN ½ CUP OF CAPERS AND PAT DRY WITH A CLEAN KITCHEN TOWEL. PREHEAT THE OIL AS DIRECTED IN THE FRIED SAGE LEAVES RECIPE AND FRY THE DRIED CAPERS IN THE HOT OIL FOR 1 MINUTE OR UNTIL THE BUDS BEGIN TO OPEN. REMOVE THE CAPERS FROM THE HOT OIL WITH A FINE-MESHED SIEVE OR STRAINER OR SLOTTED SPOON AND TRANSFER TO A PAPER TOWEL-LINED PLATE TO DRAIN. USE IMMEDIATELY.

VEGETABLES

BRAISED SPRING TORPEDO ONIONS

TORPEDO ONIONS ARE AN ITALIAN HEIRLOOM VARIETY WITH A RED-DISH-PURPLE SKIN. THEY RESEMBLE A SMALL SPRING ONION OR A LARGE GREEN ONION. THE BULBS OF THE TORPEDO ONIONS ARE ELONGATED IN SHAPE, RESEMBLING A TORPEDO OR SPINDLE. IF TORPEDO ONIONS ARE UNAVAILABLE, YOU CAN SUBSTITUTE SMALL SPRING ONIONS WITH SIMILAR RESULTS.

6 MEDIUM SPRING TORPEDO ONIONS, SPLIT IN HALF LENGTHWISE
2 TABLESPOONS OLIVE OIL
2 TABLESPOONS WATER
6 FRESH THYME SPRIGS
PINCH OF SALT

Preheat the oven to 400°F.

Place the onions in an 11 x 7-inch baking dish, cut side down. Add the olive oil, water, thyme sprigs, and salt to the onions and cover the dish tightly with aluminum foil. Bake the onions at 400°F for 25 to 30 minutes or until the bulb end is tender. Remove the onions from the oven and set aside to cool completely.

VARIATIONS:

TO MAKE **BRAISED SPRING VIDALIA ONIONS**, SUBSTITUTE 6 MEDIUM SPRING VIDALIA ONIONS FOR THE TORPEDO ONIONS AND PROCEED AS DIRECTED.

TO MAKE **BRAISED FENNEL**, CUT 2 LARGE (1¼ POUNDS) FENNEL BULBS IN HALF, LEAVING THE CORE INTACT. CUT EACH HALF INTO EIGHT ½-INCH-THICK WEDGES AND PROCEED WITH THE RECIPE AS DIRECTED, BRAISING THE FENNEL FOR 40 MINUTES OR UNTIL TENDER.

BLANCHED JUMBO ASPARAGUS

Bring a large pot of boiling salted water to a boil over high heat. Prepare an ice water bath by filling a large bowl halfway with ice and a small amount of water. Remove about ½ inch from the base of the jumbo asparagus stalks. Using a vegetable peeler, peel the asparagus bases until the tough, woody part is removed. Add the peeled asparagus stalks to the boiling water and cook for 1½ to 2 minutes or until bright green and tender. Drain and immediately plunge the asparagus into the ice water bath, stirring occasionally, until well chilled. Remove the chilled asparagus and pat dry. Refrigerate the blanched asparagus for up to three days.

VARIATIONS:

TO MAKE **BLANCHED BABY CARROTS**, TRIM THE TOPS OFF BABY CARROTS, LEAVING ABOUT ½ INCH OF THE TOPS. PEEL THE CARROTS AND BLANCH IN BOILING SALTED WATER FOR 3 TO 4 MINUTES OR UNTIL TENDER. PROCEED WITH THE RECIPE AS DIRECTED.

TO MAKE **BLANCHED PARSNIPS**, PEEL THE PARSNIPS AND CUT INTO EQUAL SIZE PIECES, ABOUT ½ INCH THICK. BLANCH THE PARSNIPS FOR 2½ TO 3 MINUTES OR UNTIL TENDER. PROCEED WITH THE RECIPE AS DIRECTED.

ROASTED RED BEETS

YIELD: 6 SERVINGS

4 LARGE (½ POUND) RED BEETS, TRIMMED
¼ CUP OLIVE OIL
¼ CUP WATER
6 FRESH THYME SPRIGS
PINCH OF SALT

Preheat the oven to 400°F.

Place the beets in a small baking dish. Add the olive oil, water, thyme sprigs, and salt to the beets and cover the dish tightly with aluminum foil. Roast the beets at 400°F for 1 hour to 1 hour and 15 minutes or until tender. Remove the beets from the oven and set aside to cool completely before peeling.

VARIATIONS:

TO MAKE **ROASTED RED BABY BEETS** TRIM THE TOPS OFF 12 SMALL BEETS (ABOUT 1 POUND), LEAVING ½ INCH OF THE STEMS INTACT. PROCEED WITH THE RECIPE AS DIRECTED, ROASTING THE BEETS, COVERED, AT 400°F FOR ABOUT 30 MINUTES OR UNTIL TENDER. SET THE BEETS ASIDE TO COOL BEFORE PEELING.

TO MAKE **ROASTED YELLOW BABY BEETS** TRIM THE TOPS OFF 12 SMALL BEETS (ABOUT 1 POUND), LEAVING ½ INCH OF THE STEMS INTACT. PROCEED WITH THE RECIPE AS DIRECTED, ROASTING THE BEETS, COVERED, AT 400°F FOR ABOUT 20 MINUTES OR UNTIL TENDER. SET THE BEETS ASIDE TO COOL BEFORE PEELING.

TO MAKE **ROASTED BABY CHIOGGIA BEETS** TRIM THE TOPS OFF 12 SMALL BEETS (ABOUT 1 POUND), LEAVING ½ INCH OF THE STEMS INTACT. PROCEED WITH THE RECIPE AS DIRECTED, ROASTING THE BEETS, COVERED, AT 400°F FOR ABOUT 30 MINUTES OR UNTIL TENDER. SET THE BEETS ASIDE TO COOL BEFORE PEELING.

TO MAKE **ROASTED BABY TURNIPS**, PEEL 12 SMALL BABY TURNIPS (ABOUT 1½ POUNDS) AND PLACE IN A SMALL BAKING DISH. PROCEED WITH THE RECIPE AS DIRECTED, ROASTING THE TURNIPS FOR 30 TO 35 MINUTES OR UNTIL TENDER.

TO MAKE **ROASTED SHALLOTS**, PLACE 1 POUND WHOLE, UNPEELED SHALLOTS IN A SMALL BAKING DISH AND PROCEED WITH THE RECIPE AS DIRECTED, ROASTING THE SHALLOTS FOR 25 TO 30 MINUTES OR UNTIL TENDER. SET THE SHALLOTS ASIDE TO COOL SLIGHTLY BEFORE PEELING.

TO MAKE **ROASTED CIPOLLINI ONIONS**, PLACE 1 POUND WHOLE, UNPEELED CIPOLLINI ONIONS IN A SMALL BAKING DISH AND PROCEED WITH THE RECIPE AS DIRECTED, ROASTING THE ONIONS FOR 25 TO 30 MINUTES OR UNTIL TENDER. SET THE ONIONS ASIDE TO COOL SLIGHTLY BEFORE PEELING.

TO MAKE **ROASTED FINGERLING POTATOES**, PLACE 1½ POUNDS SMALL FINGERLING POTATOES IN A SMALL BAKING DISH AND PROCEED WITH THE RECIPE AS DIRECTED, ROASTING THE POTATOES FOR 40 MINUTES OR UNTIL TENDER.

BALSAMIC ROASTED RED ONIONS

MAKES ABOUT 3 CUPS

4 FRESH THYME SPRIGS
½ CUP PLUS **2** TABLESPOONS BALSAMIC VINEGAR
½ CUP OLIVE OIL
2 LARGE RED ONIONS, WITH PEEL ON, CUT INTO **8** WEDGES
½ TEASPOON KOSHER SALT
¼ TEASPOON FRESHLY GROUND BLACK PEPPER

Preheat oven to 350°F.

Place the thyme, vinegar and olive oil in a shallow baking dish. Place the onion wedges, skin side down in the vinegar mixture. Season the onions lightly with salt and pepper. Cover the baking dish with aluminum foil and bake for 35 to 40 minutes, or until softened but not falling apart.

Cool the onions slightly before removing the onion peels. Slice the wedges into 1/4-inch thick strips and return the strips into the balsamic mixture. The onions can be used immediately or refrigerated for up to five days until ready to use.

APPENDIX
SOURCES GUIDE

One of our most common customer requests is for access to the same ingredients professional chefs use. This section of the book is intended to provide you with access to our favorite "disproportionately" passionate purveyors that have become the real heroes in our restaurant. It is their dedication to what they do that enables us to prepare the quality of food that we offer at the Hot and Hot Fish Club. This in turn makes them an extension of our restaurant family. We hope that in your search for superior ingredients, this guide inspires you to find committed food artisans in your own community that will help to enhance the meals you prepare for your friends and family.

ANSON MILLS
1922-C Gervais Street
Columbia, SC 29201
(803) 467-4122
www.ansonmills.com
Antebellum coarse grits, antebellum fine or coarse cornmeal, polenta, wheat flour, Carolina Gold rice, farro, and handmade rustic coarse toasted stone cut oats

AVERIETT BRANCH FARM
JOHN H. WESSON, AGRICULTURAL PROFESSIONAL
736 Old Farm Road
Sylacauga, AL 35151
(256) 404-4088
abfarms@hotmail.com
www.averiettbranchfarm.com
Produce, such as figs, squash, squash blossoms, okra, tomatoes, and eggplants

BENTON'S SMOKY MOUNTAIN COUNTRY HAMS
ALLAN BENTON
2603 Highway 411 North
Madisonville, TN 37354
(423) 442-5003
www.bentonshams.com
Smoked and unsmoked country hams including whole hams, center cut hams, and biscuit pieces (They also carry prosciutto and smoked country slab and sliced bacon.)

BIRMINGHAM FARMER'S MARKET
344 Finley Avenue West
Birmingham, AL 35204
(205) 251-8737
www.alabamafarmersmarket.org
Numerous vendors selling melons, okra, tomatoes, peaches, field peas, strawberries, peppers, muscadines, scuppernongs, and much more

BUDDY WARD & SON'S SEAFOOD AND TRUCKING INC., LLC
OWNER TOMMY WARD
(850) 653-8522
www.13milebrand.com
13-Mile Brand products, including shucked and unshucked fresh oysters, Alligator Point clams, and shrimp

CAJUN GROCER
www.cajungrocer.com
Live crawfish, peeled crawfish tail meat, tasso, prepared boudin, and andouille sausage

CHAI'S ORIENTAL FOOD STORE
2133 7th Avenue South
Birmingham, AL 35233
(205) 324-4873
Asian produce and condiments

THE CHEF'S GARDEN®

FARMER LEE JONES

9009 Huron-Avery Road

Huron, OH 44839

(800) 289-4644

www.chefsgarden.com

Produce including lettuces and greens, beans, tomatoes, potatoes, peppers, root crop vegetables, microgreens, squash blossoms, and apple cider

COOSA VALLEY MILLING

McEWEN & SONS BRAND

30620 Hwy 25 South

P.O. Box 439

Wilsonville, AL 35186

(205) 669-6605

www.coosavalleymilling.com

Cage-free farm eggs; stone-ground yellow, white, and blue cornmeal; grits; and polenta

CRESCENT MOON ORGANIC FARMS

FARMER JACK SIMMONS

P.O. Box 141

Sopchoppy, FL 32358

(850) 559-2000

www.crescentmoonorganicfarms.com

Organic produce, including lettuces, herbs, berries, squash, eggplants, persimmons, pumpkins, onions, garlic, potatoes, and beans

EARTHBORN POTTERY

TENA PAYNE

5520 Rex Ridge Road

Leeds, AL 35094

(205) 702-7055

www.earthbornpottery.net

Custom tabletop designs

EARTHY DELIGHTS

www.earthy.com

Fresh and preserved chestnuts, fresh and dried mushrooms, chocolate (such as El Rey and Dagoba), truffle oil, and Vialone Nano rice

FROMAGERIE BELLE CHÈVRE

TASIA MALAKASIS

26910 Bethel Road

Elkmont, AL 35620

(256) 423-2238 or (800) 735-2238

www.bellechevre.com

Artisanal goat cheeses, including Montrachet-style goat cheese logs, marinated goat cheese, fromage blanc (fresh goat cheese), and goat cheese crumbles

FUDGE FAMILY FARMS

HENRY FUDGE

13181 Sugar Plum Land

Madison, AL 35756

www.fudgefamilyfarms.com

Whole or half heirloom breed hogs

GARFRERICK FARMS AND GARFRERICK CAFÉ

FARMER DAVE GARFRERICK

(256) 831-0044

Organic produce, including heirloom tomatoes, peppers, eggplants, corn, and fresh herbs

HASTINGS CREATIONS

OWNERS CHRIS AND IDIE HASTINGS

2180 11th Court South

Birmingham, AL 35205

(205) 933-5474

www.hotandhotfishclub.com

All-Purpose Herb Salt, Seafood Salt, Ancho Pork Salt, Poultry Salt, Pork Rub, Hot and Hot Signature Blend Coffee, Red Mountain Honey, and Miss Belle's Peanut Butter Doggie Biscuits

HOLLOW SPRING FARM

THE BENNETT FAMILY

620 Mt. Olive Drive

Pell City, AL 35125

hollowspring@hotmail.com

Mulberries, dewberries, wild strawberries, eggplants, tomatoes, wild ginger, sassafras, wild persimmons, heirloom pumpkins, and oyster mushrooms

JONES VALLEY URBAN FARM
DIRECTOR EDWIN MARTY
P.O. Box 55357
Birmingham, AL 35255
(205) 439-7213
www.jvuf.org
Organic produce and flowers

LA CAJA CHINA
www.lacajachina.com
Pig roasting equipment and grills

LOUISIANA CRAWFISH COMPANY
140 Russell Cemetery Road
Natchitoches, LA 71457
(888) 522-7292 or (318) 379-0539
www.lacrawfish.com
Live crawfish by the pound, boiled crawfish, and peeled crawfish tail meat

MANICARETTI ITALIAN FOOD IMPORTERS
www.manicaretti.com
Italian food products including dried pastas (pappardelle, saffron fettucine, orecchiette, and orzo), gnocchi, Agrumato brand lemon oil, Agrumato brand orange oil, extra-virgin olive oil, balsamic vinegar, aged balsamic vinegar, and saba

MISS SCARLETT'S
P.O. Box 1488
Burlingame, CA 94011
(800) 345-6734
www.missscarlett.com/index.html
Miss Scarlett's fiery hot devils pepper stuffed olives

NUESKE'S APPLEWOOD SMOKED MEATS
Rural Route #2, P.O. Box D
Wittenberg, WI 54499
Orders: (800) 392-2266 Service: (800) 720-1153
www.nueskes.com/about
Smoked hams and slab and thick-cut Applewood smoked bacon

OSPREY SEAFOOD
33 Pier, Suite 25
San Francisco, CA 94111-1041
(415) 291-0156
Wholesale fish and seafood company that will sell to general public on occasion

PENZEYS SPICES
www.penzeys.com
Assorted spices, seasonings, and herbs

PETALS FROM THE PAST
OWNERS JASON AND SHELLEY POWELL
16034 County Road 29
Jemison, AL 35085
(205) 646-0069
www.petalsfromthepast.com
Specializing in antique rose bushes and heirloom shrubs as well as fresh produce, including figs, apples, pears, persimmons, satsumas, muscadines, scuppernongs, blueberries, blackberries, and assorted fresh herbs

PUNTA CLARA KITCHEN
P.O. Box Drawer 49
Point Clear, AL 36564
(800) 437-7868
www.puntaclara.com
Fig preserves

RED MOUNTAIN HONEY
OWNER TENA HOLCOMBE
(205) 933-5474
www.hotandhotfishclub.com
The Red Mountain Honey can be purchased online through Hastings Creations.

SALUMERIA BIELLESE
376 8th Avenue
New York, NY 10001
(212) 736-7376
www.salumeriabiellese.com
Assorted cured meats including guanciale, sausages, and salamis

SNOW'S BEND FARM

DAVID SNOW AND MARGARET ANN TOOHEY

P.O. Box 317

Coker, AL 35452

www.snowsbendfarm.com

Organic produce, such as greens, beans, field peas, radishes, squash, cabbage, turnips, onions, okra, leeks, rutabagas, and more

SWEET GRASS DAIRY

19635 US Hwy. 19N

Thomasville, GA 31792

(229) 227-0752

www.sweetgrassdairy.com

Artisan cow and goat cheeses as well as related pantry items

V. RICHARDS

OWNERS RICK LITTLE AND T. LYNN ADAMS

3916 Clairmont Avenue

Birmingham, AL 35203

www.vrichards.net

Market and café selling organic groceries, produce, meats, seafood, cheese, wine, and baked goods (They carry a wonderful brand of blonde verjus called Fusion Napa Valley Verjus.)

WILD AMERICAN SHRIMP

(843) 937-0002

www.wildamericanshrimp.com

Provides links for where to purchase certified Wild American Shrimp in various states

- IDIE'S LARDER -

As chefs, we are often asked what type of products we stock in our home pantry. We decided to list some of our favorite ingredients. It can serve as a guide for setting up your own home pantry and cooking through our book or as a way to elevate and enrich your own cooking style.

BUTTER

Troyer brand hand-rolled salted Amish butter and unsalted organic butter

CONDIMENTS

Tamarind sauce, wasabi paste, pickles, olives, capers and caper berries, Miss Scarlett's Fiery hot devils (pepper stuffed olives), French green picholine olives, black niçoise olives, and kalmata olives, preserved Meyer lemons, Punta Clara Kitchen fig preserves

NUTS AND DRIED FRUITS

Pistachios, lightly salted peanuts, Marcona almonds, walnuts, chestnuts (when in season), currents, and dates

OILS

All-purpose olive oil and Agrumato brand extra-virgin olive oil, lemon oil, and orange oil

VINEGARS

Sherry vinegar, balsamic vinegar of Modena, red wine vinegar, and blond verjus

DRIED PASTAS

Rigatoni, spaghetti, ditali, seashells, and orzo (all Rustichella D'Abruzzo brand, if possible) and hand-rolled dried pasta

CHOCOLATE

Callebaut white and dark chocolates, El Rey and Dagoba milk chocolate

BAKING SUPPLIES

Madagascar vanilla beans, dark brown sugar, light brown sugar, confectioners' sugar, turbinado, lemon sugar, McEwen & Sons rolled oats, baking soda, baking powder, Naturally More all-natural peanut butter, molasses, and Red Mountain honey

FLOUR

White Lily, King Arthur All-Purpose flour, Anson Mills Whole Wheat flour, masa harina, McEwen & Sons coarsely ground yellow cornmeal

COFFEE AND BEVERAGES

Hot and Hot Signature Blend coffee, organic earl grey tea, La Perruche sugar cubes

SAUSAGES AND CURED MEATS

Tasso, guanciale, boudin, Conecuh sausage, prosciutto, pancetta, mortadella, bresaola, and slab bacon

GRAINS AND DRIED BEANS

Farro, quinoa, couscous, Carolina Gold rice, Arborio rice, Vialone Nano rice, brown rice, dried black beans, and dried great Northern beans

SEASONINGS AND SPICES

Investing in a spice grinder and grinding whole spices as you need them will extend the shelf life of your spices.

Kosher salt, coarse and fine sea salt, fleur de sel, Hastings Creations seasoning salts and pork rub, whole black peppercorns, cayenne pepper, whole allspice, cinnamon sticks, Idie's homemade pickling spice, whole nutmeg, cardamom, juniper berries, cloves, star anise, cumin seeds, fennel seeds, smoked paprika, sweet paprika, hot paprika, ground Ancho chili powder, curry powder, dried Ancho chili peppers, and dried Arbol chili peppers

CANNED GOODS

Anchovies, San Marzano crushed tomatoes, tomato paste, oil-packed tuna, low-sodium organic beef, chicken, and vegetable broth

CHEESES

Fresh chèvre, farmer's cheese (or ricotta), Parmigiano-Reggiano, Pecorino Romano, and blue cheese

FRESH HERBS

Rosemary, bay leaves, thyme, chives, parsley, basil, oregano, and sage

We like to purchase all of our herbs fresh and then dry them in glass jars along our kitchen window for later use. Freshly dried herbs provide a more intense flavor than jarred dried herbs that may have been stored for long periods of time.

TREATS

Our dogs are an important part of our family life and we always stock our homemade brand of Miss Belle's Peanut Butter Doggie Biscuits

HOT AND HOT INDEX

A

Allen, Dwayne, 37
Alligator Point clams, 297, 308
ANCHOVIES, 340
 Rouille, 340
 Salt-Cured Anchovies, 239
Anson Mills, 25, 26, 148, 353, 354, 380
Apalachicola Bay, 36–37
Apalachicola oysters, 192–93
APPETIZERS AND SNACKS
 Basket of Fried Greens (Celery Fritters), 224–25
 Boiled Peanuts, 21
 Hot and Hot Cheese Plate, 291–96
 Hot and Hot Seafood Spring Rolls with Coconut Curry Dipping Sauce, 139
 House-Cured Bacon-Wrapped Figs with Bitter Greens and Walnuts, 92
 Hushpuppies, 360
 Nantucket Bay Scallop Seviche, 237
 Oyster Shooters, 180–81
 Rabbit Tamales with Black Bean Salsa, 31–33
 Roasted Squash Blossoms with Blue Crab, Cherry Tomatoes, and Cucumbers, 30
 Roasted Young Chicken Breast with Blackberry Vinaigrette, 34
 Seared Foie Gras with Brioche Bread and Wild Persimmon Jam, 141
 Shrimp and Corn Fritters with Chive Aïoli, 27
 Study of Heirloom Tomatoes with Eggplant and Sweet Grass Dairy Goat Cheese, 90
APPLES, 215
 Apple, Almond, and Endive Salad with Creamy Herb Dressing, 132–33
 Apple and Rosemary Croustade with Caramel Sauce, 211
 Baked Cumberland Spur Apples with Nutmeg Ice Cream, 160
 Hot Mulled Apple Cider, 129
April, 83, 248, 275
Arepa Cake, 46–47, 360
Arnold, Mike, 80–81, 83
ARTICHOKES
 Braised Artichokes, 373
 Roasted Pork Loin with Farro, Artichokes, and Parmesan, 254

ARUGULA
 Arugula Salad with Pancetta-Wrapped Goat Cheese, 91
 Arugula Sylvetta Salad with Garlic Bruschetta, 329
 Grouper with Tomato, Avocado, and Grilled Vidalia Onions with Basil-Lime Vinaigrette, 96–97
 House-Cured Bacon-Wrapped Figs with Bitter Greens and Walnuts, 92
 Pancetta-Wrapped Local Kiefer Pear Salad with Saba and Arugula, 135
 Pan-Seared Wild Salmon on Three-Bean Salad with Cherry Tomatoes and Basil Aïoli, 100–101
 Three-Bean Salad, 94
Asian markets, 38
ASPARAGUS
 Blanched Jumbo Asparagus, 377
 Dad's Grilled Chicken with Summer Vegetables, 103
 Grilled Cobia with Alligator Point Clam Vinaigrette, 298–99
 Grilled Jumbo Asparagus with Head-On Florida Hoppers and Preserved Lemon Vinaigrette, 284–85
 Grilled Wild Turkey Breast with Grilled Vegetables and Sauce Gribiche, 309
 Pan-Seared Pompano with Spring Vegetable Risotto and Pea Tendrils, 304
 Spring Vegetable Salad, 282–83
August, 71–74
AVOCADOS
 Green Goddess Dressing, 94, 347
 Grouper with Tomato, Avocado, and Grilled Vidalia Onions with Basil-Lime Vinaigrette, 96–97
 Hearts of Palm Salad with Pink Grapefruit and Avocado, 184–85
 Shrimp and Avocado Salad with Carolina Gold Rice, 25

B

BACON. *See also* Guanciale; Pancetta
 Bacon-Wrapped Shad Roe with Anson Mills Grits and Caper Brown Butter Sauce, 306–7
 Cracklin' Cornbread, 171
 Dove Breasts Wrapped in Benton's Bacon, 168–69
 Hot and Hot Tomato Salad, 67, 83–87, 94
 House-Cured Bacon-Wrapped Figs with Bitter Greens and Walnuts, 92
 Lady Peas, 172–73
 Soft-Shell Crab BLT, 28–29

BANANAS

Banana Bavarian Cream, 364

Hot and Hot Doughnuts Espresso Cream and Brittle, Banana Bavarian Cream Filled and Chocolate Orange Glazed, 257–59

BEANS. *See also* Black beans

Bobwhite Quail, Sausage, and White Bean Cassoulet, 198

Braised Vegetarian White Beans, 371

Braised White Beans, 369

Fudge Farms Pork and Beans with Braised Greens, Cracklin' Cornbread, and Chowchow, 156–57

Pan-Seared Wild Salmon on Three-Bean Salad with Cherry Tomatoes and Basil Aïoli, 100–101

Three-Bean Salad, 101

BEEF

BBQ Beef Short Ribs on Sweet Corn Succotash with Cracklin' Cornbread, 105–7

Grilled Beef Sirloin on Potato Galette with Mixed Baby Greens, Balsamic Onions, Blue Cheese, Tamarind Sauce, and Chive Aïoli, 104

Grilled NY Strip with Poached Farm Egg, Parmigiano-Reggiano, and Truffle Oil, 200, 202–5

Homemade Meatballs, 375

Idie's Homemade Spaghetti and Meatballs, 218–19

Jim's Oxtail Soup, 233

BEETS

Chef's Garden Beet Salad with Goat Cheese and Citrus Vinaigrette, 138

Chocolate Devil's Food Cake with Vanilla Ice Cream, 260–61

Grilled Black Grouper in Winter Vegetable Quinoa, 249

Roasted Baby Chioggia Beets, 378

Roasted Red Baby Beets, 378

Roasted Red Beets, 378

Roasted Yellow Baby Beets, 378

Smoked and Grilled Quail with Winter Vegetables and White BBQ Sauce, 143

Spring Vegetable Salad, 282–83

Bennett, Chris, 22–23, 141, 144, 230, 313, 381

BEVERAGES

Blond Mary, 76

Blood Orange Martini, 176–77

Bog Sucker, 126–27

Fig-Infused Bourbon "Toddy," 128

Fig-Infused Small-Batch Bourbon, 128

Ginger Martini, 230

Honey Tangerine Mojito, 230

Hot and Hot Pomegranate Cocktail, 178

Hot and Hot Spicy 'Tini, 277

Hot Mulled Apple Cider, 129

JP's Pomerita, 75

Norman Drive Lemonade, 75

Pineapple-Sage Lemon Celebration, 276

Southern Lemonade Cocktail, 20

Watermelon Martini, 20

Birmingham, Alabama, 18, 57, 83

Botanical Gardens, 74, 110

Farmers' Market, 17, 80–81, 380

Red Mountain, 110

Zoo, 74

BLACK BEANS

Black Bean Salsa, 350

Braised Black Beans, 371

Rabbit Tamales with Black Bean Salsa, 31–33

BLUE-VEINED CHEESE

Bibb Lettuce Salad with Candied Pecans, Cambozola, and Pomegranate Vinaigrette, 147

Blue Cheese-Stuffed Olives, 277

Grilled Beef Sirloin on Potato Galette with Mixed Baby Greens, Balsamic Onions, Blue Cheese, Tamarind Sauce, and Chive Aïoli, 104

Hearts of Escarole Salad, 186

BREADCRUMBS

Fresh Breadcrumbs, 353

Herb Breadcrumbs, 356

BREADS, 175

Cracklin' Cornbread, 171

Garlic Bruschetta, 329

Herb Croutons, 356

Raspberry and White Chocolate Bread Pudding with Raspberry Coulis, 52–55

BROCCOLI RABE. *See* Rapini

BROTHS. *See* Stocks and broths

Buddy Ward & Son's 13-Mile Seafood Company, 191, 192–93, 380

C

CAKES

Chocolate Devil's Food Cake with Vanilla Ice Cream, 260–61

Lavender Pound Cake with Meyer Lemon Glaze, 316

Molten Chocolate Lava Cakes, 321

CANDY

Candied Peanuts, 363

Candied Pecans, 364

Chocolate Truffles, 318

Cranberry and Pistachio Torrone (Nougat), 226

Espresso Brittle, 364

Sesame Brittle, 296

CAPERS
    Fried Capers, 376
Carolina Gold rice, 25, 26, 94, 148–49, 251, 353
CARROTS
    Blanched Baby Carrots, 377
    Grilled Black Grouper in Winter Vegetable Quinoa, 249
    Smoked and Grilled Quail with Winter Vegetables and
        White BBQ Sauce, 143
    Spring Vegetable Salad, 282–83
    Whole-Roasted, Free-Range Chicken with Winter
        Vegetables, 208–9
Carter, Carol, 110
Carter-Holcomb Apiary, 110
CAULIFLOWER
    Cauliflower Soup with White Truffle Oil, 183
    Fried Cauliflower (Cavolfiore Fritto), 222
    Heirloom Cauliflower Gratin with Roasted Chestnuts
        and Parmesan Cream, 188–89
CELERY ROOT
    Celery Root Slaw, 370
    Seared Day Boat Scallops with Celery Root Slaw and
        Tamarind Sauce, 194
Chai's Grocery, 38, 380
CHEESE. *See also* Blue-veined cheese; Goat cheese
    Cheese Plate with Local Fruit and Wine, 326
    Cousin Joe's Cheese Pizza, 220
    Hot and Hot Cheese Plate, 291–96
Chef's Garden, 30, 136–37, 240, 381
CHESTNUTS, 175, 187
    Heirloom Cauliflower Gratin with Roasted Chestnuts
        and Parmesan Cream, 188–89
CHICKEN
    Chicken and Conecuh County Sausage Gumbo, 273
    Chicken Stock, 335
    Dad's Grilled Chicken with Summer Vegetables, 103
    Ida Mae's Homemade Chicken Noodle Soup, 231
    Oven-Roasted Chicken Breasts on Anson Mills Grits with
        Local Scuppernongs, Muscadines, and Verjus, 155–56
    Roasted Young Chicken Breast with Blackberry
        Vinaigrette, 34
    Whole-Roasted, Free-Range Chicken with Winter
        Vegetables, 208–9
    Whole-Roasted Baby Chicken with Crawfish and Tasso
        Jambalaya, 312
CHOCOLATE
    Chocolate-Black Pepper Cookie with Cardamom, 317, 320
    Chocolate Caramel Mousse, 317, 318
    Chocolate Devil's Food Cake with Vanilla Ice Cream,
        260–61
    Chocolate Orange Sauce, 362

Chocolate Pots de Crème, 319
    Chocolate Truffles, 318
    Elton's Chocolate Soufflé with Crème Anglaise and
        Whipped Cream, 56–59
    Hot and Hot Chocolate Sampler, 317–21
    Hot and Hot Doughnuts Espresso Cream and Brittle,
        Banana Bavarian Cream Filled and Chocolate Orange
        Glazed, 257–59
    Molten Chocolate Lava Cakes, 321
    Raspberry and White Chocolate Bread Pudding with
        Raspberry Coulis, 52–55
    White Chocolate Sauce, 362
Christmas celebrations, 175, 177, 216–27
CHUTNEYS. *See* Condiments, relishes, and chutneys
CLAMS, 297
    Alligator Point Clam Paella, 308
    Grilled Cobia with Alligator Point Clam Vinaigrette,
        298–99
    Low-Country Pirlou with Clams, Sausage, Shrimp, and
        Carolina Gold Rice, 148–49
    Southern Bouillabaisse, 245–47
Cleveland, Ohio, 71–73, 175, 232
Clymer, Pennsylvania, 71, 72, 232
Coconut Curry Dipping Sauce, 338
COLESLAWS AND SLAWS
    Asian Vegetable Slaw, 38
    Celery Root Slaw, 370
    Creamy Coleslaw, 369
    Fennel Coleslaw, 170
COLLARD GREENS
    Fudge Farms Pork and Beans with Braised Greens,
        Cracklin' Cornbread, and Chowchow, 156–57
Comer, Donald, 315
CONDIMENTS, RELISHES, AND CHUTNEYS. *See
    also* Sauces
    Basil Pesto, 350
    Black Bean Salsa, 350
    Chowchow, 349
    Green Tomato Chutney, 294–95
    Peach Mojo, 351
    Preserved Meyer Lemons, 351
    Tapenade, 349
Conecuh County, Alabama, 142, 273
Conecuh Sausage Company, 273
COOKIES
    Chocolate-Black Pepper Cookie with Cardamom, 317,
        320
    Macadamia Nut Biscotti, 365
    Shortbread Cookies, 210
    Sweet Italian Cookies with Lemon Glaze, 227

CORN
    Arepa Cake, 360
    BBQ Beef Short Ribs on Sweet Corn Succotash with
        Cracklin' Cornbread, 105–7
    Cracklin' Cornbread, 171
    Creamed Field Peas and Summer Squash Salad, 64
    Grilled Corn on the Cob, 65
    Hot and Hot Tomato Salad, 67, 83–87, 94
    Rabbit Tamales with Black Bean Salsa, 31–33
    Shrimp and Corn Fritters with Chive Aïoli, 27
CORNMEAL
    Cracklin' Cornbread, 171
    Fry Mix, 353
    Hushpuppies, 360
    Warm Johnny Cakes with Blackberries and Buttermilk
        Ice Cream, 108–9
CRABS AND CRABMEAT, 275
    cleaning soft-shell crabs, 28
    Deviled Crab, 120–21
    Fried Soft Shell Crabs, 376
    Hot and Hot Fish Fry with Fennel Slaw, Hushpuppies,
        and Spicy Rémoulade, 150–51
    Low-Country Pirlou with Clams, Sausage, Shrimp, and
        Carolina Gold Rice, 148–49
    Pawleys Island crabbing, 115
    Roasted Squash Blossoms with Blue Crab, Cherry
        Tomatoes, and Cucumbers, 30
    She-Crab Soup, 278
    Soft-Shell Crab BLT, 28–29
    Southern Bouillabaisse, 245–47
CRACKERS
    Oyster Crackers, 358
Cranberry and Pistachio Torrone (Nougat), 226
CRAWFISH
    Crawfish Bisque, 279
    Crawfish Boil, 263, 265–67
    Crawfish Risotto with Preserved Meyer Lemons, 240–41
    Oven-Roasted Duck Breast on Crawfish Risotto with
        Spicy Ham Hock Broth, 45
    Whole-Roasted Baby Chicken with Crawfish and Tasso
        Jambalaya, 312
CREAM
    Whipped Cream, 367
Creek boy, 17, 37, 49, 115
CRÈME ANGLAISE
    Vanilla Crème Anglaise, 361
CRÈME FRAÎCHE
    Cilantro Crème Fraîche, 352
    Garlic Crème Fraîche, 352

    Homemade Crème Fraîche, 352
    Honeysuckle Crème Fraîche, 352
Crescent Moon Organic Farm, 280–81, 381
CROUTONS
    Herb Croutons, 356
Cumberland Spur apples, 160, 215
CUSTARDS. *See* Puddings and custards

D

December, 175
DESSERTS. *See also* Cakes; Candy; Cookies; Ice cream;
  Pies and tarts; Sorbet
    Baked Cumberland Spur Apples with Nutmeg Ice Cream,
        160
    Chocolate Caramel Mousse, 317, 318
    Chocolate Pots de Crème, 319
    Elton's Chocolate Soufflé with Crème Anglaise and
        Whipped Cream, 56–59
    First-of-the-Season Strawberry Shortcakes with
        Honeysuckle Crème Fraîche, 51
    Hot and Hot Chocolate Sampler, 317–21
    Hot and Hot Doughnuts Espresso Cream and Brittle,
        Banana Bavarian Cream Filled and Chocolate Orange
        Glazed, 257–59
    Raspberry and White Chocolate Bread Pudding with
        Raspberry Coulis, 52–55
    Rhubarb and Strawberry Tapioca Pudding, 50
    Saffron Rice Pudding with Sauternes Poached
        Persimmons, 162–63
    Warm Johnny Cakes with Blackberries and Buttermilk
        Ice Cream, 108–9
DOVES
    Dove Breasts Wrapped in Benton's Bacon, 168–69
    hunting trips, 125, 166–67, 187
Ducasse, Alain, 136
DUCK
    Duck Confit and Warm Mushroom Salad, 243
    Oven-Roasted Duck Breast on Crawfish Risotto with
        Spicy Ham Hock Broth, 45
DUMPLINGS. *See* Pasta, noodles, and dumplings

E

EGGS, 204
    Grilled NY Strip with Poached Farm Egg, Parmigiano-
        Reggiano, and Truffle Oil, 200, 202–5
    Poached Eggs, 374

ESPRESSO

Espresso Brittle, 364

Espresso Cream, 363

Hot and Hot Doughnuts Espresso Cream and Brittle, Banana Bavarian Cream Filled and Chocolate Orange Glazed, 257–59

Evans, Margaret, 248

F

FARRO, 254

Roasted Pork Loin with Farro, Artichokes, and Parmesan, 254

February, 229, 248

FENNEL

Braised Fennel, 377

Fennel Coleslaw, 170

Fennel Mashed Potatoes, 368

Grilled Veal Liver Steak with Fennel Mashed Potatoes, Onion Rings, and Tamarind Sauce, 158

Hot and Hot Fish Fry with Fennel Slaw, Hushpuppies, and Spicy Rémoulade, 150–51

Pan-Seared Flounder with Shaved Fennel Salad, Olives, and Valencia Oranges, 194

Steamed Mussels with Fennel, Leeks, and Winter Savory, 140

FIELD PEAS

Baked Shovel Nose Lobsters with Cherry Tomato and Field Pea Salad, 102

basic recipe, 372

BBQ Beef Short Ribs on Sweet Corn Succotash with Cracklin' Cornbread, 105–7

Creamed Field Peas and Summer Squash Salad, 64

Hot and Hot Tomato Salad, 67, 83–87, 94

Lady Peas, 172–73

Spring Vegetable Salad, 282–83

FIGS

Fig-Infused Bourbon "Toddy," 128

Fig-Infused Small-Batch Bourbon, 128

Fig Preserves, 116

Four Fig Tarts with Lemon Verbena Ice Cream, 112–13

House-Cured Bacon-Wrapped Figs with Bitter Greens and Walnuts, 92

FISH, 275. *See also* Anchovies; Flounder; Tuna

bream, 60

Fish Stock, 334

Fried Bream "Swimming French Fries" with Lemon Mayonnaise, 60, 62–63

Grilled Black Grouper in Winter Vegetable Quinoa, 249

Grilled Cobia with Alligator Point Clam Vinaigrette, 298–99

grilling tips, 95

Grouper with Tomato, Avocado, and Grilled Vidalia Onions with Basil-Lime Vinaigrette, 96–97

Hot and Hot Fish Fry with Fennel Slaw, Hushpuppies, and Spicy Rémoulade, 150–51

Hot and Hot Seafood Spring Rolls with Coconut Curry Dipping Sauce, 139

Pan-Seared Pompano with Spring Vegetable Risotto and Pea Tendrils, 304

Pan-Seared Wild Salmon on Three-Bean Salad with Cherry Tomatoes and Basil Aïoli, 100–101

Salt-Roasted Sea Bream or "Orate," 327

Sautéed Halibut on Purple Mashed Potatoes with Brown Butter Vinaigrette and Fried Capers, 153

Southern Bouillabaisse, 245–47

Whole-Roasted Mingo Snapper on Pipérade with Herb Croutons, 302–3

Whole Roasted Snapper with Vidalia Onions, Lemon, Basil, and Extra-Virgin Olive Oil, 39

Whole-Roasted Speckled Trout, 123

Florida Panhandle, 115, 297

FLOUNDER

buying tip, 35

giggers, 36–37

Herb-Crusted Flounder with Watercress Salad and Lemon Butter Sauce, 35

Pan-Seared Flounder with Shaved Fennel Salad, Olives, and Valencia Oranges, 194

FOIE GRAS

Seared Foie Gras with Brioche Bread and Wild Persimmon Jam, 141

Folks, A. D., 297

Fraser, Hugh, 18

Frisée lettuce, 138

FRITTERS

Basket of Fried Greens (Celery Fritters), 224–25

Hushpuppies, 360

Shrimp and Corn Fritters with Chive Aïoli, 27

Fromagerie Belle Chèvre, 234–35, 326, 381

Fry Mix, 353

Fudge, Henry, 144–45, 381

Fudge Family Farms, 144–45, 381

G

Gaines, Charles, 125

Garfrerick, Dave, 12, 88, 89, 90, 295, 381

GINGER, 230

Ginger Martini, 230

Ginger Simple Syrup, 362

GOAT CHEESE, 234–35

Arugula Salad with Pancetta-Wrapped Goat Cheese, 91

Chef's Garden Beet Salad with Goat Cheese and Citrus
    Vinaigrette, 138
Sliced Ruskin Tomatoes with Basil and Goat Cheese, 67
Study of Heirloom Tomatoes with Eggplant and Sweet
    Grass Dairy Goat Cheese, 90
Winter Density and Red Starr Bibb Salad with Warm
    Belle Chèvre Herb Toast, 236
Goodrich, Bill, 187
Goodrich, Fran, 187
GRAPES
Muscadines, 125, 154–55
Muscadine Sorbet, 159
Oven-Roasted Chicken Breasts on Anson Mills Grits with
    Local Scuppernongs, Muscadines, and Verjus, 155
Scuppernongs, 125, 154–55
Scuppernong Vinaigrette, 343
GRITS
Anson Mills White Antebellum Grits, 354
Bacon-Wrapped Shad Roe with Anson Mills Grits and
    Caper Brown Butter Sauce, 306–7
Hot and Hot Creamy Shrimp and Grits with Country
    Ham, 43–44
McEwen and Sons Yellow Stone-Ground Grits, 354
Oven-Roasted Chicken Breasts on Anson Mills Grits with
    Local Scuppernongs, Muscadines, and Verjus, 155
GUANCIALE, 93, 144
Tomato Guanciale Pasta, 93

H

HAM. *See also* Prosciutto
Hot and Hot Creamy Shrimp and Grits with Country
    Ham, 43–44
Oven-Roasted Duck Breast on Crawfish Risotto with
    Spicy Ham Hock Broth, 45
Spicy Ham Hock Broth, 336
Whole-Roasted Baby Chicken with Crawfish and Tasso
    Jambalaya, 312
Harris, Frank, 126
Harvest moon, 125
Hastings, Angelica, 49
Hastings, Charlie, 125, 130, 275
Hastings, Chris
    Christmas celebrations, 175, 177, 216–27
    creek boy role of, 17, 37, 49, 115
    culinary philosophy of, 6, 11–12, 83
    family celebrations, 229
    flounder gigging experience, 37
    Hastings Creations, 381
    hunting trips, 6, 125, 126, 130, 166–67, 229, 275
    Pawleys Island summers, 17, 37, 115, 237
    relationship with mother, 49
Hastings, Granzie, 185
Hastings, Ida Mae "Idie"
    Christmas celebrations, 175, 177, 216–27
    culinary philosophy of, 6, 11–12, 83
    dad, celebration of life of, 200
    family celebrations, 229
    Hastings Creations, 381
    summers with Grandma Morano, 71–73
Hastings, John, 245
Hastings, Steven, 123
Hastings, Vincent, 6, 74, 115, 125, 130, 166–67, 175, 200, 216,
    260
Hastings, Zeb, 6, 74, 115, 125, 130, 166–67, 175, 200, 216, 314
Hastings Creations, 381
Hearts of Palm Salad with Pink Grapefruit and Avocado,
    184–85
Holcomb, Tina, 110, 382
Hollow Spring Farm, 22–23, 230, 381
Honey, 110
HONEYSUCKLE BLOSSOMS
Honeysuckle Crème Fraîche, 352
Honeysuckle Simple Syrup, 362
Hot and Hot Fish Club
    chef's counter, 83, 88
    culinary philosophy of, 12, 18, 83
    history of, 18
    rules of, 19
Hunting trips, 6, 125, 126, 130, 166–67, 229, 242, 275

I

ICE CREAM, 74
Baked Cumberland Spur Apples with Nutmeg Ice Cream,
    160
Buttermilk Ice Cream, 366
Chocolate Devil's Food Cake with Vanilla Ice Cream,
    260–61
Cinnamon Ice Cream, 366
Four Fig Tarts with Lemon Verbena Ice Cream, 112–13
Lemon Verbena Ice Cream, 366
Molasses Ice Cream, 366
Nutmeg Ice Cream, 366
Pecan Tart with Molasses Ice Cream, 212–13
Plum and Nectarine Galette with Vanilla Ice Cream, 111
Sweet Potato Fried Pies with Cinnamon Ice Cream, 161
Vanilla Ice Cream, 366
Warm Johnny Cakes with Blackberries and Buttermilk
    Ice Cream, 108–9

Indian peaches, 215
Ingredients, fresh and local
    autumn produce, 125
    foraged and wild-harvested ingredients, 17, 23, 49, 118,
        125, 275, 313
    magic of food, 6, 12, 49
    seasonal cooking, 125
    sources guide, 380–83
    sourcing local ingredients, 282
    spring produce, 275
    success of meals made with, 11–12, 83
    summer produce, 17

J

JAMS AND PRESERVES
    Fig Preserves, 116
    Wild Persimmon Jam, 361
January, 229, 263
Jefferson County Farmers' Market (Birmingham Farmers'
    Market), 17, 80–81, 380
Johnson, Ben, 126
Jones, Bob, 136
Jones, Bobby, 136
Jones, Lee, 30, 136–37, 381
July, 71–74
June, 17

K

Keller, Thomas, 136

L

La Caja China, 270–71, 382
LAMB
    Braised Lamb Shanks with Orecchiette Pasta and
        Gremolata, 252–53
    Roast Leg of Lamb with Ratatouille, Tapenade, and
        Garlic Crème Fraîche, 48
Lark Creek Inn, 11, 24, 136, 238, 260
Lemonade stand, 74, 75
LEMONS
    Braised Lamb Shanks with Orecchiette Pasta and
        Gremolata, 252–53
    Citrus Vinaigrette, 344
    Crawfish Risotto with Preserved Meyer Lemons, 240–41
    Fried Bream "Swimming French Fries" with Lemon
        Mayonnaise, 60
    Herb-Crusted Flounder with Watercress Salad and
        Lemon Butter Sauce, 35

Lavender Pound Cake with Meyer Lemon Glaze, 316
Lemon Buttermilk Tarts with Wild Strawberries and
    Mulberries, 23, 314–15
Lemon Butter Sauce, 341
Lemon Dijon Vinaigrette, 346
Lemon Sugar, 367
Meyer Lemon Meringue Tart, 255
Meyer lemons, 249
Meyer Lemon Vinaigrette, 346
Norman Drive Lemonade, 75
Pineapple-Sage Lemon Celebration, 276
Preserved Lemon Vinaigrette, 345
Preserved Meyer Lemons, 351
Shrimp Gazpacho with Lemon Oil, 77, 94
Southern Lemonade Cocktail, 20
Sweet Italian Cookies with Lemon Glaze, 227
Lenoir, Edna, 80, 81
Lenoir, George, 80
Lenoir, Gregory, 80
Lenoir, Vernon, 80
Leo's Deli, 49
Lifestyle menus, 12
    Beach Dinner at the "Happy House," 118–23
    Crawfish, Football, Beer, and Boudin with the Staff and
        Friends, 229, 263–73
    Father-Son Dove Hunt, 166–73
    Italian Christmas with the Moranos, 216–27
    Outdoor Sunday Picnic and Fly-Fishing, 60–67
    When in Rome, 323–29
LIMES
    Basil-Lime Vinaigrette, 96–97
    Citrus Vinaigrette, 344
    Grouper with Tomato, Avocado, and Grilled Vidalia
        Onions with Basil-Lime Vinaigrette, 96–97
LOBSTERS, 102
    Baked Shovel Nose Lobsters with Cherry Tomato and
        Field Pea Salad, 102
Low-Country Pirlou, 148–49

M

Macadamia Nut Biscotti, 365
Magic of food, 6, 12, 49
Malakasis, Tasia, 234–35, 381
March, 248, 275
Marino, Joseph, 323
MASA HARINA
    Arepa Cake, 360
MASCARPONE CHEESE
    Espresso Cream, 363
May, 17, 83

McCullough, Bruce, 40–41
McEwen, Frank, Jr., 204
McEwen & Sons, 204, 354, 381
McMillan, George, 143
Memory cuisine, 6, 83, 229, 305
Microgreens, 240
Mills, Robert, 18
Mint Simple Syrup, 362
Morano, Emma, 72, 179
Morano, Ida, 179
Morano, Jenny, 72
Morano, Jim, 71, 72, 73, 128, 200–201, 232, 233, 316
Morano, Joe, 73
Morano, Rosina Maria Scerbo, 71–73, 175
Morano, Vincenzo, 71
MULBERRIES
Lemon Buttermilk Tarts with Wild Strawberries and Mulberries, 23, 314–15
Murrels Inlet, 18
MUSHROOMS
Braised Veal Cheeks with Potato Gnocchi and Chanterelles, 206–7
Duck Confit and Warm Mushroom Salad, 243
Morel and English Pea Risotto with Lemon Oil, 286
Porcini Mushroom Pasta, 328
Roasted Porcini Mushrooms with Bresaola, Mustard Greens, and Lemon Oil, 146
Saffron Pappardelle with Wild Oyster Mushrooms and Parmesan, 152
Wild Turkey Salad with First of the Season Morels and Watercress, 289
MUSSELS, 140
Low-Country Pirlou with Clams, Sausage, Shrimp, and Carolina Gold Rice, 148–49
Southern Bouillabaisse, 245–47
Steamed Mussels with Fennel, Leeks, and Winter Savory, 140
MUSTARD GREENS
Braised Mustard Greens, 170
Roasted Porcini Mushrooms with Bresaola, Mustard Greens, and Lemon Oil, 146
Slow Roasted Pork Shoulder with Fall Vegetable Gratin and Mustard Greens, 199

N

NECTARINES
Plum and Nectarine Galette with Vanilla Ice Cream, 111
NOODLES. *See* Pasta, noodles, and dumplings
November, 175

O

October, 125
Ogden, Bradley, 11, 24, 105, 136, 238, 260
OKRA, 80
Fried Okra Baskets with Chive Aïoli, 67
Hot and Hot Fried Okra Basket with Chive Aïoli, 82
Ida Mae's Pickled Okra, 78–79
OLIVES
Blue Cheese-Stuffed Olives, 277
Pan-Seared Flounder with Shaved Fennel Salad, Olives, and Valencia Oranges, 194
Roast Leg of Lamb with Ratatouille, Tapenade, and Garlic Crème Fraîche, 48
Tapenade, 349
ONIONS
Braised Spring Torpedo Onions, 377
Braised Spring Vidalia Onions, 377
Fried Onion Rings, 373
Grilled Beef Sirloin on Potato Galette with Mixed Baby Greens, Balsamic Onions, Blue Cheese, Tamarind Sauce, and Chive Aïoli, 104
Grilled Veal Liver Steak with Fennel Mashed Potatoes, Onion Rings, and Tamarind Sauce, 158
Grouper with Tomato, Avocado, and Grilled Vidalia Onions with Basil-Lime Vinaigrette, 96–97
Prosciutto and Spring Vidalia Onion Salad with Parmesan Vinaigrette, 287
Roasted Cipollini Onions, 378
Whole Roasted Snapper with Vidalia Onions, Lemon, Basil, and Extra-Virgin Olive Oil, 39
ORANGES
Blood Orange Martini, 176–77
Chocolate Orange Sauce, 362
Citrus Vinaigrette, 344
Dried Orange Slices, 367
Grilled Quail on Local Cress and Blood Orange Salad, 242
Hot and Hot Doughnuts Espresso Cream and Brittle, Banana Bavarian Cream Filled and Chocolate Orange Glazed, 257–59
Pan-Seared Flounder with Shaved Fennel Salad, Olives, and Valencia Oranges, 194
Valencia Orange Vinaigrette, 345
Osprey Seafood, 238, 239, 244, 382
OYSTERS, 192–93
Baked 13-Mile Oysters with Jalapeno, Lime, and Cilantro Butter, 191
Hangtown Fry with Local Spinach and Pancetta, 190
Oyster Shooters, 180–81
Oyster Stew, 182

P

Palladin, Jean-Louis, 136

PANCETTA, 144. *See also* Guanciale
    Arugula Salad with Pancetta-Wrapped Goat Cheese, 91
    Hangtown Fry with Local Spinach and Pancetta, 190
    Pancetta-Wrapped Local Kiefer Pear Salad with Saba and Arugula, 135

Pantry items, 384–85

Parnell, Liz, 234

PARSNIPS
    Blanched Parsnips, 377
    Parsnip Purée, 369
    Seared Nantucket Bay Scallops with Parsnip Purée and Citrus Sauce, 244

PASTA, NOODLES, AND DUMPLINGS
    Braised Lamb Shanks with Orecchiette Pasta and Gremolata, 252–53
    Ida Mae's Homemade Chicken Noodle Soup, 231
    Idie's Homemade Spaghetti and Meatballs, 218–19
    Porcini Mushroom Pasta, 328
    Potato Gnocchi, 359
    Saffron Pappardelle with Wild Oyster Mushrooms and Parmesan, 152
    Saffron Pasta Dough, 357
    Sweet Potato Tortelloni with Toasted Pine Nuts, Brown Butter, and Fried Sage, 196–97
    Tomato Guanciale Pasta, 93
    Tuna Marinara with Rigatoni, 222

Pastry Dough, 358

Patterson, John "JP," 75

Pawleys Island, 148
    original Hot and Hot Fish Club, 18
    summers at, 17, 37, 115, 237

PEACHES, 80, 215
    Ancho-Rubbed Pork Chops with Arepa Cake and Peach Mojo, 46–47
    Peach Mojo, 351

PEANUTS
    Boiled Peanuts, 21
    Candied Peanuts, 363

PEARS
    Hearts of Escarole Salad, 186
    Pancetta-Wrapped Local Kiefer Pear Salad with Saba and Arugula, 135

PEAS
    Morel and English Pea Risotto with Lemon Oil, 286
    Spring Vegetable Salad, 282–83

PEA TENDRILS, 275

Pan-Seared Pompano with Spring Vegetable Risotto and Pea Tendrils, 304

PECANS
    Bibb Lettuce Salad with Candied Pecans, Cambozola, and Pomegranate Vinaigrette, 147
    Candied Pecans, 364
    Pecan Tart with Molasses Ice Cream, 212–13

PEPPERS
    Chowchow, 349
    Dad's Grilled Chicken with Summer Vegetables, 103
    Dave's Summer Salad, 89
    Hot and Hot Spicy 'Tini, 277
    Ratatouille, 94, 370
    Whole-Roasted Baby Chicken with Crawfish and Tasso Jambalaya, 312
    Whole-Roasted Speckled Trout, 123

PERSIMMONS
    Saffron Rice Pudding with Sauternes Poached Persimmons, 162–63
    Seared Foie Gras with Brioche Bread and Wild Persimmon Jam, 141
    Wild Persimmon Jam, 361

Petals from the Past, 215, 272, 382

PHEASANT
    Oven-Roasted Pheasant Breast on Hunter-Style Risotto, 250

Picnics, 74

PIES AND TARTS
    Apple and Rosemary Croustade with Caramel Sauce, 211
    Four Fig Tarts with Lemon Verbena Ice Cream, 112–13
    Lattice-Top Cherry Pie, 114
    Lemon Buttermilk Tarts with Wild Strawberries and Mulberries, 23, 314–15
    Meyer Lemon Meringue Tart, 255
    Pecan Tart with Molasses Ice Cream, 212–13
    Plum and Nectarine Galette with Vanilla Ice Cream, 111
    Savory Pastry Dough, 358
    Sweet Pastry Dough, 358
    Sweet Potato Fried Pies with Cinnamon Ice Cream, 161

Pineapple-Sage Lemon Celebration, 276

PISTACHIOS
    Cranberry and Pistachio Torrone (Nougat), 226

PIZZA
    Cousin Joe's Cheese Pizza, 220

Placerville, California, 190

Plum and Nectarine Galette with Vanilla Ice Cream, 111

POMEGRANATES AND POMEGRANATE JUICE
    Bibb Lettuce Salad with Candied Pecans, Cambozola, and Pomegranate Vinaigrette, 147
    Hot and Hot Pomegranate Cocktail, 178

JP's Pomerita, 75
Pomegranate Sorbet with Shortbread Cookies, 210
Pomegranate Vinaigrette, 343
PORK, 144
    Ancho-Rubbed Pork Chops with Arepa Cake and Peach
       Mojo, 46–47
    Braised White Beans, 369
    Cajun-Style Boudin Sausage, 268–69
    curing and smoking, 142
    Fudge Farms Pork and Beans with Braised Greens,
       Cracklin' Cornbread, and Chowchow, 156–57
    Homemade Meatballs, 375
    Idie's Homemade Spaghetti and Meatballs, 218–19
    Roasted Pig: How to, 263, 270–71
    Roasted Pork Loin with Farro, Artichokes, and Parmesan,
       254
    Slow Roasted Pork Shoulder with Fall Vegetable Gratin
       and Mustard Greens, 199
POTATOES
    Braised Veal Cheeks with Potato Gnocchi and
       Chanterelles, 206–7
    Fall Vegetable Gratin, 372
    Fennel Mashed Potatoes, 368
    German Potato Salad, 266, 272
    Grilled Beef Sirloin on Potato Galette with Mixed Baby
       Greens, Balsamic Onions, Blue Cheese, Tamarind
       Sauce, and Chive Aïoli, 104
    Grilled Veal Liver Steak with Fennel Mashed Potatoes,
       Onion Rings, and Tamarind Sauce, 158
    Potato Gnocchi, 359
    Purple Mashed Potatoes, 368
    Roasted Fingerling Potatoes, 378
    Sautéed Halibut on Purple Mashed Potatoes with Brown
       Butter Vinaigrette and Fried Capers, 153
    Smoked and Grilled Quail with Winter Vegetables and
       White BBQ Sauce, 143
    Spring Vegetable Salad, 282–83
    Whole-Roasted, Free-Range Chicken with Winter
       Vegetables, 208–9
Powell, Arlie, 215
Powell, Jason, 215, 382
Powell, Shelley, 215, 382
PRESERVES. *See* Jams and preserves
Prince Edward Island mussels, 140
Prosciutto and Spring Vidalia Onion Salad with Parmesan
    Vinaigrette, 287
PUDDINGS AND CUSTARDS
    Banana Bavarian Cream, 364
    Chocolate Pots de Crème, 319
    Pastry Cream, 365

Rhubarb and Strawberry Tapioca Pudding, 50
Saffron Rice Pudding with Sauternes Poached
    Persimmons, 162–63
PUMPKINS, 125, 129, 130–31
    Cinderella Pumpkin Soup with Fried Sage and Lemon
       Oil, 129

Q

QUAIL, 229, 242
    Bobwhite Quail, Sausage, and White Bean Cassoulet, 198
    Creamed Bobwhite Quail "Old School" over Carolina
       Gold Rice, 251
    Grilled Quail on Local Cress and Blood Orange Salad, 242
    Smoked and Grilled Quail with Winter Vegetables and
       White BBQ Sauce, 143
QUINOA, 249
    Grilled Black Grouper in Winter Vegetable Quinoa, 249

R

RABBIT
    Braised Rabbit with Vegetable Ragout, 310–11
    Rabbit Tamales with Black Bean Salsa, 31–33
RAMPS, 275, 304
    Pan-Seared Pompano with Spring Vegetable Risotto and
       Pea Tendrils, 304
RAPINI
    Grilled NY Strip with Poached Farm Egg, Parmigiano-
       Reggiano, and Truffle Oil, 200, 202–5
    Sautéed Rapini, 221
RASPBERRIES
    Raspberry and White Chocolate Bread Pudding with
       Raspberry Coulis, 52–55
    Raspberry Coulis, 363
Ratatouille, 94, 370
Red Alae sea salt, Hawaiian, 90
Red Mountain Honey, 110, 382
RELISHES. *See* Condiments, relishes, and chutneys
Rhubarb and Strawberry Tapioca Pudding, 50
RICE
    Alligator Point Clam Paella, 308
    Anson Mills Carolina Gold Rice, 353
    Basic Risotto, 355
    Carolina Gold rice, 25, 26, 94, 148–49, 251, 353
    Crawfish Risotto with Preserved Meyer Lemons, 240–41
    Creamed Bobwhite Quail "Old School" over Carolina
       Gold Rice, 251
    Low-Country Pirlou with Clams, Sausage, Shrimp, and
       Carolina Gold Rice, 148–49

Morel and English Pea Risotto with Lemon Oil, 286
Oven-Roasted Duck Breast on Crawfish Risotto with Spicy Ham Hock Broth, 45
Oven-Roasted Pheasant Breast on Hunter-Style Risotto, 250
Pan-Seared Pompano with Spring Vegetable Risotto and Pea Tendrils, 304
Saffron Rice Pudding with Sauternes Poached Persimmons, 162–63
She-Crab Soup, 278
Shrimp and Avocado Salad with Carolina Gold Rice, 25
Whole-Roasted Baby Chicken with Crawfish and Tasso Jambalaya, 312
Roberts, Glenn, 25
Rome, family trip to, 323

S

SABA, 135
Pancetta-Wrapped Local Kiefer Pear Salad with Saba and Arugula, 135
SAGE LEAVES
Fried Sage Leaves, 376
SALAD DRESSINGS AND VINAIGRETTES
Balsamic Vinaigrette, 346
Basil-Lime Vinaigrette, 96–97
Blackberry Vinaigrette, 34
Brown Butter Vinaigrette, 341
Chervil Vinaigrette, 346
Chive Dressing, 347
Citrus Vinaigrette, 344
Creamy Herb Dressing, 346
Extra-Virgin Olive Oil Vinaigrette, 344
Green Goddess Dressing, 94, 347
Grenache Vinaigrette, 344
Herb Vinaigrette, 348
Lemon Dijon Vinaigrette, 346
Meyer Lemon Vinaigrette, 346
Parmesan Vinaigrette, 346
Pomegranate Vinaigrette, 343
Preserved Lemon Vinaigrette, 345
Scuppernong Vinaigrette, 343
Sesame Vinaigrette, 345
Valencia Orange Vinaigrette, 345
Walnut Vinaigrette, 345
SALADS. *See also* Coleslaws and slaws
Apple, Almond, and Endive Salad with Creamy Herb Dressing, 132–33
Arugula Salad with Pancetta-Wrapped Goat Cheese, 91
Arugula Sylvetta Salad with Garlic Bruschetta, 329
Bibb Lettuce Salad with Candied Pecans, Cambozola, and
Pomegranate Vinaigrette, 147
Chef's Garden Beet Salad with Goat Cheese and Citrus Vinaigrette, 138
Creamed Field Peas and Summer Squash Salad, 64
Dave's Summer Salad, 89
Duck Confit and Warm Mushroom Salad, 243
Endive Salad with Kumquats and Pecorino, 272
German Potato Salad, 266, 272
Grilled Jumbo Asparagus with Head-On Florida Hoppers and Preserved Lemon Vinaigrette, 284–85
Grilled Quail on Local Cress and Blood Orange Salad, 242
Hearts of Escarole Salad, 186
Hearts of Palm Salad with Pink Grapefruit and Avocado, 184–85
Mama's Tomato Salad, 122
microgreens, 240
Pancetta-Wrapped Local Kiefer Pear Salad with Saba and Arugula, 135
Pan-Seared Wild Salmon on Three-Bean Salad with Cherry Tomatoes and Basil Aïoli, 100–101
Prosciutto and Spring Vidalia Onion Salad with Parmesan Vinaigrette, 287
Roasted Porcini Mushrooms with Bresaola, Mustard Greens, and Lemon Oil, 146
Shrimp and Avocado Salad with Carolina Gold Rice, 25
Sliced Ruskin Tomatoes with Basil and Goat Cheese, 67
Spring Vegetable Salad, 282–83
Three-Bean Salad, 94
Watercress Salad, 35
Wild Turkey Salad with First of the Season Morels and Watercress, 289
Winter Density and Red Starr Bibb Salad with Warm Belle Chèvre Herb Toast, 236
Salt, Hawaiian red alae, 90
San Francisco, California, 11–12, 38, 244, 323
SAUCES. *See also* Condiments, relishes, and chutneys; Crème Fraîche
Ancho Chili Sauce, 337
Basic Aïoli, 342
Basil Aïoli, 342
BBQ Sauce, 336
Caramel Sauce, 363
Chive Aïoli, 342
Chocolate Orange Sauce, 362
Cocktail Sauce, 223
Coconut Curry Dipping Sauce, 338
Lemon Butter Sauce, 341
Lemon Mayonnaise, 60
Raspberry Coulis, 363
Rouille, 340

Sauce Gribiche, 337
Spicy Rémoulade Sauce, 339
Summer Tomato Sauce, 339
Tamarind Sauce, 338
Wasabi Aïoli, 342
White Barbecue Sauce, 337
White Chocolate Sauce, 362
SAUSAGE
Bobwhite Quail, Sausage, and White Bean Cassoulet, 198
Cajun-Style Boudin Sausage, 268–69
Chicken and Conecuh County Sausage Gumbo, 273
from Conecuh County, Alabama, 142
Low-Country Pirlou with Clams, Sausage, Shrimp, and Carolina Gold Rice, 148–49
Oven-Roasted Italian Sausage, 221
Sausage Stuffing, 374
SCALLOPS, 194
Hot and Hot Fish Fry with Fennel Slaw, Hushpuppies, and Spicy Rémoulade, 150–51
Nantucket Bay Scallop Seviche, 237
Seared Day Boat Scallops with Celery Root Slaw and Tamarind Sauce, 194
Seared Nantucket Bay Scallops with Parsnip Purée and Citrus Sauce, 244
Southern Bouillabaisse, 245–47
Scerbo, Louie, 71
Scerbo, Theresa, 71
Scerbo Morano, Rosina Maria, 71–73, 175
Schulze, Richard, 148
September, 125
Sesame Brittle, 296
Sgreccia Grocery Store, 72
Shad, 275, 305
SHAD ROE, 275, 305
Bacon-Wrapped Shad Roe with Anson Mills Grits and Caper Brown Butter Sauce, 306–7
SHALLOTS
Roasted Shallots, 378
SHRIMP
Breaded Fried Shrimp with Cocktail Sauce, 223
Grilled Jumbo Asparagus with Head-On Florida Hoppers and Preserved Lemon Vinaigrette, 284–85
Hot and Hot Creamy Shrimp and Grits with Country Ham, 43–44
Hot and Hot Fish Fry with Fennel Slaw, Hushpuppies, and Spicy Rémoulade, 150–51
Low-Country Pirlou with Clams, Sausage, Shrimp, and Carolina Gold Rice, 148–49
Shrimp and Avocado Salad with Carolina Gold Rice, 25
Shrimp and Corn Fritters with Chive Aïoli, 27

Shrimp Gazpacho with Lemon Oil, 77, 94
Shrimp Stock, 334
Southern Bouillabaisse, 245–47
wild American shrimp and the shrimping industry, 40, 383
Simmons, Jack, 280–81, 381
SIMPLE SYRUPS
Ginger Simple Syrup, 362
Honeysuckle Simple Syrup, 362
Mint Simple Syrup, 362
Simple Syrup, 362
SNACKS. *See* Appetizers and snacks
SORBET
Muscadine Sorbet, 159
Pomegranate Sorbet with Shortbread Cookies, 210
SOUPS AND STEWS
Aunt Emma's Italian Wedding Soup (Zuppa Maritata), 179
Bobwhite Quail, Sausage, and White Bean Cassoulet, 198
Cauliflower Soup with White Truffle Oil, 183
Chicken and Conecuh County Sausage Gumbo, 273
Cinderella Pumpkin Soup with Fried Sage and Lemon Oil, 129
Crawfish Bisque, 279
Ida Mae's Homemade Chicken Noodle Soup, 231
Jim's Oxtail Soup, 233
Low-Country Pirlou with Clams, Sausage, Shrimp, and Carolina Gold Rice, 148–49
Oyster Stew, 182
She-Crab Soup, 278
Shrimp Gazpacho with Lemon Oil, 77, 94
Southern Bouillabaisse, 245–47
Vegetable Minestrone with Pesto, 24
South Carolina Low Country, 18, 26, 148, 245. *See also* Pawleys Island
SPINACH
Aunt Emma's Italian Wedding Soup (Zuppa Maritata), 179
Basket of Fried Greens (Celery Fritters), 224–25
Hangtown Fry with Local Spinach and Pancetta, 190
House-Cured Bacon-Wrapped Figs with Bitter Greens and Walnuts, 92
SQUASH, YELLOW
Creamed Field Peas and Summer Squash Salad, 64
SQUASH BLOSSOMS
Roasted Squash Blossoms with Blue Crab, Cherry Tomatoes, and Cucumbers, 30
Stephens, Elton B., 57, 248, 315
STEWS. *See* Soups and stews
STOCKS AND BROTHS

Chicken Stock, 335
Fish Stock, 334
Shrimp Stock, 334
Spicy Ham Hock Broth, 336
Veal Stock, 335
Vegetable Stock, 334

STRAWBERRIES
Chris' memories, 49
First-of-the-Season Strawberry Shortcakes with
     Honeysuckle Crème Fraîche, 51
Lemon Buttermilk Tarts with Wild Strawberries and
     Mulberries, 23, 314–15
Rhubarb and Strawberry Tapioca Pudding, 50
St. Rocco's Church, 71, 72, 232, 323

STUFFING
Sausage Stuffing, 374

SUCCOTASH, 83
BBQ Beef Short Ribs on Sweet Corn Succotash with
     Cracklin' Cornbread, 105–7

SUGAR, FLAVORED
Cinnamon Sugar, 367
Lemon Sugar, 367
Vanilla Sugar, 367
Sun-Up Produce, 80–81
Super Bowl party, 229, 263–73
Sweet Grass Dairy, 290–91, 326, 383

SWEET POTATOES
Sweet Potato Fried Pies with Cinnamon Ice Cream, 161
Sweet Potato Tortelloni with Toasted Pine Nuts, Brown
     Butter, and Fried Sage, 196–97

T

Tamarind Sauce, 338
Tanglefoot, 297
Thanksgiving, 175

TOMATOES, 80–81, 275
Baked Shovel Nose Lobsters with Cherry Tomato and
     Field Pea Salad, 102
Dave's Summer Salad, 89
Green Tomato Chutney, 294–95
Grouper with Tomato, Avocado, and Grilled Vidalia
     Onions with Basil-Lime Vinaigrette, 96–97
heirloom varieties, 83, 88
Hot and Hot Tomato Salad, 67, 83–87, 94
Mama's Tomato Salad, 122
Pan-Seared Wild Salmon on Three-Bean Salad with
     Cherry Tomatoes and Basil Aïoli, 100–101
Roasted Squash Blossoms with Blue Crab, Cherry
     Tomatoes, and Cucumbers, 30

Sliced Ruskin Tomatoes with Basil and Goat Cheese, 67
Soft-Shell Crab BLT, 28–29
Study of Heirloom Tomatoes with Eggplant and Sweet
     Grass Dairy Goat Cheese, 90
Summer Tomato Sauce, 339
Tomato Guanciale Pasta, 93
Trotter, Charlie, 136

TUNA
Seared Tuna on Asian Vegetable Slaw with Wasabi Aïoli,
     38
Tuna Marinara with Rigatoni, 222

TURKEY, 275
Grilled Wild Turkey Breast with Grilled Vegetables and
     Sauce Gribiche, 309
Wild Turkey Salad with First of the Season Morels and
     Watercress, 289

TURNIPS
Roasted Baby Turnips, 378

V

VANILLA AND VANILLA BEANS
Chocolate Devil's Food Cake with Vanilla Ice Cream, 260–61
Plum and Nectarine Galette with Vanilla Ice Cream, 111
Sugared Vanilla Beans, 367
Vanilla Crème Anglaise, 361
Vanilla Ice Cream, 366
Vanilla Sugar, 367
Vawter, John, 229
Vawter, John Edward, 229
Vawter, Patrick, 229

VEAL
Braised Veal Cheeks with Potato Gnocchi and
     Chanterelles, 206–7
Grilled Veal Liver Steak with Fennel Mashed Potatoes,
     Onion Rings, and Tamarind Sauce, 158
Homemade Meatballs, 375
Idie's Homemade Spaghetti and Meatballs, 218–19
Veal Stock, 335

VEGETABLES
Braised Rabbit with Vegetable Ragout, 310–11
Dad's Grilled Chicken with Summer Vegetables, 103
Fall Vegetable Gratin, 372
Grilled Wild Turkey Breast with Grilled Vegetables and
     Sauce Gribiche, 309
Hot and Hot Vegetable Plate, 94
Pan-Seared Pompano with Spring Vegetable Risotto and
     Pea Tendrils, 304
Slow Roasted Pork Shoulder with Fall Vegetable Gratin
     and Mustard Greens, 199

Smoked and Grilled Quail with Winter Vegetables and White BBQ Sauce, 143

Spring Vegetable Salad, 282–83

Vegetable Minestrone with Pesto, 24

Vegetable Stock, 334

Whole-Roasted, Free-Range Chicken with Winter Vegetables, 208–9

VERJUS, 43

Hot and Hot Creamy Shrimp and Grits with Country Ham, 43

Oven-Roasted Chicken Breasts on Anson Mills Grits with Local Scuppernongs, Muscadines, and Verjus, 154–55

VINAIGRETTES. *See* Salad dressings and vinaigrettes

Vin cotto, 135

W

Waggoner, Bob, 136

Ward, Buddy, 192

Ward, Martha Pearl, 192

Ward, Tommy, 192–93, 380

Wasabi Aïoli, 342

WATERCRESS, 248

Grilled Quail on Local Cress and Blood Orange Salad, 242

Herb-Crusted Flounder with Watercress Salad and Lemon Butter Sauce, 35

House-Cured Bacon-Wrapped Figs with Bitter Greens and Walnuts, 92

Pan-Seared Wild Salmon on Three-Bean Salad with Cherry Tomatoes and Basil Aïoli, 100–101

Three-Bean Salad, 94

Wild Turkey Salad with First of the Season Morels and Watercress, 289

WATERMELON

Chilled Red and Yellow Sugar Babies, 122

Watermelon Martini, 20

Weinberg-Lynn, Michael, 238, 244

West Side Market, 71, 72

Woodcock hunting, 125, 126

Woodcock moon, 125

Z

Zannoni's Grocery Store, 71, 226

HOT AND HOT
FISH CLUB
COOKBOOK

- THE ORIGINAL HOT AND HOT FISH CLUB RULES -

RULE I
TIME AND PLACE OF MEETING

It is the duty of members to meet, at or about 12 o'clock p.m., at the Club House, at Midway sea shore, on each Friday, from the first Friday in June, to the last Friday, but on, in October.

RULE II
ADMISSION OF MEMBERS

Any person, wishing to become a member, must be proposed by the President, and if elected by a majority, shall, after subscribing to the rules, and paying his admission fee of fifty dollars to the Treasurer, be entitled to all the rights and privileges of a member.

RULE II
QUORUM

Not less than two-thirds of the members shall constitute a quorum for the transaction of business.

RULE IV
OFFICERS

There shall be a President and Vice-President, to preside at the meetings, and a Secretary and Treasurer, to record the proceedings, and to take charge of the funds of the Club.

RULE V
DUTIES OF THE PRESIDENT

Each member, in rotation, and in order of residences, shall act as President. He shall furnish a ham, and good rice, and also attend to the preparation for dinner, to be on table at 2 o'clock p.m., or not later than half-past 2. He must preserve order, and select sides with the Vice-President for games. If absent, he must send his ham and rice.

RULE VI
DUTIES OF THE VICE-PRESIDENT

The Vice-President shall, in addition to his dish and wine, supply the Club with water and ice, and attend to the games. If the President is absent, the Vice-President will preside, and his next neighbor officiates for him. He must also announce whether champagne will be brought at the ensuing Club meeting.

RULE VII
DUTIES OF SECRETARY AND TREASURER

The Secretary and Treasurer shall keep a record of the proceedings of Club, take charge of the funds, receive or disburse, according to the vote of the Club. He shall also keep an account of the debts due by, and to the Club, and furnish an annual report at the first meeting in October.

RULE VIII
DUTIES OF MEMBERS

Each member shall contribute at least one substantial dish for dinner, also one bottle of wine, unless it shall have been previously announced that champagne will be furnished. He must also bring not less than two knives and forks, two tumblers, two wine glasses, two plates, and one dish.

RULE IX
DUTY OF CERTAIN MEMBERS

Each unmarried member shall be permitted in rotation to furnish a pudding, in lieu of that required under Rule VIII.